T0212181

Reinventing ITIL® and DevOps with Digital Transformation

Essential Guidance
to Accelerate the Process

Second Edition

Abhinav Krishna Kaiser

Apress®

Reinventing ITIL® and DevOps with Digital Transformation: Essential Guidance to Accelerate the Process

Abhinav Krishna Kaiser
Bengaluru, India

ISBN-13 (pbk): 978-1-4842-9071-2   ISBN-13 (electronic): 978-1-4842-9072-9
https://doi.org/10.1007/978-1-4842-9072-9

Managing Director, Apress Media LLC: Welmoed Spahr
Acquisitions Editor: Celestin Suresh John
Development Editor: James Markham
Coordinating Editor: Mark Powers
Copy Editor: Kezia Endsley

Cover designed by eStudioCalamar

Cover image by Glitch Lab on Unsplash (www.unsplash.com)

ITIL® is a (registered) trademark of AXELOS Limited. All rights reserved.

Distributed to the book trade worldwide by Apress Media, LLC, 1 New York Plaza, New York, NY 10004, U.S.A. Phone 1-800-SPRINGER, fax (201) 348-4505, e-mail orders-ny@springer-sbm.com, or visit www.springeronline.com. Apress Media, LLC is a California LLC and the sole member (owner) is Springer Science + Business Media Finance Inc (SSBM Finance Inc). SSBM Finance Inc is a **Delaware** corporation.

For information on translations, please e-mail booktranslations@springernature.com; for reprint, paperback, or audio rights, please e-mail bookpermissions@springernature.com.

Apress titles may be purchased in bulk for academic, corporate, or promotional use. eBook versions and licenses are also available for most titles. For more information, reference our Print and eBook Bulk Sales web page at http://www.apress.com/bulk-sales.

Any source code or other supplementary material referenced by the author in this book is available to readers on GitHub (https://github.com/Apress). For more detailed information, please visit http://www.apress.com/source-code.

Printed on acid-free paper

To my readers,
whose constant feedback and encouragement
keeps me churning out new books...

Table of Contents

About the Author

Abhinav Krishna Kaiser is a management consultant and works as a partner in a leading consulting firm. He consults with organizations that are looking to improve, become efficient, and transform. His areas of expertise include Digital Transformation, Product Models, Agile, DevOps, ITIL, and other connected IT areas.

Abhinav is a digital transformation enthusiast who has been instrumental in driving several transformation initiatives across sectors. He has consulted with companies to change their approach from traditional to a product-led model, and these initiatives have driven companies to achieve new heights in reaching higher customer satisfaction levels.

He is one of the leading names synonymous with ITIL, and his previous publication, *Become ITIL 4 Foundation Certified in 7 Days*, is one of the top guides recommended to IT professionals looking to get into the service management field and become ITIL Foundation certified.

Abhinav started consulting with clients several years ago on IT service management, creating value by developing robust service management solutions. He is one of the foremost authorities in the area of configuration management, and his solutions have stood the test of time, rigor, and technological advancements. A natural evolution in consulting, led him from service management to Agile and DevOps and now into digital transformation and product-led models.

Abhinav has trained thousands of IT professionals on DevOps processes, Agile methodologies, and ITIL expert-level certifications. He blogs and writes guides and articles on digital transformation, DevOps, Agile, and ITIL at http://abhinavpmp.com. His first book came out in 2015: *Workshop in a Box: Communication Skills for IT Professionals*. He runs a video channel on YouTube that has garnered several thousands of views and acclaim: https://www.youtube.com/user/abhinavonthetube.

As consultants go where the clients want them to, Abhinav has traveled across the globe and has lived in the United States, Australia, South Africa, and the United Kingdom, before settling down in Bangalore. He is happily married to Radhika, and they have two children—Anagha (daughter) and Aadwik (son).

About the Technical Reviewer

 **Rajeev Kesana** brings two decades of IT industry experience, partnering with customers at Tech Mahindra, IBM Software Labs, Infosys, Capgemini, & TCS. As an accomplished leader in strategy and transformation, Rajeev has envisioned, designed, and built multiple technology-transformation-focused business units from the ground up over the years. Currently based in Hyderabad, where he resides with his wife, Chaitanya, he enjoys meditation, nature, cooking, and travelling.

Introduction

I am lucky to have worked on various transformation programs in the past 15 years. Although we didn't call it "transformation" in the 2000s, it disrupted the notions of what was considered normal, the general principles that we applied and the outcomes that we considered are time immemorial. Just as a sculptor takes a piece of monolith and turns it into something beautiful, transformation projects involve fast-paced evolutions that change the current flow into something different.

Transformation is the same in every field. The principles are common across the board. I went through a physical transformation fairly recently. I weighed around 95 kilograms (210 pounds) and I am 177 centimeters (5'8") tall. My body mass was 28 percent fat, according to a machine that measures all kinds of bodily stats. I had accepted that this was my normal; this was who I was and honestly, it never bothered me.

I was introduced to a fitness coach by my wife, who had transformed some of her friends. Although I wasn't serious at first, I decided to hire him. The regimen involved a combination of diet devoid of voluminous food and activity at the gym. The first couple of weeks were perhaps the most difficult part of transformation, with hunger eating at me. I was asked to cut down my carb intake to a fifth of what I used to consume. No chips. No pizzas. And no beer. As I saw my weight shed on a weekly basis, the cravings disappeared and so did the hunger. I longed to follow my prescribed diet, and I looked forward to my time at the gym. A few months down the line, I had lost around 25 kilograms (55 pounds) and I was down to 17 percent body fat.

The man in the mirror was transformed, but it did not happen overnight. It took a lot of discipline and will power to stay on course. My coach changed my diet every week based on the progress that I made—the importance of measurement and feedback struck me more than ever before. My weight loss was massive to begin with and slowed as the weeks passed, which is the expected to curve for any transformation, physical and digital. I have far from a perfect body, but I am in a much better place than when I started off. Digital transformations are typically like this; they don't end. At any point, you can see how much you have progressed, and new technologies, direction and pivots point towards the path where much more can be achieved.

Reinventing ITIL® and DevOps with Digital Transformation is the second edition of *Reinventing ITIL® in the Age of DevOps*. The first edition received lots of feedback from on-the-ground implementations. The ideas were the first of their kind, and that book provided solutions to thousands of ITIL projects that were moving the DevOps way. As the pandemic hit, digital transformation accelerated, and our notions of work changed with it. I added five chapters in the second edition to address this new level of evolution, whereby DevOps projects started to move into the bigger realm of digital transformation. The original chapters (with some modifications) are presented as Section I, while the new chapters covering digital transformation are in Section II. You can read this book like a story, from cover to cover, or you can use the table of contents to choose topics of interest.

In Chapter 12, I present a framework for strategizing and implementing digital transformations, called the *battle tank framework*. This framework has nothing to do with wars or the army—it illustrates various elements of digital transformation in conjunction with the parts of a battle tank. The final chapter of this book presents a product-led approach, which is quite distinct from the usual ways of working.

PART I

ITIL to DevOps

CHAPTER 1

Introduction to DevOps

New ways of working or new methodologies often come about because of a problem—yes, it all starts with a problem. DevOps too resulted from problems faced by businesses. Businesses craved quick turnarounds to their solutions. Businesses often found, in the midst of development, that they didn't have all the information they needed to make the right decisions. They wanted to make a few more changes to the requirements and still expected the delivery to happen on time. DevOps was born to solve this problem.

DevOps just didn't show up as the DevOps we have today. It evolved over time. It was clear to those who started solving the agility problem that DevOps had a lot of potential to not just solve that problem but also increase productivity by leaps and bounds. Further, the quality of the software developed had the potential to be the best. Thus, to this day, DevOps keeps evolving for the better.

DevOps is not just a methodology for developers. Operations reaps its share of benefits from DevOps as well. With increased automation, operations went from being a mundane job to an innovative one. Operations folks got a new lease on life through various tools that made their working lives a whole lot of fun, and they could look forward to integrating and configuring tools to do advanced stuff, rather than the repetitive workload that's generally associated with operations. Productivity shot up and human errors became much rarer.

Software development was carried out on the back of the software delivery lifecycle (SDLC) and was managed through waterfall project management. On the operations front, ITIL ruled the roost. Through DevOps, development and operations essentially came together to form a union. In the mix, the waterfall methodology gave way to Agile methodologies, and still people who designed DevOps processes did not have a good understanding of how ITIL would come into DevOps. A lot of noise started to circulate that the dawn of DevOps was the end for ITIL. This was plainly noise without any substance; you will learn in this book about the value that ITIL brings to the table and why DevOps cannot exist in its entirety without a framework such as ITIL.

3

© Abhinav Krishna Kaiser 2023
A. Krishna Kaiser, *Reinventing ITIL® and DevOps with Digital Transformation*,
https://doi.org/10.1007/978-1-4842-9072-9_1

The first part of the book is structured around the ITIL service management framework and explores what changes need to be made to ITIL to ease into DevOps projects. Chapter 4 covers common ITIL processes and ITIL functions with respect to DevOps and Chapters 5 through 10 provide in-depth analysis of major processes in ITIL around DevOps designs and implementations. You can use the book to readily implement ITIL in the most effective manner for it to create value in DevOps projects. The second part of the book shifts gears to transform DevOps a notch higher – into digital transformation.

This chapter briefly explains DevOps, including its principles, elements, and processes. Chapter 2 provides a snapshot of ITIL V3, including its lifecycle, phases, processes, and functions. Chapter 3 analyzes DevOps and ITIL, identifying the commonalities and conflicts that support the journey toward adapting ITIL for DevOps implementations.

What Exactly Is DevOps?

There are multiple perceptions about DevOps in the core. In fact, if you search the web, you will be surprised to find multiple definitions for DevOps. No two definitions have common aspects and elements.

I have trained thousands in the area of DevOps, and the best answer I have is that it combines the development and operations teams, and that's about it. Why does bringing two teams together create such a strong buzz across the globe? In fact, if it actually was just the culmination of two teams, DevOps probably would have been discussed in the human resources ecosphere, and it would have remained a semi-complex HR management process.

During the beginning of the DevOps era, to amuse my curiosity, I spoke to a number of people to understand what DevOps is. Most bent toward automation, some spoke of *that* thing they do in startups, and there were a very few who spoke of it as a cultural change. Interesting! Who talks of culture these days, when the edge of our seats burn a hole if we don't act on our commitments? A particular example made me sit up and start connecting the DevOps dots, and it all made sense eventually.

DevOps with an Example

Let's say that you are a project manager of an Internet banking product. The past weekend you deployed a change to update a critical component of the system after weeks of development and testing. The change was deployed successfully; however, during the post-implementation review, it threw an error that forced you to roll back the change.

The rollback was successful, and all the artifacts pertaining to the release were brought to the table to examine and identify the root cause the following Monday. Now what? The root cause was identified, a developer was pressed into action to fix the bug, and the code went through the scrutiny of various tests, including the tests that were not originally included that could have caught the bug in the functional testing stage rather than in production. All the tests ran okay and a new change was planned. It was approved by the change advisory board, and the change was implemented, tested, and green-lit.

These are the typical process activities that are undertaken when a deployment fails and has to be replanned. However, the moment things go south, what is the first thing that comes to your mind as the project manager? Is it what objective action you should take next, or do you start thinking about the developer who worked in this area, the person responsible for the bug in the first place? Or do you think about the tester who identified the scenarios, wrote the scripts, and performed the exploratory testing? It is true that most people start to think about the people responsible for the mess. Why? It is because of our culture. We live in a culture that blames people and tries to pass the buck.

I mentioned earlier about some respondents telling me that DevOps is about culture. So, what culture am I talking about in the context of this example? The example depicts a culture of blame, where the project manager is trying to pin the blame on the people on their team directly responsible for the failure. They could be factually right in pinning the blame on the people directly responsible, but I am focusing on the practice involving blaming individuals.

How is this practice different from the DevOps culture? In DevOps, the responsibility of completing a task is not considered an individual responsibility but rather a shared one. Although an individual works on a task, if the person fails or succeeds, the entire team gets the carrot or the stick. Individuals are not held responsible when we look at the overall DevOps scheme of things, and we don't blame individuals. We follow a blameless culture. This culture of blamelessness culminates from the fact that we all make mistakes because we are humans after all and far from perfect. We make mistakes. So, what's the point of blaming people? In fact, we expect that people do make mistakes, not based on negligence but from the experimentation mindset. This acceptance (of developers making mistakes) has led us to develop a system where the mistakes are identified and rectified in the developmental stages, way before they reach production.

How is this system (to catch mistakes) built? To make it happen, we brought the development and operations teams together (to avoid disconnect), we developed processes that are far more effective and efficient than what is out there (discussed in the rest of the book), and finally we took umbrage under automation to efficiently provide feedback on how we are doing (as speed is one of the main objectives we intend to achieve).

DevOps is a common phrase, and with its spread reaching far and wide, there are multiple definitions coming from various quarters. No two definitions are alike, but they do have a common theme: culture. So, for me, DevOps is a cultural transformation that brings people together from across disciplines. They work under a single umbrella to collaborate as one unit with an open mind and to remove inefficiencies.

Note   A blameless culture does not mean that the individuals who make repeated mistakes do so without repercussions. Individuals are appraised justly and appropriately and in a constructive manner.

Why DevOps?

What gave rise to a new culture called DevOps, you might ask? The answer is evolution. If you take a timeline view of software, from the 1960s up to the advent of the internet, developing software was equivalent to building a project or launching a space shuttle. It required meticulous planning and activities that were planned to be executed sequentially. The waterfall project management methodology was thus born with five sequential steps, as indicated in Figure 1-1.

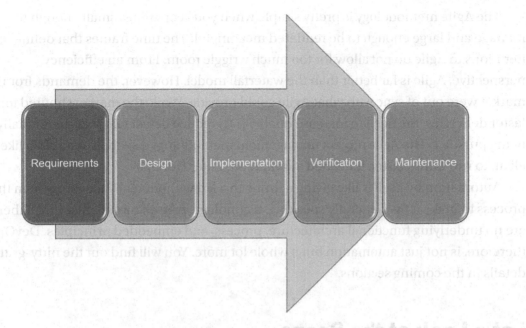

Figure 1-1. *Waterfall project management methodology*

When the Internet boomed, software was far more accessible, and this generated great demand. When the software industry started to expand, the waterfall model's limitations were exposed. The need to complete a detailed planning exercise and the sequential practice of flow seemed like an impediment to the advancement of the software industry.

Then in 2001, at a ski resort in Utah, the Agile Manifesto was born. A number of prevalent Agile methodologies came together to form a common goal that would remove the cast-in-stone waterfall sequential activities.

Agile was more fluid because all its requirements were not conceived at the beginning. It was an approach that was based on iterations, where all the project management activities just cycled over and over again. In between, if a requirement changed, that was okay because there were provisions to make changes that were not bureaucratic nor tedious in nature. In fact, the Agile methodology places emphasis on the response to changes in requirements rather than any map to be followed.

The flexibility and dynamism that came about through Agile spread its wings across the software industry. A number of software projects migrated to the Agile way of working, and to this day, there are projects that are undergoing serious coaching during this transformational phase.

The Agile methodology is pretty simple when you keep things small enough to manage and large enough to be rendered meaningful. The time frames that define iterations in Agile do not allow for too much wriggle room. From an efficiency perspective, Agile is far better than the waterfall model. However, the demands from the market were out of sync with what Agile could provide. While the market shouted for faster deliveries, the need to increase quality (i.e., reduce defect rate) was perennially being pursued. The Agile project management methodology needed something, like an elixir, to run things faster. It needed automation. Enter DevOps!

Automation by itself is like giving a drone to a kid without really teaching them the process to make it fly. Generally speaking, technology by itself has no meaning if there are no underlying functional architecture, process, and embedded principles. DevOps, therefore, is not just automation but a whole lot more. You will find out the nitty-gritty details in the coming sections.

Let's Look at the Scope

The word *DevOps* gives away the scope through its conjunction of two parts of a software lifecycle. While Agile existed mainly to put an end to the rigidity brought forth by the waterfall model, it was said that the methodology can be used for operations as well. However, without an overarching process or framework, using Agile for operations with the same rigor does not work. DevOps bridged this gap by bringing in the operational phases and developmental activities under a single umbrella and employing common processes and principles across the board.

DevOps comes into play when you start with the software development process, which is the requirements-gathering phase. It ends when the software retires from service. DevOps spans the entire software lifecycle, and if you read between the lines, you cannot just implement and execute DevOps until deployment and be done with it. It will continue to function until the software is used by its designated users. In other words, DevOps is here to stay, and stay for as long as services are delivered. So, in practice, the operational phase runs perpetually, and DevOps will deliver the required optimization and automation. The processes to run operations will be borrowed from the ITIL service management framework, and the present format of the ITIL framework will be highly customized to fit the DevOps bill. The process of how ITIL fits into a DevOps project is the heart of this book.

Note   The word DevOps came into existence thanks to Twitter. The first Devopsdays conference was held in Ghent, Belgium in 2009. While people tweeted about it, the #devopsdays tag used 11 characters out of a possible 140. To shorten it, one of the tweeters used #devops, and others followed suit. This led to what we know today as DevOps.

The Benefits of Transforming into DevOps

Many software companies have been delivering applications for a number of years now. Why do we need DevOps to tell us how we must develop?

Our services are being delivered to a number of customers, including top banks and mines around the globe. I am running just fine with my service management framework. Why DevOps?

People have lived for thousands of years. They did just fine, reproducing and surviving. What has changed in the past 100 years? We have changed the modes of transport for better efficiency, we communicate faster today, and overall our quality of life has gone up several notches. *Something is working* should not be a barrier to improvements. DevOps introduces several enhancements in the areas of working culture, process, technology, and organizational structure. This transformation is rooted in practices that were developed by like-minded organizations that were willing to experiment, and the results have vastly gone in the favor of DevOps over other ancient methodologies.

Amazon, Netflix, Etsy, and Facebook are just some of the organizations that have taken their software deliveries to a whole new level, and they don't compete with the laggards anymore. They have set new benchmarks that are impossible to meet with any other methodology.

At the 2011 Velocity conference, Amazon's director of platform analysis, Jon Jenkins, provided a brief insight into Amazon's ways of working. He supported it with the following statistics.

During weekdays, Amazon is able to deploy every 11.6 seconds on average. Most organizations struggle to deploy weekly consistently, but Amazon does more than 1,000 deployments every hour (1,079 deployments to be precise). Further, 10,000 hosts receive deployments simultaneously on average, and the highest Amazon has been able to achieve was 30,000 hosts simultaneously receiving deployments. Wow! These numbers are out of this world. And these are the statistics from May 2011. Imagine what they are able to do today!

It's just not the speed of deployments. There are several other advantages that Amazon went on to claim during the conference:

- Outages due to software deployments have gone down by a whopping 75 percent since 2006. Most outages are caused by new changes (read software deployments), and the reduction in outages points to the success achieved in deploying software changes.

- The downtime owing to software deployments has reduced drastically, by about 90 percent.

- On average, there has been an outage for every 1,000 software deployments, which is about a 0.001 percent failure rate. This looks great for a moderate software delivery organization, but for Amazon, the number seems high because of the more than 1000 deployments every hour.

- Through automation, Amazon has introduced automatic failovers whenever hosts go down.

- Architecture complexity has reduced significantly.

Insight from the State of DevOps Report

Puppet Labs publishes an annual whitepaper called the "State of DevOps Report." The report provides insight into the world of DevOps—the statistics, changes, and innovations in the past year.

In the 2021 report, Puppet Labs surveyed about 2,657 professionals, including executives, developers, testers, and other IT professionals. The trajectory of people working in DevOps takes the shape of a bell. In 2014, 16 percent of the respondents worked in DevOps, in 2017, it was 27 percent, and in 2018, it was 28 percent, which was the peak. 2019 saw 22 percent of professionals working in DevOps, with a further dip to 20 percent in 2021. It appeared as if DevOps was spreading like wildfire until 2018, and then it started to slow down. The reasoning is, as DevOps reached its zenith, the scope of changes or transformation in organizations took shape under a bigger umbrella called *digital transformations*. The dip does not indicate that fewer people are practicing DevOps, but rather that the association with DevOps started to decline and the same DevOps methodology became an integral part of digital transformation, which is discussed in part 2 of this book.

According to the report, the future of operations in DevOps/digital projects depend on the following aspects:

- *Vendor engineering*: Single service providers are the thing of the past. Organizations, however small, contract with multiple vendors for their various IT needs. Managing all the vendors begins with the contracting process and is managed throughout the lifecycle. It requires uncommon skills and is referred to as vendor engineering.

- *Product engineering*: This is the age of creating products and running companies through their products. This product-led approach (discussed in detail in Chapter 15) brings new thinking to the ways of working, starting from how organizations approach their positioning, to how their teams are stacked and the decisions they undertake.

- *Sociotechnical system engineering*: The culture of working in the digital age is changing, and the primary reason is that rapid feedback flows swiftly and directly to the source. If people are to deliver at their best, then they must be given the freedom to experiment. Performing activities out of compulsion or fear is a deterrent in the long run, and confidence levels dip significantly. It is all the more important to develop a culture where people can confidently state their minds, including being able to disagree with their leaders.

- *Managing the portfolio of technical investments*: There is an application for every use case, and teams no longer support a single application or a portfolio of applications. Support has become expensive and more importantly, hands-free. In such a scenario, it is key that the code shipped during development is free from clutter (read, technical debt). The more cluttered it is, the more expensive it is to maintain, due to instability and delays. The mitigation is straightforward: reduce technical debt. It doesn't add value, and even if the customers don't see its effect, doesn't necessarily mean that it is harmless.

11

DevOps Principles

DevOps principles are in a state of constant evolution. In fact, there are multiple versions of the principles. The most widely believed set of principles is represented with the acronym CALMS. Figure 1-2 shows a mug from a marketing campaign for DevOps featuring CALMS.

Figure 1-2. *DevOps principles (credit: devopsnet.com)*

CALMS stands for the following:

- Culture

- Automation

- Lean

- Measurement

- Sharing

Culture

There is a popular urban legend that the late Peter Drucker, known as the founder of modern management, famously said, "Culture eats strategy for breakfast." If you want to make a massive mind-boggling, Earth-shaking change, start by changing the culture that can make it happen. Culture cannot be changed using a swift process. It is embedded into human behavior and requires an overhaul of their behavior.

Here are some of the behavioral traits that we seek to change with DevOps:

- Take responsibility for the entire product and not just the work that you perform
- Step out of your comfort zone and innovate
- Experiment as much as you want; there's a safety net to catch you if you fall
- Communicate, collaborate, and develop affinity with the involved teams
- For developers especially, you build it, you run it

Automation

Automation is a key component in the DevOps methodology. It is a massive enabler of faster delivery and crucial for providing rapid feedback. Under the culture principle, I talked about a safety net with respect to experimentation. This safety net is made possible through automation.

The objective is to automate whatever possible in the software delivery lifecycle. The kinds of activities that can be efficiently automated are repetitive tasks that don't require human intelligence. For example, building infrastructure was a major task that involved hardware architects and administrators, and most importantly building servers took a significant amount of time. This time was added to the overall software delivery. Thanks to technology advancements, we have cloud infrastructure today, and servers can be spun up through code. Additionally, we don't need hardware administrators to do it. Developers can do it themselves. Wait, there's more! Once the environment provisioning script is written, it can be used to automate spinning up servers as many times as necessary. Automation has changed the way we see infrastructure.

Activities involving executing tasks such as running a build or a test script can be automated. But the activities that involve human cognizance are hard to automate today. The art of writing code or test scripts requires human intelligence, and the machines of today are not in a position to do it. In the future, artificial intelligence will be able to take on these types of activities.

13

Lean

DevOps has borrowed heavily from the Lean methodology and the Toyota Production Systems (TPS). The thinking behind the Lean methodology is to keep things simple and not overcomplicate them. It is natural that the advent of automation decreases the complexity of architecture and simplifies complicated workflows. The Lean principle aids in keeping us on the ground so we can continue working with things that are easy to comprehend and simple to work with.

There are two parts to the Lean principle. The primary issue is not to bloat the logic or the way you do things; keep it straightforward and minimal. An example is the use of microservices, which support the cause by not overcomplicating the architecture. We are no longer looking to build monolithic architectures that are cumbersome when it comes to enhancements, maintenance, and upgrades. A microservice architecture solves all the problems that we faced yesterday with monolithic architectures; it is easy to upgrade, troubleshoot (maintain), and enhance.

The second part of the principle is to reduce waste arising from the methodology. Defects are one of the key wastes. Defects are a nuisance. They delay the overall delivery, and the amount of effort that goes into fixing them is just a sheer waste of time and money. The next type of waste focuses on the convoluted processes. If something can be done by passing the ball from A to B, why does it have to bounce off C? There are many such wastes that can be addressed to make the software delivery more efficient and effective.

Measurement

If you should automate everything, then you possibly need a system to provide feedback whenever something goes wrong. Feedback is possible if you know what the optimum results should be. The only way you can find out whether the outcome is optimal is by measuring it. It is therefore key that you measure everything if you are going to automate everything!

The measurement principle provides direction about the measures to implement and the tabs to feel the pulse of the overall software delivery. It is not a simple task to measure everything. Many times, we don't even know what we should measure. Even if we do it, the *how* part can be an obstacle. A good DevOps process architect can help solve this problem. For example, if you are running static analysis on your code, the extent of passable code must be predetermined. It is not a random number; there should be scientific reasoning behind it. A number of companies allow a unit test to pass even if it parses 90 percent of the code. That's the kind of logic that must go behind measuring everything. You must be realistic about the kind of feedback that you want to receive.

In operations, parameters such as monitoring applications, infrastructure, performance, and others fall under this principle. Measurements in monitoring indicate when an event is categorized as a warning or an exception. With automation in place, it is extremely important that all the critical activities, and the infrastructure that supports them, be monitored and optimized for measurement.

There are other measurements that are attached to contracts and SLAs and are used for reporting on a regular basis. These measurements are key in the overall scheme of things.

Sharing

The final principle is sharing, which hinges on the need for collaboration and knowledge sharing between people. If we aim to significantly hasten the process of software delivery, people can no longer work in silos. The knowledge, experience, thoughts, and ideas must be into the open for others to join in the process of making them better, enhanced, and more profound.

One of the key takeaways of this principle is to put everyone who works on a product or a service on a single team and promote knowledge sharing. This will lead to collaboration rather than competition and skepticism.

There are a number of collaboration tools on the market today that support the cause. People don't even have to be co-located to share and collaborate. Tools such as Microsoft Teams and Slack help get the information across not only to a single person but to all those who matter (such as the entire team). With information being transparent, there is no reason for others to worry or be skeptical about the dependencies or the outcome of the process.

Elements of DevOps

DevOps is not a framework; it's a set of good practices. It started from a perfect storm that pooled several practices together (discussed later in this chapter), and today we consider them under the DevOps umbrella. You might have seen the elephant in Figure 1-3. The IT industry around software development is so vast that a number of practices are followed across the board. This is depicted as the elephant in the figure. DevOps, which is a cultural change, can be applied to any part of the software industry and to any activity that is being carried out today. So, you can identify any part of the elephant (say testing) and design DevOps-related practices and implement them—then you are doing DevOps!

Figure 1-3. *The DevOps elephant (credit: devopsdays.org)*

No matter where you want to implement DevOps, there are three common elements that support and enable the culture change. These three elements are indicated in the Venn diagram shown in Figure 1-4.

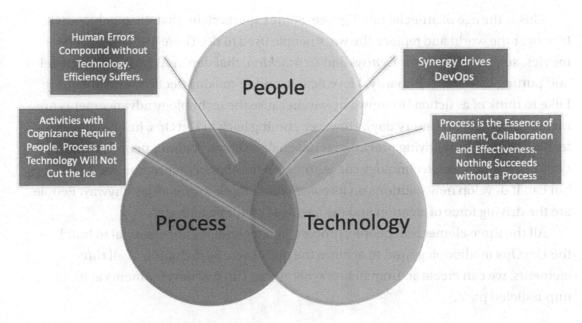

Figure 1-4. *Three elements of DevOps*

People, process, and technology are the three elements that are common to all DevOps practices. In fact, they are the enablers to affect change in the DevOps culture. Only when the three elements come together are we able to realize the complete benefits of DevOps.

Let's examine the three elements and see how they fit together. To bring in a cultural change, we most definitely need people, and people cannot operate without the aid of processes. By bringing in people and processes, we achieve the functional design to implement a DevOps solution. However, the question is whether it is efficient. Humans are known to make mistakes. We cannot avoid it. How can processes alone support humans in identifying the mistakes? There may be a way to do this, but it is most definitely not efficient. To make things move faster and in a more efficient manner, we need the technology stack to help us achieve the process objectives.

Today people talk of DevOps through the lens of technology. They throw around several tool names and claim that they do DevOps. So, the question to ponder is whether you can really do DevOps by tools alone. Can people and technology elements suffice without an underlying process? You probably guessed the answer, and the answer is no. Nothing succeeds without a process in place, not only in DevOps but in every objective that you want to achieve, IT or otherwise.

This is the age of artificial intelligence. Some experts claim that the machines will take over the world and replace the work people used to do. There are a number of movies, such as *Terminator Genisys* and *Ex Machina,* that depict AI taking over the reins and putting humans in jeopardy. I love fiction, and AI making decisions is something I like to think of as fiction (for now anyway, because the technology advancements are breaking new barriers every day). However, coming back to DevOps, just employing technology with underlying processes is not going to cut it. Without people, creation does not happen. Yes, technology can automate a number of preprogrammed activities, but can it develop new solutions on its own? I don't think so, not today anyway. People are the driving force of creation and the agents of cultural change.

All the three elements of people, process, and technology are essential to build the DevOps methodology and to achieve the objectives. By the union of all three elements, we can create an unmatched synergy that can fuel developments at an unparalleled pace.

People

The word *DevOps* is derived from the conjunction of two words, development and operations. I have already familiarized you with what DevOps is all about: a change of culture in the way we deliver and operate software. People are at the heart of this cultural transformation, and they are one of the three critical elements that enable the DevOps culture.

The development and operation teams are combined to bring about a change in culture. The thinking behind it is quite straightforward. Let's say that an application is developed and it comes to the change advisory board (CAB) for approval. One of the parties on the CAB is the operational teams. They specifically ask questions around the testing that has been performed for this software, and even though the answer from development is yes for the success rate of all the tests, the operational teams tend to be critical. They don't want to block progress, yet they find themselves in a position where they have to support software that they haven't been familiarized yet. The bugs and defects that come with the software will become their problem after the warranty period (usually between one and three months). Most important, they only have the confirmation of the developers to go by when the quality of the software is on the line.

In the same scenario, imagine if the operational teams were already part of the same team as development. Being on the same team gives them the opportunity to become familiar with the development process and the quality controls put in place. Instead of asking questions in the CAB, they can work progressively with the development teams to ensure that the software is maintainable and all possible operational aspects are considered beforehand. This is one such case study that showcases the benefit of having a single team. I talk more about it in the section titled "DevOps Team."

In Figure 1-5, you can visualize the development team on one end of the cliff, while the operations team is on the opposite end. In between the two cliffs lies an area of uncertainty where activities that fall between the two teams have a knack of being unpredictable and sparred over, generally over ownership. In other words, you want things to be either with the development team or with the operations team. There is no bridge between the teams, which can result in a lot of confusion, miscommunication, and mistrust between the two opposing teams.

Figure 1-5. *Conflict between development and operations teams*

Let's consider the priorities for both teams. The development team still has a job because there is a need to develop new features. That is their core area, and that is what they must do to remain relevant. The operations team's big-ticket goal is to keep the environment stable, in the most basic sense. They need to ensure that even if something were to go wrong, they would be tasked to bring it back to normal, in other words, maintain the status quo. So, here we have a development team intending to create new features and an operations team looking to keep the environment stable. Why does it have to be rocket science to have evolved into a methodology called DevOps that promises to shake the industry from its roots? Well, the environment is going to remain stable if there are no changes introduced to it. As long as it stays stagnant, nothing ever will bother its stability, and the operations team would have been awarded for a stellar job. But, we have the development team waiting in the wings to develop new features. New features that are developed will be deployed in the production environment. There is every chance that new features could impact the stability. So, stability is something that can never be achieved as long as new features are introduced, and the software will remain stagnant without enhancements and expansion.

A decent way to tackle this conundrum between the development and operation teams is to put them together and create channels of communication within the team members. The development and operations teams have a shared responsibility to ensure that development, testing, deployment, and other support activities happen smoothly and without glitches. Every team member takes responsibility for all the activities being carried out, which translates to the development and operation teams jointly working on the solution that begins with coding and ends with deployment. The operation teams have no reason to mistrust the test results and can confidently deploy the results onto the production environment.

DevOps Team

Along with a new way of working and the new culture comes what is called a *DevOps team*. We have so far discussed a single team consisting of the development and operation teams. An anti-pattern that has emerged in the IT industry is the creation of DevOps teams that consist of a pool of tooling professionals. A team of tool specialists is not a true DevOps team; rather, it should be a truly cross-functional team consisting of roles needed to support an application.

The Basis for a DevOps Team

DevOps does not suggest that you pool your entire set of development and operation teams together and create a DevOps team. The DevOps team must be built around an application. If application X is being developed, let all the people responsible for its development and operations be together to create one single team, which is a true DevOps team. If application X is complex and has a number of features, find a way to logically create multiple DevOps teams based on the application's features.

An Example of a DevOps Team

Application X is an internet banking program that caters to individuals and small business owners. It is currently in the development stages. Let's think of the roles that are required to support it. Today, most projects work in an Agile manner, and the development of application X will be no different. It is based on Scrum practices and employs a single Scrum team for its development. The DevOps team for application X possibly consists of the following roles:

- *Product owner (PO)*: The product owner is from the business organization and is the owner of the product backlog.

- *Scrum master (SM)*: The Scrum master leads the development as a servant leader.

- *Developer (DEV)*: Coding and unit testing are carried out by the developers.

- *Testers (TEST)*: Testers are involved in developing test scripts and executing functional and nonfunctional tests.

- *Architect (ARC)*: Architects design the software and are generally shared across multiple DevOps teams, as they are not required to play a full-time role in a single DevOps team.

- *Database administrator (DBA)*: This person does database management.

- *Application support (AS)*: This person is responsible for the support activities of the application.

- *System administrator (SYS)*: This person is responsible for configuring and managing tools.

- *Service manager (SMG)*: This person is responsible for managing services from the incident, problem, change, and other service management areas.

- *IT security (SEC)*: This person is responsible for managing aspects of IT security.

Figure 1-6 provides a typical structure of a DevOps team in which the architect is shared between the two illustrated DevOps teams.

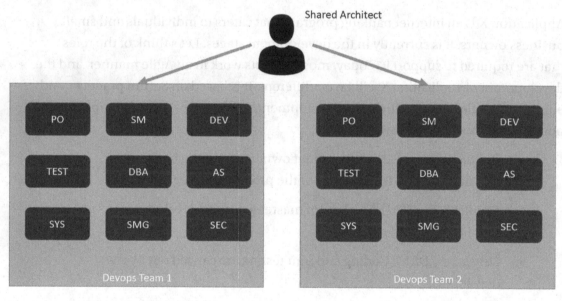

Figure 1-6. *Typical DevOps team structure*

Processes

Processes are a key component in ensuring the success of any project. However, we often find that most DevOps implementations focus more on automation and technology and give a backseat to processes that are supposed to be the basis of automation. They say that backseat driving is dangerous, so placing processes in this position and hoping that the destination will be reached in record time with no mishaps is a gamble that plays with unpredictability. Therefore, it is important that processes are defined first along with a functional DevOps architecture and then translated into tooling and automation. *The process must always drive tools and never the other way around.*

With DevOps combining different disciplines under a single banner, the processes need to be rejigged to fit the new objectives. The section covers the processes pertaining to the development area. The rest of the book is dedicated to operational processes and their union with the development processes.

Waterfall project management methodologies (such as PMI-backed Project Management and PRINCE for projects in controlled environments) are not favored in the IT field anymore. There are various reasons for this, mainly stemming from the rigidity it brings into the project management structure. Most IT projects run on Agile project management methodologies because of the flexibility it offers. According to PMI's Pulse of Profession publication, 71 percent of organizations have been leveraging Agile. Another study by PricewaterhouseCoopers, in a study named "Agile Project Delivery Confidence," reports that Agile projects are 28 percent more successful than their waterfall counterparts. This is huge considering that Agile is still new and emerging and that the waterfall methodology has existed since the 1960s.

When we talk about Agile project management, there are a number of methodologies to pick from. Scrum, Kanban, Scrumban, Extreme Programming (XP), Dynamic Systems Development Method (DSDM), Crystal, and Feature Driven Development (FDD) are some examples. However, all the methodologies are aligned by a manifesto that was formulated in a ski resort in Utah in 2001. There are a set of 12 Agile principles that provide guidance in setting up the project management processes.

In this book, I do not go into the Agile project management processes. These processes are similar irrespective of the DevOps implementation. The specific DevOps processes that are introduced on top of the Agile processes are as follows:

- Continuous integration
- Continuous delivery
- Continuous deployment

Continuous Integration

A number of developers work together on the same piece of code, which is referred to as the *mainline* in software development lingo. When multiple developers are at work, conflicts due to changes performed on pieces of code and the employed logic are quite common. Software developers generally integrate their pieces of code into the mainline once a day.

When conflicts arise, they discuss and sort it out. This process of integrating the code manually at a defined time slows down development. Conflicts at times can have drastic results with hundreds of lines of code having to be rewritten. Imagine the time and effort lost due to this manual integration. If I can integrate code in almost real time with the rest of the developers, the potential amount of rework can be significantly reduced. This is the concept of *continuous integration*.

To be more specific, continuous integration is a process where developers integrate their code into the source code repository (mainline) on a regular basis, say multiple times a day. When the code is integrated with the mainline, any conflicts, if there are any, will come out into the open, as soon as it is integrated. The resolution of conflicts does not have to be an affair where all developers sit across the codebase. Only those who have conflicts need to sort them out manually. By performing this conflict resolution multiple times a day, the extent of the conflicts is drastically minimized.

Note   The best definition of continuous integration was coined by Martin Fowler from ThoughtWorks, who is also one of the founding members of the Agile Manifesto.

Continuous integration is a software development practice whereby members of a team integrate their work frequently. Each person usually integrates at least daily, leading to multiple integrations per day. Each integration is verified by an automated build (including tests) to detect integration errors as quickly as possible. Many teams find that this approach leads to significantly reduced integration problems and allows a team to develop cohesive software more rapidly (source: https://www.martinfowler.com/articles/continuousIntegration.html).

Integrating the code with the mainline is just the beginning. Whenever the code is integrated, the entire mainline is built, and other quality checks such as unit testing and code-quality checks (static and dynamic analysis) are also carried out.

Note   A *build* is a process whereby the human-readable code is converted into the machine-readable language (executable code) and the output of a build activity is a binary.

Unit testing is a quality check whereby the smallest testable parts of an application are tested individually and in a componentized manner.

Static analysis is an examination of the source code against the coding standards set forth by the industry/software company, such as naming conventions, blank spaces, and comments.

Dynamic analysis is an examination of the binary during runtime. Such an examination helps identify runtime errors such as memory leaks.

An Illustration

Let's say a particular project has three developers, and each developer integrates their code three times a day. On a daily basis, this equates to nine integrations. As per Figure 1-7, code that is integrated gets unit tested first, followed by software builds and code quality checks. All this happens automatically whenever the code is integrated.

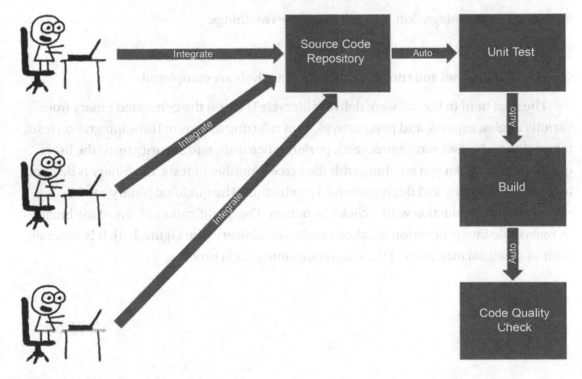

Figure 1-7. *Continuous integration*

With nine integrations on a daily basis, we are staring at a possibility of having nine unit tests, nine builds on the entire mainline, and nine code-quality checks.

Suppose one of the builds, unit tests, or code-quality checks fail. The flow is interrupted, and the developer gets down to work to fix the defect. This ensures that the flow of code is not hampered and other coders can continue coding and integrate their work onto the mainline.

In the "Technology" section, I talk about a few tools that are used to achieve this kind of an automation. They set loose the dependencies that we normally have and the impediments that are normally faced by developers.

Continuous integration allows for fast delivery of software, and any roadblocks are avoided or identified as early as possible, thanks to rapid feedback and automation. The objective of continuous integration is to hasten the coding process and to generate a binary without integration bugs.

Continuous Delivery

With continuous integration, you achieve these two things:

- A binary is generated successfully.

- Code-level and runtime checks and analysis are completed.

The next item in the software delivery lifecycle is to test the generated binary from various angles, aspects, and perspectives. I am referring to system tests, integration tests, regression tests, user acceptance tests, performance tests, and security tests; the list is quite endless. When you are done with the agreed number of tests, the binary is deemed to be of good quality and deployable into production. The qualified binary can be deployed into production with a click of a button. The qualification of any of the binaries as releasable into production is called *continuous delivery* (see Figure 1-8). It is generally seen as a natural extension of the continuous integration process.

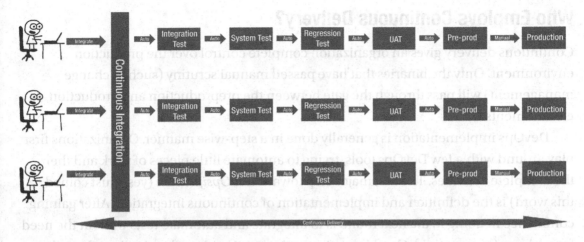

Figure 1-8. *Continuous delivery*

Figure 1-8 depicts a continuous delivery pipeline. After every successful cycle of continuous integration, the binary is automatically subjected to an integration test. When the integration test is successful, the same binary is automatically system tested. The cycle passes up to the preproduction environment as long as the tests (regression and user acceptance testing in Figure 1-8) are successful. When the same binary is successfully deployed in the preproduction environment or any other environment that comes before the production environment, the binary becomes qualified to be deployed to production. The deployment into the production environment is not done automatically, but requires a trigger. The entire cycle—starting from the code push into the source code repository up to the manual deployment into the production environment—is continuous delivery.

Figure 1-8 shows three developers integrating their code and three deployable binaries. Continuous delivery does not dictate that all three binaries have to be deployed into production. The release-management process can make a decision to deploy only the latest binary every week. Remember that the latest binary will consist of the code changes performed by all the developers up until that point in time.

The sequence of automation for the activities beginning in the continuous integration process until the production environment is referred to as a *pipeline* or *continuous delivery pipeline* in this case.

Who Employs Continuous Delivery?

Continuous delivery gives an organization complete control over the production environment. Only the binaries that have passed manual scrutiny (such as change management) will pass through the gate between the preproduction and production environments.

DevOps implementation is generally done in a step-wise manner. Organizations first play around with a few DevOps tools, trying to automate little pieces of work and then the complete activities. The first major step toward *DevOpsification* (yes, I just coined this word) is the definition and implementation of continuous integration. After gaining confidence in doing it, the next round is to integrate and automate tests without the need for a trigger (automation). Combining the test integrations into the pipeline where the binary can be deemed deployable is a big step toward achieving continuous delivery. Most organizations do not have the capability to fully implement continuous delivery as illustrated in Figure 1-8. It requires adequate focus, unparalleled talent in process and technology, and—most importantly—a concrete vision and intent to move toward automation.

Automation Testing vs. Continuous Testing

Here is more DevOps jargon for you: continuous testing. *Continuous testing* is the process where automated tests kick in after the continuous integration process. There is absolutely no human involvement during the execution of tests, not even a trigger to begin a test. Everything happens in a sequence, and the only automated trigger is a successful test of the previous activity. For example, in Figure 1-9, the automated UAT does not happen if the regression test does not succeed.

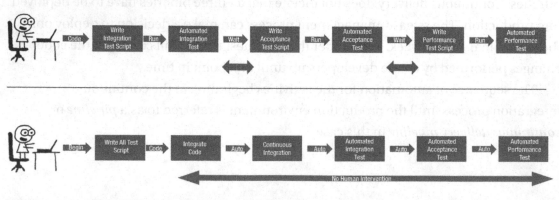

Figure 1-9. *The difference between automation and continuous testing*

The term automation testing may be familiar to you. What is the difference between the two?

Automation testing is a process in which tests are executed automatically using various automation testing tools. However, the trigger to begin the testing in an automated fashion is a manual activity.

Continuous testing is a process where the execution of tests is run through the testing tools automatically following code integration and success of the previous sequential activity. There is no manual trigger to begin a test execution.

So, what is the difference between automation testing and continuous testing?

In both the cases, test scripts have to be written by testers, and there is no difference in the manner they are written. The only difference is the execution.

Generally, in a project involving automation testing, the code is developed and built. Then the automation test script is written and fed into the testing tool and manually triggers an automated test.

In the continuous testing world, the automation test scripts are written before the coding begins, which requires a good and common understanding of the requirements. When the binary is successfully built and continuous integration cycle is successfully processed, the execution of the tests is triggered and they run automatically as well.

The advantage of continuous testing over automation testing is that the entire sequence of activities in the pipeline happens rapidly, one after another. There are no waiting periods for scripts to be ready or for the tester to press the Execute button. It is swift, leaving no room for inefficiencies of human constructs and therefore enabling faster delivery, which is the objective of DevOps.

Continuous Deployment

Continuous deployment is one step beyond continuous delivery. In continuous delivery, the deployment to production is based on a manual trigger. However, in the *continuous deployment* process, the deployment to production happens automatically, as depicted in Figure 1-10.

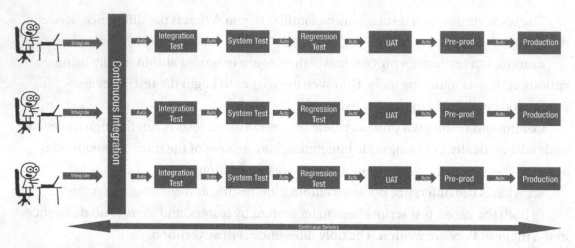

Figure 1-10. *Continuous deployment*

In Figure 1-10, as soon as all the tests are successful, the binary is deployed to the preproduction environment. When the deployment to preproduction goes as planned, the same binary is deployed into production directly. In continuous delivery (Figure 1-8), the binaries were qualified as deployable, and the release manager was in a position to not deploy every single qualified binary into production. On the contrary, in continuous deployment, every single qualified binary gets deployed onto the production instance.

You might think that this is far too risky. How can you deploy something into production without any checks and balances or approvals from all stakeholders? Well, every test that is performed and all the quality checks are qualifying binaries as deployables. It's all happening in an automated fashion. You would do the same set of things otherwise, but manually. Instead of deploying multiple times a day, you might deploy once a week. All the benefits that you derive from going early into the market are missing from the manual processes.

Let's say that one of the deployments were to fail. No problem! There is an automated rollback mechanism built into the system that rolls back the deployment within seconds. And it is important to note that the changes that are being discussed here are tiny changes. So, the chances of these binaries bringing down a system are remote.

Continuous Delivery vs. Continuous Deployment

Figure 1-11 depicts the difference between continuous delivery and continuous deployment.

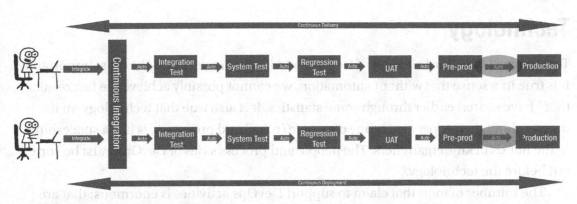

Figure 1-11. *The difference between continuous delivery and continuous deployment*

The difference lies in the final sequence, where the deployment to production instance is automatic in continuous deployment and has a manual trigger in continuous delivery.

Any organization on the journey of implementing DevOps will implement the continuous delivery process and, upon gaining sufficient maturity, will move toward the pinnacle of DevOps maturity: the continuous deployment process.

Organizations that feel a need to keep total control of their production environment through a formal structure of approvals and visibility tend to opt for continuous delivery. Banking and other financial segments fall into this category.

There are other organizations that have scaled the DevOps maturity ladder and are quite confident that the automatic deployment doesn't significantly impact their production environment, and even if something were to fail, then the rollback will be rapid too, even before anybody can notice it. Companies like Amazon, Netflix, and Google have been in this space for a while now. I shared a statistic earlier about Amazon managing a deployment every 11.6 seconds. How is it even possible? Look no further than continuous deployment.

Note   Here's a cheat sheet for continuous delivery and continuous deployment:

Continuous delivery: You can deploy.

Continuous deployment: You will deploy.

Technology

Technology is the third element of DevOps and is often regarded as the most important. It is true in a sense that without automation, we cannot possibly achieve the fast results that I have shared earlier through some statistics. It is also true that technology on its own, without the proper synchrony of people (roles) and processes, is like a spaceship in the hands of kindergarteners. The people and process sides of DevOps must be sorted out before the technology.

The number of tools that claim to support DevOps activities is enormous; that are too many to count.

Choosing the Right Tool

Not all tools can be used for all technologies, and the same tool cannot be used to carry out different types of activities. For example, if you are using the Java programming language for unit testing, you need use a tool such as JUnit. On the other hand, with Microsoft technologies, you need NUnit for unit testing.

There are tools that support multiprogramming languages, such as Jenkins and Cucumber. In fact, for the same activity and the same technology, there are multiple tool choices. It is important to weigh the capabilities and compatibilities before choosing one. For example, for the source code repository function, there are multiple good choices. Git is the most common one, and Subversion is almost as popular as Git. Both provide versioning capability for the source code and can be integrated with other toolsets for automation. Which one should you choose? If you look deeper into the technology employed, Subversion falls under the category of central version control system (CVCS), and Git is a distributed version control system (DVCS).

The underlying technology specifies where the code is stored and retrieved. CVCS employs a server-client relationship to store and retrieve the code. The developer is required to first check out the existing code, make changes, and check it back in. Under DVCS, every single developer has the entire mainline sitting on their computer. So, there is no concept of check-out and check-in. DVCS allows multiple developers to work seamlessly.

The greatest advantage of DVCS over CVCS is its availability. For DVCS to function, you don't need an active network connection, but for CVCS it is absolutely necessary. If server access is blocked, development comes to a standstill. Thus, CVCS has a single point of failure (SPOF), something that goes against the principles of DevOps, which emphasizes incessant development and maximum efficiency. Since source code is available locally in DVCS, accessing, merging, and pushing the code is much faster relative to CVCS. DVCS also enables software developers to exchange code with other developers before pushing it to the central server and, consequently, to all other developers. In fact, there are no notable disadvantages with DVCS other than perhaps the storage needs on a developer's terminal if the source code contains an elongated history of changesets.

In this example of a source code repository, I gave a glimpse of how the tools are chosen and how they must be scrutinized. The role of a DevOps architect is to find the right tool for a particular activity.

Categories of Tools

Remember the periodic table of elements? Digital.ai (formerly XebiaLabs) has replaced the chemical elements with a few DevOps tools in their respective categories in a periodic table format. Figure 1-12 shows this periodic table of DevOps at the time of this writing.

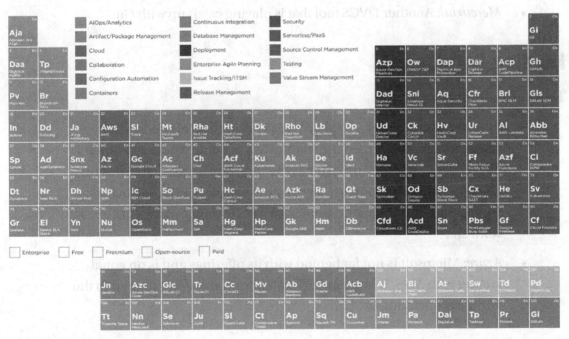

Figure 1-12. *The periodic table of DevOps (Source:* `https://digital.ai/learn/`
`devops-periodic-table/`)

If I have to categorize the toolsets, then I would probably do it based on function and the outcome that I am trying to achieve. For example, managing the source code is an outcome, so I categorize all source code repositories under a single bucket. The following sections list some categories to help you identify the right tool. They are, by no means, comprehensive.

Source Code Repositories

These are the more popular source code repositories:

- *Git*: The most popular source code repository today. Git is free and open source. However, some Git hosting providers charge you for the hosting service and the customizations that have been employed.

- *Apache Subversion*: Commonly referred to as SVN, this is open source (and free). This version-control system is losing steam because of the underlying CVCS technology. This is not apt for most DevOps implementations.

- *Mercurial*: Another DVCS tool that is playing catch up with Git.

Hosting Services

These are hosting services:

- *Amazon Web Services (AWS)*: AWS has taken the DevOps world by storm. It has transformed the way hosting is done, where consumers pay only for what they use. The AWS ecosystem is vast, and Amazon offers its own set of tools for carrying out various DevOps activities. For example, AWS CodeCommit is an AWS instance of the Git software.

- *Azure*: Microsoft is not far behind with its offerings and is on equal footing with AWS. It hosts multiple platforms and is not limited to the Windows operating system.

- *Google Compute Engine*: Can you leave out Google when talking about hosting and state-of-the-art tooling solutions? The solutions offered on all hosting services are high quality, so in most cases, cost becomes a factor in choosing one over the other. At the time of this writing, Google Compute Engine offers the cheapest prices across multiple segments.

Orchestrators

Automation is achieved through the orchestration of various toolsets. Orchestrators create workflows through which pipelines can be defined, along with various parameters that set the criteria for progression into the next activity. These are orchestrators:

- *Jenkins*: Jenkins is the most popular orchestrator, as it works across platforms and technologies. It can talk to most tools through various plug-ins. The best part is that the tool is free and comes with massive community support.

- *UrbanCode Deploy*: UrbanCode Deploy is an IBM product that is a powerful orchestration tool. Its compatibility with mainframe systems is its biggest advantage. The tool can also carry out automated deployments, which Jenkins achieves through orchestration with other tools.

- *Bamboo*: Bamboo is from Atlassian and is not free. Like Jenkins, it works across platforms and supports multiple technologies.

Deployment and Environment Provisioning

These tools do deployment and environment provisioning:

- *Ansible*: Ansible is a popular tool for automated deployments, environment provisioning, and configuration management. The concept of infrastructure as code (IAC), whereby infrastructure can be built by scripts, is handled through Ansible. Other toolsets in this category also effectively manage IAC.

- *Puppet*: Puppet comes in two versions: open source with limited features and a full-blown enterprise version. It is perhaps the most popular tool in this category.

- *Chef*: This is similar to Ansible and Puppet. Facebook uses Chef for its deployments and for managing the configuration of applications and infrastructure.

Testing

There are a number of types of testing, and in this section, I highlight some popular testing tools that are employed in DevOps implementations.

- *Selenium*: This is the most popular functional testing tool. It works across platforms and technologies and integrates seamlessly with all the major orchestration tools. It is open source.

- *Cucumber*: Cucumber runs automated acceptance tests (such as UAT without the user). It provides support for behavior-driven development (BDD), which is a development methodology that is driven by writing the test script first and then the code. The test scripts are written in a natural language called Gherkin.

- *HP LoadRunner*: LoadRunner by HP is a testing tool for measuring system behavior and performance under load. Performance testing is considered nonfunctional testing, whereby the quality aspects of an application are scrutinized.

Is DevOps the End of Ops?

With the introduction of continuous integration, continuous delivery, and continuous deployment, the focus has been to plug the defects, increase the quality, and not sacrifice the efficiency. The thinking behind the notion of DevOps ending the operational activities is based on the premise that a lack of defects will not give rise to operational work. If there are no defects, there are potentially no incidents or problems, which translates to a massive reduction in operational work. Another example is if we implement continuous deployment, the change and release management processes as we know them will be automated to a great extent and will diminish the need for approvals and subsequent approvals, release planning, and release deployment.

Let's get one thing straight: no matter how much you try using technology and automation, defects will always exist. The number of defects will go down due to the rapid feedback and automation, but to state that all the defects will be identified and rectified is absurd. With the reduction of defects, the amount of operational work will definitely go down. With the argument around change and release management processes, the execution of changes and releases can be automated through continuous delivery and continuous deployment, but the planning bit will always remain in the human realm. To an extent, the operational work involving change and release management processes are starting to go down as well.

Innovation is a double-edged sword. With the introduction of tools and automation, there is a new operational requirement to set up and configure the tool stack and to maintain it as long as the project is underway. This is an operational activity that is added to the traditional operations work. While some areas have seen a reduction, there are new ones that have sprouted to take their place. The manual, repetitive, and boring activities are going away. In their place, exciting DevOps tooling work has come to the fore and is making the operational roles all the more lucrative.

So, if you are an operational person, it is time to scale up and scale beyond managerial activities alone. The new wave of role mapping requires people to be *technomanagerial* in talent and be multiskilled. T-shaped resources, not only for operations but also in development, are being sought after. I-shaped resources must look toward getting acquainted with areas of expertise that complement their line of work.

With the advent of DevOps, there is a turbulence created in software projects. It is a good turbulence because it seeks to raise the level of delivery and to make teams, rather than individuals, accountable for the outcomes. From an operations front, it is clear that their role has gone up a couple of notches, whereby the mundane, boring, and repetitive activities have been replaced with imaginative and challenging jobs such as configuring pipelines, integrating toolsets, and automating configuration management. The nature of operations work has changed but not the role they play as guardians of environments and troubleshooters of incidents and problems. DevOps has not meant the end of operations but rather rejuvenated it to an exciting journey that will keep the wits of people working in operations alive.

Summary

Treat this chapter as DevOps 101. The basis and origins of DevOps are happenstance, but the principles it uses are supported by thousands of enthusiasts who have improved and transformed the thinking of rapid delivery. Continuous integration, continuous delivery, and continuous deployment form the basic processes and maturity levels in DevOps. The structure of DevOps teams is unified to encourage collaboration and remove the silo culture. Technology plays a significant part through the automation it brings in. But at the heart of it all, DevOps is a culture that promotes blamelessness, experimentation, and collaboration.

CHAPTER 2

ITIL Basics

The Information Technology Infrastructure Library (ITIL) is the most popular framework to deliver services. It has become a standard of sorts, and most service-based organizations have implemented one form of ITIL or another.

The objective of the ITIL framework is to provide guidance on how services have to be defined, developed, built, and operated. The framework provides a detailed lifecycle of phases, from inception to operation, in a methodical fashion, which some construe as loaded or heavy (something not considered favorably today). No matter what the critics say, ITIL is complete and absolute and takes into account all perspectives of a service; it is a valuable ally for a service management organization. The entire process of setting up ITIL in organizations may take anywhere from 6 to 18 months, depending on the volume and complexity.

I have practiced ITIL for more than 20 years, and when I look at the length and breadth of the framework, it amazes me how holistically it has grown over the years. I wrote a book on the subject, called *Become ITIL 4 Foundation Certified in 7 Days* (Apress, 2020). This book is a foundational course in ITIL for those who intend to get into the service management industry. The additional aim of the book is to aid readers in becoming ITIL Foundation certified (within seven days, considering professionals have a day job). If you want a deeper understanding of the ITIL framework, I highly recommend that you read the book. This chapter is meant to provide the absolute basics of ITIL, which is the foundation for the building that I am about to construct in the rest of this part.

IT Service Management and ITIL

There was a time when there was business and then there was IT. Businesses had their set of practices, and IT was a supporting agent, helping businesses achieve their tasks. IT supplied businesses with a word processor for drafting contracts and the ability to compute complex formulas. Without IT, businesses could survive, although surely with some inconvenience.

39

© Abhinav Krishna Kaiser 2023
A. Krishna Kaiser, *Reinventing ITIL® and DevOps with Digital Transformation*,
https://doi.org/10.1007/978-1-4842-9072-9_2

Today, the world of business has been turned on its head. You take IT out of business and the business will cease to exist. In other words, there is no business without IT. Businesses rely on IT for its sustenance, and IT is not a support function anymore. Rather, it is a partner that enables businesses to achieve their goals and succeed in beating their competitors. Try to think of a midsize business where IT is not be involved. I know your results came up blank. To reiterate, IT is a part of the business, and there is no looking back.

IT service management is defined as the implementation and management of quality IT services that meet the needs of and deliver value to the business. IT services are provided by IT service providers (the entity that provides IT services to internal and external customers) through an appropriate mix of people, processes, and information technology.

There is increased pressure on IT to deliver on its services. IT must deliver services that not only meet its objectives but also do it effectively and efficiently. And it must be done at a minimal cost. The competition in the IT service management industry is fierce. You have some of the biggest names playing ball, cutting IT costs, and providing best-in-class service. The world of IT service management is challenging with ever-changing technology, and it's exciting with innovative ideas coming into play. At the same time, it's a race that can be won only if you couple technology with management.

The Conception of ITIL

The history of ITIL is nebulous and inconsistent. It started sometime during the late 1980s as a collection of best practices in IT management. A department in the UK government, known as the Office of Government Commerce (OGC), sanctioned the coalition. Basically, the best practices of various IT departments and companies in the United Kingdom were studied and documented. It is believed that most of the initial practices that constituted ITIL came from IBM.

The first version of ITIL was bulky and lacked direction with a compilation of more than 30 books. The second version of ITIL was cut down to nine books in 2000 but mainly revolved around two books: service delivery and service support. The ITIL certifications were based on these two books as well. ITIL V2 introduced ten processes, five each from service delivery and service support. I started my ITIL journey with ITIL V2.

ITIL V2 was process-centric. IT organizations were expected to operate around the ITIL processes. The processes were interconnected but lacked a broader vision and a flow to move things along.

The shortcomings and inadequacies in V2 gave rise to ITIL V3 in 2007. It has 24 processes, spanning the entire lifecycle of a service, from conception up to a point where the service runs on regular improvement cycles.

ITIL V3 came out with five books, each book spanning a lifecycle phase of an IT service. ITIL V3 has penetrated most IT organizations. Even conservative IT organizations have embraced the ITIL V3 service management framework with open arms. The framework is rampant in the industry today and enjoys the monopolistic nature, except for Microsoft, which adheres to a derivative version of ITIL, the Microsoft Operations Framework.

In 2011, ITIL V3 received a minor update where a couple of new processes were added along with some minute changes in definitions and concepts. This version of ITIL is referred to as ITIL 2011, and some people refer to it as ITIL V3 2011, indicating the version and the revision year. ITIL in this version has 26 processes and four functions.

In 2017, a new version (V4) was announced. The date was set two years later, and in February 2019, a phase-wise release of ITIL 4 started. It started with the ITIL Foundation publication and the announcement of the ITIL Foundation examination, and in the next few months, individual modules were announced. The entire set of ITIL 4 modules came out in 2020. In my view, ITIL 4 should have come out at around 2015, which was the prime time when DevOps had taken shape and several eulogies for ITIL V3 were sung. Several experts from all areas of IT predicted ITIL's doom. They felt that ITIL V3 was quite archaic and did not fit the needs of the digital age. They are right about it, and until ITIL V3 was adapted to work in DevOps projects, it was not going to work - which is exactly what the first part of the book intends to cater to.

Figure 2-1 depicts ITIL versions over the years.

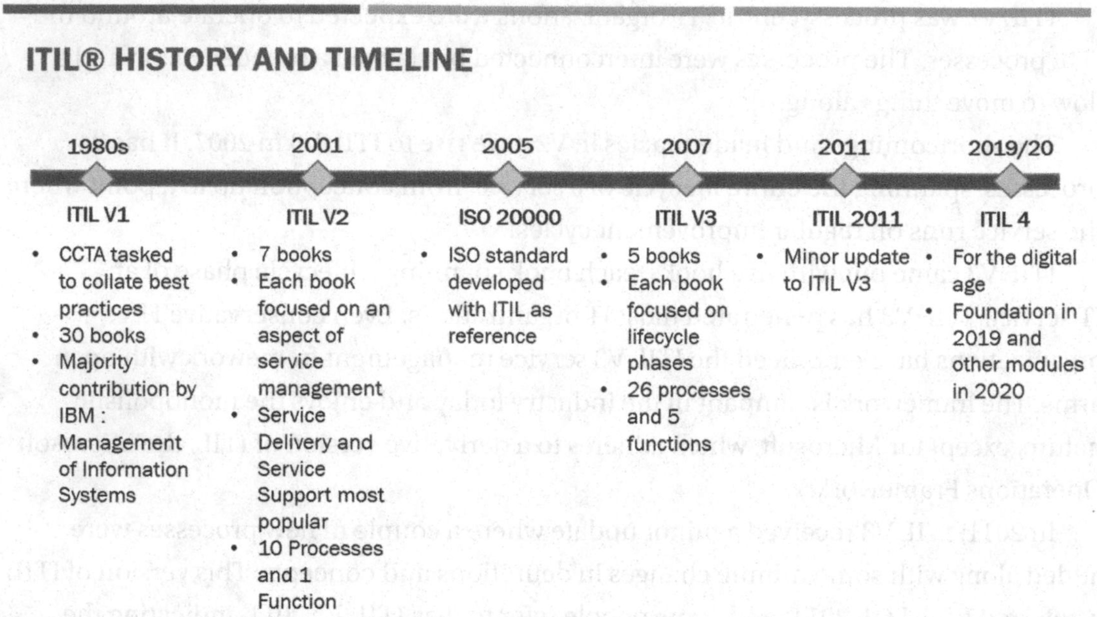

ITIL® HISTORY AND TIMELINE

1980s	2001	2005	2007	2011	2019/20
ITIL V1	**ITIL V2**	**ISO 20000**	**ITIL V3**	**ITIL 2011**	**ITIL 4**
• CCTA tasked to collate best practices • 30 books • Majority contribution by IBM : Management of Information Systems	• 7 books • Each book focused on an aspect of service management • Service Delivery and Service Support most popular • 10 Processes and 1 Function	• ISO standard developed with ITIL as reference	• 5 books • Each book focused on lifecycle phases • 26 processes and 5 functions	• Minor update to ITIL V3	• For the digital age • Foundation in 2019 and other modules in 2020

Figure 2-1. *ITIL over the years*

Note   Although ITIL 4 is the latest version, the guidance provided in ITIL V3 is most prevalent. Although a number of companies looked at moving into the new version, the general feeling was that it was apt for the digital age, but it consisted of principles that need to be accounted for, like value chains and value streams, and the guidance provided around practical implementation was insufficient. In this book, I address the topic of ITIL 4 but recommend new strategies and process changes based on ITIL V3 2011.

Competition to ITIL

ITIL has been dominant for the past two decades. There are no other service management frameworks that are competing for space. It is quite lonely in the club of service management frameworks. Why do you think this is the case? A lot of things have worked in ITIL's favor. It has a single objective—to deliver value to the business. To deliver unparalleled value, it has adopted the following characteristics:

- ITIL is based on best practices.

- ITIL is nonprescriptive.

- ITIL is vendor and technology neutral.

- ITIL is nonproprietary.

As mentioned in the previous section, best practices are collated from various organizations. Some organizations may be doing a great job of gathering requirements, while others focus on identifying improvements. So, when you take the best of such organizations and bring that together, you have knowledge that is enviable.

Proprietary knowledge, on the other hand, stays within close quarters, and fewer heads have been banged together to come up with proprietary knowledge, which may be good, but it's not as diverse and experienced as public frameworks such as ITIL.

Proprietary knowledge is developed for the sole purpose of meeting the organization's objectives. It is not meant to be adapted to meet other organizations' objectives. Moreover, if you are adopting proprietary knowledge, you are expected to pay a fee or royalty of some kind. Public frameworks are free. When you can get an all-you-can-eat buffet for free, why would you pay for dinner à la carte?

Understanding Services

ITIL is a framework that is centered on IT services. So, it is imperative to first understand the meaning of a service, according to ITIL. Here is the official definition of an IT service:

A service is a means of delivering value to customers by facilitating outcomes that customers want to achieve, without the ownership of specific costs and risks.

The best way to understand anything that is complex is to break it into parts. This is my method for understanding the concept of IT services.

The first section of the definition states: "means of delivering value to customers by facilitating outcomes that customers want to achieve."

IT services in ITIL are defined from a customer viewpoint. Essentially, an IT service must deliver value to the customer. The value delivered must be something that the customer considers as helpful. Let's take the example of an IT service that is quite common across the board: the Internet. An Internet service delivers value to customers to help them achieve their objectives. So, it fits the bill of what an IT service is all about.

If the Internet service provider (ISP) were to provide speeds upward of 100MB per second for a customer who only checks emails, it would be overkill. The high speeds offered by ISPs are generally appreciated by gamers and social networking users. In contrast, the customer who uses the Internet service for checking emails does not find any special value between a high-speed Internet and a normal Internet connection. But for a user who hogs a lot of bandwidth, it is valuable. To summarize, the value of an IT service is derived from the customer's standpoint. So from this example, value to one customer may not be value to another.

Now the last part of the definition states: "without the ownership of specific costs and risks."

The customer enjoys the service but does not pay for specific costs. Instead, they pay for the service as a lump sum. For example, in the Internet example, the customer pays for the high-speed Internet a fixed sum every month, not a specific price for the elements that make up a service, such as the infrastructure that supports it, the people who maintain and design, and the other governmental regulation costs. Instead, the customer just pays an agreed amount.

The final part of the definition states that the customers do not take ownership of the risks. Yes, but the Internet service provider does. What are some of the risks that exist in the IT world pertaining to ISPs?

- Fiber cuts

- Availability of support technicians

- Infrastructure stability among others

The customers protect themselves against the risk of enjoying services through service level agreements (SLAs) to guarantee service at certain minimum levels (fit for use and fit for purpose).

Service Types (Components)

A service can be broken into three components. Essentially what a service provides is the heart of a service; the component is called as the *core service*. The core service is customer-facing; however, the core service is powered by sets of services called *enabling services*, which is the final component. Finally, the core service is embellished with other service to make it more attractive (the third and final component), called *enhancing services*.

So, these are the components of a service:

- Core service

- Enabling service

- Enhancing service

Figure 2-2 illustrates the three components of a service.

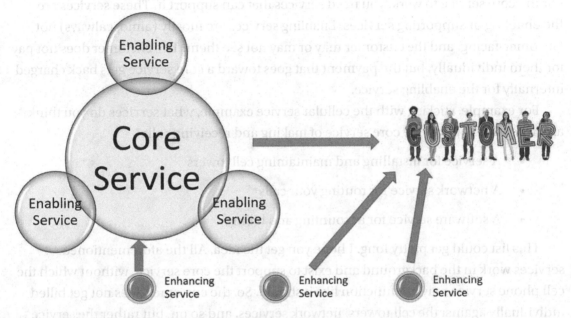

Figure 2-2. *Types/components of a service*

Core Services

A core service is at the heart of the service that is delivered to the customer. It delivers the basic outcomes that the customer is interested in. The value representation for the customer starts with the core service, and it is the main driver that the customer is willing to pay for.

For example, say a customer signs on with a cellular service provider to make and receive calls on the go. The most basic service that a cell phone service provider offers is the ability to make and receive calls. This is the core service. If the service provider fails to deliver the telephony functionality to the customer's satisfaction but instead focuses on other add-ons such as high-speed Internet, the customer will still be unhappy because the core service, the reason behind the customer's decision to pay for the service, has backfired.

Enabling Services

For the core service to work, you need services that can support it. These services are the enabling or supporting services. Enabling services are mostly (almost always) not customer-facing, and the customer may or may not see them. The customer does not pay for them individually, but the payment that goes toward a core service gets back charged internally for the enabling service.

For example, sticking with the cellular service example, what services do you think are needed to support the core service of making and receiving calls?

- A service for installing and maintaining cell towers

- A network service for routing your calls

- A software service for accounting and billing

This list could get pretty long. I hope you get the idea. All the aforementioned services work in the background and exist to support the core service, without which the cell phone service may not function like it should. So, the customer does not get billed individually against the cell towers, network services, and so on, but rather the service the customer enjoys comes with a price tag attached to it.

Enhancement Services

Enhancing services provide the excitement factor to the customer. They add on to the core service, providing a number of services that most often excite the customer into paying more for the service. The enhancing services may not function on their own, so it is necessary for them to be piggybacked on the core service for their deliverance.

A core service can exist without enhancing service, but the reverse is not possible. The presence of enhancing services differentiates the service provider from others in the market.

For example, the customer can make and receive calls. What else? When looking at the service brochure, the customer was more interested in what else the service provider could offer as the calling part was a given. It offered 4G Internet, Internet hotspots around the city, voicemail, SMS, and others. These additional features help the customer make a decision in choosing the service provider.

Understanding Processes

ITIL is made up of processes. Just as with services, you cannot get into the nitty-gritty of ITIL if you don't understand the concept of a process. I give you some examples to emphasize its importance so that your foundation is strong for what you have to build on for your career. For the official definition, ITIL defines a process as follows:

> *A structured set of activities designed to accomplish a specific objective. A process takes one or more inputs and turns them into defined outputs.*

You can envision a process as a set of activities that you need to perform, one after another, to achieve something. Each activity that you perform sets the precedence for the next one and then the next. The objective of a process would be to achieve an output that is along the expected lines and as desired.

Now for a simple and digestible example. A process is similar to a recipe for cooking a dish. In a recipe, you have several steps that you need to follow, as instructed, to get the dish you desire.

Let's look at this recipe for an egg omelet. It goes something like this:

- *Step 1*: Break a couple of eggs into a bowl.

- *Step 2*: Whisk them until they become fluffy.

- *Step 3*: Add salt and pepper to the mixture.

- *Step 4*: Heat a nonstick frying pan and melt some butter until it foams.

- *Step 5*: Pour the egg mixture into the pan and tilt the pan until it covers the base.

- *Step 6*: Cook for a minute or two and flip the omelet and cook it for a minute more.

- *Step 7*: Serve the omelet hot with toasted bread.

You need to follow the steps to make an egg omelet. You cannot interchange any two steps to get the same output. In IT language, this is the *process* to make an egg omelet.

The main aspect of a process is the interconnectivity between the individual steps, and collectively, all the steps work toward a common goal, or a common objective that is desired.

Note   All processes must have an input, a trigger, and an output. A trigger will initiate a process to kickstart, and the provided inputs are processed to provide a predictable output. In the recipe example, eggs are the input, and hunger or the need to have breakfast is the trigger. The finished product of the omelet is the output.

Understanding Functions

Before I discuss functions, let's take a look at organization structures. It is quite common these days for there to be teams with people who have expertise in one area. Examples could be the networking team, the UNIX team, the Windows team, the Java team, and the web development team. It is also in vogue that teams are carved out based on the depth of knowledge. An example would be a Network L1 team (junior), Network L2 team (senior), and Network L3 team (expert teams, the architects). L1 teams consist of people with less experience, and the tasks they are asked to take care of are quite basic and administrative in nature. For an L2 team, it gets a little more complicated, and they could be asked to troubleshoot and diagnose outages. An L3 team could be your top-notch team that not only provides support when L2 needs it but also helps architecting networks.

The teams that I have been referring to are known as *functions* in ITIL, nothing more, nothing less. There are only four functions that are defined in ITIL, and all of them come into play during the entire lifecycle of ITIL framework. The official definition of a function is as follows:

> *A team or group of people and the tools or other resources they use to carry out one or more processes or activities.*

Functions in ITIL

All the functions are defined in the service operations publication. The list of functions is as follows:

- Service desk
- Technical management
- Application management
- IT operations management
  - IT operations control
  - Facility management

Processes vs. Functions

There are processes, and there are functions in ITIL. While there are 26 processes, there are only four functions. Processes don't run by themselves. They need people to carry out the individual process activities in traditional ITIL (you will find out later how processes can be automated later in this book in DevOps). And the people the processes look for come from functions. To state it simply, functions provide the resources needed by the processes to complete their objectives.

Within the organization where you work, there are verticals—say banking, retail, and insurance. There are processes that cut across all the verticals of the organization such as human resources. The people in the verticals perform their role in the human resources process, which is horizontal cutting across all verticals, even though they are part of a function. This is an example of how a process leverages functions for carrying out the set objectives.

Figure 2-3 illustrates the intersection between processes and functions. You can replace the functions with the verticals in your organization and the processes with the common processes such as travel process, promotion processes, and others, to establish a better understanding.

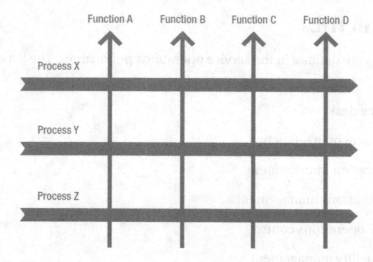

Figure 2-3. *Intersection between processes and functions*

ITIL Service Lifecycle

ITIL was derived from various high-level activities that encounter an IT service, and each of these high-level activities was introduced as phases in the ITIL service lifecycle. The five phases are as follows:

- Service strategy
- Service design
- Service transition
- Service operations
- Continual service improvement

These five phases are represented in Figure 2-4. The figure shows service strategy at the core to indicate the importance and involvement of a sound strategy in the inception of IT services. Service strategy provides guidance around existing and new IT services. Surrounding service strategy includes service design, service transition, and service operations. Service design provides the direction pertaining to the realization of a service. The IT services that are identified in the service strategy are defined and designed, and blueprints are created for its development. These designs are built, tested, and implemented in the service transition phase. After implementation, the services move into a maintenance mode. Maintenance of services is handled by the service operations phase. Continual service operations envelop the other four phases. The depiction shows that all four phases present opportunities for improvement, and the continuous service improvement will provide the means to identify and implement improvements across the service lifecycle.

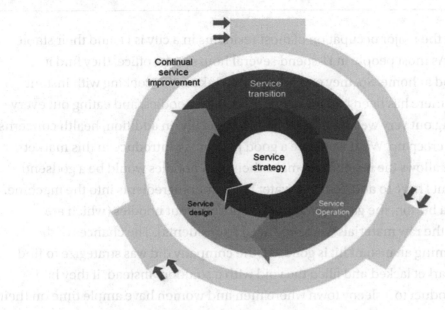

Figure 2-4. *ITIL service lifecycle*

Did you notice that every phase in ITIL has *service* in it? This is not happenstance but rather strongly indicates that ITIL is service-centric, and it revolves around services that provide value to customers.

Service Strategy

Service strategy is at the core of IT services. It is the heart of service management. The main intent of ITIL and IT service management is to create value for customers. The value creation starts at the service strategy lifecycle phase.

In this phase, the question "why do it?" is posed before the question "how to do it?". The core intent of this phase is to develop a strategy and create services that add value to customers. For the service provider organization to flourish financially, everything must be business as usual at the end of the day.

Note   Business as usual is commonly abbreviated as BAU. It refers to employees of an organization completing their respective day-to-day tasks in a normal way. Exceptions and ad hoc changes to the work done does not count as BAU.

Let's say that the major occupation of most residents in a city is IT, and their staple food is noodles. As most people in IT spend several hours at the office, they find it difficult to fix food at home. So, they end up ordering takeout or cooking with instant noodles. Of late, there has been bad press against instant noodles, and eating out every day is not working out very well for the residents financially; in addition, health concerns are beginning to creep up. What would be a good product to introduce in this market?

A gadget that allows the residents to make their own noodles would be a godsend, where the residents have to add flour, oil, water, and other ingredients into the machine. And at a click of a button, the gadget would start churning out noodles (which are healthy because the raw materials were produced by residents). The chances of the this gadget becoming an instant hit is good. All the company did was strategize to find out what their market lacked and filled the void with a solution. Instead, if they had marketed this product to a sleepy town where men and women have ample time on their hands to fix their own food and healthy noodles are available on every shelf across the stores in the town, the same company would have had to shut down shop quite early in the game.

In short, strategy is not a silver bullet. Every problem will have a different solution, and identifying this solution is a strategy that is bound to make or break companies.

The most important aspect of service strategy is to understand the customer, identify the customers' needs, and fill those voids. If the provider can do this, even a dim-witted service or product would take off exponentially, until someone else finds a competing service or a product to counter yours.

To give with another non-IT example, let's say that a landowner identifies a location in a popular neighborhood that lacks a decent mall. Building one would be like striking gold; you would have customers waiting to lap up what you have to offer once it is built. This move can potentially be termed a successful strategy.

Specifically, with ITIL, the service strategy's role is to provide guidance on creating value through IT services. The idea is to introduce services that have the potential to succeed and garner market share.

Service Strategy Processes

The following processes are listed in the ITIL service strategy publication:

- Strategy management for IT services
- Service portfolio management
- Demand management
- Financial management
- Business relationship management

Service Design

At the end of the service strategy lifecycle phase, leadership has provided direction and guidance on which services to offer. The outcome of the service strategy is like the idea that an entrepreneur comes up with. Whether the idea will come to fruition will become known in time.

The service design lifecycle phase answers the question "How do I do it?". It takes the idea and comes up with solutions and designs that give wings to the ideation process set forth in the previous phase.

The success of a service depends primarily on the service design phase. While strategy plays an initial part, the solution to make it happen is equally important.

Tablet computers have existed for a long time. My earliest memory of one was the Palm Pilot in the 1990s, and I started using Windows-based tablet PCs in the early 2000s. They were commonly called *personal digital assistants* (PDAs). But it was not until the introduction of iPads in 2010 that led to an explosion in the demand for the touch-capable portable computing devices. They stepped in and became synonymous with tablet computers.

What are the differences between an iPad and all the other personal handheld devices that came before? In my opinion, it is the iPad's design that made the difference. The strategy was out there since the 1980s, but the design wasn't great. This is my interpretation of the tablet computer history and its relation to design; others may see it differently. The key takeaway is to highlight the importance of design. Before I end this topic, I will honorably mention Android tablets, which are competing with iPads neck to neck. There is nothing better than two good designs fighting for acceptance on a strong foundation built on a wise strategy.

Revisiting the non-IT example that I used with service strategy, after identifying the location, the landowner will have to hire the best architects to bring the most value money can buy on the land that is most sought after. The architectural designs that the architects come up with become the blueprint showing what things will look and feel like once they are realized.

Service Design Processes

The following processes are listed in the ITIL service design publication:

- Design coordination
- Service level management
- Availability management
- Capacity management
- Supplier management
- Information security management
- Service catalog management
- IT service continuity management

Service Transition

The output of the service design is a set of design documents giving you the designs pertaining to all aspects of a service. The next task is to develop the service based on the designs. In the ITIL world, this is called the *service transition*, where the designs are transitioned into production environments through development, testing, and implementation.

The service transition lifecycle phase answers the question "What do I develop and deploy into production?" To achieve the objectives of service transition, you could employ service design lifecycle activities, hardware delivery lifecycle (HDLC) activities, or any other framework that delves into building a system/service and deploying it into the intended environment. ITIL is flexible like that; it can integrate seamlessly with any of the frameworks you can throw at it.

Going back to the non-IT example, there are architectural drawings from the previous design phase. These designs are handed over to a qualified builder to construct the mall as per the architectural designs. The builder constructs the mall in this phase as per the plan and brings it to a state where it could be operationalized. This is exactly the role of the service transition phase.

Service Transition Processes

The following processes are listed in the ITIL service transition publication:

- Change management
- Release and deployment management
- Knowledge management
- Transition planning and support
- Change evaluation
- Service validation and testing
- Service asset and configuration management

Service Operations

Service operations is the most popular phase of the ITIL service lifecycle. The reasons are twofold.

- Operations run for a long time. I am trying to avoid the word *infinite* here, as there is nothing guaranteed in this world. So, in effect, operations run for a long time, which translates into most service management practitioners working on the service operations lifecycle phase.

- As the phase runs the maximum amount of time, it has the maximum number of touch points with the customer. Moreover, operations is considered to be the first point of interaction for a customer on a regular basis.

Service operations entail maintenance and making sure the services are running as per the plan—the status quo is achieved. Under service operations, there are no new development or deployments, only maintenance. When I say no deployments, I will clearly differentiate that from regular patching or some releases being deployed for maintenance issues. Some maintenance activities could include doing health checks, fixing issues when they arise, and ensuring recurring activities are scheduled and run as planned.

Drawing on the previous example, the mall owner takes possession of the mall, rents out the shops, and sets the ball in motion for it to run smoothly. For it to be operationalized, they need to hire people who can manage various areas of the mall and employees who can carry out day-to-day tasks, such as cleaning, security, marketing, and so on. They also need to set up daily/weekly/monthly/yearly activities as required activities to keep the mall functioning. Examples could include monthly generator checks, security audits, four-hour restroom janitorial services, and so on. Do you get the drift?

By looking at this simple example, you can easily see the activities that are needed in operations. The operations phase in IT service management is a lot more complicated and requires plenty of minds to work out its various aspects.

Service Operations Processes

The following processes are listed in the ITIL service operations publication:

- Incident management

- Problem management

- Event management

- Request fulfillment management

- Access management

Continual Service Improvement

The final phase in ITIL is continual service improvement. While I call it the final phase, it does not necessarily come into play after the service operations phase. If you look at Figure 2-4 closely, you will observe that this phase encircles the other four phases. There is meaning to this. This phase takes input from any of the other phases to carry out its process activities. You can also say that it does not fit in the lifecycle phases because it does not roll once the previous phase has completed its delivery, but will feed improvement opportunities to the previous phases. But remember that this is the phase that keeps the ball rolling, or the service breathing.

I strongly believe that if something does not grow, it is as good as dead. This is true with careers, bank accounts, or anything else you might think of, except of course our waists! This concept applies to services too; if they do not improve over time, IT services wither away and something else takes their place. The objective of the continual service improvement (CSI) phase is to identify and implement improvements across the four lifecycle phases; whether they are improvements in strategies, designs, transition, or operations, CSI is there to help. It is also the smallest phase of all the phases in ITIL.

In keeping with the example, in the fully functional mall, you might have thought that general maintenance should be sufficient for upkeep and ongoing operations. This may be good for a brief period, but not for long-term care. Other malls are competing with this one in terms of amenities, stores, parking availability, and aesthetics, among others. If this mall does not improve over time, customers are going to lose interest, and sales will start to dwindle. So, to keep up with the growing demands, the mall owner must find ways to make the mall exciting to shopkeepers as well as to customers, perhaps by providing space underground for a public transit station, valet parking for certain customers, free high-speed Internet for customers, and moving walkways.

These improvements need not happen overnight; it can be a process that takes place over days and months. But the important thing is to keep improving the mall on a regular basis.

Continual Service Improvement Process

The following process is listed in the ITIL continual service improvement publication:

- Seven-step improvement process

Note   It takes an extremely mature service organization to implement all five phases. Generally speaking, service design, transition, and operations are the most commonly implemented phases, followed closely by continual service improvement. Service strategy is sparse.

ITIL Roles

ITIL is a harbinger of employment. It has introduced a number of roles, all useful and necessary, that are the most sought after in the IT industry today. As mentioned, ITIL has 26 processes, and each of these processes needs to be owned, managed, and practiced. Automation has its place in ITIL, but machines cannot do what people can, even in the age of machines ruled by Skynet!

Note   According to Wikipedia, Skynet is a fictional neural net–based conscious group mind and artificial general intelligence system that features centrally in the *Terminator* movie franchise and serves as the franchise's main and true antagonist.

Every ITIL process brings to the table at least a couple of roles (process owner and process manager). So, it brings plenty of employment opportunities, plus customers would be happier dealing with people with the right skillset and with the organization that has clarity over people owning and managing respective areas. So, with 26 processes in the pipeline, you are looking at more than 50 distinct roles, at a minimum.

At a framework level, there are four roles that can be applied to various services and processes. The roles are that of a service owner, process owner, process manager, and process practitioner.

Service Owner

Earlier in the chapter, I explained what a service is. This service, which provides value to the customer, must have an owner to ensure somebody has accountability. The person who owns the service from end to end and the person without whose consent no changes would be done is the service owner.

In the mall example, the mall owners are accountable to the shopkeepers and the customers. The owners own the place, so they put their signature on all changes being made to it; in other words, the mall owner approves enhancements and modifications and decommissions if any. They are the service owner in ITIL terminology.

Process Owner

A process is a set of coordinated activities that exist to meet the defined objectives. This process, or the series of coordinated activities, needs an owner, someone who has a finger on the pulse to check whether the process is fit for the purpose and that it is subjected to continuous improvements.

This person is the process owner and is accountable for the process deliveries, be it in terms of effectiveness or efficiency.

In the mall example, several processes will be defined and implemented. One such process is maintaining the diesel generators. The maintenance process could go something like this: weekly general checks on Sundays at 10 p.m. and detailed monthly checks on the first Sunday of each month at 11 p.m. Checks are done based on a checklist. If minor repairs are identified, they are carried out during the maintenance window. If a major repair is identified, a suitable window is arranged, all the necessary resources are mobilized, and repairs are carried out by a specialist team. This diesel generator process cannot be orphaned. It needs somebody to own it and ensure that it is meeting its objective, which is to work without outages.

Process Manager

You know what a process is and who the owner is. It is unlikely that an owner will actually manage things on their own. They will hire people who can manage the process for them.

Process managers ensure that the processes run as per their design and achieve what they're meant to. Since they are close to the work, they are in a good position to suggest improvements to the process owner. A decision to accept or reject the suggestions is made by the process owner.

A process manager is accountable for the operational management of the process, which means coordinating activities between various parties; monitoring, developing, and publishing reports; and, as mentioned earlier, identifying improvement opportunities.

In the diesel generator maintenance process, the process owner hires an electrical engineer to manage the maintenance activities and to report on the outcomes. The maintenance manager is responsible for ensuring that the technicians involved have the right skillset and are following the right set of instructions in carrying out the maintenance activities. If the manager finds that the weekly checks are not adding value, they can suggest to the process owner to shelve the weekly checks and schedule them for every two weeks. As mentioned earlier, the decision to make the checks every two weeks is made by the owner, not the manager.

Process Practitioner

Anyone who plays a part in the process is a process practitioner. This may be the manager or the owner or someone who may not be part of the process hierarchy. To rephrase, people who are responsible for carrying out one or more activities in a particular process are process practitioners.

In the generator maintenance process, technicians have the responsibility to check the generators based on a checklist. They are process practitioners. It is also likely that the technician is a process practitioner for multiple processes, depending on the number of processes they are acting on. For example, they could also be responsible for electrical maintenance, electrical repairs, and elevator maintenance, thus being a process practitioner in each of these processes.

RACI Matrix

In an organization, it is important that roles and responsibilities be clearly defined. When there is ambiguity over responsibilities for activities, it often leads to inefficiency within the system. You might have seen in your own organization that a lack of clarity over roles and responsibilities can end up in a mess, where both of the perceived responsible parties duplicate activities or both leave them for the other to act on.

RACI is an acronym for Responsible, Accountable, Consulted, and Informed. According to the ITIL service management framework, these four types of roles can be used to define all responsibilities and ownership in an organization.

- *Responsible*: The person who is responsible for carrying out the activity gets this tag. This person actually completes the work. Examples could be your process manager and process practitioner, who are responsible for managing activities and performing deliveries, respectively.

- *Accountable*: This is the person who owns the activity. This person is the decision-maker. Examples are the service and process owners. It is important to remember that although in the real world you could have joint ownership, in the world of ITIL, there is no joint ownership. An activity has a single owner. It can never be shared by two individuals.

- *Consulted*: In any organization, you have subject-matter experts who need to be consulted before and during activities. These people play the role of a catalyst in the service management organization. They do not own anything, nor do they get their hands dirty in the actual operations. But, they do provide their expertise in the successful execution of the activity. Examples are corporate lawyers and technical architects.

- *Informed*: There are the people who like to soak in the information. They do not have any role in the activity but want to be informed of the progress or the lack of it. They are, in other words, stakeholders without the power to make decisions. Examples are users and senior management.

An Example of RACI

Table 2-1 shows an example of how a RACI matrix looks. It has activities to be performed as part of a process in several rows. Those who play a role in the process make up the columns. You get a matrix by putting the activities and the roles together.

Table 2-1. *RACI Matrix Example*

Activities	Mall Owner	Maintenance Manager	Maintenance Engineer	Customer
Schedule maintenance activities	C	AR	I	
Sponsor maintenance activities	AR			
Perform maintenance activities		A	R	I
Communicate to customers	A	R		
Fix issues with diesel generator	I	AC	R	

In the example, the activity "Schedule maintenance activities" is owned and performed by the maintenance manager (AR represents Accountability and Responsibility in the respective cell). So, both the accountability and responsibility lie with them. For this activity, they are consulting (represented by C) with the mall owner on suitable dates and informing (represented by I) the maintenance engineer on the maintenance schedule.

Let's look at the final activity: "Fix issues with diesel generator." In this activity, the accountability lies with the maintenance manager, but the person performing the fixing is the maintenance engineer. The engineer consults with the manager regarding this activity, as the manager is experienced in diesel generators. The mall owner is merely informed of this activity.

Tips on RACI Creation

Developing a good RACI matrix takes experience and good insight into the activities on hand. However, there are a few ground rules that will aid you in your RACI creation endeavors:

- For every activity, you can have only one person accountable.

- Responsible, consulted, and informed can be spread across multiple roles, although I have not illustrated this in the example.

- A single role can don various hats, such as accountable and responsible for "Sponsor maintenance activities" by the mall owner.

- Accountable and responsible are mandatory for every activity.

- Consulted and informed are optional. If you are not informing anyone of an activity, you may not have the informed role for the particular activity. "Sponsor maintenance activities" is an example.

- Identify and document as many activities as possible in the RACI matrix, as long as the activities have specific deliverables coming from it.

ITIL V3 and ITIL 4

ITIL 4 is not a new wine in an old bottle. Although the principles of the ITIL remain strong, the nuances of the framework are contrasting. While the former tries to build a story like Jeffrey Archer, the new is dynamic and explosive like Tim Ferris' brilliance. In other words, the resemblance is limited to individual processes rather than the story and context built around them.

There are several changes but I am not going to discuss all of them in here. Maybe I need an entire book to expound on it. The big ticket items are discussed in the following sections.

The Service Lifecycle Is Dead

On expected lines, the service lifecycle has been done away with. It was the lack of a traditional lifecycle that led the call for a new ITIL.

The void left by the service lifecycle has been taken up by not one concept but two. Service value system and service value chain are the new concepts that drive the delivery of services. Service value chain roughly tries to cover for service lifecycle but takes the PDCA flavor with the planning, acting, vetting, and corrective actions.

Introducing Practices

In ITIL, processes rule the roost. All activities happen through processes. In fact, the service lifecycle is comprised of various processes to deliver service phase objectives. However in ITIL 4, it is practices that take center stage, but not as prominently as the processes did.

Practices are more than processes. One does not replace the other nor is one a mere reflection of the other. A process was meant to take in certain inputs and when the trigger kicks in, a set of activities were designed to take place. And finally there is an output. A practice is an extension of a process. It not only defines the activities but also brings together various entities, capabilities, and tools to accomplish the set objectives.

We had a concept called functions in ITIL V3, which were the teams executing various processes. In the previous ITIL version, I had a section dedicated to fuse processes and functions. I imagined the functions running as horizontals while the processes were verticals and they intersected as a mesh—because people and teams were needed to run the processes. I don't include that section in this book. Guess why? There are no functions in ITIL 4. The functions are fused within the process and the outcome can roughly be termed a practice.

Imagine having a problem management team in your organization. It is a function. What do they do? They work on the problem management process to meet its objectives. Not just the problem management team, you needed other technical teams to deliver the objectives. They were part of the different distinct functions

To collaborate better and to deliver value efficiently, ITIL 4 has introduced the concept of practices. That's the problem management practice in this instance. It's a system whose objective is to deliver all the problem management outputs.

Service Has a New Definition

In ITIL V3, *service* is defined as a means of delivering value to customers by facilitating outcomes customers want to achieve without the ownership of specific costs and risks. The onus was on the service provider to create value for the customer; the customer does not have to own the risks or individual costs for unit items. The customers pay a certain agreed amount for the service and get the service without worrying about the service's inherent risks or the underlying cost of individual elements that make up a service.

ITIL 4 has changed the definition of a service. It is a means of enabling value co-creation by facilitating outcomes that customers want to achieve, without the customer having to manage specific costs and risks. The difference might look trivial but the meaning and implication is huge.

Today a service provider cannot tuck away services and deliver them to the customer in isolation. Any service can become valuable only if there is ample direction and feedback from the customer, the primary person who uses the service. Hence the definition has rightly included *co-creation*.

Governance Is a New Kid on the Block

In ITIL V3, governance was not embraced with open arms in my opinion. Yes we had the governance process to ensure that the service management work was governed to the hilt and things didn't go in unwanted directions. But there was no explicit mention or a process or a function to define it. It was always the outsider looking in.

Things have changed for the better in ITIL 4. Governance has a proper seat at the table. The only way a service management framework (or any other management framework) can get governance defined and implemented correctly is by giving it focus and defining its objectives. More on this in Chapter 5.

Automation Is In

Activities that does not require cognizance, intelligence, or decision making brain cells can theoretically be run by machines. This makes even more sense if these activities are repeatable. Automation is the key to launching and running any service because services are not simplistic anymore. There are multiple integrations and managing every single driver can only be achieved if they are entrusted to the machines. So, automation is to be embraced and not looked at as an opponent to job creation.

ITIL V3 toyed with the idea of event management tools. It was not full blown but the intentions were clear. ITIL 4 has taken this to the next level by defining a guiding principle that couples optimization and automation.

Summary

This chapter was meant to be a refresher course on ITIL. You read about the history of ITIL, its origins, and its present form. ITIL's foundation is based on services. The success of ITIL implementation is dependent on how well the services and its components are defined. ITIL V3's lifecycle is the centerpiece of ITIL implementations, and they move in a sequential manner—starting with service strategy and then service design, service transition, service operations, and continual service improvement. ITIL draws boundaries through the RACI matrix, which defines the roles and responsibilities of the various parties involved. ITIL V3 and ITIL 4 have several fundamental differences, which have pros and cons. ITIL V3 is sequential but the implementation guidance is rock solid. ITIL 4 provides the principles of applying ITIL to the digital realm, but it stops short of providing guidance on implementation.

CHAPTER 3

ITIL and DevOps: An Analysis

Chapters 1 and 2 introduced DevOps and ITIL as independent frameworks/ methodologies, and I consciously did not make an effort to combine the two entities. This chapter analyzes them together. It dissects the big ticket conflicts and sets the tone for the rest of the book. In other words, it encourages creating a union between the two rather than replacing one with the other. Chapters 1 and 2 clearly specify that the two are leaders in their own respective areas, and developers cannot reasonably replace one with the other. The question of replacement has arisen because the newer of the two, DevOps, steps on ITIL's foot and claims to take over certain (or all) aspects of service management.

Today the reality is that ITIL is (almost) everywhere in some form or another. The majority of development projects run on Agile today, and the normal extension of it, DevOps, is being talked about at great length. However, the implementations are far and few. One of the prime reasons for this is because of the ambiguity that exists between product development and service management. Wherever DevOps is being implemented (with the exception of Amazon, Netflix, and others I discussed in Chapter 1), it is being restricted to the development side of things. The time is right to make DevOps whole by removing the uncertainty and ambiguity (see Figure 1-4), and that is the reason for this book's existence. The book is titled *Reinventing ITIL and DevOps with Digital Transformation*, and it's a practical approach to implementing ITIL in DevOps projects. However, this book is so much more than what this title suggests, because it realizes the DevOps principles to the fullest and will make DevOps a potent force for years to come.

© Abhinav Krishna Kaiser 2023
A. Krishna Kaiser, *Reinventing ITIL® and DevOps with Digital Transformation*,
https://doi.org/10.1007/978-1-4842-9072-9_3

Product vs. Services

Traditionally speaking, the IT industry is like a magnet that has two opposing poles: products and services. So, you are running either a development project or a maintenance one. The people involved on the development side of things have different skillsets, and the support personnel have their own unique talents.

Figure 3-1 indicates this IT magnet, featuring products on the left and services on the right.

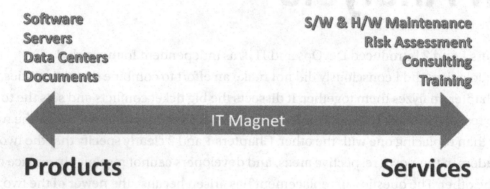

Software
Servers
Data Centers
Documents

S/W & H/W Maintenance
Risk Assessment
Consulting
Training

IT Magnet

Products   **Services**

Figure 3-1. *IT magnet*

Products (discussed in detail in Chapter 15) are typically tangible—in a digital way, meaning that a digital/physical deliverable is produced. They can be consumed either now or at a later point in time. Services, on the other hand, are intangible—it is the experience that is the result of consuming a service. More important, a service is consumed in the present, rather than getting serviced for future needs. I am not referring to purchasing services for an advanced period of time but rather experiencing something. For example, you can head to a bakery and purchase a quiche. That's a product. You can choose to eat it now or later. The experience of eating it can be experienced only when you bite into it. This is a service.

Referring to Figure 3-1, some examples of products include software, servers, data centers, and documents. All the products can be purchased one time and be used now or later. On the other end of the IT magnet are the services. Maintaining the software and the hardware that is either purchased or developed falls under services. Other examples include conducting risk assessments, consulting, and training. All these services can be experienced only in the present.

The product industry depends heavily on the service industry because the products that are developed or purchased need servicing on a regular basis. Take, for example, a car that you purchased this summer. You paid the dealer a certain amount of money and purchased the car. The transaction between the consumer and the product manufacturer for all practical purposes is done. The car, however, needs to be maintained on a regular basis. For somebody not so hands-on like me, I depend even more on the auto service stations to maintain the oil and other fluid levels in my car and to check the various parts of the car every six months.

The auto service station, as the name indicates, is a service provider and it gets business every time I choose to experience the service. There is an open debate about whether the product industry is more profitable or whether it is the service industry given that the service industry comes into play as long as the product is relevant. The other school of thought is that the product replication and the profit by numbers make the product industry a better proposition. I don't see this debate being settled anytime soon!

The reality is that although we have products and services, the gulf between the two is shrinking fast. The ideological differences between the two industries don't benefit the consumer, who is facing the heat from the divide. The cost of producing products and living off the profits is no longer feasible, as there are intense price wars between competitors. For the service provider, the cost of providing services is rising, but the market conditions do not allow them to charge higher rates. Neither the product manufacturers nor the service providers can survive in the present market. So, how do they survive?

The answer is that the product and service industries bring together their resources and capabilities to become a *solution provider,* as illustrated in Figure 3-2.

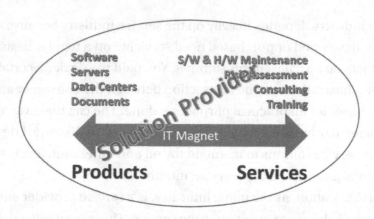

Figure 3-2. Solution provider

How does this work? Does it mean that an organization that develops products starts providing support as well? Not really. This model has been in place for some time, whereby the product manufacturer extends support for their products for a certain period of time. This is a failed model; in addition, this organization is nothing but two entities (products and services), and the gulf—instead of existing between different organizations—exists within the same organization.

A solution provider brings together products and services with an aim to solve the needs of the customers. The solution is developed based on the problems faced by the customers and the specific requirements. In other words, it is customized to ensure that the customers get focused value from the overall delivery of products and services and at an optimized cost.

Today you will find that the gap between products and services is quite narrow, and the solution to customers' needs and problems is being addressed by joining products and services. The outcome of this marriage is popularly known as *XaaS*—which refers to anything as a service. Specific popular examples include software as a service (SaaS), platform as a service (PaaS), and infrastructure as a service (IaaS). In the XaaS model, every customer need turns into a service, including products. So in essence, the marriage of products and services has given birth to the *product as a service*.

There are several advantages of the XaaS model. Referencing Chapter 2 on the topic of services, the definition of a service is as follows:

> *A means of delivering value to customers by facilitating outcomes that customers want to achieve, without the ownership of specific costs and risks.*

In the XaaS model, the customer gets to enjoy the product without the ownership costs, the need for constant upgrades, and the risks associated with it. In exchange, the customer pays regular "rent" to use the product as a service. Office 365 is an excellent example; it falls under the SaaS model. I get to use all the programs that fall under Office 365 for a regular monthly or yearly fee. When Microsoft upgrades the program, I get the upgrades for free. To start using the Office product, I don't need to spend capital upfront, which was the traditional model. Earlier, I used to purchase Office products, and in a couple of years, my version became extinct and I was forced to purchase a new license or upgrade the existing one at a cost.

Another use case is that of startup companies that require servers and datacenters. They now have the luxury of the IaaS option where they can reroute their precious capital into other parts of the organization rather than spending it all on infrastructure. Instead, they pay a monthly or yearly fee.

Turning our attention back to DevOps and ITIL and their mutual existence, the solution is to bring the two together to get the best results. DevOps can be seen as the product side of the IT magnet, and ITIL is definitely on the service side. DevOps is the right approach to providing the solution to customers rather than products, but for it to happen, there is a need for a solid service management framework such as ITIL. The XaaS model works if the product management and delivery are powered by DevOps and the ongoing services through ITIL.

We don't have other options. The best industry models must come together to boost the IT industry from sinking in waste and provide customers with the best possible outcome. The value to customers is based on their perceptions. ITIL identified this aspect a long time ago and put in place various service-management parameters that manage the customer expectations, thus ensuring customer satisfaction. The volatile market conditions and the blitzkrieg of technological advancements require a software development process that can turn on a dime as the wind changes direction. This is made possible through DevOps implementations. Finally, the XaaS model has greatly benefited the solution providers as well as the customers—it's a win-win situation. From all fronts, there is a desire to combine various natural elements, and this is exactly what I am trying to accomplish in this book, by bringing the two magnetic poles together and creating a bond that's bound to take the IT industry into the next decade.

Big Ticket Conflicts

Not all is well with how things stand at the moment between DevOps and ITIL. Importantly, the conflicts between the two must be identified before going into solution mode (Chapter 4 onward). ITIL has been around for a while now, and DevOps is relatively the new kid on the block. So, just as we have generation gaps among people, these gaps exist in frameworks as well, leading to certain big ticket conflicts, covered in this section. The minor issues are a culmination of the major conflicts; therefore, I expect them to be resolved through dialogue and perspective of the bigger picture.

Which Is It: Sequential vs. Concurrent?

ITIL V3 was conceived in the age of waterfall management, and DevOps is anti-waterfall—meaning that it's Agile in nature. The five phases of ITIL are strictly sequential in nature. Unless you have a service strategy, you cannot develop new services. Unless you have defined services, you cannot think of designing, building, and implementing them. Only after they are implemented and handed over formally can they be maintained. So, the fruits of the labor are visible only during the service operations phase, because the rest of the time, the service is in its development stages and is adding no value to the customers.

This is the point of inflection as far as DevOps in concerned. DevOps is based on Agile, which is *anti-sequential*. Therefore, DevOps expects some form of output right away. How can you do it in ITIL given that the service developmental works are a long consummated process? As I mentioned earlier, this is the time for identifying conflicts and not resolving them.

Let's Discuss Batch Sizes

With the sequential nature of ITIL, the outcome is one big piece of delivery that contains all the pieces of the puzzle required to solve the IT service conundrum. This worked fine for services for the most part, but product delivery today mostly deals with small batches. Every sprint delivers a piece of software that can be independently tested, demonstrated, and verified. The suspense around what is going to come out at the end of the long-winded cycle does not exist in a DevOps-run project.

The longer the batch size, the riskier the proposition. What if the requirements were misunderstood all along and, in the end, you produce something the customer never wanted? Either it would be too late to go back and make changes or the road to completion would have plenty of rework. Either way, the customer ends up being unsatisfied. This is where DevOps pitches in with its small batches. If there are any changes to be done, you make them before you start.

It's All About the Feedback

Delivering small batches alone to find out whether the direction you are taking is right is not enough. You need the feedback to come through rapidly so that you are on the right course.

In ITIL, there is never any talk of formal feedback until you get to the final phase, which is continual service improvement. I am not suggesting that people who follow ITIL don't take feedback seriously, but I am pointing out that the framework has missed an important element that's one of the core pillars for satisfying customers.

The small batches that are produced in a DevOps cycle are followed by a feedback cycle, whereby feedback is sought every step of the way, and it comes in the form of test results, acceptance tests, and demonstrations to the customer. Considering that the two-week sprint cycle is the most common, even if you were going off-course, the amount of rework that you may be expected to perform is equivalent to the two-week sprint. This too is arrested by the presence of a product owner who is from the customer's organization and who is part of the team and knows exactly what the team is working on at any point in time. By contrast, in ITIL (where feedback is not formalized until you hit the improvement cycle), if the service development takes a quarter to half a year, the entire effort will be wasted if it's not as the customer demanded.

The Silo Culture

The ITIL service management framework defines functions that are teams where people with similar skillsets are housed. In other words, every team represents a silo of people with similar talents. As and when they are required to work on process activities, they get pulled into the process role, and then they are sequestered back to their homes. There is the logic behind this. People with similar skillsets, when housed together, can help each other in terms of capability improvement and can work as a team to deliver results.

In DevOps, as covered in Chapter 1, teams are strictly cross-functional and are formed around a product or a project. They are aligned to the product or project alone, and this helps ensure that all the right people needed to build and support a product are sitting in the same group and not spread across the organization with differing lines of reporting structure. By housing the cross-functional teams together, teams invariably understand all aspects of the product, and this helps deal with issues and other parts of delivery.

Clearly, ITIL and DevOps are divided over how the team structure should look. It definitely makes sense to put all the similar talented people together to ensure skill development and capability improvement. But is this structure focused on the product and the customer? Is everybody on the team intimately close to the product to ensure speedy delivery? These are some loopholes that are clearly present in the ITIL world.

It makes sense to build cross-functional teams to get to know the product better. If they are part of the team since inception, the intimacy with the product deepens and helps support the customers in an effective manner. However, does everybody on the team have a role to play throughout the lifecycle of a product? That is the answer to seek! The answer will be along the lines of no. So, what do you do with them? In IT, we don't bench people as we did a decade ago. How do you ensure that the intimacy with the product is maintained and yet the resources are utilized optimally? This is a challenge that comes up often in DevOps projects, and the answer lies in a *metateam*.

What Is Configuration Management?

The word *football* does not indicate the same sport around the world. In the United Kingdom and many other countries, it refers to "soccer," which is played with a perfectly round ball. In the United States, however, football is a different game altogether, played with an oval-shaped ball and somewhat similar to rugby. Likewise, the word *configuration management* has different connotations in ITIL and DevOps.

In ITIL, a *configuration management system* (CMS) is a collection of databases of service-related data. It contains configuration management databases, incident records, problem records, change records, known error databases, and everything else that goes into the service management system.

The word *configuration management* is commonly used to refer to source code management (SCM) in the software development industry, and it has trickled down to the DevOps scheme of things as well. The repository consisting of source code, the strategy, and implementation around branches and the way updates are done to the repository are all under the purview of configuration management in DevOps.

So, it is quite apparent that configuration management has different meanings in both areas. When you try to bring the two systems together, which one would you probably go with? The ITIL configuration management has critical configuration management database (CMDB) information, which is considered the foundation for setting up services. DevOps configuration management refers to the source code itself, which is at the heart of software development. So, you cannot replace one with the other. This is a serious conflict that requires an amicable solution if you plan for a long game with the two frameworks.

Continuous Deployment Makes Release Management Irrelevant

As introduced in Chapter 1, the continuous deployment process directly deploys the package into the production system when all tests are green. This is the domain of control for the change and release management processes, and by deploying directly without any governance and controls, there is a perception that the change and release management processes become irrelevant.

The ITIL change and release management processes are a trusted set of processes that ensure that the changes going into production are well-tested, and it also brings together all the stakeholders in a huddle to decide the merits and demerits of a potential change. Careful planning around changes by all stakeholders can potentially ensure that the changes are beneficial to the organization and do not disrupt any of the existing setup unless they are designed that way.

By going around these governance processes, DevOps through the continuous deployment process is setting a bad precedent that is uncontrolled and perhaps malevolent to the ecosystem. The general perception is that development teams rejoice over fewer governances, and operations teams feel antsy about this whole DevOps thing! The market we are in today roots for speed and dynamism. In fact, more and more organizations are withering away when they are unable to cope with the speed of change. So, organizations have opted to ride the DevOps rollercoaster and take chances with rapid deployments. In fact, continuous deployment may not be feasible for all types of organizations. Some, such as banks and other financial institutions, have legal and regulatory approvals in their workflow that hold them back by opting for trigger deployments rather than continuous deployment.

Continuous deployment going around the approvals of change management is a premature judgment call. ITIL change and release management provide the precious governance layer around the changes going into the ecosystem. It would take an artist to bring both together and stitch them up seamlessly, and I have taken up the cudgels to be that artist. There are ways to rein in continuous deployments through the change and release management processes, and Chapters 9 and 10 look at them in detail. The truth is that we need both. Continuous deployment is the future, and it differentiates market leaders from the rest.

Union of Mindsets

DevOps is a philosophy. It's a new culture and with it comes a new mindset. The DevOps mindset aims to speed up software delivery through collaboration and working in small batches, aided by automation. The thought process is that working swiftly in smaller batches will help deliver incrementally, and even if something were to go wrong, the damage would be trivial. Rolling it back is a simpler task as well, with a good chance that nobody on the other end (read, end users) even notices.

Although never mentioned thus far, service management (aka ITIL) has a mindset too. The framework is built heavily around the customers, and the mindset is around creating value to customers through services. ITIL ensures that a customer's perception of value takes precedence over what it really is, and customers always get what they want. Across the five phases, ITIL ensures that value creation is at the heart of services, and this is a great sign of things to come when we place the service management framework over the DevOps mindset. DevOps is highly centered on the customer because, in the Agile methodology, the customer is part of the development team. The customer role, referred to as a *product owner* (PO), works with the team from inception to the end, helping to build a set of requirements and prioritize them, as well as providing regular feedback and supporting the team every step of the way.

The union of mindsets puts all other conflicts on the back burner. It does not matter if one is sequential and the other is concurrent because at the heart of both, the customer is elevated to a new high. As long as true north points to the customer, frameworks and philosophies blend like fresh strawberries and milk in a strawberry milkshake. The taste gets better only when the individual elements of the milkshake do not reveal themselves as strawberries, milk, or sugar. Likewise, ITIL and DevOps have all the ingredients to come together to create synergy and support what customers want when they want it and maintain those wants seamlessly. The union of mindsets, despite the differences, is illustrated in Figure 3-3.

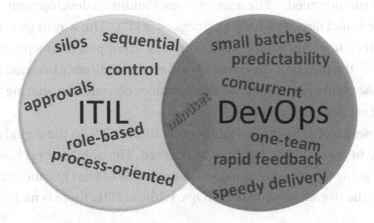

Figure 3-3. *The union of mindsets*

The Case for ITIL Adaptation with DevOps

Some experts believe that ITIL is a 20-year-old framework that does not fit into the Agile scheme of things, which is viewed as dynamic, fast-paced, and innovative. Further, the argument goes on to state that ITIL is bulky, rigid, and strictly sequential. The problem these proponents state is that ITIL is a framework for services and service-based organizations. With the advent of DevOps, the line between development and support is closing in, and a service-oriented framework doesn't fit into a hybrid (development and operations) way of working. Before ITIL, development ran on a waterfall model, and support drew inspiration, practices, and processes from ITIL. With the conglomeration of development and operations, waterfall has already made way for Agile project management methodologies. And ITIL too will have to buckle in. But what is its replacement? There is none, because DevOps infuses plenty of enthusiasm in the development practices, and the interest wanes during the operational practices.

The proponents against the ITIL framework are rather biased. Without an occupant in the wings, the existing tenant is being driven out. A big gaping hole will be the outcome if their will is the way. Their arguments seem one-sided, as the obvious benefits derived from having ITIL are often sidelined.

ITIL is a framework that has met the rubber on the road more than any other organized set of practices for more than three decades. The framework has adapted to the changing world and adopted the best practices from the industry to be the be-all and end-all. ITIL v3 came out in 2007, with a minor update four years later. (ITIL 4, which was released in 2019, is a reference guide more than anything else.) So, can a decade-old framework still suit our needs? The answer is yes. Fluidity in development and being Agile does not conflict directly with the principles of ITIL. The way to go about building a service does not change, but what essentially needs to happen is for a prominent person in ITIL to identify the pieces of the framework that can be directly inserted into the DevOps processes and to delicately tweak a few more bits without altering the meaning or objectives of service management.

With the absence of any other suitable competitor to ITIL in the digital age, there is no question whether ITIL still needs to be pursued. The only factor is how quickly companies are going to recognize the operational needs of DevOps and blend the ITIL framework into the overall scheme of DevOps. Without ITIL, there is no DevOps!

Note   Gene Kim, the author of *DevOps Handbook*, says that DevOps being in opposition to ITIL is a misconception. Even releasing more than 10,000 deployments a day requires processes. What goes against the DevOps objectives are the approvals.

To Conclude

Many experts believe that ITIL may be humongous in terms of the literature and may be sequential, but it is well known that ITIL does not prescribe the sequence of activities nor does it dictate the bureaucracies to be involved. Instead, the framework provides the phases in which a service needs to be developed to ensure that all aspects of a service are addressed during the formational stages.

Jayne Groll, the CEO of the DevOps Institute, says that within the more than 2,000 pages of ITIL publications, there are no implications or directions to suggest that the ITIL processes must be developed in a complex manner and that it must follow certain bureaucracies (such as obtaining approvals before embarking onto the next stage). She further goes on to state that DevOps does not diminish the value of ITIL. Instead, it validates and matures it by connecting the dots between Agile, Lean, automation, and other related frameworks.

Matthew Skelton from Skelton Thatcher Consulting believes that DevOps has much to learn from ITIL, including identifying and addressing dependencies, putting emphasis on service level agreements (SLA), and developing service strategies. On the other hand, ITIL can learn plenty from DevOps, such as collaboration between various teams, effective event management by modern monitoring toolsets and metrics, and the rapid responses to incidents.

Kaimar Karu, head of ITSM at Axelos, is of the opinion that ITIL has things to adapt from DevOps—mainly on the people front. DevOps can help with better communication, collaboration, and customer focus.

In the next few chapters, the focus is on the solutions to the problems and conflicts listed in this chapter. Furthermore, the remainder of the book takes on the integration of the ITIL framework and DevOps practices. I worked in the area of ITIL for several years and have helped organizations create value through service management designs based on ITIL processes. The ITIL processes are grounded in maturity, and there is nothing fundamentally wrong with them. In the era of swift turnarounds and automation, the existing processes have to be adapted to the ITIL way of working. You will see in the chapters dedicated to individual processes that the principle underlying the processes does not change; the meaning and its objectives stay firm to what it is meant for. But the way it is designed and executed has been altered to make it more dynamic and Agile.

The adaptations that I have recommended are just one way of looking through the adaptation lens. There are more ways of doing things. In the spirit of ITIL, where the framework avoids prescribing a way of designing and operating, I stick to the same philosophy with my material so you can adapt it further to your organizations, designs, and processes.

Summary

This chapter looked at ITIL and DevOps from chapter to verse. While ITIL has a legacy that has evolved over the years, DevOps is considered modern. ITIL was built on the waterfall project management model, where things flow sequentially from one activity into another. Whereas DevOps (and Agile) is about building or working toward the goal in the form of iterations—generally delivered in small batches. ITIL is strong in its foundation and its concepts are timeless. DevOps is the culmination of brains that aimed toward rapid development and nothing else. Integrating these two elements can only result in a powerful force.

CHAPTER 4

Integration: Alignment of Processes

From this chapter on, we start aligning the ITIL service management framework with a DevOps project. The exciting bit starts here! The exercise involves looking at ITIL holistically and identifying the phases and processes that can stay as is and those that need to realigned.

Although ITIL offers great insights and learning, I do not reframe DevOps processes, methodology, or philosophy to fit the ITIL framework just so it sounds better.

Analysis of ITIL Phases

ITIL is broadly categorized into five phases, and at least four of them are sequential in nature. The fifth one is an overarching phase. The sequential phases are as follows:

- Service strategy
- Service design
- Service transition
- Service operations

Continual service improvement is the overarching phase that is invoked at any time during the four phases. Figure 4-1 shows the phases of ITIL.

© Abhinav Krishna Kaiser 2023

A. Krishna Kaiser, *Reinventing ITIL® and DevOps with Digital Transformation*,
https://doi.org/10.1007/978-1-4842-9072-9_4

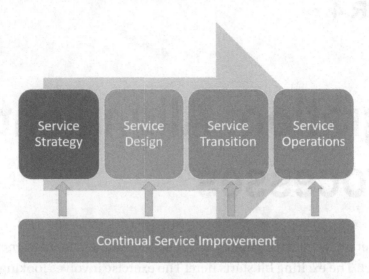

Figure 4-1. *ITIL phases featuring sequential and overarching phases*

These phases are designed and aligned in a logical manner, where the service ideation and inception happen right at the beginning. The business providing the services determine the service applicability, the cost of its development, the return on investment, and the market segment, among other tasks. This is done in the service strategy phase. After the sponsors support the finalized service, it goes into the design stage. During the service design phase, the various design elements of a service are put together. Here, the service is developed on paper—something like a blueprint. The next logical step is to take this blueprint and get something out of it. This is the service transition phase, whereby the service is built and implemented based on the designs. This could involve training and hand-holding along with the services build. After the implementation of a service, the service needs to be maintained to ensure that it runs as it was designed. This is the service operations phase. Throughout the four phases, there are opportunities for improvement, and the continual service improvement phase is firmly focused on the four phases in order to identify improvement opportunities and execute any feasible improvements.

The obvious problem is its sequential nature. Let's say that the business heads conceive a service takes about a month, with the design and transition phases lasting about six to eight months. Within the nine-month period, a lot can change. The service that was conceived may become irrelevant, or it may have to be overhauled to meet a different market segment. This drawback is typical of a project executed in the waterfall style of project management. The obvious solution is to turn it into the Agile style of functioning, whereby the service elements are designed and executed in sprints. However, adapting service development into an Agile style may not be a simple task.

Analysis: Service Strategy Phase

Let's take another look at the processes in Figure 4-2.

Service Strategy
- Strategy Management for IT Services
- Service Portfolio Management
- Demand Management
- Financial Management
- Business Relationship Management

Figure 4-2. Service strategy processes

Strategy Management for IT Services

When it comes to strategizing, plenty of research is needed to decide what can be deemed a service. It requires plenty of footwork in terms of crunching the numbers and identifying whether it is worth offering a particular service. It also requires identifying the competition and defining a unique factor that will help the organization's service stand out from the crowd. All of these activities and the related ones are carried out under the strategy management for IT service process.

This process, although associated with IT, is a business process. Every business starting with a new product or service has to do the groundwork if it wants to be sure that the product or service will trounce the competition. The flexibility of the Agile way of working is that the end-to-end strategizing need not be done before the rest of the processes kick in. As long as the big ticket features are known, that is probably sufficient for the high-level design to take place. The same concept can be applied to the deliverables of the strategy management for IT services process.

Let's say that a business wants to offer cloud services as part of its renewed strategy. The market is already crowded with a number of players, and there are some top guns like Microsoft Azure, Amazon Web Services (AWS), and Google Cloud Platform (GCP). The new cloud service must be competitive, either in terms of pricing or features, or both, to stay relevant. While the basics of a cloud service remain well known, the strategizing is done around the differentiator. For the service design to kick in, is it necessary that the entire strategy be known? Not really. The design can start at a high level, and the basic architecture can be put in place by the time the strategy is well conceived. The differentiators or the enhancements can be on top of the basic design. This technique will help the business quickly move from inception to the design stage and subsequently to build and service release.

Note   A *service backlog* is a list of all the basic, intermediate, and advanced features that need to be designed, built, and implemented to deploy a service.

DevOps primarily deals with building (the service transition phase) and maintaining (the service operations phase) products and services. Therefore, the strategizing and design processes are taken care of under the Agile project management framework. This ensures that the product backlog consists of all the elements of the product. In this case, the service backlog consists of all the basic, intermediate, and advanced features that have been identified.

Figure 4-3 illustrates how a service can be built from the ideation phase to the deployment stage in an Agile manner.

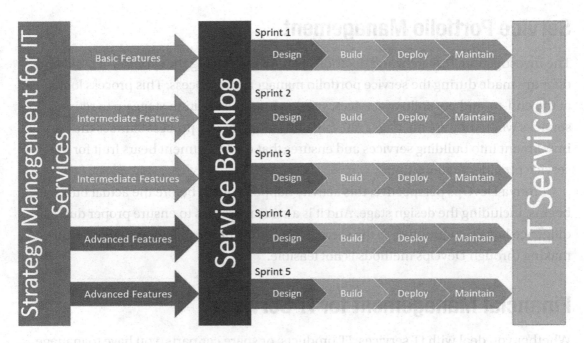

Figure 4-3. *Service development the Agile way*

Let's say that the basic features are known early and there is clarity around what goes in, which is usually the case in terms of basic features. An example could be cloud infrastructure to set up servers on the fly using an infrastructure-as-code (IaC) model. The basic features make up the initial items in the service backlog. In Sprint 1, the design of the service with the basic features is completed. This is followed by the build (development) and implementation (deployment). A service can be offered with the basic (but core) features to start with. With the design, development, and deployment of the core feature, we have just created the first piece of the IT service. Whether the basic service can be offered to a select group of customers is a business decision.

Likewise, when the intermediate and advanced features are formalized, they are populated in the service backlog and subsequently designed, built, and deployed. The service is developed progressively rather than in a big-bang approach.

After deploying services, the system needs to be maintained to ensure the status quo. The operational activities kick in to ensure the services run smoothly. The activities that you see in Figure 4-4 between the service backlog and IT service usually represent the scope of DevOps.

Service Portfolio Management

The investigation, research, and decisions behind identifying the services to build and offer are made during the service portfolio management process. This process looks at the end-to-end portfolio of services, starting from the ideation stage up to retiring services when they are no longer relevant and valuable. The process sources the investment into building services and ensures that the investment bears fruit for the service provider organization.

From a DevOps perspective, this activity happens much before the actual build begins, including the design stage. And it is a critical process to ensure proper due diligence before committing to the service. Therefore, proposing to hasten decision-making through DevOps methods is not feasible.

Financial Management for IT Services

Whether you deal with IT services, IT products, or spare car parts, you have to manage the finances. This includes developing a budget to operate within, keeping tabs on where the money is spent, and charging back as necessary. At a high level, this is common in most industries, and it is no different in the IT services sector. The financial management of IT services takes care of budgeting, accounting, and chargebacks for services.

The financial side of a service takes place in the service strategy phase; however, this process comes into play in all phases. While the budgets are set up before the actual work begins, accountability of expenditures happens throughout the lifecycle. Chargebacks happen when necessary. As mentioned, this happens everywhere, and it is no different in a DevOps project where high-level budget estimates are made for the build and test phases—because the Agile processes try to couple finances loosely with the project deliverables. From a DevOps standpoint, nothing needs to change the way it is set up in ITIL.

Demand Management

Demand management is an interesting process and is not too common in most service-based organizations. The process gathers inputs from various sources to feel the pulse for the upcoming demand for services. For example, if the customer plans to add several hundred more users to the lot, the service provider must be aware of this ramp-up to ensure that the services (such as Internet bandwidth, storage allocation, account creation, and so on) are scaled by the time the ramp-up is done.

So, how is this relevant to a DevOps project? Consider this: as part of the build activities, or even before the build can start, a number of prerequisites need to be in place. How will these demands be addressed without a mechanism that is in alignment with the DevOps way of working? I know that in most organizations, getting the right kind of people, tools, and especially environments on time is a major challenge. Most of these resources are showstoppers, and they make or break organizations. So, how can you align the needs of the project with the demand management process?

The ITIL demand management identifies demand for services by preempting and identifying patterns to better serve customers through uninterrupted and optimized service delivery. In a DevOps project, my recommendation is to extrapolate the reach of the demand management process to look into all the demands of a DevOps project. Be it in the human resource area, or tools, or anything else that is needed to run the project, demand management steps in.

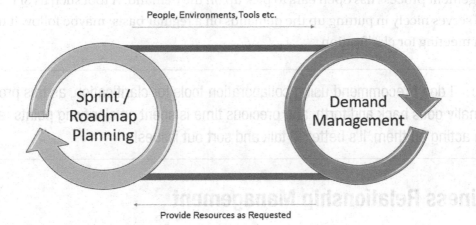

Figure 4-4. Demand management alignment

When you plan the roadmap for a DevOps-styled implementation, you do certain due diligence to identify what type of people you need, the environment setup, tools, work locations, and other work enablers. The demand management process in this setup must be as lean as possible to ensure that provisions are made for speedy deliveries. Today, some of the environments and tool setups are managed on the cloud, and the developers and DevOps engineers can spin environments along with the required toolset at the snap of a finger. However, some organizations are skeptical, and provisioning environments is still done in the traditional way. So, if you are to going to work in a DevOps project, the demand management process must make commitments to use the full extent of technology to remove any blockers that exist. When it comes to people and work locations, it's a different matter altogether. Companies don't maintain a massive bench strength anymore, and brick-and-mortar offices come at a premium. There is more onus on the demand management process to ensure that the people sourcing and other enabling processes are optimized and focused on speed and quality.

Most of the demands generally get sorted out during the roadmap planning. No matter how detailed the plan is, calculations go awry. During the build process, there might be new requirements that need to be sourced. Therefore, there should be constant alignment between the sprint planning process and demand management to get new demands (if any) every two weeks and fulfill them in a decent amount of time. It should work both ways.

The sprint planning sessions must identify what is needed in the next sprint or a couple of sprints from now, and a governance structure should ensure that the demand management process has open ears to pick up on the demand. A tool such as Slack or Trello serves nicely in putting up the demands on a regular basis; maybe follow it up with a meeting for clarification.

Note   I don't recommend using collaboration tools for clarification, as this process normally goes back and forth, and precious time is spent on clarifying points rather than acting on them. It's better to talk and sort out issues!

Business Relationship Management

The business relationship management process ensures that sufficient hooks are drawn between the customer and the service provider organization at strategic and tactical levels. This ensures that the customer feedback is immediately dealt with, and when there is a need for new products and services, the business relationship management can jump in to offer services to meet the needs. This is a relatively new process brought in to support the service level management process in the service design phase.

The tenets of managing customers are more or less the same in every industry, but maybe even more so in a DevOps project. Decisions at a strategic level can affect the product or service delivered, so it is imperative that you are aware of the customer's needs and address any feedback.

> **Note**   In a Scrum team setup, the product owner is the customer who works with the DevOps team. They provide regular feedback during the various Scrum ceremonies. Gathering feedback and acting on it is a good example of business relationship management activities (not all) in action.

Analysis: Service Design Phase

The service design phase comes immediately after the service has been identified to be developed or enhanced, and the overall design of a service is done here. Making it relevant to a DevOps project, this phase provides the architectural and enterprise design to the service or product being delivered in DevOps style.

Figure 4-5 shows the service design processes.

Service Design

- Design Coordination
- Service Catalog Management
- Service Level Management
- Availability Management
- Capacity Management
- IT Service Continuity Management
- Information Security Management
- Supplier Management

Figure 4-5. *Service design processes*

Design Coordination

Design coordination is the umbrella process for all design activities. It is a process that manages the complete design activities, including aligning with the strategic initiatives, the business requirements, and the management of budgets, resources, scope, quality, and schedule. To state it simply, design coordination is a process for managing the project of developing service designs.

Most organizations that implement ITIL don't try to call the design coordination process out and plan to meet its objectives. The process just happens under the guise of project management. There is nothing specific about coordinating design in the ITIL framework. However, when we look at designing services for a DevOps project, we can definitely enhance this process to fare better.

For starters, in Agile and DevOps, options are good. We don't like to concretize anything right at the beginning and put all our money on a single solution. I borrow the concept of coming up with multiple design options from the Scaled Agile Framework (SAFe). SAFe introduced a set-based design (SBD), whereby the requirements and design options are flexible, even during the development stages. By staying flexible, the design can pivot from one option to another based on the market conditions, the value generated, and expenses, among other factors.

In a traditional world of design, after the requirements are drawn and fully analyzed, the blueprint of the service (design) is drafted, run by all stakeholders, and finalized. This is referred to as a *point-based design*, as depicted in Figure 4-6.

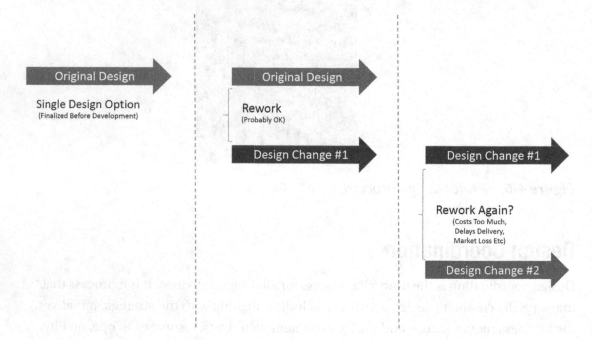

Figure 4-6. Point-based design

Typically, in a point-based design, a single design option is finalized, and the design team gets to work materializing it, indicated in the left column of Figure 4-6. At some point in the development stages, the original design might require changes, and these alterations are done on the fly by getting certain approvals. There is a certain amount of rework, but the overall project plan is factored for such rework, which is still considered normal. In Figure 4-6, the altered design is indicated as Design Change 1, indicating a decent amount of rework.

However, as the development comes close to ending and as the transition to the real world begins, the stakeholders realize that Design Change 1 is no longer fully relevant to the current market conditions and to what they had assumed a few months/years back. The design needs to change, and that needs to be followed up with a major amount of rework. Questions pop up at this moment: Is it really worth it? What if something were to change between now and the development completion of Design Change 2? What is the return on investment from all this rework?

There is a good chance that the service that needs to go through massive amounts of rework might never see the light of day.

What if there were multiple designs to work with from the beginning? What if you could pivot during the development stages from one design to another? The set-based design has the answer (see Figure 4-7).

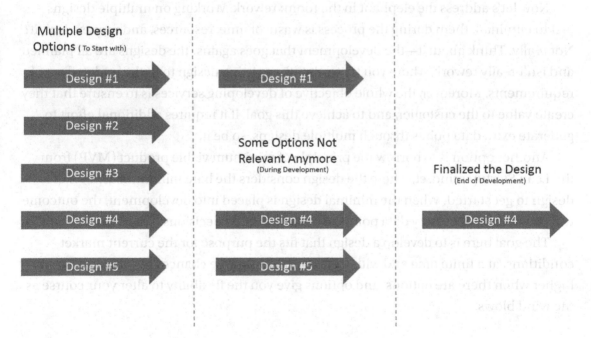

Figure 4-7. Set-based design

In the set-based design, you don't finalize on a single design. You come up with a set of possible designs, which gives you the leverage to pivot from one design to another, even late in the game. This is illustrated in the first column, showing five different designs.

The development begins with all five designs. When you do this, you start with aspects of design, which helps when deciding which design options to drop. Figure 4-7 shows that Designs 2 and 3 are no longer relevant.

As you continue working on the other designs, and as you come closer to completion, it is clear that some designs can't make the cut, and you finalize Design 4.

In a set-based design, instead of finalizing at the beginning and working your way making changes to the design, you start with multiple options and eliminate designs that don't fit the purpose and the use. This process gives you a better handle on adapting to the current market conditions faster and allows you to make informed decisions as you move through the process. Most importantly, you don't have to live with a mistake that you made months earlier in deciding on one design over the other but rather make a decision when you have all the data points.

Now let's address the elephant in the room: rework. Working on multiple designs just to eliminate them during the process is waste of time, resources, and money, isn't it? Not really. Think about it—the development that goes against the designs are all planned and isn't really rework, where you try to alter the existing design to fit the updated set of requirements. Moreover, the whole objective of developing services is to ensure that they create value to the customer, and to achieve this goal, if it requires additional effort to generate extra data points through multiple designs, so be it!

Another option is to borrow the principle of minimum viable product (MVP) from the Lean Startup mindset, where the design considers the bare minimum aspects of a design to get started. When the minimal design is placed into development, the outcome will provide the necessary data points to make informed decisions.

The goal here is to develop a design that fits the purpose for the current market conditions, at a finite time and with a planned budget. The chances of success is much higher when there are options, and options give you the flexibility to alter your course as the wind blows.

Service Catalog Management

The service catalog management is a key process in the ITIL framework. It provides a single view of all available services for the customers to choose from. Think about the service catalog as a menu in a restaurant that gives you a list of all available dishes. Likewise, a service catalog for a service provider gives customers the necessary information on what is being offered and what is in the pipeline.

Service catalog management exists to ensure that the service catalog is current and up to date and provides all the pertinent information to the customer. This works well in the ITIL framework and can continue to do so in a DevOps project.

There is a second thread to service catalog management, which is more technical in nature. It is referred to as a *technical service catalog*. This is an internal service catalog that provides the internal teams with pertinent information on who is supporting the service and what the dependencies are.

For example, if I were to offer WordPress as a service to the customer, on the back end, multiple teams make up this service. The cloud infrastructure team takes care of the underlying servers and networks. The application team provides support for the WordPress application. The database team supports the MySQL database. All three teams work in conjunction to provide the WordPress service. If any of the underlying services that power the WordPress service go down, the WordPress service goes down as well. Therefore, it is important to map the service dependencies, and the technical service catalog maps the service dependencies and keeps it updated.

In a DevOps project, technical service catalogs are as important as the service catalog (visible to customers). Based on its availability and accuracy, DevOps can be a lot more effective at churning out incident fixes, identifying dependencies, and mapping components and modules. In a typical DevOps project, the role of a technical service catalog is often not recognized, which leads to delays from analysis that identifies the dependencies. A DevOps project can be a lot stronger and more effective with the implementation of the service catalog management process.

The service asset and configuration management (SACM) process is an extension of the technical service catalog management process, and it maps the dependencies to its granularities. Chapter 6 is dedicated to this process.

Service Level Management

The service level management process is like a score-keeper. It is responsible for measuring the levels of services delivered to customers, and before it can measure them, the process agrees with the customers on the level of service that is to be offered.

The service level management process works closely with the business relationship management discussed in the "Analysis: Service Strategy Phase" section earlier in this chapter. While the business relationship management works at a strategic and tactical level, the service level management works at an operational level.

This process seeks to understand the service level requirements (SLRs) from the customer and translate them into service level agreements (SLAs), which will be used as a rulebook for measuring and reporting the numbers. The SLRs determine the contingencies to be provided in the architecture (such as high-availability architecture) and the resources to be onboarded, and this eventually has bearing on the cost of services.

The service level management process under ITIL was meant to measure the various aspects of a service, mostly on the operational front. DevOps is a combination of development and operations. While the operational measurements hold water in DevOps, the development measurements need to be factored in during customer discussions and negotiations. Generally, in a DevOps project, discussions around key performance indicators (KPIs) and expected measurements are done at a contractual level, without a process defining the ins and outs of the data sources and measurement of performances. The service level management can be a valuable ally for DevOps projects in identifying the KPIs and keeping a tab on how things move along.

Agreement of service levels happens at multiple levels. The agreement with customers are referred to as SLAs, and an internal agreement in the same organization is called an *operational level agreement* (OLA). Typically agreements with suppliers also have SLAs, along with underlying contracts (UCs).

DevOps is all about speed and quality. To enable speed, multiple toolsets are employed across various environments. They are usually managed by separate teams. Therefore, it is imperative that the agreements (either OLA or SLA) exist to ensure guarantees for speedy deliveries.

Availability Management

The availability management process ensures that the services delivered to customers are available as mandated by the service level agreements. The premise is that no matter how great the offered service is, it is not worth anything if the users are unable to access it. This process ensures that the underlying architecture—the infrastructure and application—are built to the expected rigors of the service.

After the service levels are agreed on by the service level management, the availability management kicks in to build a service that meets and perhaps surpasses the expected levels of a service. For example, building a service for 99.99 percent availability can look very different for a similar service built for 99.9999 percent availability. The difference between the two is minuscule, running in decimals, yet the impact on architecture could be massive. For 99.9999 percent availability, the architects have to factor in multiple layers of contingencies to ensure that even multiple failures do not take down the service. The cost of services offered at 99.9999 percent availability is multiples of the cost of services offered at 99.99 percent availability.

Managing availability in an ITIL project is similar to that of a DevOps project. Both offer services, and both have to abide by the service levels pertaining to availability. However, there are additions as always in the DevOps world. First, most environments are on public clouds, and this could be a challenge in terms of setting availability targets. Then, the presence of multiple environments to provision for builds and tests requires a tightened grip over the availability designs, even for environments that are not customer-facing. Also, multiple tools are employed in DevOps projects, and they too need to be hosted and be available as per the DevOps team's needs. Any laxity in the availability management of test environments or tools will result in the delayed delivery of services, which in turn will affect the overall delivery levels set forth by the service level management process.

Therefore, it is important that the availability requirements are carefully analyzed to be in perfect alignment with the delivery rate and the speed at which the team can deliver.

The other aspect to consider is over-delivering on availability. As mentioned about the cost earlier, every single decimal adds exponentially to the cost of services. So, building an architecture that over-delivers in terms of availability is not bound to be cost-effective, which is detrimental to the business angle of services.

Capacity Management

Although capacity management is placed in the service design phase in the ITIL framework, the process extends its arms across the entire lifecycle. It exists to ensure that the services offered have sufficient capacity to produce value. As a service provider, you might be offering a top-of-the-line, full-featured service (say, cloud services), but if there isn't sufficient capacity (bandwidth and disk space), then the service will be useless after all. Therefore, capacities must be ensured for maximum utilization of a service, and the process plays a significant role in value creation for customers.

Note   In the traditional architecture design principles, the design will also leave room for growth and uncertainty; however, in the DevOps world, the demand might vary because of changing business requirements and a shortened service/product lifecycle.

The capacity management works proactively in planning for various aspects of capacities and in reacting to capacity-related incidents and problems. It is a process that takes control over anything to do with capacity across the entire lifecycle of a service or product.

Capacity management comes in three flavors:

- Business capacity management
- Service capacity management
- Component capacity management

Business Capacity Management

The business capacity management flavor tends to the business's needs for ensuring sufficient capacities. It works primarily in the service strategy phase and is responsible for understanding the demands of the customer, and it works closely with the demand management process in identifying patterns of business activity to accurately plan for current and future capacities.

In a DevOps project, business capacity management plays a key role in ensuring that the scale-up and scale-down of deliveries are done in a seamless fashion, by monitoring the demand and supporting the scale plans.

The process can also help provide guidance on the scale of workload coming the project's way. Think about the incoming requirements as a funnel. The customer throws in a bucket a list of the requirements to be brought forward to production. The funnel size determines the incoming flow and the outcome. Therefore, insights around what comes in can help alter the funnel size as needed. On the flipside, a scale-down insight will help optimize and reduce the overall cost of delivery. Figure 4-8 illustrates the funnel concept.

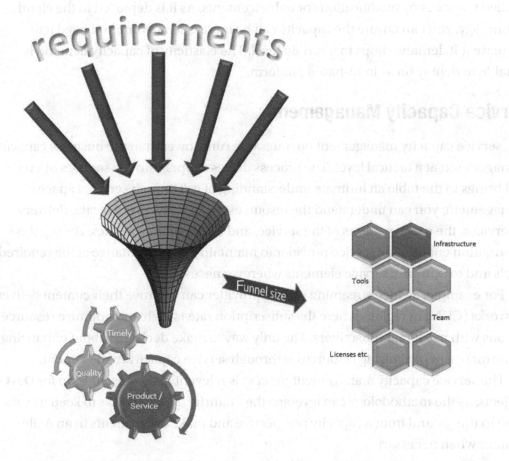

Figure 4-8. *Business capacity management*

In Figure 4-8, requirements come thick and fast through the opening. The service or product delivered will depend on the size of the funnel, which is indicative of the infrastructure, tools, team strength, and licenses, among other things, that must be delivered. The delivery is a product or service, and without any riders, a product or service does not add any value. What if a service is delivered that's reeking of bugs or

97

a product is delivered two years too late? It is critical to deliver when the product is expected to be delivered, and an agreed level of quality must be maintained as a hygiene factor. All this is possible if and only if the funnel size alterations are made quickly and effectively. For this to happen, business capacity management is a vital cog in the entire chain link.

The ITIL business capacity management is well-defined to address the capacity concerns coming from the business. For DevOps, the existing process can be readily applied without any modifications or enhancements. As it is deployed in the cloud technology, you can ensure the capacity can be increased anytime you need it or decrease it if demand drops to a certain level. The elasticity of capacity demand is suitable to deploy on a cloud-based platform.

Service Capacity Management

The service capacity management operates one rung lower than the business capacity management: at a tactical level. The process delves deeper into the services offered and brings to the table an intimate understanding of it. Through service capacity management, you can understand the resources that are leveraged for the delivery of services, the usage patterns of the service, and all the other statistics. Having this information enables the service provider to maintain the performance at the required levels and to optimize service elements wherever necessary.

For example, a video streaming service provider can improve their content delivery networks (CDN) in regions where the subscription rate is high and optimize resource at regions with moderate subscribers. The only way to make decisions about enhancing performance or optimizing resources is through service capacity management.

The service capacity management process is relevant in its present form for DevOps projects, as the methodology can leverage the maturity of the process to keep its ears close to the ground from a capacity perspective and make adjustments in an Agile manner when necessary.

Component Capacity Management

The final subprocess that operates at the runway level (operations) is component capacity management. In this subprocess, the scope isn't to measure the performance of the service from end to end but rather to look internally at the various configuration items that make up the service.

Component capacity management is an important subprocess, as the tactical and strategic capacity management processes rely on the data from the ground to make decisions on the top.

In a DevOps project, where a service depends on the infrastructure and applications, every cog being capacity managed is a given. The additional components that need to be capacity managed are the tools and the various nonproduction environments that are set up to manage the quality show.

IT Service Continuity Management

The IT service continuity management (ITSCM) process supports the business continuity management (BCM) process by ensuring that the business functions identified in the BCM are sufficiently recovered in the agreed upon timelines.

This process is invoked mostly when there are disasters of epic proportions and the service offered to customers is probably going to be impacted for long periods of time. Long-running incidents without any resolution in sight can fall under the scope of ITSCM too.

The service provider would have prearranged recovery options such as having real-time data replication on servers sitting across the ocean or running empty fully equipped offices to helicopter in people from affected regions as necessary. There are different types of recoveries, but what is more important is to identify the type of recovery needed and to make plans for it. The inspiration to identify the type of recovery can be drawn from the BCM.

The ITIL ITSCM process is meant for services that are offered and used by customers and deemed critical to customer's business. The process framework is mature and has demonstrated time and time again that it meets the objective and is valuable to the customer. So, I see the ITIL ITSCM process delivering the same sets of values in a DevOps project for services that are under the purview. On the development side of DevOps, the code, database, and tool configurations are most critical, and if there are backup and recovery mechanisms in place, that should be enough for most projects. Some projects might insist that development and testing not stop even in the wake of the disaster, given the stringent timelines running against market conditions. In such cases, the DevOps architects must plan for recoveries of code, data, pipelines, and environments. They must also explore provisions for developers to work in alternative settings, such as working over the raw Internet from the comfort of their homes.

Nowadays, the job of architects is less challenging, as the cloud platform can offer lots of features for fast recoveries, backup, and dual-site hosting during disaster recovery operations.

Information Security Management

Information security is a key aspect of IT today, and everything that we do digitally is looked at from the perspective of security. To manage the customer information that is used in delivering the services, the information security management process is in place.

The information security management follows the footsteps of the overall business, the customer's business security controls, and legislative controls, if any. In ITIL, information security is comprised of the following:

- *Confidentiality*: Confidentiality is about ensuring that only authorized personnel have the right to access data. It is about protecting information from unauthorized parties.

- *Integrity*: Data that is accurate, trustworthy, and consistent has integrity. Data gets transmitted at some point in the lifecycle and gets read and modified across the lifecycle. The data must stay true to what was transmitted at all times. In essence, integrity is about protecting the data against change from unauthorized parties.

- *Availability*: Data may be well-protected from access by unauthorized people, but it must also be available to authorized parties, when needed. Denial of access to data is one of the security concerns and is categorized as a data breach. The service provider must guarantee availability by ensuring that infrastructure is well-architected, and the security protocols protect the right to privacy and safeguard against modifying confidential data.

This is generally referred to as CIA and is illustrated in Figure 4-9.

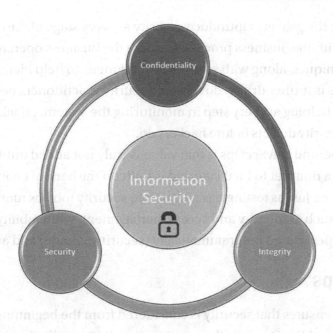

Figure 4-9. *Information security elements (CIA)*

From a DevOps perspective, CIA is too basic for service operations. From a development standpoint, security has a lot more standing, and there are two philosophies currently that are ruling the security space in DevOps projects: DevSecOps and Rugged DevOps.

DevSecOps

The philosophy behind DevSecOps is that everyone involved in development is responsible for security. This includes the businesses, developers, tools administrators, testers, and product owners, among others.

Traditionally, security was considered after the product was developed and functionally tested. It was a phase in the development process, and this was in the waterfall world. In Agile, security activities must be done in an iterative manner. The problem is that security has always been considered a major roadblock for speedy delivery and IT innovation. So, in many cases, security becomes an afterthought. There are various instances of security lapses like in Twitter and Facebook, which are the result of laidback security controls.

In DevSecOps, the goal is to introduce security at every stage of the development process. It starts with the business processes, where the business operators are given the tools and techniques, along with security practitioners, to help identify security requirements. This is further drilled down with security practitioners being part of the DevOps team and helping at every step in monitoring the system, attacking the system, and identifying security defects before hackers do.

The thinking behind DevSecOps is that value is truly not added until security has been part of it. It's a mindset to inculcate and is built on the back of cooperation between various stakeholders. Just as testing has shifted left, security too has moved with it. Now security activities such as identity and access management, vulnerability scanning, and firewalling can be performed programmatically (security as code) and automated.

Rugged DevOps

While DevSecOps ensures that security is considered from the beginning stages of development, Rugged DevOps puts the onus on security over all other activities. In other words, between development, operations, and security, Rugged DevOps prioritizes security over the other two.

In Rugged DevOps, the security framework is first established, and all the other successive and subsequent activities work within the boundaries of security. This promotes an increase in trust, transparency, and a better understanding of risk probabilities.

The objective is to get solid, secure code, and the Rugged DevOps mindset places stringent controls to achieve this. One of the practices is to perform a penetration test at every stage of development. The Rugged DevOps Manifesto is as follows.

> *I am rugged because I refuse to be a source of vulnerability or weakness.*
>
> *I am rugged because I assure my code will support its mission.*
>
> *I recognize that my code will be attacked by talented and persistent adversaries who threaten our physical, economic, and national security.*

Supplier Management

No single service provider can provide end-to-end customer services. The service provider will employ other service providers to provision customer services. For example, a cloud service provider will require dedicated network connectivity, which is a specialty of different types of service providers. The cloud service provider will require hardware, and there are hardware manufacturers that indirectly help provision services. The network service providers and hardware manufacturers are referred to as *suppliers* in ITIL as they are not directly contracted by the customer but rather by the service provider to offer a service. Suppliers are managed with the supplier management process. The trend today is adopting another framework that's an offshoot of ITIL called *service integration and management* (SIAM). This framework deals with the management of services in a multivendor environment that is common for most organizations today.

One of the main objectives of the supplier management process is to get the most out of the money paid to suppliers. However, in project management circles, we often ensure that suppliers don't get squeezed, and in the end, the contractual situation becomes favorable to both. From a DevOps perspective, we employ a number of suppliers, and the money expended is not everything. We need to build a healthy relationship with suppliers to influence their feature pipeline. For example, let's say that a configuration management tool that you use requires an additional feature such as self-healing with some added controls. If your relationship with the supplier is healthy, you stand a chance in prioritizing the supplier's feature development list, which will eventually be beneficial to you. To sum up, in any project, especially with a DevOps philosophy, it is paramount to maintain relationships, promote collaboration (even with suppliers), and keep an open communication channel with all involved parties.

Other supplier management objectives are about managing suppliers through contracts and measuring performance on a regular basis. These are what you would expect from a supplier management process, and the ITIL supplier management process ticks all the boxes.

Analysis: Service Transition Phase

In the service design phase, all the aspects of design are carried out. In the DevOps adoption, however, some of the processes that appeared in the design are carried out throughout the development lifecycle. Considering that high-level designs are in place, it's time that the rubber starts to meet the road. This is the service transition phase where the actual development of services begins.

The processes involved in the service transition phase are indicated in Figure 4-10. Some of the processes have dedicated chapters for DevOps project adoption.

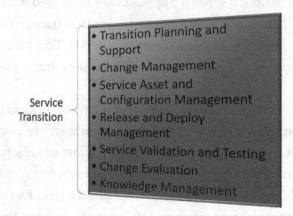

Figure 4-10. *Service transition processes*

Transition Planning and Support

Transition planning and support makes up the project management side of the service transitioning activities. The process ensures that all the deliverables promised in the service transition service lifecycle are delivered as per the scope, the time, and the cost. This process is quite specific to the service transition phase. In DevOps projects, the service transition and service operations phases work hand in hand, and the process and specific project management side of transitions will make way for Agile to step in and take over the entire project lifecycle.

In effect, the transition planning and support will cease to exist in its present form and will become part of the entire Agile process that primarily defines and dictates the transitioning activities.

Change Management

Chapter 9 is dedicated to the change management process.

Service Asset and Configuration Management

Chapter 6 is dedicated to the Service Asset and Configuration Management (SACM) process.

Release and Deployment Management

Chapter 10 is dedicated to the Release and Deployment Management process.

Service Validation and Testing

A service or product that is built needs to be tested to ensure its quality. This includes functional tests to prove that the service or product is fit for use and nonfunctional tests (such as performance and security) to prove that the service is fit for purpose. These tests are within the scope of the service validation and testing process in ITIL.

In the ITIL publication, value creation is defined as a product that is fit for purpose and fit for use. Value is derived based on the functionality delivered through a service and the warranty aspects, including nonfunctional parameters such as security, capacity, availability, and continuity. Figure 4-11 defines the value creation principle.

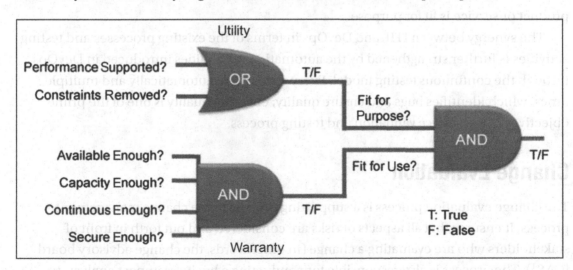

Figure 4-11. Value creation (image credit: ITIL.org)

This aspect of value creation in DevOps is the continuous testing that is performed after the binary is built. I briefly addressed the testing activities in Chapter 1. Testing ensures that the product or service conforms with requirements and meets all the nonfunctional requirements. The DevOps testing process (continuous testing) fits like a hand in glove with the ITIL value creation, as illustrated in Figure 4-12.

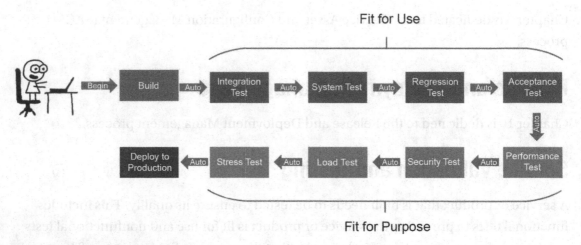

Figure 4-12. *Value creation through continuous testing*

In Figure 4-12, tests such as integration, system, regression, and acceptance are functional in nature, and in ITIL terminology, a test ensures that the service or product is fit for use. The tests indicated in the bottom row—such as performance, security, load, and stress—are conducted based on nonfunctional requirements and ensure that the product or service is fit for purpose.

The synergy between ITIL and DevOps in terms of the existing processes and testing activities is further strengthened by the automation capabilities introduced in DevOps through the continuous testing model. Every test is done automatically and multiple times, which identifies bugs and ensure quality; ensuring quality is one of the prime objectives of the service validation and testing process.

Change Evaluation

The change evaluation process is a supporting process to the change management process. It ensures that all aspects of risks are considered and put forth in front of stakeholders who are evaluating a change (in other words, the change advisory board [CAB]). The process is also responsible for conducting a business impact analysis to identify the true nature of business impact based on the potential change, which once again provides ammunition for the CAB to make a decision.

While carrying out business impact analysis and conducting thorough investigations are good practices, they must not get in the way of speedy delivery and innovation. In DevOps, the changes made are smaller in pieces and are done multiple times to arrest the probability of business impact due to a change going south. In other words, changes are done much more rapidly, and if a change brings about an unwanted situation, it is rolled back immediately. Since these changes are small, the chances of one hurting the business is minimal. This is one of the insurances that exists in DevOps for delivering rapidly. In essence, the process around thorough investigation may not happen in depth, but it needs to be done for every user story that is developed.

The concept of minimum viable product (MVP) is borrowed in most DevOps projects. This concept comes from the Lean Startup methodology. In an MVP approach, you first build a service or a product that is as basic as it can be, but provides the opportunity to conduct tests such as business impact analysis and various forecasts. This is done to get a feel for how the final product might impact the business, positively and negatively.

So, in a DevOps project, change evaluation is not done exclusively but is embedded within the change and release management processes.

Knowledge Management

Knowledge is most valuable in all areas of study, be it ITIL, DevOps, or civil engineering. It must be built, protected, and managed to have complete command over of products and services and to make sound decisions. The knowledge management process in ITIL is defined with the sole purpose of managing the knowledge in organizations.

A product or a service is built over a period of time and goes through multiple iterations. The people responsible for development and testing change over time and are replaced by others. The incumbent knowledge with the team is precious; it helps the team make changes efficiently and resolve incidents effectively. But if a new team is tasked to do the same, the knowledge management system is the only bridge that can scale up the new team to the incumbent team's familiarity with the products and services.

The objective of ITIL knowledge management process is to ensure that the knowledge of services is preserved in a knowledge management database and is updated when changes are made. It also attempts to prevent reinventing the wheel because of an effective knowledge management system.

The process ticks all the boxes in the list of features and activities that you look for in a knowledge management system. It is ample and has demonstrated that it works well with the ITIL framework, and the same process can be implemented for a DevOps project as well. However, there is a subtle difference. Agile projects encourage less documentation than traditional projects. The DevOps team uses a less formal way to maintain the knowledge, by coding in a way that tells the story, plus writing comments in the code (to make the code more readable), sharing knowledge in wiki pages or user community forums, or even just taking screenshots and videos to capture knowledge. It can be quite challenging to locate the knowledge in the DevOps world, as it is not as straightforward as with traditional projects, where everything is documented and a keyword search can reveal the results.

Analysis: Service Operation Phase

The service transition phase deploys the product or service into production, and now it is up to the service operation phase to maintain the status quo.

Figure 4-13 shows the processes in the service operation phase.

Figure 4-13. *Service operation processes*

Event Management

The event management process monitors various strategic points in the infrastructure, applications, and services and keeps a close watch on events that are preprogrammed. Only through event management can a fast resolution be put in place, which reduces the downtime and increases value to the customers.

The process depends heavily on tools to monitor devices and services. DevOps deals with a lot of tools, including ones that fall into the monitoring space. The ITIL event management process provides guidance on the process to identify the critical points, monitoring controls, and the subsequent set of actions to be done based on the event. All this can quickly and readily be consumed by a DevOps project, as there is no dedicated guidance in DevOps to support the setup of monitoring systems and event detection mechanisms.

The ITIL event management process can be applied to the DevOps toolsets as well to ensure that the rapid delivery mechanisms aren't affected because of failing tools and infrastructure. It is also key to establish types of events to help understand the criticality of the events generated. Talking of types of events, ITIL defines three:

- *Informational event*: This event conveys information that is mostly transactional, such as an administrator logging into a server or a completion of a batch job. The outcome of an informational event will not have any subsequent actions attached to it. At most, an email could be sent out to certain stakeholders.

- *Warning event*: A warning event indicates that something is unusual; however, it is not an exception or an error yet. As the event name indicates, it gives a heads-up that an anomaly is about to happen. Examples include the CPU utilization nearing peak load and an administrator password keyed in incorrectly multiple times. The subsequent action after an event can be a low-priority incident logged and automatically assigned to the designated team.

- *Exception event*: When something goes down or is untoward, it is an exception. Urgent action impends after an exception event. Examples include cloud services that are down and data that is downloaded to an unknown IP. Following an exception event, a high-priority or a critical priority incident is raised, and the resolution teams spring into action.

There is no rule that events must be categorized in this way. ITIL is based on good practices and on the experiences of multiple organizations. These three types of events have served well over the years; hence, they find a place in this book. Plus, the examples that I provided are based on my experience and what I think must be categorized under information, warning, and exception. For your organization, you can start defining events using a blank slate. You can define as many types of events as you want—as long as there is a clear demarcation between the types of events.

Note   Monitoring and event management might be talked about in the same vein, but there is a subtle difference. Monitoring is the activity pertaining to keeping a close watch on the device statuses. Event management deals mostly with the aftermath of an event detection. It deals with identifying meaningful notifications and taking appropriate actions.

Incident Management

Chapter 7 is dedicated to the incident management process.

Request Fulfillment

The request fulfillment process is defined to fulfill the service requests placed by the users, customers, and other concerned stakeholders. This process is often confused or is badly combined with the incident management process. The request fulfillment process serves service requests, and the incident management process serves incidents. Service requests and incidents are different beasts altogether.

An incident is a disruption to a service, either in full or partially. Generally, it pertains to downtimes and outages. A service request, on the other hand, has nothing to do with outages. It is a request placed to obtain something over and above the service that is already offered. Examples of service requests include access requests to a SharePoint portal, requests for a new laptop, and requests to unblock a certain IP from a firewall.

In a DevOps project, there are plenty of tools, databases, systems, and repositories. Projects may require new tools, upgraded environments, access to team members, and new configurations. All these fall under service requests and under the ITIL request fulfillment process. The process has matured over the years, and in the present form, it is apt for a DevOps project.

Problem Management

Chapter 8 is dedicated to the problem management process.

Access Management

Access management is an offshoot of the information security management and request fulfillment processes. While accesses to tools, systems, and repositories fall under the confidentiality clause of the CIA, access management is also a service request that is managed through the request fulfillment process.

The access management process exists to execute the policies set forth in the information security management process, and it diligently acts on service requests in providing, modifying, and removing access to users and other stakeholders.

In my view, the access management process is a minor process that could have been done away with in the ITIL 2011 publication. It does not add significant value to the ITIL framework, and the activities stated in the process are duplicates of what is already defined under the request fulfillment process. At best, access management could have been a subset of the request fulfillment process. I have not seen many organizations implement access management separately, but if an organization feels the need to do so for a DevOps project, so be it.

Continual Service Improvement

The continual service improvement (CSI) lifecycle phase stretches across all other phases. The scope of CSI is any of the other activities in the other four phases. The objective is to ensure that the services don't stay stagnant but rather improve gradually and steadily. There is just one process in this phase, which is indicated in Figure 4-14.

Continual
Service
Improvement

• The Seven-Step Improvement Process

Figure 4-14. *The CSI process*

The Seven-Step Improvement Process

The seven-step improvement process is the only process in the continual service improvement service lifecycle phase. This is because the process is generic and can be applied to any situation, any process, and any activity to come out on the other side with an improvement opportunity.

It is important to note that improvements are an integral part of ITIL. If a service stays stagnant without anything to show in terms of improvements, it is pretty much guaranteed that the service is on the decline. A competitor is likely to come up with something better, and any service that lacks improvements is due to be left playing catchup. So, without a doubt, improvements are a necessity in ITIL. And all improvements, either directly or indirectly, point to an increase in value delivered to the customer, and this and only this will keep the service afloat.

Figure 4-15 shows the seven-step improvement process.

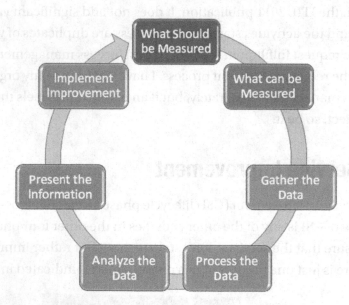

Figure 4-15. *Seven-step improvement process*

The seven-step process follows a logical model, whereby the succeeding activity builds on top of the first, and all the seven actions are aimed at identifying and implementing improvements. It all starts with what the strategy is, in other words, what you are trying to improve. This points directly to the IT vision that has been set forth. Once you know where you want to be, then in the second step, you check whether it is feasible to find that data points that you need. If you are unable to measure something, then probably you have an improvement right there—go back to the design table and enable measuring the data points as needed to achieve the targets.

Steps 3, 4, and 5 assume that you have the data that you need, and the data is processed and analyzed so that the mere raw data ends up being information that you can use by Step 6, where the analysis is presented back to the decision-makers. When a decision is made to improve, the final step is to go ahead and implement it. The key here is that the process does not stop with one iteration. It keeps chugging along. This model of continuous cycles of improvements is an indispensable factor when we consider alignment with DevOps. DevOps loves iterations, as it makes sense to keep doing small things over and over again to achieve big targets. Secondly, improvements are the only way DevOps is going to remain relevant and address the various challenges that face projects.

This natural alignment between the seven-step improvement process and DevOps comes in handy, as the process can be readily applied, in its present form, to any aspect of a DevOps project and you can get tangible results out of the cycle. As the nature is cyclic and iterative, you can probably read into the process as a step toward the future and a stepping stone into the DevOps world.

Summary

This chapter looked at the union of individual ITIL processes through the eyes of DevOps. Upcoming chapters recommend a number of process changes for major processes, such as incident and problem management processes. This chapter discussed other minor processes and processes that do not change much within the prism of DevOps.

CHAPTER 5

Teams and Structures

Processes provide guidance for objectives to be met and outcomes to be delivered on time. They provide the directions necessary for an organization to succeed. However, processes are not executed by machines—people are required to carry them out. People are extremely unpredictable, and their analog nature does not guarantee outcomes, no matter how well processes are laid out. Therefore, it is imperative that teams be set up for maximum chances of success. The setup for success starts with the team's structure. The team's motivation, orientation, and enthusiasm stem from this structure. The teams and their structure are the focus of this chapter, which is aimed at delivering faster outcomes with higher accuracy.

Note In ITIL 4, there are no processes or functions. Processes and functions added a layer of complexity that offered no benefits to those trying to define processes and team structures.

ITIL's processes represented a series of activities and workflow necessary to turn an input into an output. Functions were team structures that provided the resources for carrying out the process activities. Practices and functions engaged in a matrix arrangement where processes called on different functions to carry out process activities. In ITIL 4, the ITIL processes and functions are put together to work in unison as a practice.

A *practice* is defined as a set of organizational resources designed to perform work or accomplish an objective. Practices are based on a set of organizational resources that could be people, infrastructure, software, or processes. These resources are aligned/designed in order to achieve a specific objective. The keyword is a specific objective, and not general. If you create a practice for making burgers, it does not create anything other than burgers. If you want to make a burrito, you need a different practice.

© Abhinav Krishna Kaiser 2023
A. Krishna Kaiser, *Reinventing ITIL® and DevOps with Digital Transformation*,
https://doi.org/10.1007/978-1-4842-9072-9_5

A Plunge Into ITIL Functions

Functions in ITIL are the silos that teams are spread across. Each function represents a group of people with different skillsets. As introduced in Chapter 1, the functions in ITIL are represented in Figure 5-1.

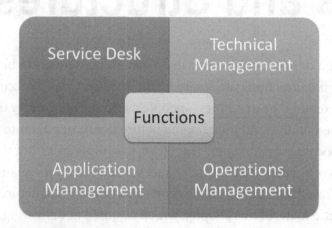

Figure 5-1. *Functions in ITIL*

Service Desk

The service desk is an integral component of the ITIL framework, and most ITIL implementations prioritize the design and implementation of the service desk and its associated processes. It is a group of people who act as the face of the service provider organization to users, suppliers, other service providers, and even customers. The service desk is the single and first point of contact for the identified stakeholders. If you have a problem with your mobile phone bill, you call your cell phone service provider, and the person on the other end of the line is from the service desk.

As the service desk serves as the single and first point of contact, it often becomes the face of the service provider organization. Therefore, it becomes an activity of utmost gravity to ensure that the service provider is fit to represent the service provider organization with professional etiquette. Generally, an organization's image depends on the service desk. Just think about it. If your cell phone provider's service desk gave you the cold shoulder about a genuine problem you are facing, would you measure the service provider's performance based on this interaction? Definitely you would, even if the service had been immaculate up until now, because a single interaction can break a solid foundation built over the years.

The service desk is the first line of support for the service provider organization apart from being the first point of contact. If the service desk cannot resolve an incident or fulfill a service request, it is escalated to the second line of support and then the third if the second line is not in a position to resolve. In an organization that supports an application, generally the first and second lines of support offer configuration changes. If the resolution requires changes to the code, it is pushed to the third line of support. The third line of support is part of the DevOps team in a DevOps organization. This is represented in Figure 5-2.

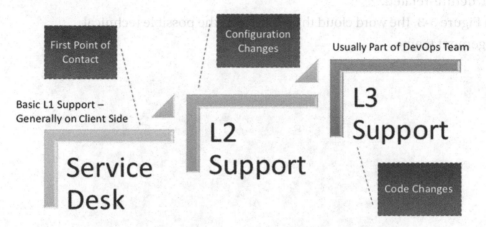

Figure 5-2. Functional escalation from service desk to L3 support

This chapter discusses the DevOps team and its role in the overall service desk.

Note   There are multiple types of service desks that are in vogue. The most prominent ones are local service desks that serve a particular location, centralized service desks that are located centrally to serve multiple locations, and distributed (virtual) service desks that are spread across multiple locations. In the last case, the call is routed depending on the requestor's geography and issue.

Technical Management

Technical management is a functional grouping of all the technical (infrastructure) teams. The organization structure is built around the specialization of individuals. The thinking behind this organization structure is to place people with similar skillsets in groups. Server teams, network teams, database teams, and data center teams, among others, usually make up technical management function. In Figure 5-2, the L2 and L3 teams could possibly come from the technical management function if the incident is infrastructure-related.

In Figure 5-3, the word cloud throws light on the possible technical management teams.

Figure 5-3. *Technical management teams*

The premise behind setting up a separate technical management silo is to ensure that the functional grouping will promote knowledge sharing between professionals with similar skillsets. This silo is their home, the base where they are groomed, mentored, and mature over time. When a project or a process activity comes calling, they are deployed into action. After completion of the project or process activity, they return to their familiar habitat.

This type of an organization is called a *matrix organization,* where the people are placed in silos and are deployed into projects when needed. When the project is done, they go back to their silo. They typically have dual reporting, one from the silo and the other from the project. This is not ideal but is commonly employed in most organizations.

The ITIL framework promotes placing people with similar skillsets in separate teams or silos. They don't distinguish between people who have stepped into the field and the architects. Everybody is in the same silo. The rationale is that the architects require the help of the operational professionals to design better, and the maintenance personnel may require the support of architects in their activities. However, most organizations today do not subscribe to this organizational framework, but rather keep architects and operations separate.

Application Management

Technical management is to the IT infrastructure as application management is to applications. Similar to technical management catering to IT infrastructure, application management specializes in software management (development and support).

Application management is a function that houses professionals who work on software development and maintenance activities. They represent a silo that provides resources for various software-related activities involving application practices such as requirement gathering, analysis, design, coding, and testing. Figure 5-4 illustrates a few application management teams that could exist.

Figure 5-4. *Application management teams*

Apart from providing resources to meet process objectives, one of the main tasks of application management is to make decisions on buying third-party software or building it in-house. Based on the requirements, options available on the market, commercials, and other factors, the application management function is expected to decide whether the service provider is better served buying commercial off-the-shelf (COTS) software or building their own. For example, if an organization needs a ticket management system and looks at the COTS options, ServiceNow, BMC Remedy, or HP Service Manager might be a better bet than building a product with in-house developers. But if an organization needs a specific workflow management solution and if the customization on the available COTS products is expensive and time-consuming, it makes sense to opt for an in-house solution.

Within application management, there are two areas: application development and application management. Application development is involved in developing new software or enhancing existing software, whereas application management maintains the software in its designed state. They take care of incidents as they come and don't get into the specifics of making significant changes to the software. The distinction in ITIL is very clear; you need people with different attitudes and skillsets to carry out application development and application management activities. It is prudent to identify the resources and move them into their respective silos.

The thinking behind different silos for application development and application management is in stark contrast to what DevOps believes in, which is "one team, one software." The DevOps team and its objectives are covered later in this chapter.

IT Operations Management

Operations is often seen as a launch pad for professionals getting into the IT sector. It is viewed from the prism of complexity and is rated pretty low, which is the primary reason for professionals to be put into operations, which signifies the bottom rung of the IT career ladder. However, this notion is not true. Operations cannot be done by everybody, especially newbies. It is a specialist job and requires a different set of skills to expect the unexpected and to learn rapidly from mistakes. For operational roles, you need people who are wired different so they can understand the underlying root causes from repetitive actions and the analysis carried forth to look for permanent solutions. In ITIL, the IT operations management function is tasked with managing the service operations.

There is a lot of strategy in the beginning, followed by planning and implementation. But the actual execution of the plans are done by the IT operations management function. People under operations management interact fairly regularly with customers, and their attitude and zeal to keep the engine running can have an effect on the customer.

Within operations, the ITIL framework defines two distinct subfunctions:

- IT operations control
- Facilities management

IT Operations Control

IT operations control is the subfunction where IT infrastructure operations are executed. I mention IT infrastructure specifically because the application management group handles the operations of software-related operational activities.

Some frequent activities that are performed here are monitoring, running operational bridges, taking backups and performing restorations, managing batch jobs, printing, and keeping an eye on the performance of all systems.

A number of operations activities today can be fully automated to ensure efficiency and standardization and to avoid human errors and biases. Automation is one of the key aspects of DevOps, whereby you try to avoid people carrying out repetitive activities with the sole aim of utilizing people power where it is really needed.

Operations in an integral part of DevOps teams, and the scope of the IT operations control function is purely based on the operational activities pertaining to IT infrastructure. On a DevOps team, operations folks find a place, but they are mostly from the application maintenance front. Managing physical IT infrastructure is done outside a DevOps team, as it is a common activity that serves multiple DevOps teams. However, within the DevOps teams, the IT infrastructure operations teams is involved in spinning up environments, managing them, and ensuring that the environments (or lack of) don't end up being a bottleneck for speedy delivery. This is all made possible through advancements in technology, whereby servers can be created through code—a concept known as infrastructure as code (IaC). Environments can be created by writing scripts, and with the help of tools such as Puppet and Ansible, they can be spun up in a matter of minutes and hours as opposed to weeks and months of effort gaining approvals and manually processing environments.

Facilities Management

The second subfunction in IT operations management is facilities management. As its name suggests, this function takes care of facilities that are key to running IT services, such as data centers, control rooms, workspaces, recovery sites, and generators, among others.

The facilities management function is an overarching entity for all the teams and people involved in the delivery of IT services. They are the enablers for DevOps and other teams to deliver. They remain independent and outside the purview of DevOps teams.

DevOps Team Structure Revisited

Chapter 1 briefly introduced the DevOps team, as illustrated in Figure 5-5.

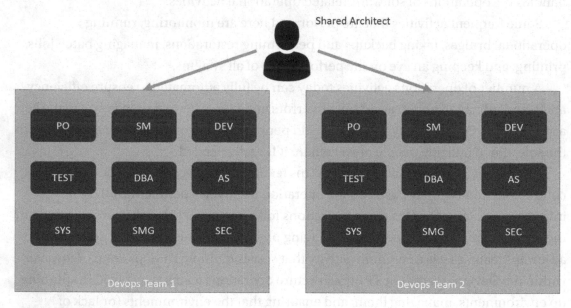

Figure 5-5. *DevOps team structure*

On this DevOps team, everybody associated with product development is placed together in the same team and is asked to make the best use of the aligned goals and objectives to intensify delivery and minimize rework (generally owing to defects). This structure is inspired by the Toyota Production System concept of *Obeya* (from the Japanese 大部屋, which translates to "large room" or "war room"), where in the time of crisis, all stakeholders are brought into the same room to quicken decision-making. When all the decision-makers are sitting across from each other, there is no need to wait for decision-makers to give their okays at their leisure. Likewise, when all the people connected to the development and support of a project are together in the same room, the need to formally hand decisions between teams to "pass the buck" does not arise.

Given that the shared responsibility is enforced, people on a DevOps team cannot point fingers at each other, as everybody becomes responsible for everything delivered, or a lack thereof.

Traditional Model

Let's examine how this is different from the traditional sense of setting up teams that is defined in the ITIL functions and in waterfall's matrix organization. In a traditional organization, people with similar skillsets are placed on the same teams and verticals and are called into action when needed. The people are always temporarily assigned to projects and are pulled back to the home base at the end of the engagement.

Consider Figure 5-6, which depicts a typical matrix organization where practices denote various verticals consisting of resources with similar skillsets. The illustration considers development, testing, server, database, project management, and architecture the practices. Digging deeper, the development practice will have multiple teams based on the technology, which I generically called Team 1, Team 2, and Team 3. This could be a Java team, Microsoft team, a web development team, and so on. Likewise, each of these practices can be subdivided based on technology, which is the most common practice of organizing teams within enterprises.

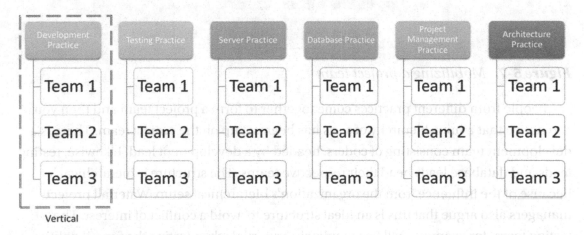

Figure 5-6. *Matrix organization*

Let's say that a project team is mobilized to develop an application. Some of the team members from each practice come together to form a project team. This is illustrated in Figure 5-7. In this illustration, I picked up developers, testers, database admins, an architect, and a project manager. Note that the server administrators from the server practice were not placed on the project team because the infrastructure is considered an enabler and it stays outside the project governance. During project planning, the infrastructure setup is considered a dependency, and this dependency is likely to turn into a risk in due time since a discrete governance model is a formula for failure. Likewise, there could be other dependencies, but considering that infrastructure is most essential, keeping it outside the project governance is a risk waiting to materialize.

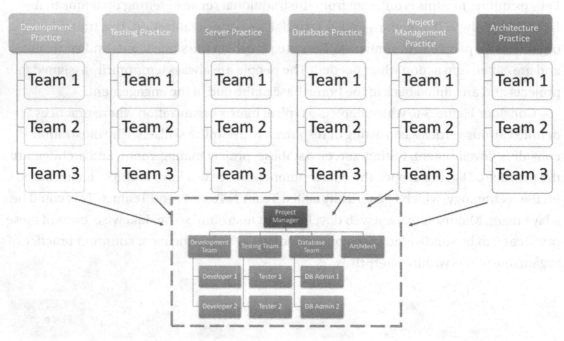

Figure 5-7. *Mobilizing a project team*

People from different practices come together to form a project team and then you can notice that a mini-hierarchy of sorts has been set up on the project team. There is a development team consisting of coders, headed by a development lead. Likewise, testing leads and database leads head their respective teams. The structure is hierarchical because of the influence from the organization's hierarchical setup. Waterfall project managers also argue that this is an ideal structure to avoid a conflict of interest. The testing team, for example, will be completely impartial when testing the functionalities, as they are under different leadership, and they are not obliged to push it through. I examine this argument under the Agile model.

The Agile Model

The Agile model, more specifically the Scrum framework, guides you to maintain smaller teams, and each of these teams is homogenous and hybrid with developers, testers, a Scrum master, and a product owner. These teams are called Scrum teams in the Scrum framework. This is illustrated in Figure 5-8.

Figure 5-8. *Scrum team*

There are a few seemingly major differences between a traditional model of team organization and a Scrum-based organization.

Flat Hierarchy

The Agile team organization is as flat as a pancake. There are no layers, as clearly visible in the traditional model. Flat organizations help transmit and receive information between team members because of the lack of hierarchy, which helps promote better collaboration between team members. Collaboration is one of the key asks of the Agile framework, whereby the entire team works as a single unit.

A flat organization is not a panacea for all of an organization's hierarchical problems. It works the best if the teams are smaller and are well-adapted to freely share information. Therefore, for a Scrum team using this flat structure, the recommended team size is between six to nine members—that's it! These numbers are based on experiments and the experiences of various project management experts in the field.

You might wonder how you can manage with a maximum of nine resources for bigger projects. The answer is to form multiple Scrum teams with homogenized setups. In other words, every Scrum team will have a dedicated Scrum master, a product owner, a business analyst, developers, and testers. Each Scrum team will be responsible for the development of a particular feature or a module to ensure that they work independently, with minimum dependencies as much as possible. For example, if you are building an Internet banking application, Scrum Team 1 is tasked with the development of fund transfers, Scrum Team 2 with credit rating checks, and Scrum Team 3 with the debits and credits feature. All three teams are going to come together to form a single application, but managing each of these modules or features independently on a homogenized team provides the project team with the best chance of success.

No Project Manager

In Figure 5-8 you might have noticed that there is no project manager. This is not a mistake but is by design. You don't need project managers if the team is self-supervised and is able to work synchronously on their own. To help with the synchrony, a new role of a Scrum master has been introduced. The Scrum master, unlike the project manager, is not a manager who keeps people in check while they work. The primary role of a Scrum master is to help the Scrum team in their developmental activities by removing impediments that come in the way of hurdles. A Scrum master is a servant leader who leads the team members by helping them succeed. Think about it as a cross-country relay, where the racers are required to cross several bumpy terrains to win the race. The Scrum master essentially removes the bumps from the way of the racers to ensure that they drive swiftly and come out on top. The actions are generally attributed to leaders, and the Scrum master is doing this not by commands but rather by service.

Single Team

In the traditional model there were mini-hierarchies: development team, testing team, and database team. The logic is to keep each of these teams independent of the others to ensure ample wriggle room to do their work and to ensure there is no conflict of interest. The traditional modelers did not want to have a situation where the testers would pass all the tests owing to the pressure of release timelines. The logic is sound, but can there be a better way to manage it? On the downside, handovers between each of these teams were sluggish and often not seamless. A lot of time and effort went to waste in trying to explain the reasoning behind the codes and the test failures between teams. For example, during the coding phase, only the coders are given the requirements, and then the coders pass on the developed code to the testers and at that stage explain the requirements. How much information is passed in this game of Chinese whispers? The testers tested based on what they understood, but received that information from second and third parties.

The answer to this problem that materialized more often than not was to build a single team with all the roles fused in. You create a single team and not multiple teams as was the case in the traditional team. Remember that the teams are small in the Agile case, so a large traditional model team typically translates into multiple Scrum teams. When you fuse team members with different skillsets into a single team, the next thing on the agenda is to provide shared responsibility, where everybody on the team has equal ownership of product or feature delivery. This means you cannot have a situation where the developers did extremely well but the testers failed to test on time. When there is any kind of lapse at any stage of the development lifecycle, the entire Scrum team takes responsibility. When shared responsibility is the principle for judging the team members on their work products, conflicts of interest simply disappear. They do not arise because the entire team wants to see the product succeed and will not be in a position to compromise on what they see as substandard.

Product Owner

Apart from the role of a Scrum master, which is new, there is another role introduced in the Agile organization: the product owner. The product owner is the sole owner of the product backlog, which is the list of requirements that need to be developed. The product backlog consists of all the nuts and bolts that need to go into the product or feature. The product owner owns this list and is the person who prioritizes this list to help the Scrum team pick up items from the product backlog during sprints. If any clarifications are needed on the requirements, the product owner is ready to help the Scrum team.

How is it that the product owner has a complete grasp of the requirements, and how is it that the product owner knows what priority item needs to be picked up? Although the product owner is part of the Scrum team, he/she is from the business (customer) organization. The proximity of a business representative who owns the requirements list helps the development team develop better, faster, and to the requirements. In the traditional model, the customer always sat outside the project organization and was brought in only during testing and demonstrations, which was at the end of the project lifecycle. In the Agile model, the customer or a customer's representative takes a seat on the project team and works with the development team closely in realizing the requirements. This change in stance in terms of where the customer sits prevents the gulf of mismatch between what was asked for and what was delivered.

Predictability

Predictability may not be a good feature for individual's personality, but for projects, it is a top-notch character trait to possess. In a traditional model, a project might run for a few weeks, and another project might drag on for a year or two. The cycles of development, testing, and other associated activities happen at different times, depending on the project plan, which was carefully laid out well before the project is due to begin. Over a period of time, contexts change, and the project plan changes along with it. This seems to bring in plenty of uncertainty to the mix with long project timelines and multi-angle changes bearing their ugly effect on deliveries.

The top motto of the Agile project management methodology is not to freeze everything at the beginning, but to keep things fluid, transparent, and flexible to adapt to things that change. Predictability is the last thing you would associate with Agile, right? Wrong! Although Agile is flexible enough to pick up whatever gets pushed up the list by the product owner, most elements in the framework have a predictable nature.

For example, the sprint length is two weeks, starting on the first Monday and ending on the second Friday. On the first day of the sprint cycle, you have a *sprint planning* session where the entire team comes together to estimate and plan what can be achieved during the two weeks. On the last day of the sprint (the second Friday), the developed product is showcased to stakeholders, and feedback is received. Also, on the same day, the team sits together and does a post-mortem called a *sprint retrospective* to understand what went right and what went wrong during the sprint and to identify ways of not repeating the mistakes and to optimize the delivery. So, come what may, every second Friday, the customer stakeholders are aware that a demonstration of the developed product (however small) is on schedule. No matter what happens in the market, the sprint length remains the same, and the sprint plans are drawn up for the two-week estimates and delivered accordingly within the two-week window. This is the predictable side of Agile project management, which provides a roadmap for customers on what to expect and what to commit.

The DevOps Model

The Agile model is self-sufficient. It is a single homogenous team that has all the elements of development built into it. Once the software is released into production and is accepted by operations, the Agile team gives up its baby for adoption and washes its hands of it. The team that developed it knows the product intimately, so why give it up to another team to manage? Logic does not support it, but there are certain sections of the IT community that believe operations is rookie work and experienced hands shouldn't be doing it.

Let's take this argument one step further. If this product were to break down, experienced hands require X amount of time to recover it, and the rookies, because of their relative inexperience of the product, require about four times as much time (the numbers put forth in this argument are factionary; there are no studies to suggest that it takes four times the effort). The amount of time taken to resolve the issue is the downtime during which customers cannot use the product or the service. This downtime can translate into penalties based on the SLAs, negative perception of the service provider, and bad-mouthing of the service provider to other potential customers. Given that the time taken to resolve an issue can be significantly more with a separate operations team, will service provider organizations sacrifice perception and avoid penalties for the sake of engaging experienced hands only on developmental activities? This sounds absurd! This is one of the prime reasons that the concept of DevOps took shape and the DevOps team was born to break all barriers that exist.

Composition of a DevOps Team

The objective of a DevOps team is to build a team that is the alpha and the omega of a product or a service. We look at this team for all its needs. The thinking behind this is not to scatter the knowledge across teams but to groom and build it under a single umbrella that is close quartered.

The DevOps team introduced in Chapter 1 is the target team we try to build that has both the development and operational team members. It is a team that is going to coexist between sections of IT that are considered to be on different poles—the development and operations teams.

Another illustration of a DevOps team is provided in Figure 5-9. The DevOps team is a conglomerate of three different teams. The first is the Scrum team discussed in the previous section under the Agile model. The second is the application management function from ITIL; this is the team that is involved in managing and maintaining the application. The final parts of the DevOps team are the other functions that help with nonfunctional aspects of a product, such as IT security, tools automation and configuration, and service managers who manage the various service management activities and also act as a conduit between the DevOps team and the customer organization on operational aspects. The formation of a DevOps team is decided by the product, the service, the service provider organization, and the contracts that were signed. The team composition presented here is for illustration purposes only. For example, if you don't need a service manager to be part of the DevOps, so be it. Somebody else can pitch in to take the role, or maybe a shared team can manage service management activities. The same is true for all activities coming under other functions. However, the roles coming under the Scrum team and the application management teams are a fairly standard setup for a DevOps team, and it can be said that they are the permanent members of the team.

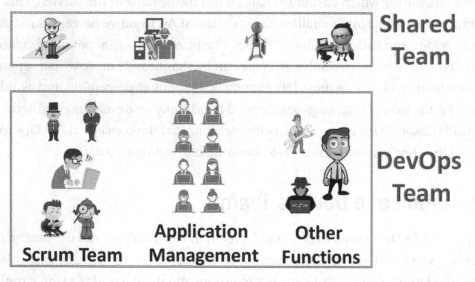

Figure 5-9. *DevOps team composition*

Another team is introduced in Figure 5-9, the shared team. The shared team consists of a set of functions that must be carried out in a DevOps workload, but a dedicated team member carrying out the function is not the best use of that person's costs. Therefore, we create a shared team for functions such as architecture, IT infrastructure, consultants, and domain experts, when they support multiple DevOps teams. In effect, their time will be shared between multiple DevOps teams, and they must manage their time and expectations with the DevOps teams on their availability and delivery. I have always found this challenging, especially when you have significant deliveries to make. But we don't have a choice today with the onus on cost reductions; for example, a dedicated consultant or a dedicated domain expert is a major waste of resources if they don't have full-time work.

Consider Figure 5-10, which features the scope of a team's reach in an organization to provide a sense of how people are spread across teams.

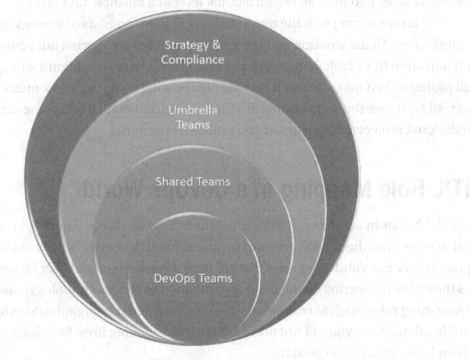

Figure 5-10. *Team scope in an organization*

The DevOps teams are on the lowest rung in terms of the breadth of scope covered, meaning that they are pretty much restricted to the product and service they develop and manage. They are focused on their product, and they are 100 percent dedicated to supporting the product placed in their scope. They don't get into the development or problem-solving of other products and services.

The shared teams, on the other hand, have a wider reach than a DevOps team. The name *shared teams* suggests that the resources on the shared teams support multiple DevOps teams. For example, a software architect may provide architectural support to multiple DevOps teams, which is fairly common.

The next layer in the hierarchy of scopes consists of the umbrella teams. These are teams that carry out their work across multiple projects and services. They don't restrict themselves to limited teams but rather do it for an entire program or an organization depending on the size of the organization. Some examples include the capacity management activity, which is generally done at a larger level considering that the capacities of infrastructure and network are generally shared across multiple projects. Another example is the asset management activity. Managing assets (such as laptops) is generally governed from an organizational level or a business unit level.

The topmost rung with the maximum scope space consists of strategy and compliance. All the strategic and compliance activities are carried out across the organization by default, rather than at a lower level. An organization's strategy will affect all projects, DevOps or not, so it is at the highest rung on the scope-o-meter. Compliance as well is strategized and planned at a higher level, although it will come down to individual projects being audited and put under the lens.

ITIL Role Mapping in a DevOps World

ITIL V3 brings in a number of roles across its five publications. Figure 5-11 shows the list of roles from the service provider organization. It deliberately does not include the practitioner roles and other roles that are from the customer and user community, as they have no bearing on the mapping with the DevOps methodology. Also, the lower-rung roles, such as coordination roles, usually exist in organizations but not in publications. Also, you will not find the list of roles coming from functions, as I discussed them in detail in earlier sections.

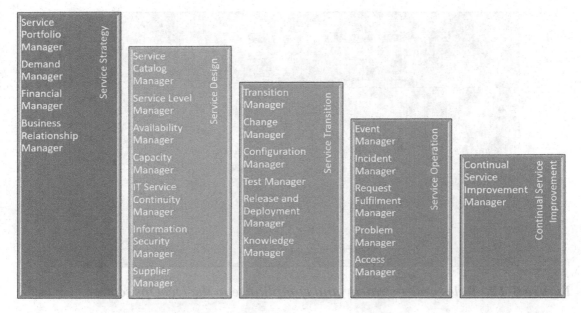

Figure 5-11. *ITIL roles*

Strategy and Compliance

The roles that appear in the service strategy lifecycle phase of ITIL can be directly mapped to the strategy and compliance role structure in the DevOps model, as the ITIL roles performed are at a strategic level and the DevOps scoping is for strategic activities along with compliance.

Figure 5-12 indicates the ITIL service strategy roles in the DevOps scope of activities. The role of a quality manager is not explicitly named in the ITIL publications. However, to manage the compliance of related ISO standards, such as ISO 20000 and ISO 27001, you need a head to lead the quality function.

Figure 5-12. *Roles under strategy and compliance in the DevOps scope*

Umbrella Teams

Umbrella teams are the set of activities that you perform that affect the entire organization or business unit. These activities are common across the board, and they level the playing field. For example, a change policy/process is generally common for all technologies and business units in mature organizations because this is the process that controls what goes in and what doesn't. I talk more about this later in the book. Figure 5-13 shows the roles that are generally placed in umbrella teams.

Most ITIL roles go under the umbrella teams scope, as the activities they manage are common across the entire organization or business, and it makes more sense to keep them standardized. The criteria for roles to be placed under the umbrella teams is that the policies and processes stay common across the organization or the business unit.

Figure 5-13. *Roles under umbrella teams scope*

Shared Teams

Shared teams work at a DevOps team level but across multiple DevOps teams. The strategy behind coming up with the shared teams is to ensure that costs are splurged on various roles, especially when the workload is not 100 percent. Some of the roles indicated in Figure 5-14 can easily move into the DevOps team scope depending on the product and scale of the project.

You will find that some of the roles, such as configuration manager and knowledge manager, find representation under shared teams as well; they were previously featured under umbrella teams. They find double representation because the role under umbrella teams sets the tone for how the configurations and knowledge databases are developed and managed, and the execution is done at a shared teams scope.

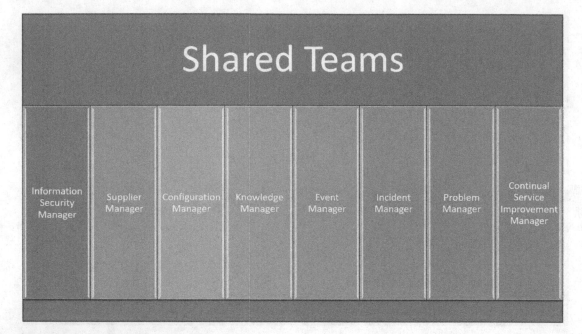

Figure 5-14. *Roles under shared teams scope*

DevOps Teams

The DevOps teams are mostly made up of people who work on the ground, close to the development and operations teams. You will find that some roles are common to the shared teams and umbrella teams. If a specific role is in the DevOps teams, it can be absent from the shared teams scope, and vice versa. Figure 5-15 showcases the roles under the DevOps team's scope.

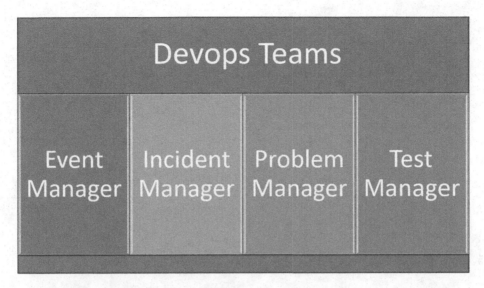

Figure 5-15. *Roles under the DevOps teams scope*

Note that this mapping is a guide only, because every organization has its own chemistry and trying to combine a standard set of elements goes against the nature of DevOps.

Summary

An organization thrives on backing a powerful operating model. An operating model is partly defined by the teams, the structures, and their responsibilities. While ITIL has clearly segregated teams to work as functions in a matrix type of an organization, there are nuances in DevOps models that do not work well in silos. This chapter transformed the functions and roles defined in ITIL into the DevOps ways of working.

CHAPTER 6

Managing Configurations in a DevOps Project

Most projects fail because of a lack of configuration management and control over the various components that make a project tick. Configuration management is the foundation upon which a project is built. Building a shoddy foundation will logically result in the walls and roofs of the project crumbling down in record time. Configuration management plays a significant role for systems made up of multiple components that are integrated with other systems and run on multiple dependencies. Sound familiar? Most systems today are complex, owing to the need for integration and its respective data sources and data consumers. In such a complicated setup, it is imperative that systems be driven by configuration management, which projects rely on heavily. In this context, those are DevOps projects.

ITIL's service asset and configuration management process has matured over the years and has been powering the service industry for a number of years. The first half of this chapter delves into the ITIL configuration management process. It follows up with what constitutes configuration management in a DevOps project and provides the details around how they can work in unison.

ITIL Service Asset and Configuration Management Process

The ITIL service asset and configuration management process has served as the spine for IT services over the years, and within ITIL, the process has matured with each version. It is a process that defines whether a service provider succeeds in delivering IT services and defines the longitude of the services offered.

139

© Abhinav Krishna Kaiser 2023
A. Krishna Kaiser, *Reinventing ITIL® and DevOps with Digital Transformation*,
https://doi.org/10.1007/978-1-4842-9072-9_6

The concept of configuration management is simple enough. Configuration management gives you a blueprint of IT services, the architecture underneath, and the dependencies. It provides an accurate reflection of the connected pieces and dependencies. It is this network of components that make the service work, and having it in a form that's alive and accessible gives you ammunition to make changes to services with ease, identify business impact with minimal analysis, and resolve outages in a jiffy. These are the tools that you need to be a valid player in today's market, where changes happen on the fly and customer wish lists change faster than ever.

A project without accurate and dynamic configuration management is a nightmare. Imagine making changes to one part of the system without understanding the impact they could cause on other, dependent systems. This happens commonly in the software development industry. It is not uncommon that architects are baffled when they have certain dependencies and defects crop up through the regression of acceptance testing quite late in the development lifecycle. This is a blunder of sorts because there is a good likelihood that software delivery might not happen as per the promised schedule, and if the development teams try to cram in fixes at the last minute, defects pop up. If only the architects had a working configuration management process in place, they could have identified everything that needed to be changed and could have avoided the negativity that emanates from failures.

Objectives and Principles

In short, the service asset and configuration management process exists to ensure that the various moving parts of a service are identified, registered, and maintained as long as the service is operational. The principle behind the process is to identify the smallest piece of a component that can be uniquely identified and managed and to connect such components with each other to build a service model. Once a service model is built, it needs to be maintained as long as needed to support the restoration of services, to identify the business impact, and to make changes to the service.

Service Assets and Configuration Items

There are two parts to this process: service assets and configuration items (CIs). Service assets are individual elements that make up a service. The entire lifecycle of the service assets—beginning with initiation, the changes it undergoes, and finally retirement—is managed, controlled, and tracked in the service asset and configuration management process. Examples of service assets are software, licenses, monitors, laptops, data centers, and servers.

A service asset is any resource or capability that could contribute to the delivery of a service. A configuration item is a service asset that needs to be managed in order to deliver an IT service.

A configuration item is a fundamental component of a service that can be configured, tracked, accounted for, and controlled. For example, in an email server involving servers, routers, and MS Exchange applications, each server, router, switch, application, and firewall can be considered a CI. Why? Because these CIs can be tracked, controlled, accounted for, and audited.

Not every service asset is a CI, but every CI is a service asset.

Who decides what can or cannot be a CI? This is a decision made by the configuration architect based on the nature of the services, its interfacing to other processes such as incident and change management processes, and most importantly the cost. For example, a server can be considered a CI. Conversely, each of the components of a server such the processor, memory, and hard drives can be considered CIs, which necessarily alludes to a lot more effort (and cost) in coming up with the configuration management and maintaining it. Therefore, generally the decision is left to the architect to make a judgment call on what level a CI should be considered. The general practice is to measure the value derived by delving deeper into the services for deriving CIs.

Every CI has a number of attributes attached to it. Attributes are various details that are recorded against a CI, such as owner, location, date of commission, status, and configuration. All these attributes are controlled through change management. This is the layer of control that ensures that the configuration management remains accurate and nobody can make changes to it without the approval and consent of the change management governance.

Any service asset that is critical or that directly impacts a service is a configuration item. This definition gives rise to a number of types of CIs that could potentially be leveraged in a service provider organization. Human CIs (workforce management), document CIs (document management), business CIs (the business processes that connects business side of things), software CIs (business applications and in-house developed software), and hardware CIs (servers and routers) are some examples. An architect can choose to include only IT elements (such as software and hardware) or go shopping for human CIs through HR departments and document CIs through document management teams. It is entirely the architect's decision on how to manage the CIs appropriately.

Scope of Service Asset and Configuration Management

As the name of the process suggests, there are two main parts to the service asset and configuration management (SACM) process: asset management and configuration management.

The asset management part of the SACM process is where the accountability of all the service assets happens. Under this, the service assets are identified, accounted for, managed, and controlled. The type of assets that will be individually managed will be at the discretion of the service provider organization.

For example, a service provider might decide to include the monitor as part of a desktop so as to not manage the monitor individually but under the whole unit of a desktop computer.

The question to ask is how well a service provider can manage the service assets, without any compromises to the users, to the service provider personnel, and to the services. Based on this, the service design lifecycle phase determines whether certain service assets are within or outside the scope of individual management. Remember that every asset has to be managed. Whether they are managed individually or as a group is at the service provider's discretion.

In most organizations, service assets have a financial value associated with them. The user group that enjoys the service will be charged for the assets leveraged. For example, if I am using a laptop, each year my business unit is billed a certain amount of money for the laptop that I use. Of course, it is notional charging, where an actual exchange of money does not take place. But, it is a good practice to keep track of assets and their financial information across the organizational units.

On the other hand, the scope of configuration management is based on services that potentially impact business by the lack of it, or even in its degraded state. The scoping of which services to be included in the configuration management process is decided by the architect.

Introducing the CMDB, CMS, DML, and DS

To manage the service asset and configuration management process, you rely on a number of databases with varying relevance and significance.

Configuration Management Database

A *configuration management database* (CMDB) is a repository containing all the CIs, including their relationships. For example, in a CMDB model, the dependency between the CIs can be defined through relationships such as "runs on" and "supported by."

In the CMDB, you can have multiple services, the individual CIs, and their relationships. Most modern ITSM tools, such as ServiceNow and BMC Atrium, offer placeholders to record the upstream and downstream impacts. If you pick up a service and want to use it visually to see how CIs connect, you will see an array of connections between the CIs. Using this visual image, other processes such as incident management can troubleshoot incidents with ease, and processes such as change management can identify upstream and downstream impacts with a click of a button. Imagine if this were not in place; the whole activity involving analysis and troubleshooting would be tough.

In an organization, you can have multiple CMDBs depending on the requirements, business structure, and customer obligations. For example, you can have a CMDB for business units A, B, and C; a CMDB separately for customer ABC; and yet another CMDB for internal infrastructure and software. There is no limit, as long as the logic makes sense to manage, control, and simplify matters.

Configuration Management System

The *configuration management system* (CMS) is the super database that contains all the CMDBs and more in its ecosphere. It is the layer that integrates all the individual CMDBs along with other databases in the IT service management space, such as known error databases, incident records, problem records, service request records, change records, and release records. Figure 6-1 provides an illustration of a CMS.

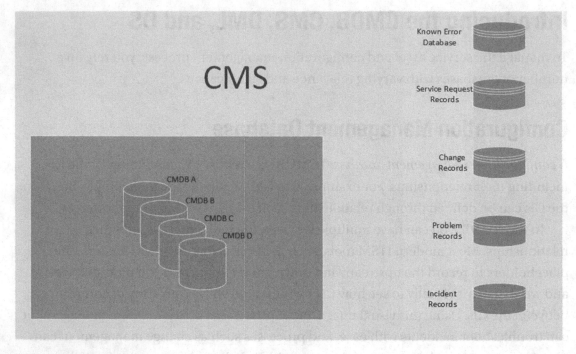

***Figure 6-1.** Configuration management system*

It is possible that some CIs in a CMDB talk to other CIs in another CMDB. The overview of all the relationships between the CIs is provided in the CMS.

The CMS holds the CI data as well as other databases such as incident records, so service providers and customers alike can utilize the CMS to identify all the incidents raised against a CI and the number of times they have failed on a regular basis.

Definitive Media Library and Definitive Spares

The *definitive media library* (DML) is a repository for storing all licensed copies of procured software and software developed in-house. The repository can be an online one or a physical one, but it needs to be access controlled.

The software that is accepted into the DML is controlled by the change management process, and only copies authorized by change management into the DML are allowed to be used during the release and deployment management process. The software that gets into the DML is expected to be analyzed, quality tested, and checked for vulnerabilities before being accepted.

In the case of a physical DML where CDs, DVDs, and other storage media are used, it is expected that the storage facility is fireproof, can withstand the normal rigors of nature, and is secure against media thefts.

The DML is ideally designed during the service design lifecycle phase, and the following are considered during the planning stages:

- Medium to be used and the location of the master copies to be stored

- Security arrangements for both online and offline storage

- Access rights, including who has access and how it is controlled

- The naming convention for the stored media to help in easy retrieval and tracking

- What types of software go into the DML, for example, source codes or packages

- Retention period

- Audit plan, checklist, and process

- Service continuity of DML if disaster strikes

The *definitive spares* (DS) is a repository for storing hardware spares. Generally, all organizations store a certain amount of stock, mostly pieces of critical infrastructure, to be used to quickly replace hardware in case of an incident. Also, stocks are needed for the operational consumption and ever-increasing demands of the customer.

Like DML, a DS must be secured, tracked, managed, and controlled. However, change management generally does not get involved in controlling the items that go in and out of the DS, as the gravity of compromising intellectual property and master copies of licensed versions can be messy compared to hardware spares. The SACM process oversees the overall functioning of the DS.

Service Asset and Configuration Management Processes

The service asset and configuration management process is a complex process with technical and logical flavors playing a big part in its definition and implementation. At a high level, the process can be explained in five steps, as shown in Figure 6-2. Translating these five steps into a full-fledged process is a different matter altogether. The architect behind configuration management must be well versed in the technicalities surrounding the service, have a good understanding of the contractual requirements, and must be an expert in ITIL to understand the interfaces of configuration management with other processes.

I have been developing configuration models and processes for a long time now, and still the field amazes me, as there is always something new to learn, such as new technologies or a complicated contractual requirement such as a report on the number of cores for servers. I might write a book in the future on ITIL configuration management as the bookshelves look barren when it comes to configuration management and the techniques to implement it. This section only talks about it from a high-level view.

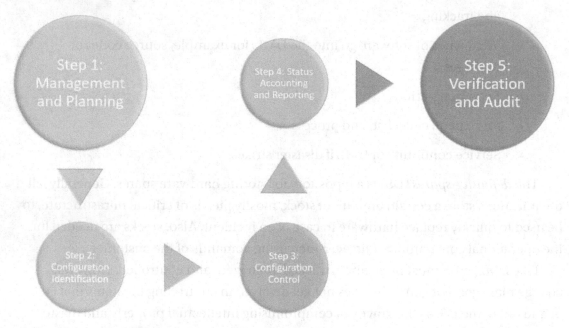

Figure 6-2. SACM process

Step 1: Management and Planning

Configuration plans play a major role in the SACM process. The plans lay out the various elements of the configuration management that needs to be considered in the implementation. There is no set template for plans to be formed, and every plan is customized for the services in scope and the customer/interfacing process requirements.

A configuration architect will lead the planning exercise by giving structure to the configuration model and defining various elements of configuration management that are fit for use and fit for purpose throughout the service management lifecycle. This is by no means an easy exercise. In terms of the timeline, a good plan might take as much time as the overall implementation of the process.

Before this step, the architect must identify all stakeholders and sit down with each one to understand the stated and unstated requirements. Contract documents are one of the major sources of requirements. After gathering all requirements and analyzing them for configuration management elements, a plan has to be defined with the following items:

- The scope of SACM (what services are in and which ones aren't)
- Sources of requirements and how they translate into specific configuration management decisions
- Interfaces with other process (specifying the exact nature along with the handshake details)
- Principles around which the configuration management will be built
- Identification of risks and dependencies
- Involved suppliers and their scope in the SACM process
- Identified tools
- Tools to be integrated between systems and suppliers
- Service assets and configuration items along with their attributes
- Configuration identification and control mechanisms
- Configuration management roles and their authorized accesses
- Other elements as needed

Step 2: Configuration Identification

A good plan gives way to a seamless identification of configuration items. Based on the identified configuration items and their respective attributes and data sources, the CIs are identified for the defined scope.

Identifying CIs is a tedious and time-consuming process, depending on the complexity of the services and the configuration management database. It is an activity where different parts of the organization must come together to identify the right set of CIs and register them accurately in the CMDB. For example, the data center teams, the tools team, and the configuration management team must work in close collaboration to capture the identified CIs from the data center into the CMDB. Tools help capture CIs accurately and quickly. There was a time when we were manually capturing CIs based on the service architecture. Many times, by the time we acquired the architecture diagrams, captured the CIs, and registered them, the CIs involved had been modified or replaced. Or new CIs were introduced into the architecture. This was a risk that we were running against when manually identifying CIs.

However, today things are a lot more advanced, and most CIs are captured automatically using discovery toolsets such as Service Watch, ADDM, and Dynatrace. The discovery tools can even identify the relationships between CIs (such as a software using a database). The manual activity in this whole process is to validate the data to ensure its integrity.

Step 3: Configuration Control

When all the configuration items are identified and the service models are built, they are not going to remain constant forever. They can change at every turn, such as when tweaking configurations, replacing modules, or even changing the architecture. For the configuration management to stay relevant and useful, the CIs that are identified and built must remain accurate at all times. A tight control net must be weaved around the CMDB to ensure that all changes to the database happen through a defined process that is streamlined and without loopholes.

Since configuration identification takes a good amount of time, it is likely that the configurations will change before they officially get into the configuration control stages. Therefore, it is practical to set up the control processes, and when configurations are identified, they automatically go into the pipeline that's controlled by the defined control processes. If control processes kick in sequentially, it is likely that you will look down the barrel to find the changes in the CMDB even before you claim a stabilized CMDB build.

The control processes are generally concerned with the following:

- When the CMDB will be modified (trigger and input)
- How it will be done
- Who does it
- Handshakes with other processes

Generally speaking, a good configuration management control process will initiate making changes to the CMDB on the back of a change ticket. After making the changes to the CMDB, the data is verified with the live environment to ensure that the change performed is as proposed in the change plan. For example, if a change ticket is raised to upgrade the hard drive on a server to 2TB, but instead the hard drive inserted is 1GB, configuration management must identify the mismatch and have mechanisms flag it to all concerned. So, configuration management is not just a database to store data but is also a validation tool that can help organizations achieve total control.

Step 4: Status Accounting and Reporting

The configuration items that make up the CMDB have lifecycle states. Let's say that a server is ordered, procured, and delivered to the service provider. When the server gets delivered, generally it is registered in the CMDB with the status of "in store." When it is built or tested, the status may change accordingly. When the server makes it to production, it takes the state "active" or "live." When it's time to send it for maintenance, the status gets changed accordingly. When it's at the end of its life, the server gets decommissioned with a status of "decommissioned." Finally, it is discarded as e-waste, and the server ends up with a final status of "disposed."

All the status changes must be defined and controlled. For the status to change from decommissioned to disposed, let's say the acceptance criteria is that the hard drive must be wiped clean and degaussed. Unless this is done, the status will not change to disposed. Likewise, between the status changes, there are input, acceptance, trigger, and output criteria. The status accounting activity is responsible for ensuring that every change in state for a CI is recorded, and at any point in time, a clear lifeline as a CI traverses through states is available.

Based on the data recorded, reports can be generated to provide an accurate representation of the CMDB ecosystem. A number of reports are generally developed as part of the service asset and configuration management process. A few include configuration baseline and snapshots, active CIs in production, CI changes that are unauthorized, and CI changes performed in a specified period.

Step 5: Verification and Audit

The CMDB is built and used by the service management teams on a day-to-day basis for all their needs. But how do we know that the data residing in the CMDB reflects the true representation of the configuration items in production? For all we know, somebody could have made changes to some of the servers and switches without updating the changes in the CMDB. The verification and audit activity ensures that the accuracy of the CMDB is checked on a regular basis.

This activity can happen in multiple ways. Today we have automated auditing tools that monitor CIs in production and compare them to the CMDB values. If they don't match, a flag goes out to the concerned teams indicating the anomaly. This is perhaps the most efficient way to verify the accuracy of the CMDB.

Then there are CIs that cannot be audited automatically, such as racks on a chassis and server mounts. These need to be audited physically. In this case, an auditor walks into a data center and picks up a random set of servers and switches to be audited physically. The CMDB indicates its physical location. The auditor walks up to its physical location and checks whether the server/switch sits where it is meant to.

Physical audits are limited to geographical attributes of a CI. However, there was a time when the entire audit was done physically. An auditor would ask the administrator to log into a server and then would check for the configuration matches physically. Gone are those days, as physical checks have been replaced by remote audits. The auditor remotely connects with the administrator to audit the configurations of CIs instead of being physically present at the data center.

When the audit is complete, an audit report is written, highlighting the lapses and providing a list of actions aimed at improving the accuracy of the CMDB. The lapses are referred to as nonconformances (NCs). A certain period of time is given to the accountable teams to fix the lapses and to come up with a preventive measure to ensure such inaccuracies don't occur again. Anomalies between the CIs in the field and the CMDB happen mostly because of unauthorized changes and the lack of CMDB changes on authorized changes.

Why Configuration Management Is Relevant to DevOps

Configuration management is at the heart of service management and is solely responsible for the efficient resolution of incidents and to provide an effective map for identifying true business impact. DevOps is not much different from ITIL when it comes to the maintenance of products and services. The other half, development, also has plenty of dependency on configuration management, as you will find out later in this chapter.

Development is not a stand-alone activity and cannot be done in isolation. Systems talk to one another and exchange data. With configuration management in place, it makes it much easier for developers to identify the connecting bits and develop with ease and efficiency.

Some of the development projects that I was involved with, sadly enough, did not have the luxury of a CMDB or a map that gave them an accurate representation of web services, databases, and views. So, any development done on one part of the software resulted in something else breaking on the other end. The worst part was that such defects came to the fore only during regression testing toward the later part of the development and testing lifecycle. This essentially led to a few panic moments for the development team, put a big question mark around the quality of the product, and delayed the project release.

DevOps is based on the premise of speeding up the development cycle and increasing the quality of the product, apart from efficient operational activities. For faster cycles of development, something like a CMDB is absolutely essential to be able to have all the information you need.

I cannot implement DevOps processes in a project until I have a working configuration management in place—something like a CMDB that gives me a view of the application and infrastructure integrations. In a software development project, configuration management is a whole lot more than just something like a CMDB. There are other moving parts that require additional management of configurations, which I discuss in the next section.

Configuration Management in a DevOps Sense

Is configuration management relevant at all today in the age of cloud and automation? Detractors say that everything is on the cloud; resources are allocated dynamically, and at the click of a button, environments are spun up. So, why do you need to maintain the configurations and attributes if they are subject to change in a whiff?

It is true that the way we used to stack up servers has changed; in fact, it has been transformed. We no longer depend on server teams to create virtual machines and load operating systems and the set of standard settings and applications. At a click of a button, environments are created within minutes, and the resources of the server are shared between multiple server boxes. They are logically pooled to create an environment on the cloud. The question to ask, rather than point to automation is, what configuration is going into the making of the environment? How does the one-click environment creation tool know what parameters and configurations to use in the environment? The answer is quite simple: configuration management based on ITIL.

Consider Figure 6-3, which depicts a simple configuration management system in the DevOps world. The environment today generally lies in the cloud, and the cloud infrastructure gives you the ability to scale and descale on demand without any physical changes done to the underlying infrastructure. Furthermore, all the applications and their dependencies are deployed and maintained automatically, who gives no scope for any uncontrolled changes to creep in. The underlying configuration management that starts with the cloud infrastructure, the codebase, the binaries, and the dependencies, among others, provides a real-time blueprint of all things configuration in a DevOps project, and this will power projects to develop freely and with flair.

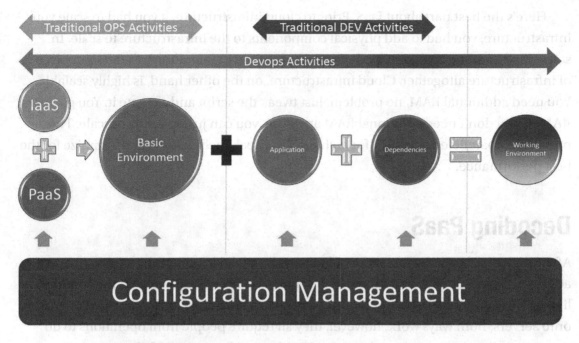

Figure 6-3. *DevOps configuration management*

Decoding IaaS

Traditionally building a server—which involved racking it on a chassis, hooking all the cables up, and allocating a subset of the box as a virtual machine—was the role of somebody working in operations. Today, with the advent of the cloud and automation, server creation is dynamic and can be done with a few keystrokes. The physical activities involving server racking and connecting cables are still and will always be a manual activity in a data center. I don't see robotics taking over this activity! However, building a server with specific hardware configurations is fully automated today.

To build a server, a script needs to be written with the required configurations, and the script is then executed with tools such as Vagrant or Pivotal Cloud Foundry. Writing a script is a one-time activity, and it can be executed as many times as needed to create additional servers, which is generally referred to as *one-click server creation*. In fact, infrastructure-as-a-service (IaaS) providers such as AWS, Azure, and Google Cloud have created an intuitive interface to enable semi-technical people to build their own servers by playing around on their GUIs.

Here's the best part about IaaS. Prior to cloud infrastructure, if you had to scale your infrastructure, you had to add physical components to the infrastructure to scale. In some cases, adding could not be done, which resulted in migration to a different piece of infrastructure altogether. Cloud infrastructure, on the other hand, is highly scalable. You need additional RAM, no problem. Just tweak the script and execute it. You got extra RAM. If you don't need additional RAM anymore, you can just as easily descale. This provides unparalleled flexibility for architects to tweak their designs and optimize for the best performance.

Decoding PaaS

After a server is built, the first order of business is to load an operating system on it. This activity was traditionally carried out by installing the operating system at the command line or via friendly GUIs. Or, operating systems can be installed by loading preset images onto servers. Both ways work; however, they all require people from operations to do them, and since it was a manual process, it took a good amount of finite time.

This is where PaaS comes in to automate the process of installing the platforms (operating systems). Once the server is ready, running a script yet again with platform characteristics enables the setup of an operating system at the snap of a finger. You can also configure OS-level configurations such as enabling group policies, installing standard antivirus software, monitoring, and other agents as specified by the organizational policy.

PaaS is also flexible. If you want to change a configuration across a server farm, you just need to change the script and execute it. Changes to thousands of servers can happen in an instant, saving hours of manual dispensation. Tools such as Ansible, Puppet, and Chef help with installing and maintaining software configurations.

Application Deployment and Configuration

In Figure 6-3, I indicate that the combination of IaaS and PaaS basically gives you a bare shell environment on which applications and their dependencies are loaded to complete the setup of the environments, in other words, testing and production. The application deployment was traditionally done manually, and the application was configured with its dependencies and database connections. This was traditionally the activity that the development team used to perform in testing environments and was mimicked by operations teams on production environments.

Automation has significantly changed the way we deploy and configure applications. The tools that I discussed for use with PaaS are capable of delivering application packages along with all the necessary configurations at the click of a button.

So, does this mean that the development team's role has been trimmed to development and testing alone? In a sense, yes. We expect developers to focus on their core areas and leave the repetitive activities for tools to execute. In addition, unnecessary human errors are eliminated in the age of automation.

Underlying Configuration Management

In Figure 6-3, all the configuration activities performed have a common link: configuration management (and, more specifically, ITIL's configuration management). Let's break this down.

To perform IaaS (in other words, build a server), you need to know what configurations you need to employ. How would you get this information? You can get it from the architects or configuration management plans, if it's a new development. What if it's a system that has existed for ages and has been modified, changed, and upgraded several times over the years, and none of the blueprints carry the exact specifications of the server. In this case, where can you get the server specifications? Logging into each one of them and getting the details or even running a monitoring and discovery script is not too dependable. What you need is a live database that has been updated with the true configurations of the server over the years: the configuration management database. The CMDB, which is at the heart of configuration management, has all the answers that IaaS toolsets need to build the server.

Even after the server is built all the way up, the configurations still need managing. Whether the configuration data lies in the configuration management toolset or the CMDB, it does not matter. The configuration management toolset can work as a federated CMDB to ensure that the CMDB has all the data available in a single database.

Likewise, PaaS takes configuration details from the CMDB to complete its tasks, and the application deployment and its dependencies can be effortlessly identified in a CMDB using the existing relationships between various CIs. So, the whole network of application dependencies can be brought together, stitched, and deployed to make the environment whole again with minimum effort, ensuring maximum productivity for the involved teams.

Once everything is set up, the working environment goes into the CMDB as a CI or a bunch of CIs with relationships and is managed until its retirement.

Automation in Configuration Management

Cloud infrastructure changes to the configuration happen quite rapidly. If the configuration management is to remain updated, it needs to be updated as rapidly as the changes. That is where the automation in configuration management comes in to play.

Making changes to configurations, although done quite rapidly with minimal lead time—requires governance. Something like the change management process to govern the changes done to ensure that it does not disrupt services. There is a special provision in change management called *standard changes* where changes are preapproved after a thorough assessment of business risks, which allows changes to be carried out with minimal lead time.

I talk about standard changes in detail in Chapter 9. However, for now, assume that changes are done on the back of standard change tickets. You can make CMDB updates automatically based on the standard changes instantly after the change has been deemed successful. This way, the CMDB data remains accurate with the environment at all times, thanks to the automation you employed to make it happen.

One way to visualize this happening is that the CI where the changes are going to happen are registered in the standard change. The CI is referenced from the CMDB. So, when the change is carried out, the referenced CI gets a trigger to change its configuration. But where does this configuration data come from? It might come from the change ticket. However, more accurate sources of configuration changes are the monitoring toolsets that you use to keep your finger on the pulse. These tools pick up changes to the configurations, confirm whether there is a change ticket associated with them, and if there is, go ahead and update the CMDB directly. *Voila!* Suppose that the change carried out is an unauthorized one (no change ticket to back it up). In that case, automation helps flag the unauthorized changes to the relevant parties. In fact, automation can go one step ahead too. Based on the lack of a change ticket, the configuration toolsets like Ansible and Puppet can self-correct the configurations to undo the changes. So, thanks to automation, you can fully ensure that no unauthorized changes take place in the ecosystem. The CMDB data remains accurate and provides a true reflection of the network of CIs in the data center and the rest of the ecosystem.

Who Manages DevOps Configurations?

The activity involving building a server—virtual machines, group policies, and the operating system—has always been part of the operations space. The server teams were responsible for discharging the duties related to building the server up to its operating system. In some cases, they even deployed the applications manually, tweaked the services involved, and set up applications.

As mentioned, servers are built in a completely different way today. Building a server has been codified using scripts, and writing scripts can be seen as an activity that might fall under the developer's realm. So, it begs the question of whether the activity of building servers requires hardware engineers (read, operations).

This is a common trap that people who try to dissect DevOps fall into. We are no longer dealing with Dev and Ops teams anymore. We are dealing with DevOps teams, where the team works as one unit to get the job done. If the developers can write scripts and execute them to build servers, then so be it. While they build a server, they are carrying out an operational activity and not a developmental activity. The same person wears different hats while executing different activities in this case. Therefore, in a DevOps team, it is important not to differentiate people based on Dev and Ops but rather recognize them as a collective unit—a unit that collaborates to bring the best of both worlds into building and maintaining a product.

To conclude, the DevOps team manages configurations related to the CIs that come under its scope. We don't call someone the configuration analyst or manager because they manage configurations. In fact, in a DevOps project, at a DevOps team level, we don't even like to manage configurations manually but rather automate them so that changes happen automatically and keep up with the rate of change. When new CIs are introduced, a central configuration management team that is accountable for the overall design and maintenance of the CMDB is brought into the loop for seamless additions and possible deletions.

Comprehensive Configuration Management

In DevOps, configuration management has a wider scope than a typical services organization would require. For operations to run, a services organization with a good working CMDB will be utterly satisfied, as it gives them the foundational support to resolve incidents quickly and to assess the business impact accurately. For development teams to be satisfied, it's a different kettle altogether. The superset of configuration management, which is indeed what a DevOps project requires, is the comprehensive configuration management.

Comprehensive configuration management (CCM) is meant to be a single source of truth for a DevOps project. Data integrity is integral to the success of any project, and this is accomplished in DevOps through CCM, which maintains the entire product, project, and service information. To extend this concept, no information pertaining to a DevOps project can reside outside the CCM.

Comprehensive configuration management consists of three parts, as shown here (and illustrated in Figure 6-4):

- Configuration management database

- Source code repository

- Artifact repository

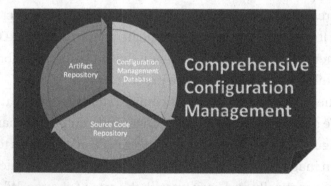

Figure 6-4. *Comprehensive configuration management*

The idea behind comprehensive configuration management is simple enough. The entire lifecycle of DevOps starts with development and continues to exist with operations. Therefore, the configurations for a DevOps project start with the configurations around managing source codes and the branching strategies. The binaries generated need to be managed with care and with nitpicky organizational skills. In DevOps, we recommend that developers check in the code multiple times a day, resulting in multiple builds and binaries. Not all the binaries end up getting pushed to various environments. Therefore, it is critical to segregate the builds that get pushed to production and those that don't make the cut. Binaries are stored in an artifact repository, which is part of comprehensive configuration management.

Configuration Management Database

A Configuration Management Database (CMDB) comes with multiple views—one that is beneficial to operations, one for developers, and maybe another as a superset of all information such as a complete CMS view.

The developer's view of the CMDB can possibly have the various integrations of the software, including the data sources, data consumers, residing environment (servers), databases, and database instances. The operations view will possibly go deeper into the infrastructure, and the CMDB of the data sources and data consumers will have all the possible information to troubleshoot incidents and to identify root causes of problems. So, although a CMDB is a vast repository of data, it is possible to customize the views to ensure that the developer or operational personnel using it does not get drained from data overload.

A CMDB is essential for a development team's day-to-day activities, as it helps to draw a blueprint of all integrations. This will help the architect plan the development activities better, with no element of surprise coming in the latter part of the development process. It helps developers write better code considering all the possible integrations and avoids defects due to regression issues. The overall quality of the software improves because of fewer defects, and most importantly it avoids rework and boosts the development team's productivity.

For operations, a CMDB is like pure gold. When incidents or problems are raised against the application, it helps the team to troubleshoot the issue faster and thus reduce the downtime of the service. During the planning of enhancements as well, an accurate business impact can be drawn with a CMDB in place.

To summarize, a CMDB is an inherent part of any project, be it ITIL-driven services or DevOps-powered software development projects. Building and maintaining a CMDB is an onerous task and involves a significant portion of the budget investment. However, the value gained by it outweighs the money spent building and maintaining it.

Figure 6-5 shows a CMDB. In the illustration, services, applications, databases, and servers are represented by the different colored boxes. Service 1 depends on Application A, as shown by the arrow. Application A leverages Database 1. Both Application A and Database 1 reside on Server A.

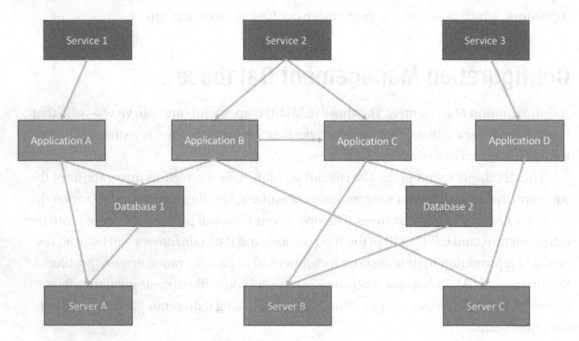

Figure 6-5.   *Another illustration of a CMDB*

In a real CMDB, however, the arrows mean something different from the relationships described. For example, an application generally uses a database; this is the relationship between the two entities. An application residing on a server leads to a dependency on the relationship. The relationship around the data flow between applications (indicated between Application B and Application C) is one of the data dependencies.

CMDB for Change Management

The CMDB is particularly useful when you are trying to change any of the applications, databases, or servers.

Let's say you want to make a change to Application B. To make the change, you must first do an impact assessment. A CMDB helps in performing impact assessments, and in Figure 6-5, suppose changes are done to Application B. The impact assessment will read that any changes done to Application B will impact Application C, as the data is flowing through it.

Today, software development seldom happens in isolation. The software to be developed either is an improvement over existing code or is getting plugged into an enterprise network of applications. Therefore, it is critical that the impacts are assessed correctly, and a CMDB is a great help in this area.

CMDB for Provisioning Environments

Another application of a CMDB in DevOps is in environment provisioning. Today we can spin up environments on the go with tools such as Ansible in our scripts. When you key in the exact configuration of the production server, the environment-provisioning tools create a prod-like server with the click of a button.

But how is it that you are going to obtain the complete configuration of a server? The most straightforward way is to refer to a CMDB.

Let's say Server C is a production server that needs to be replicated. In the CMDB, the Server C entry will provide the complete configuration of the server, which is a great help in creating provisioning scripts such as with Playbooks (compatible with Ansible).

CMDB for Incident Management

The CMDB also has other benefits, such as supporting the incident management teams during incident resolutions. The CMDB readily provides the architecture of applications and infrastructure, which is used to troubleshoot and identify the cause of the issue.

Source Code Repository

A source code repository (SCR) is a critical element of a DevOps project, as the entire basis for delivering software quickly starts with the organization of the SCR and its related scripts. The SCR has never been included or referred to in the ITIL publications because the design and maintenance of services depended on the production instance of the application rather than the means to achieving the application instance. If you are strictly from an ITIL background, you will find that the SCR is a completely new subject that was never addressed in any of the ITIL versions and publications. The SCR is an integral part of the CCM, and to make configuration management whole again for DevOps projects, it is critical that you understand the nuances of the SCR and include it during the design and implementation of the configuration management process for DevOps projects.

Basics of a Source Code Repository

A source code repository hosts the codebase used when developing an application. It is a version control system that allows multiple versions of the source code to be stored, retrieved, and rolled back at any point in time. This will act as an insurance against code changes that potentially could break the application. An SCR is the single source of truth for the entire project team, and it is also the medium that allows the team to collaborate and work as one unit. Source code repositories are also called *version control systems*, and the management techniques involved are referred to as *source code management*.

The objective of an SCR is to bring about a clear understanding of the constituents of different versions of a software. If you were going to release software version 4.4, then what exactly does it consist of, the contents of the release notes? To control the software and its configuration, this information is critical. In addition, every version change that was done to the SCR has a name associated with it, a timestamp, and a summary of changes performed. This showcases the evolution of a software and will come in handy during firefighting exercises.

What Can Be Stored in a Source Code Repository?

This is a million-dollar question. SCR in principle is a repository where files are stored and code changes are performed with features to allow collaboration. In a repository, typically anything and everything can be stored. This includes documents, libraries, contracts, databases, and the source code, of course. However, the best practice is to restrict the SCR to store the codebase, build scripts, test scripts, deployment scripts, stored procedures, and configuration files.

An easy way to remember is that data that is readable by humans goes into an SCR. Anything that isn't readable goes into an artifact repository. This is just a broad principle. There could be some exceptions to this rule.

Good Practices for Achieving DevOps Objectives

A DevOps project can be deemed successful if it can accelerate the speed of delivery and reduce the defect count. For this to happen, some good practices around source code management are necessary.

In Chapter 1, when I discussed the process of continuous integration, I wrote of the need for developers to check their code in at regular intervals. This is absolutely necessary. However, even before we go into the length of delivery, it is important to lay down a hygiene factor involving storing source codes and other scripts that are stored on a source code repository. First, all source code and scripts must be stored in an SCR and nowhere else. I have seen some developers store code locally and check it into an SCR when needed. This is not a good practice if a team is involved (which is generally the case) in the software development. No files should be stored locally, and code changes done on a local machine must be checked into an SCR in short batches to obtain fast feedback and allow other developers to make adjustments according to the code changes, or vice versa.

An SCR is a safety net that helps you experiment. Since it is a version control system, any mistakes you make can be undone at the click of a button. In DevOps projects, experimentation is encouraged, and an SCR ensures that no matter what you screw up, you can always go back to the previous state without working your sweat glands.

Choosing a Source Code Repository Tool

There are a number of commercial off-the-shelf (COTS) and open source repositories available today. Architects who are implementing DevOps projects are spoiled for choices with differing feature sets, which makes choosing one all the more complex. Before we get into the tools that are used today and the benefits behind them, we need to understand the architecture and principle behind these toolsets.

Source code repositories or version control systems come in two different architectural standards. Traditional SCRs fall under the architectural standard called a *centralized version control system* (CVCS). The concept is straightforward. The source code is stored in a centralized repository and can be accessed by all authorized developers. At any point in time, one of the developers can check out the code, make changes, and check the changes back into the repository. This is illustrated in Figure 6-6.

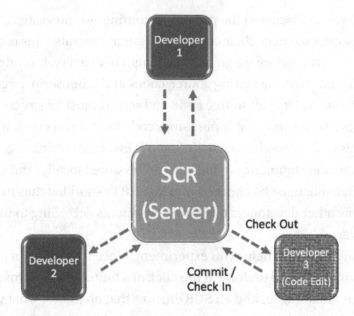

Figure 6-6. *A centralized version control system*

In a CVCS, the codebase is stored centrally on a server, and developers can access it to make changes and check it back in, something similar to the traditional file repositories such as Microsoft SharePoint. When a developer makes a change to the codebase, other developers have to pull the changes to their local systems, and the incremental changes appear in the local repositories. The positive aspect of a CVCS is that the developers are not expected to store local copies of the codebase, and as soon as they are connected to the network, they can access the server and pull the entire codebase. This is also one of the main disadvantages. Suppose the network or the repository is down; the developers cannot do anything but wait for the systems and networks to come back up. This affects the productivity and hence the project timelines. This shortcoming is taken care of in the modern architecture of an SCR: a *distributed version control system* (DVCS).

A DVCS is far more flexible, as the codebase is stored locally in every developer's machine, and it is updated directly from the server as well as from other developers, which is similar to how torrent downloads work. So, even if the network to the SCR server or the server itself is down, the developers can work on their local copies and share their changes dynamically with other developers. The SCR server is no longer a single point of failure in a DVCS architecture, as is the case in CVCS. This is illustrated in Figure 6-7.

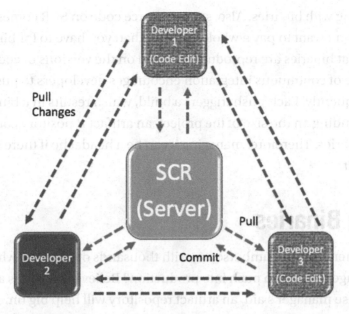

Figure 6-7. *Distributed version control system*

Another thing to note between the two architectures is that in DVCS you see that two developers are concurrently making changes to the codebase, while in CVCS, the codebase is locked when a single developer checks it out. In DVCS, concurrent working is one of the major pluses and is a differentiating factor in being the SCR architecture of choice in DevOps projects.

Because developers don't depend on a server for pulling and committing their changes, the whole process of development is much faster, and it promotes collaborative working, which are sweet words to hear for any DevOps project.

Tools that run on the CVCS architecture are Subversion (SVN), CVS, and Perforce. SVN is perhaps the most popular of the CVCS toolsets and is quickly being replaced by DVCS ones such as Git and Mercurial.

Artifact Repository

An artifact repository is a database that stores primarily binaries. In addition to binaries, you can store libraries and product- and project-related documents. All machine-readable documents go into an artifact repository and not into a source code repository, primarily because artifacts are bigger, and the collaborative features of an SCR are overkill for dealing with binaries. Also, storing source code on SCR comes at a premium price, and you don't want to pay a whole lot more than you have to for binaries—for the simple reason that binaries are reproducible based on the versions of codebases.

The principle of continuous integration encourages developers to push code to the mainline frequently. Each push triggers a build, which results in a binary getting generated. Depending on the size of the project, an artifact repository could end with thousands of binaries. Therefore, managing it can be a headache if there is no proper strategy around it.

Managing Binaries

Binary management can be cumbersome; with thousands of binaries, which one should the release manager choose to push into production? Believe me, this is an undesirable task. To the release manager's aid, an artifact repository will help big time.

An artifact repository comes with two logical partitions for storing and managing binaries:

- Snapshot

- Release

Every time a build is successfully run, the binary that is generated is stored in the Snapshot repository. But not all of the binaries are pushed into production unless the project adopts the continuous deployment methodology. The binary that is pushed into the production is first moved into the Release partition before being deployed into production, as illustrated in Figure 6-8.

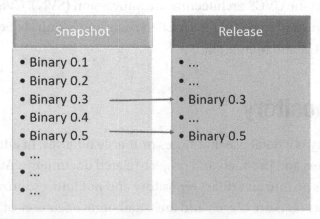

Figure 6-8. Artifact repository logical partitioning

Figure 6-8 demonstrates that various binaries are generated every time the build is successful. The binaries in this example are named Binary 0.*x* and are stored in the Snapshot partition. Not every binary is promoted into production.

The binaries that are promoted get moved into the Release partition from the Snapshot partition. In this example, that includes Binary 0.3 and Binary 0.5.

This is key to the release management process. Let's say that Binary 0.5 is deployed into production, and the deployment fails. As a fallback step, the deployment must roll back to the previous version.

The previous binary versions used are stored in the Release partition, making planning and executing releases efficient.

Without a logical partition, imagine the planning and effort it would take to identify the previous version in production and roll it back.

Summary

Configuration management is the most important process in ITIL and the spinal cord of DevOps projects to operate in an autonomous fashion. Getting configuration management right will have bearing on the health and wellbeing of the project. Configuration management in DevOps can be referred to comprehensive configuration management that consists of configuration management database (CMDB), source code repository, and artifact repository. Identifying, capturing, and maintaining data across each of these repositories is crucial.

CHAPTER 7

Incident Management Adaptation

Whenever somebody refers to IT service management or ITIL, the first issue that comes up is the incident management process. No matter how far away one might be from the service management area, they always seem to be quite familiar with the process and its relevance. It is a highly popular process that finds its rightful place in every organization. Since this process makes or breaks an organization's service delivery, service providers often give plenty of weight to the process, and as a result, the incident management process is perhaps the most mature of all the ITIL processes.

This chapter assumes that you are new to the concept of incident management, so the first couple of sections provide insights into the world of incident management from an ITIL perspective, which is the baseline that we are going to draw for the DevOps adaptation. If you are well versed with the incident management process, you can skip ahead to the DevOps adaptation sections.

However, in my experience as an ITIL trainer, ITIL practitioner, and ITIL consultant, I find that many people believe that they know incident management but their understanding is further away from the ITIL's version. The rationale behind my supposition is that ITIL practitioners often believe that an incident management implementation in their respective organizations to be absolutely correct, which is not often the case. Most organizations tweak and turn the process to their advantage, and there is nothing wrong in doing that. But, when it comes to an individual's understanding of incident management, the person must draw a clear line between what the incident management baseline is and what is implemented in their organizations. With this logic, I recommend you read all the sections in this chapter to get a better handle on the ITIL incident management process and its adaptation in a DevOps environment.

© Abhinav Krishna Kaiser 2023
A. Krishna Kaiser, *Reinventing ITIL® and DevOps with Digital Transformation*,
https://doi.org/10.1007/978-1-4842-9072-9_7

What Is ITIL Incident Management?

The main aim of incident management is to reduce downtime once a service is disrupted. The process does not get into the areas of prevention and thus reduction of downtime but rather is a process that lives and breathes in the reactive realm and jumps into the ring when the service is down. Let's look at some examples of services. Cable TV, Internet, and electricity are some services we subscribe to, and the expectation is that they must be available around the clock. Let's say that you come back tired from work, get a cold beer from a fridge, and sit down in front of TV to enjoy your time. If the cable TV service goes down, then obviously you cannot enjoy the service that you are paying for. In this instance, your service is down, which is a disruption to the service you were meant to enjoy. However, just because the service is down does not mean that incident management is at play. Perhaps your service provider does not even know that your service is down. When you lodge a complaint, an incident is logged against your cable TV account, and the incident management process is triggered.

Since you are logging the incident, it is considered reactive incident management, as you are reacting to a reported incident. Suppose your service provider had a mechanism to monitor cable TV connections in real time and the cable TV service goes down in the afternoon. The service provider would soon enough know about the outage and can raise an incident without being called in. The process that deals with monitoring and acting on various states of monitoring is the event management process. The event management process monitors various critical points for defined changes of state, and when the change of state refers to a loss of service (or degradation), an incident gets logged automatically (capability exists), and the incident management process takes over from the event management process. This is proactive incident management where the incident is logged even before users have identified anomalies in the system.

Incident Management Is Vital

The incident management process plays a vital role in any service provider organization. It is the process that influences customer perception, it is the process that ensures that customers aren't at a disadvantage because of the lack of services, and it is the process that opens the communication channel on a regular basis with customers and keeps a lid on expectations before the steam blows all over. Therefore, the incident management process must be developed and implemented with utmost precision to ensure that the customer's sensibilities are understood and that restorers are deployed to work when needed. This is the area where DevOps can have a momentous role, as the integrated DevOps teams provides the incident manager with the best of resources/staff to be parachuted into an incident resolution when needed. This luxury of having knowledgeable and capable resource-handling incidents in a non-DevOps incident management process is generally rare.

Incident Management Is the First Line of Defense

I see incident management as the first line of defense. The service desk is the first point of contact, you might think. That's true! The service desk plays a role as first-line support. When they cannot resolve the incident, they pass it onto L2 and L3. More often than not, the incident management process can find a resolution and bring the service back online—whether it involves tactics that are permanent in nature or are temporary is not of significance. At times when critical incidents emerge or when a temporary resolution is applied, the problem management process picks up the slack to perform a detailed investigation and to apply a permanent solution. I will talk about problem management later in this book.

Digging Deeper Into Incident Management

Incident management is a vast topic, and with the maximum number of IT service management professionals working in this process, it has grown a lot in terms of maturity and the ways of working. Although the section title says, "digging deeper into incident management," I am just going to skim the surface of the incident management process and provide a basic understanding of what the process entails.

Objectives and Principles

The main objective of the incident management process is to restore the service to its normal self as quickly as possible—the focus being on speed rather than on how it's achieved, as long as it's not disruptive. Speed is critical because the service is down, and a service that is not enjoyed by the users and customers has the potential to lead to business losses. In turn, the service provider gets penalized based on the signed contracts.

Note   Here's the definition of an *incident* from the ITIL publication: "An unplanned interruption to an IT service or reduction in the quality of an IT service."

Let me provide an example to illustrate the means of resolution over permanency. Let's say that the printer located in your bay has run out of juice and you need to print something out for an upcoming meeting. You register an incident, as per the standard process, but it takes a couple of days for a new ink toner to arrive and another day for it to be installed. You don't have that kind of time on your hands, and moreover incident management frowns on delays such as this. Therefore, the incident analysts help you install a printer that is in the adjacent bay, which will enable you to print before the meeting. Here, by providing a temporary solution, users are unaffected for long periods of time, and the work gets done as it should seamlessly—maybe with a little blip. On the back end, new toner is ordered, and its installation is processed. It's a win-win situation. This temporary solution is referred to as a *workaround,* as it does need to be tweaked again to fix the problem permanently. You cannot expect users to use the printer in the adjacent bay going forward—indefinitely.

To emphasize the point, the objective of incident management is to make sure that the service comes back to normal state as soon as possible, no matter how it's resolved. To ensure that the applied fix is stable and long standing, there are other processes that are held accountable.

What Constitutes an Incident?

Any disruption to a service is an incident. When we say *service*, we refer to services that are in the active state and services that are currently available and being enjoyed by the user community. Suppose a service is being designed and something in the process goes wrong. This cannot be an incident. It could be a defect or a bug that needs to be fixed using the software lifecycle management process. The incident management process must be strictly applied to the services that are live.

There are exceptions, but they must have a rationale. Suppose a software development team encounters an issue with the system testing environment. They go ahead and raise an incident. Why? The software developers and testers are the users (internal customers) of the testing environment service that is put into place to develop applications.

Another scenario is when the tool that monitors the health of the network switches is down. You still register an incident although the customer's service is unaffected. Why? If you consider monitoring a service, it's a service that has an internal service provider involved. Second, the lack of a monitoring tool is a risk that poses greater danger to services—delayed incident detection and hence longer downtime.

Who Can Register Incidents?

So far we have discussed two instances:

- Users report incidents based on their observation or experience of service degradation or lack of service usability.

- Monitoring tools keep a close to real-time watch on the service, and as soon as it veers from the normal, an incident is automatically registered.

Users reporting incidents is highly reactive, and a fact surfaces that the service provider does not know whether the services are running as they should. It is highly ineffective in terms of maintaining service uptime, although the downtime of services is calculated generally based on the registered incidents. Monitoring agents reporting incidents is a highly recommended option and is often employed in most services. The monitoring toolsets often keep track of services or devices and employ a set of criteria for registering incidents. This system is effective because many times, incidents are identified and rectified even before the users get wind of them. I would not call it proactive as opposed to reactive when users report incidents, but in the reactive quadrant, this provides the best chance of resolving incidents quickly—which directly serves the purpose of the incident management process.

There are two types of monitoring services available—active monitoring and passive monitoring. *Active monitoring* refers to monitoring toolsets that monitor critical points of a service or a device and register an incident during anomalies. Examples of monitoring tools include Dynatrace, AppDynamics, Splunk, and Nagios. The second type is *passive monitoring*, where the devices such as switches and routers have a built-in capability to capture data and report it to another system that studies the data and decides to take action based on the study. Passive monitoring is often not an effective partner for the incident management process to keep downtime in check. A third-party monitoring tool (active monitoring) has a fair chance of staying outside the realm of the infrastructure, applications, and network, and report back on health accordingly.

Apart from users and monitoring tools reporting incidents, there's a third source as well. IT staff who are working toward maintaining services (infrastructure, application, and networks) are required to report incidents when they observe them. Like users, IT staff reporting incidents is ineffective as well, but nonetheless it is an option to keep the IT staff aligned with the overall objectives of the incident management process.

A Typical Incident Management Process

It is important to understand the general set of activities that are followed to achieve the incident management objectives. As mentioned, ITIL is based on the value derived from various organizations, and incident management is one of the founding processes. The typical process is based on the common set of activities performed across organizations. Figure 7-1 illustrates a typical incident management process in line with the ITIL service operation publication.

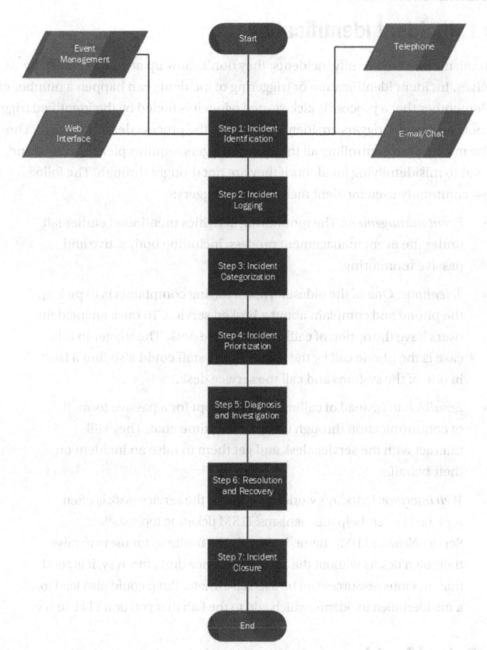

Figure 7-1. *Typical incident management process*

Step 1: Incident Identification

A mechanism needs to identify incidents; they don't show up at your doorstep by themselves. Incident identification or triggering of incidents can happen a number of ways. Remember that a process is kick-started when it is fueled by the identified triggers. It is important that all triggers are identified during the process definition stage. The more the merrier, but controlling all the known triggers requires plenty of effort and could lead to misidentifying incidents if they are not thought through. The following are the most commonly used incident management triggers:

- *Event management*: The monitoring activities mentioned earlier fall under the event management process, including both active and passive monitoring.

- *Telephone*: One of the oldest forms of raising complaints is to pick up the phone and complain about a broken service. To raise an incident, users have the option of calling the service desk. The trigger in this case is the phone call by the users. The IT staff could also find a fault in one of the systems and call the service desk.

- *Email/chat*: Instead of calling, users can opt for a passive form of communication through email or real-time chat. They still interact with the service desk and get them to raise an incident on their behalf.

- *Web interface*: In today's world of cutbacks, the service desk is often replaced by self-help mechanisms. ITSM ticketing tools such as ServiceNow and BMC Remedy provide the frontend for users to raise their own tickets without the aid of the service desk. In a way, it is good that precious resources can be used elsewhere. But it could also lead to a misidentified incidents, which add to the flab that you don't like to see.

Step 2: Incident Logging

All incidents that are identified should be logged, with a timestamp that is unalterable. Incidents are generally logged directly into the tool by the user if there is a web interface. The event management tools can also create incidents based on the threshold levels and the designed algorithms. The service desk raises incidents on behalf of end users when they call, email, or chat about their issues.

An incident ticket has a number of fields associated with it, primarily to support the resolution of the incident and to control the various parameters and pull reports as necessary. The following are some common fields that are found on incident tickets:

- Incident number (unique)
- End user name
- End user team name
- Incident logger name
- Time of logging the incident
- Incident medium (phone/chat/web/email)
- Impact
- Urgency
- Priority
- Category
- Related CI
- Incident summary
- Incident description
- Assigned resolver group
- Assigned engineer
- Status
- Resolution code
- Time of resolution/closure

Step 3: Incident Categorization

Not all incidents fall in the same bucket. Some incidents are server based, some network, and some application/software. It is paramount to identify which bucket the incident falls into, as the incident categories determine which resolver group gets assigned to resolve it.

For example, if there is an incident logged for the loss of Internet, you need the network team in charge of handling network issues to work on it. If this incident gets categorized incorrectly, say into applications, the incident will be assigned to a resolver group that specializes in software troubleshooting and code fixes. They will not be able to resolve the incident. They would have to recategorize it and assign it to the right group. The resolution would then take longer, and this defeats the purpose of the incident management process. So, it is absolutely imperative that the team that is logging the incident is specialized in identifying the incident types and categorizes them correctly.

In case of autologged incidents, event management tools are designed to select a predetermined category that does not falter. User-raised incidents are automatically categorized based on the keywords mentioned in the incident summary and description. It is quite possible that the incident could be categorized incorrectly in this scenario, but in the interest of automation, this is the price you have to pay.

Step 4: Incident Prioritization

Earlier I discussed incident prioritization. This is the step where the process of incident prioritization is acted upon. The service desk measures the urgency and impact and sets the incident priority. Event management tools have the ability to set the right priority based on an algorithm. User-created incidents are normally assigned a default priority, and the resolver group changes the priority once it begins resolving the incident. Incident priorities are not set in stone. They can be changed throughout the lifecycle of an incident. It is possible that the end user hyped the impact of the incident and raised a higher-priority incident. During the resolution process, the resolver group validates the impact and urgency and alters the priority as needed. Some critical incidents are monitored after resolution. The observation period could see the priority pushed down until closure.

Step 5: Diagnosis and Investigation

The service desk performs the initial diagnosis of an incident by understanding the symptoms of the incident. The service desk tries to understand exactly what is not working and then tries to take the user through some basic troubleshooting steps to resolve the incident. This is a key substep, as it provides the necessary data points for further investigation on the incident. It is analogous to a doctor asking you about the symptoms you have: Do you have throat pain? Do you have a cough? Do you have a cold? Do you have a headache? You get the drift. Likewise, the service desk is expected to ask a series of questions to provide the necessary information to resolve the incident quickly, which is the objective of the incident management process.

Not all incidents can be resolved by the service desk. They are functionally escalated to the next level of support, generally referred to as level 2, or L2. The L2 group is normally part of an expert group, such as the server group, network group, storage group, or software group. The resolver group diagnoses the incident with the available information and, if needed, calls the user to obtain more information. It is possible that the service desk's line of questioning could be on the wrong path, and perhaps the resolver group must start all over again by asking the right set of questions. Investigation of the incident digs deeper into the incident by understanding one or more of the following thought processes:

- What is the user expecting to obtain through the incident?

- What has gone wrong?

- What are the sequence of steps that led to the incident?

- Who is impacted? Is it localized or global?

- Were there changes performed in the environment that might have upset the system?

- Are there any similar incidents logged previously? Are there any known error database (KEDB) articles available to assist?

Step 6: Resolution and Recovery

Based on the investigation, resolutions can be applied. For example, if the resolver group determines that a particular incident is not localized, there is no reason for it to resolve the incidents on the user's PC, but rather it starts troubleshooting in the server or network. Or perhaps it brings in the experts who deal with global issues. The success of resolution rides on the right path of investigation. If the doctor you are seeing prescribes the wrong medicine because the line of investigation was completely way off, the chances of recovery are close to nil, aren't they?

For incidents that are widespread in nature (affecting multiple users), once the resolution is applied, various tests have to be conducted by the resolver group to be absolutely sure that the incident has been resolved, and there is generally a recovery period to observe the incident and be on the lookout if anything were to go wrong again.

In some of the accounts that I have handled in major incident management, it was a regular practice to keep major incidents open for at least a week, to observe, and to hold daily/hourly meetings with stakeholders to check the pulse and to keep tabs on things that could go wayward.

Step 7: Incident Closure

When an incident is resolved, it is normal practice to confirm with the user before closing the incident ticket. The confirmation is generally made by the service desk, not the resolver group. So, the process for post-resolution of an incident is that the incident is assigned to the service desk for confirmation and closure of the incident. Some organizations think that this step adds too much overhead to the service desk and prefer to forgo this confirmation. They keep the incident in resolved status for maybe three days. An email is sent to the user stating that the incident has been resolved, and if they feel otherwise, they are expected to speak up or to reopen the incident. If there is no response in three days, the incident would be auto-closed. I like doing this and have been a proponent of the auto-closure system as confirmation can be overbearing and, from a user's standpoint, irritating to the customer to receive calls just to ask for confirmation.

After an incident has been closed, a user satisfaction survey goes out asking for feedback on the timeliness of the resolution, the ease of logging incidents, and whether the user was kept informed of the incident status throughout the lifecycle.

Major Incidents

Major incidents, as the name suggests, are severely impacting incidents that have the potential to cause irreparable damage to the business. So, the ITIL service management suggests that major incidents be dealt with through a different lens. This can be done by having a separate process, a more stringent one, of course, with stricter timelines and multiple lines of communication. Many organizations institute a separate team to look into major incidents and hire those with specialized skillsets to be exposed to the pressure that the job inherits.

The people who work solely on major incidents are called *major incident managers*. They have all the privileged powers to mobilize teams and summon management representatives at any time of the day (or night). They run the show when there is a major incident and become completely accountable for the resolution of the incident. The pressure on them is immense, and it calls for nerves of steel to withstand the pressure from the customer, service provider senior management, and all other interested parties.

I once worked as a major incident manager and was heading a major incident management team not too long ago. The job entailed keeping the boat afloat at all times, and any delays from my end could potentially jeopardize the lives of miners across the globe. During a major incident, there could have been two or three phones buzzing with action, emails flying daggers into my inbox, and chat boxes flashing and roaring. It is a good experience when you think about it in hindsight and a time I will cherish.

To track, manage, and chase incident-related activities, there are incident managers who keep tabs on all occurrences. When a major incident hits the queue, none of the groups takes responsibility, but they call in the experts (major incident managers) to manage the situation. In some cases, the service desk and incident managers might validate the incident priority before calling the major incident line.

It is good practice to let the whole service provider team and the customer organization know that a major incident is in progress to make sure that everybody knows that certain services are down and to avoid users calling the service desk to report the same incident. A few good practices in this regard include sending emails at the start and end of major incidents, flashing messages on office portals and on ticket logging pages, and playing an interactive voice response (IVR) messages when users call the service desk.

Incident Management in DevOps

Whenever we talk of DevOps and the operations side of it, we are mostly referring to incident management and a methodology that caters to maintaining services from a downtime reduction standpoint. Making incident management work in a DevOps project is critical for the DevOps model to work. If we can get incident management right, the rest of the components in the DevOps methodology flow like molten lava.

This section not only looks at the process to be employed but also drills down to the management of the DevOps team—the jugglery between incidents and user stories and everything else that can make or break the incident management process in a DevOps project.

Before you delve deeper into the aspects of incident management in DevOps, the setting you need to consider is the *one team* concept. This is a team consisting of the traditional application development and application management teams fused into a single being. It is illustrated in Figure 7-2. I am not highlighting the other roles that I did in Chapter 5, as the focus of this section is to emphasize the formation of a single team that is responsible for both development and maintenance activities. This team is the alpha and the omega of the product you are supporting or the service you are delivering.

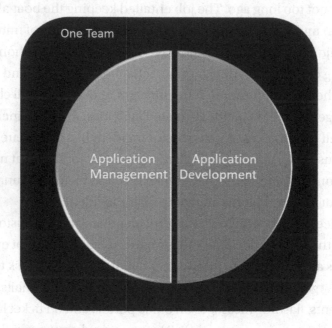

Figure 7-2. *One team concept*

Agile Project Management

There are multiple types of inputs for a DevOps team. They can come in the form of user stories for developing new features, or can come through the service management pipeline in the form of incidents and problems. The DevOps team must cater to all recognized types of inputs.

User Stories

The inputs for an application development team are generally requirements from the customers. In the Agile world, we call these user stories and not requirements. Is it the same wine in a fancier bottle? No. User stories are the goals that the users want to achieve from their own perspectives. User stories are written in the form of users explaining what they want the software to do in various contexts. Here are some examples of simple user stories:

- I want to get suggestions when I start typing in the search box.

- I want the desktop background to refresh every hour.

- I want to see the logo as I scroll down the web site.

User stories can be specific and more to the point. They help developers by providing a context, action, and expectation. The *given-when-then* template is often used to define user stories.

- *Given* specifies a context.

- *When* provides the action that you are going to take in the defined context.

- *Then* sets the user's expectation when the action is taken in the defined context.

Here's an example:

- *Given* I sign into a shopping website

- *When* I type **puppy** in the search bar

- *Then* a list of products with the keyword puppy will appear on a full page

Simply put, the requirements for a development team come in the form of user stories. The expectation from a user story is that it is a piece of work that can be completed within a sprint. But it is likely that the piece of work coming in is too complicated to be completed in a sprint cycle. These bigger pieces of work are referred to as *epics*, and they are further broken down into user stories. Development of epics can run across multiple sprints. Epics are broken into multiple user stories, and the development of user stories is planned to be done in a single sprint.

Incidents

When there are incidents reported for a service supported by a DevOps team, the incident eventually trickles down onto the laps of the team for its resolution. The team that works on the user stories could be tasked with resolving incidents as well.

Problems

Although incidents and problems are mentioned in the same vein, more often than not, they are a different species. Chapter 8 goes into the depths of problem management in a DevOps project. Identifying the problem is one of the inputs in a DevOps team, and the nature of work coming from a problem is to triage the underlying cause of complex or nagging issues. Once the root cause is known, a permanent solution is applied to avoid repeatability.

Sprints

In Agile project management methodology, we work in smaller chunks at a time, referred to as *sprints*. A sprint could last anywhere from two to four weeks. The idea behind a sprint is not the same as the phases in the waterfall project management methodology. The activities performed in a sprint are the same as the other sprints. However, the prerequisite activities completed before the actual development—such as requirement gathering, environment setup, and environment design—are done before the sprint cycle kicks in and are usually referred to as Sprint 0. The nature of sprints is illustrated in Figure 7-3.

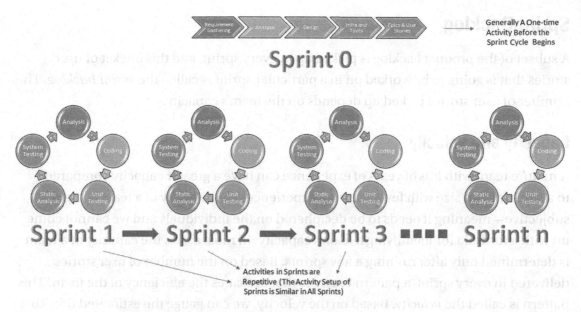

Figure 7-3. *Nature of sprints*

There can be as many sprints as needed to develop a product. There are absolutely no restrictions. However, in the Scaled Agile framework, there is a concept of an Agile release train (ART), which supports long-running projects by clubbing the planning and execution in chunks, usually between eight and twelve weeks. Usually an ART will encompass about four to five sprints, and each ART has a planning session involving all stakeholders, governance to manage multiple sprint activities, and a review session toward the end of the cycle.

Sprint Planning

The master list of all user stories is stored in a bucket called the *product backlog*. Not all the requirements are well known before the development commences. A good chunk of the requirements are added during the project, which is the premise of Agile project management: to keep an open mind for changes to come midway through the project. Agile teams must embrace changes during the development cycle with open arms, and that's precisely why a holistic planning exercise is planned in iterations, and the exercise is called *sprint planning*. If the sprint is two weeks, the planning exercise will determine what can be achieved during the two weeks only, and not more.

Sprint Backlog

A subset of the product backlog is picked up in every sprint, and this bucket of user stories that is going to be worked on in a particular sprint is called the *sprint backlog*. The number of user stories picked up depends on the team's capacity.

Capacity and Velocity

A mature team with lots of years of experience can have a greater capacity compared to a similar team size with fewer years of experience. The capacity of a team is highly subjective—meaning it needs to be deciphered on the individuals and we cannot come up with a formula for identifying a team's capacity. In most cases, the capacity of a team is determined only after running a few sprints. Based on the number of user stories delivered in every sprint, a pattern emerges that indicates the efficiency of the team. This pattern is called the *velocity*. Based on the velocity, we can gauge the estimated time to complete all the user stories in the product backlog. Velocity is one of the key metrics used in Agile project management.

Determining Complexity

Not all user stories are similar in complexity. Some user stories require a few hours of development, while others may need a few days. Calculating the velocity based on the number of user stories does not accurately reflect on the team's performance. Therefore, we measure the complexity of user stories with story points. Story points are an abstract unit of measurement for user stories that loosely indicate their complexity, the duration to complete development and testing, and the dependencies involved. Every user story is associated with certain story points, and the process of associating user stories with story points is called *story point estimation*.

Estimation Technique: Planning Poker

The estimation process is not a straightforward activity. There is no formula to help with it. Story points are determined based on relative comparison with other user stories. For example, creating a login page can be estimated to be one story point in project A, in which a blogging engine is getting built. But on another project involving the same login page for an Internet banking site, the login page user story could have three story points.

The estimated story points for user stories depend solely on the complexity of the other story points. There are several ways of coming up with the estimation. The most popular one is through the game of planning poker.

The game of poker is played with each team member given a set of playing cards bearing numerical values—usually the Fibonacci series (1,2,3,5,8,13,21...). The user stories in the product backlog are laid out to identify the simplest and least complex user story, and this user story is given one story point. Based on this user story's complexity, the other user stories are measured. If the login page is one story point, how complex is the summary page where various data sources have to be called in? Say that it is five times as complex, so five story points are given to it.

How do you determine whether it is five times more complex or eight times more complex? Who can determine this? This is where the game of planning poker comes in handy. The team is seated around the table along with the product owner, each with their own set of Fibonacci-numbered cards. First they all agree on the simplest user story. Conflicts within team members on what constitutes the simplest work story are sorted out through discussion. If there is no consensus, it is put to vote, and the user stories with maximum backing are considered the simplest. The simplest user story is given a weight of one story point.

The product owner then goes on to pick the next user story from the product backlog and explains what is expected, which provides a fair idea to the team on its complexity. Now each of the team members measures the user story against the simplest user story. If the simplest user story has a complexity of X and if the user story that is being considered for estimation is five times as complex (5X), then the playing card number bearing the numerical value 5 is drawn. Each team member pulls the playing card based on their perception and keeps it face down on the table. When everybody has drawn a card, the card is turned up, and discussions begin to deliberate the complexity and to arrive at a consensus on its complexity and the associated story points. It is likely that one developer might select three story points while another selects five story points. Each of the developers has to provide a rationale for their complexity estimation; this can either compel the other team members to change their vote or stick to their points of view. This exercise might seem to take time, but underneath, it is beginning a conversation around the user stories, and it is bringing the team together in arriving at a decision. It is like a jury that deliberates on a verdict hoping to arrive at a consensus.

DOR and DOD

There are several user stories in the product backlog. How do you know which ones to pick? As mentioned earlier, the product owner is the only person who can call the shots and prioritize requirements. However, what is the acceptance criteria for a user story to be picked up into a sprint? We call this minimum criteria the *definition of ready* (DOR), which means having all the ducks in a row in perfect order before being considered for development.

How do you know that the user story that is picked up in a sprint is delivered? What is the agreement upon completion of a user story? This common agreement upon completion of development is called the *definition of done* (DOD). DOD refers exactly to the series of actions that are undertaken before signaling it as done. For example, in a project, the DOD could be as follows:

> Analysis ➤ Coding ➤ Unit Testing ➤ Static Analysis ➤
> System Testing

So whenever a user story goes through this cycle successfully, it is considered done. But for another project, the DOD could be this:

> Analysis ➤ Coding ➤ Unit Testing

In this case, the team is expected to run unit tests successfully before the user story is considered delivered.

In both the examples, there is no right or wrong definitions of done. It is an agreement between the customer and the software development organization as far as what constitutes done and stick with it throughout the lifecycle of the product.

Sprint Planning for a DevOps Team

The sprint planning session is in play. We have identified that the inputs are user stories, incidents, and problems. So, all the three inputs make up the product backlog, and it is represented as an input funnel, as shown in Figure 7-4.

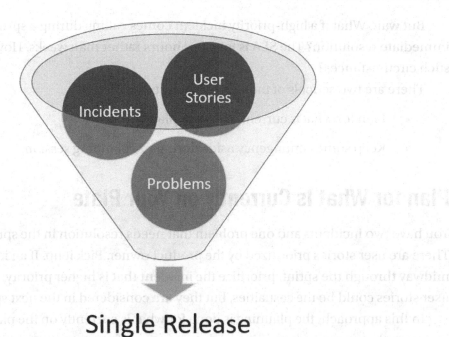

Single Release

Figure 7-4. *Input funnel for a DevOps team*

Incidents and problems have a SLA associated with them; delays in resolving incidents could lead to SLA breaches and penalties. So, during the planning session, it might be prudent to pick up incidents that are closer to breaching. If I have four incidents, two breaching their SLAs in the next three weeks and the other two breaching in about five weeks, I will probably pick the two incidents that are breaching the SLA in three weeks.

Let's say that the team capacity is 40 story points. They have identified the two incidents that need to be resolved during the sprint. The incident resolution's complexity is identified using story points. In this case, let's say that it amounts to four story points. So, they have another 36 story points for problems and development activities.

There is one problem in the product backlog whose SLA is nearing the breaching levels, so they decide to pick it up as well. The problem is worth ten story points. So, the team has about 26 story points left for the delivery of user stories.

The team then goes on to pick user stories amounting to 26 user stories or fewer. One of the working principles in planning is that the identified load never exceeds the team capacity. This means that the team cannot choose more than 26 user stories. In other words, when the capacity is 40 story points, the load must be less than 40 story points.

189

But wait. What if a high-priority incident comes calling during a sprint that requires immediate resolution? The SLA is for a few hours rather than weeks. How do you plan for such circumstances?

There are two schools of thought for such scenarios:

- Plan for what is currently on your plate.

- Keep some contingency aside during the planning session.

Plan for What Is Currently on Your Plate

You have two incidents and one problem that needs resolution in the sprint, so take it up. There are user stories prioritized by the product owner. Pick it up. If an incident comes midway through the sprint, prioritize the incident that is higher priority. One or more user stories could be the casualties, but they are considered in the next sprint.

In this approach, the planning is done for what is currently on the plate, and incidents that come midway railroad the execution of some parts of the delivery, which is deemed okay considering that incidents pertain to the disruption of services. But in terms of identifying the team's performance, team morale could take a hit. You planned for 39 story points in a sprint, but you delivered only 26 because of the midway incident. It kind of throws the sprint and planning off-balance. But, I have seen this kind of a setup used in organizations, and it does fairly well if the product is quite stable.

Keep Some Contingency Aside During the Planning Session

In the second method, a certain amount of contingency is kept aside during the planning session for midway incidents. For example, during the sprint planning session, the team could consider that the planning will be done for 35 story points instead of 40. The remaining five story points are a contingency measure for incidents that require immediate assistance.

In my experience, I have seen that with operations, nothing goes precisely as planned. There's always something coming back to you, either for code changes or to answer certain queries. It is good to keep some contingencies to ensure that the operational side of things is given equal priority. Moreover, even developmental activities can benefit from some amount of contingency. After the DOD, the incremental delivery of the product could go in for a performance test, a security test, or even an acceptance test. The feedback from any of these tests can mean additional development in future sprints. A decent amount of contingency will take this a long way.

How much contingency should you keep? The answer is in the metrics. Analyze the high-priority incidents you received for the product in the past year. Identify the frequency of occurrence and the average complexity of the work that was involved. Marrying the two will give you a contingency measure to consider during planning sessions. Do a similar analysis for development activities outside the purview of sprints. Measure the frequency of feedback and the average amount of rework that is needed. A combination of rework and incident expectancy will give you a good idea of the contingency to consider.

The Scope of the DevOps Team in Incident Management

Incidents come in all shapes and sizes. Not all are the same, and most importantly, not all incidents need to be handled by the DevOps teams. Normally in operations, we call different levels of support L1, L2, L3, and L4 (and so on). The various levels define the complexity and indicate the team responsible for resolution.

Levels of Support

To keep things simple, I consider only three levels—L1, L2, and L3. L1 defines basic support such as answering user queries, scheduling batches, and taking backups, among others, that are performed through an administrative page. To carry out these activities, no coding experience is necessary. In fact, the only experience that is technically needed is to follow the instructions exactly. On the soft skills front, there's plenty more to address, as the service desk is usually responsible for the L1 type of support.

When an incident is identified at a higher level than what the service desk is capable of doing, the service desk immediately transfers the ticket to the next line of support, L2, without trying to fix it themselves. By trying things in support, we invariably waste time, which translates to an extension of downtime and the customer not being happy. So, as soon as the incident complexity is identified, it gets pushed to the next level.

191

The second level of support, L2, is one over the service desk. This team provides a configuration level of changes to the product and involves incidents pertaining to IT infrastructure and connectivity. The teams that are best suited to handle the configuration level and infrastructure changes are shared teams. These shared teams work across products and services, and they are best placed to support at a L2 level.

The next level of support, L3, involves code changes. In this case, it includes architectural changes as well. Architectural changes are usually referred to as L4s. So, any code changes to be affected can be done only by the L3 support team. The L3 support team has access to the codebase and the necessary skillsets and setup to make changes to the code. Remember that making changes to the code is like a surgeon cutting into your skin to access your organs. Not all doctors can do it nor do they have an environment or setup to perform such operations. Your surgeon is like L3 support, a general physician like L1, and a specialist like a L2 support. The L3 support or the L3 team is the DevOps team, in other words, the blended team that does application development and application management.

Figure 7-5 illustrates the different levels of support—L1, L2, and L3. I use an inverted pyramid to indicate the levels because the areas under the L1, L2, and L3 levels of support are directly proportional to the volume of incidents handled by each of the support teams. In my experience, most of the incidents that come through require basic knowledge for resolution, L1, by service desk. Among the ones left over, a lion's share of the incidents are resolved through configurational changes. Only a small percentage of incidents actually flow through to the L3 team, which is the DevOps team.

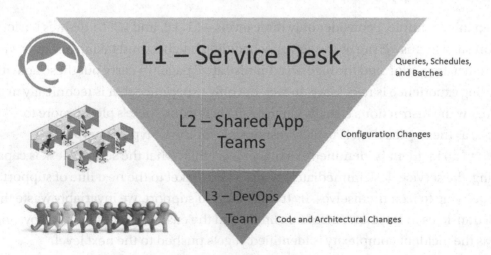

Figure 7-5. *L1, L2, and L3 support structure*

An incident that requires code support flows into the service desk. The service desk identifies that the incident pertains to code changes. Do they transfer the ticket to the DevOps team? The answer is no. The service desk does not and cannot make a decision on an incident requiring code changes. They don't have the necessary skillsets to make that decision. Therefore, their only functional escalation is to the L2 team. The L2 team, the technical management function as per the ITIL publication, is better able to recommend code changes. They transfer incidents to the DevOps team.

Does the DevOps team accept all incidents that come into their bucket? The answer is once again no.

The incident manager comes into the picture when incidents hit the DevOps incident bucket. They review the incident, analyze it, and determine whether the incident requires code changes or whether it can be resolved through changes in the configuration files. If it's the latter, the incident is pushed back to the L2 support team, and if it requires changes to the code, the incident manager gets the pertinent information (to meet the DOR) to populate the product backlog with the incident.

Incident Flow

From my experience, about 60 percent of incidents are resolved either at the service desk or by using tools that can resolve incidents automatically without human intervention. About 30 to 35 percent of incidents need configuration level of changes. And only a small percentage of incidents flow through to the DevOps team, requiring changes to the code. Remember that the code usually does not break services. There are plenty of layers above the code build, such as configuration, infrastructure, and network, that can cause incidents.

Note   It is a good practice to pass the configuration changes through the CI-CD pipeline to ensure that the development and test environments are similar to the production environments and to identify any regression issues. Also, changes performed by L2 should be reviewed by L3 teams during sprint retrospectives, in order to reflect on the changes and identify any improvement opportunities.

I was involved in a couple of projects where the L2 support was combined with the DevOps team. With L2 in DevOps team, the team had to resolve more incidents than the actual development work. The morale of the team went from being quite high to terribly low because most of the time they were consigned to working on configurational changes rather than the actual work that coders do. After this experience, it was pretty clear to me that L2 must stay outside of a DevOps team.

Knowledge Management at the Core

One important key ingredient that is missed time and again is the knowledge around the product, the history, and all that is necessary to maintain and upgrade. It is in fact as important as the configuration management, but it is often given a secondary life, with the key phrase being *if there is time*. Development is given the priority and so is everything else that contributes directly to the service or the product. When it comes to creating and maintaining knowledge, people just don't have the time. And when an incident comes calling, the developers sit for a detailed session of analysis trying to identify all the dependencies and the logic behind the application design. This analysis time eventually eats into the incident resolution time, extending the downtime and failing the objective of the incident management process.

If the intent is to make incident management effective and efficient, then start with the knowledge management along with the configuration management. Time and again I have seen projects not even maintain the bare necessities such as design documents. The remedy to the problem starts with governance. Agile project management preaches minimum documentation with an emphasis on developing a working software. So, determining what the minimum documentation should look like needs to come from project governance. For a DevOps project that covers both development and operations, the documentation around the product/service must be specific, easy to retrieve, and regularly updated.

ITIL's Knowledge Management

In fact, ITIL's knowledge management process is quite powerful and has the ability to provide credence to the management of knowledge in a DevOps project. The process exists to ensure that the service delivery is done in an efficient manner and the knowledge is available when it is needed. The whole premise is around ensuring knowledge exists to support the process and not that the knowledge needs to be there because you created something new.

I have heard from a few project managers that the whole idea of maintaining knowledge is done so that the organizations get ISO certified. They say that they maintain knowledge just for the sake of it. This statement is so untrue. Let me peel it open like an onion. The ISO certifications are based on standards that have shown results and that are widely accepted. The controls in the ISOs are a culmination of what the industry determines is relevant and something that is absolutely necessary for the project to perform. Consider the example of a risk register, a document where you record project risks along with its respective owners, mitigation plans, and other pertinent details. You tend to revisit the document when needed, especially after major changes. Let me remind you that risks stand in the way of project success and failure, and maintaining one will help you understand the project risks and be prepared for them when they materialize. It is better to be ready than be surprised.

What Knowledge to Maintain

Every project is different, and every project caters to different domains. The technology is different, which changes the composition of the documents that one maintains for a projects.

Generally speaking, in a development project, you should maintain a number of documents including the following:

- Contracts signed with the customer
- High-level requirements
- Design and analysis documents
- Test strategy and test plan
- Project and release plans
- Financial plans and tracker
- Estimation schemes and trackers
- Balanced scorecards
- Release notes
- Training and support documents

From a support perspective, the following documents are generally maintained:

- Service level agreement

- Support documents with cheat sheets

- Knowledgebase of issues encountered

- Root cause analysis and proactive measures undertaken

- Improvements implemented

- Reports

To me, the most critical documentation that you can maintain in a DevOps project is the code itself. No, I am not talking of the comments in the code but the way the code is written. Just like how this book is divided into chapters and subheadings, well-written code can also be placed under chapters covering the various functionalities it is trying to achieve. The marks of well-written code are the following:

- *Simplicity*: Do not introduce complex loops, but rather keep the code simple.

- *Readability*: Anybody (other coders) reading the code must be in a position to understand what it is indeed doing.

- *Maintainability*: It should be easy to make changes and debug.

- *Efficiency*: If you can convey a message with fewer words, that's the way to do it; likewise, the logic that can be realized with fewer lines of code is efficient (tools like SonarQube help in this regard).

- *Clarity*: Code must tell the story, and you must put in all the effort for the story to reveal itself by using meaningful class and method names.

Knowledge Storing and Retrieval

Creating documentation is one part of the story; it is like a story that develops nicely, and everything solely depends on the climax. If the developed knowledge is not easily retrievable, then it's not the climax everybody is waiting for. What is the point of creating knowledge if nobody knows how to retrieve it? What good is a story if the ending is shoddy?

I have seen organizations use certain folder structures on Microsoft SharePoint and other file repositories. When it is first set up, everything is hunky dory, and after a period of time, disuse and laziness sets in. The folder meant for placing release notes stays stagnant, while release notes are stored on local drives and emails. The document tracker remains unread and unmodified until an audit is announced. Why do you think this problem happens?

To me this is a problem that we create. The structure with files, file updates, check-in, checkout, and sync issues are all adding to the problem. It is so complex that developers would rather analyze from the beginning rather than search in the so-called knowledge base.

What does work well is an integrated system with everything stored in the same place. You don't have the hassle of switching applications, and everything can be done with one touch. Lovely, isn't it? If you are using Jira as your project management tool, imagine a file repository built into Jira, where files can be stored directly against the design task or the user stories. Life would be much simpler. Creating and storing documents is a whole lot of fun, and retrieval is super friendly as well. The problem of nonmaintenance does not arise, as everything is right in front of your eyes. By the way, you can get this functionality on Jira through an add-on from the Atlassian Marketplace, but it is not as good as the real thing. I am comparing it against ServiceNow, the service management tool. In ServiceNow, a separate knowledge management module exists where articles can be created or files uploaded, just like how you would do it on a weblog. The best part is the integration with the rest of the ServiceNow system. When you create an incident, you key in an incident summary and provide a brief of the issue. Based on the keywords, the system automatically searches the knowledge base and displays relevant knowledge base articles. Analysts and technicians working on incidents have access to knowledge at their fingertips, and they didn't even have to search for it. This makes a big difference in utilizing the maximum power of knowledge management.

The DevOps Incident Management Process

Earlier in the chapter, you looked at a typical incident management process based on industry best practices. I also mentioned that the incident management process is generally adapted for organizations that implement them based on their services, stakeholders, and comfort level. For a DevOps project, the typical incident management process goes through some adaptions, but overall it remains the same in spirit and in principle. With the DevOps incident management process, you cannot deviate too much from the normal, a sign that is good news for existing application management projects looking to go the DevOps way.

The DevOps incident management process is illustrated in Figure 7-6. The sequence of activities is indicated with seven-pointed stars.

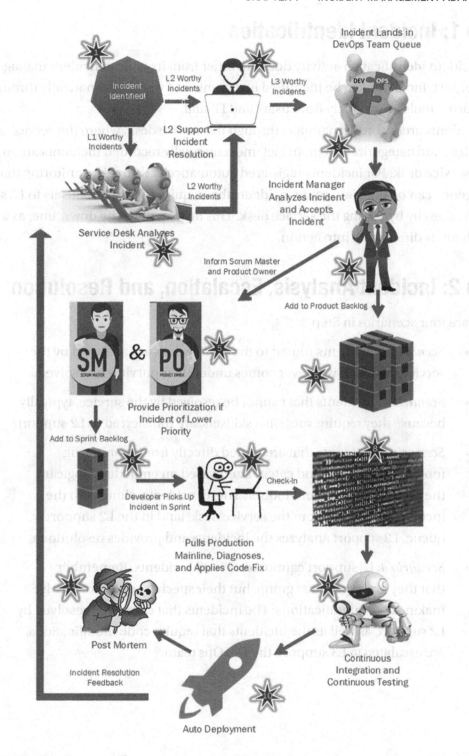

Figure 7-6. *DevOps incident management process*

Step 1: Incident Identification

The incident identification activity does not differ from its typical incident management counterpart. Incidents can be identified in a number of ways, automatically through monitoring tools or manually from users and IT staff.

Incidents are recorded manually through the service desk, where the service desk prioritizes and categorizes them. In fact, most manually recorded incidents are routed to the service desk. For incidents registered automatically through monitoring tools, intelligence can be built into route incidents that require specialist skillsets to L2 support directly, thereby bypassing the service desk. This helps reduce the downtime, as a better abled team is directly put into action.

Step 2: Incident Analysis, Escalation, and Resolution

There are four scenarios in Step 2:

- *Scenario 1*: Incidents routed to the service desk are analyzed by the service desk, and whatever comes under their purview is resolved.

- *Scenario 2*: Incidents that cannot be resolved by the service, typically because they require specialist skillsets, are transferred to L2 support.

- *Scenario 3*: Incidents that are routed directly from monitoring tools are prioritized and categorized based on embedded logic in the service management toolset. These incidents, along with the incidents escalated from the service desk, land in the L2 support queue. L2 support analyzes the incidents and provides resolutions.

- *Scenario 4*: L2 support cannot resolve all incidents. Remember that they are a specialist group, but their specialty does not involve making code modifications. The incidents that cannot be resolved by L2 support, as well as the incidents that require code modifications, are escalated to L3 support, the DevOps team.

Step 3: Incident with DevOps Team

This is the step where things get interesting compared to a normal service management practice. Usually there is a specialist L3 support team, the application management team that exists only to manage the services such as the resolution of incidents requiring code modifications. In the DevOps incident management process, the incident has been passed onto the DevOps team, which is primarily a development team.

Try to imagine the amount of specialty that the DevOps team brings to the table for incident resolution. The software developers have intimate knowledge of the software, and this will reduce downtime rapidly and ensure that the incidents are resolved as quickly as possible, meeting the objective of the ITIL incident management process.

Step 4: Incident Manager Analyzes and Accepts Incidents

As per the roles and structures discussed in Chapter 5, the incident manager is part of the DevOps team. However, if the DevOps team is fairly small without a full-time workload for an incident manager, the person can be placed in a shared role as well.

The incident manager is well aware of the product that is being developed and managed. Generally, in ITIL, incident managers are reactive folks, and they act on the incident when it comes in and, during the course of the incident, understand the intricacies of the product. However, in the DevOps incident management process, incident managers are part of the DevOps team that works with the developers. So, they are well versed with the product, and this expanded knowledge gives them a better handle on incidents that could possibly come in. This knowledge gives them the power to manage incidents throughout the lifecycle with precision and can help direct and manage multiple teams to align toward incident resolution swiftly and with a purpose.

All incidents that come to the DevOps team go through the desk of the incident manager. This person analyzes the incident, and after confirming that it requires coding-specific skillsets, the incident is accepted. If the incident manager decides that the incident can be resolved by the L2 support and does not require changes to the code, the incident manager can send the incident to L2 support. In certain cases, if the L2 support is unable to resolve the incident even if the incident does not call for changes to the code, the incident manager accepts the incident in the DevOps team queue.

Accepting an incident involves two things:

- Adding the incident to the product backlog. Generally, the service management tool for registering and tracking incidents and the product backlog tool are separate toolsets. For example, ServiceNow is a service management tool for registering and tracking incidents, and Jira is a tool for managing the product backlog. The DevOps team generally does not work on the service management tool, as the product backlog is their single source of truth. Therefore, the incident details need to be moved into the product backlog. This can happen through a connector (B2B bridge). In this case, Atlassian Marketplace is one of the providers for connectors between ServiceNow and Jira. The incident that is accepted by the incident manager is moved over to the product backlog with a click of a button. If no such connector exists, the incident manager might have to manually register the incident in the product backlog.

- After accepting the incident, the incident manager must inform the product owner and the Scrum master about the addition of the incident in the product backlog. The Scrum master or the product owner does not decide whether an incident can make it to the product backlog; that decision lies with the incident manager. However, both parties need to be notified, as they need to start planning for incident resolution.

Steps 5 and 6: The Incident Is Prioritized and Added to the Sprint

The Scrum master is responsible for adding incidents to the sprint backlog. Before doing that, the product owner will analyze the incident and determine its priority. For example, if the incident is low priority with an SLA of 25 business days, then the product owner might prioritize it lower for it to be accommodated in the upcoming sprint and not be included in the ongoing one. If the incident is major, with an SLA counted in hours rather than days, the product owner will prioritize the incident over all others, and it will be included in the current sprint.

The Scrum master will add the incident in the sprint backlog depending on the priority. If a high-priority incident pops up, the incident is immediately added to the sprint backlog. If a lower-priority incident comes in, it can wait for the next sprint or the sprint after, depending on the SLAs attached to it and the prioritization of the product owner. When the incident is added to the sprint backlog, the Scrum master engages the Scrum team and the incident manager to resolve the incident. If it is a major incident, the priority is communicated, and the best developers or a group of developers get into action for speedy resolution.

Steps 7 and 8: The Scrum Team Makes Code Changes and Checks In

When the sprint backlog is populated with the incident (and only then), the Scrum team will start working on it. In most instances, incidents are added midway through the sprint, which is usually not common in any other development project involving the Scrum methodology. However, in DevOps, this is accepted and valid. To make way for the incident, there is a certain amount of contingency added during the planning sessions. During stable periods and change freeze windows, a minimal amount of contingency is added during sprints. When releases are being deployed into production or whenever partner systems are being modified, there is a certain expectation of regression hitting the project, which allows for additional effort going into the contingency bucket.

The developer is usually briefed by the incident manager on the history and facts around the incident, which might help the developer re-create the issue and could possibly lead to faster resolution.

The developer might be working on a development branch, but for the incident, the developer will pull the production codebase (mainline). Whatever modifications done to the code will be done on a separate branch and not on the development branch.

Let's consider the Illustration of a mainline featuring release 1.3 in Figure 7-7. The development for the next release (R 2) is carried out on a development branch. All developers are working on the development branch. Midway through the sprint, an incident lands in the sprint backlog, and one of the developers picks up the incident from the backlog.

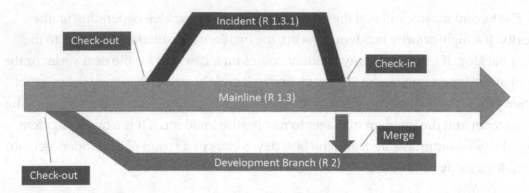

Figure 7-7. *Development and incident resolution in parallel*

The developer will make changes based on the production codebase, such as R 1.3 on a separate branch (R 1.3.1), and not on the development branch. When the code changes are done, the code is checked back in to the production mainline, considering that the incident needs to be resolved at the earliest. If the code changes performed go through the testing phase successfully and are deployed without any issues, the developers working on the development branch have to merge the code changes performed in R 1.3.1 (incident) onto the development branch before continuing their coding activities. This is an important step and ensures that the incident fixes (code changes) completed between R 1.3 and R 2 aren't missed when R 2 is deployed. Second, there is a probability that some of the code changes performed for the incident fix could lead to merge conflicts and will need to be resolved before any build and test activities.

Step 9: Continuous Integration and Continuous Testing

In Chapter 1, I explained the continuous integration process and the concept of continuous testing in a fair amount of detail. At this point in the process, the developer checks in the code, and the automation built into the development system kicks off the build activity, followed by unit testing, static analysis, and other activities pertinent to continuous integration.

After a successful build and code reviews, the binary goes through a rigorous testing process. In DevOps, we hoot for continuous testing where various tests such as system, integration, regression, performance, and other types of testing are done automatically, generally in a sequential manner. For this to happen, the various test scripts must be ready before the code check-in. This requires a certain amount of maturity in terms of DevOps processes for the project team. While this capability is built, project teams opt for automation testing, where the test triggers are done manually when the test scripts are ready. Automation testing does not require test scripts to be in place before the code check-in.

Step 10: Auto Deployment

Most DevOps-savvy organizations have auto deployment in place, which deploys the package at a click of a button.

In the incident management process, it is important to tweak the release policies to support a reduction of downtimes. The release policy must be flexible enough to allow deployments without too many riders and outside the schedule of releases. Only then does the whole setup of bringing in incidents within the development teams' workload make sense. Most organizations' release policy states that the changes to software can be made only during minor and major releases. Emergency changes are usually frowned upon and are viewed as exceptions in most organizations practicing ITIL service management. However, in DevOps-led projects, there are no exceptions; instead, there's only common sense. If a service or part of a service is down, then you need to bring it up as soon as possible. For this to happen, if you need to deploy a package, so be it. What's the fuss over it? Amazon would ask. We do it multiple times a minute!

Following deployment, there are some sanity checks performed, some automatic and some manual. These checks are mandatory to ensure that the basic and critical parts of the system are working as they should. Nobody likes to make changes, even the Amazons and Netflixes. When a new package hits production, smoke tests are done to ensure that the scent of production did not drive the binary on a lunatic path (just saying)!

When the sanity checks wave the green flag, the incident manager informs the service desk to take the incident to closure by seeking confirmation from the user who logged the incident. If there is no user involved in this incident creation, the appropriate customer contact is made aware of the resolution.

Through Steps 5 to 10, the incident manager is actively monitoring the incident. The person provides support and seeks updates from team members on a regular basis. The incident manager also keeps the customer updated on the progress and the expected date of resolution at all time. This communication with the customer is extremely critical, as a loss of service generally results in revenue losses, and no business takes loss of revenue kindly. In my experience as a major incident manager, I have come across customers who have lost their cool, and the situation is far from pretty.

Step 11: Post-Mortem

The whole incident management process would be undone if there were no checks in place to identify the reason for the incident. However, this investigation is not done at a detailed level, as the problem management process is tasked with investigations around service breakages. The incident management process conducts a fairly quick, though not thorough, investigation into the incident to determine the reasons behind the issue. This is an important step in the DevOps methodology, as the lessons from the investigation could forewarn the team of another incident or could reveal potential weaknesses in the code and the logic. However, the post-mortem does not involve pointing fingers at individual members of the DevOps team, pinpointing them for the lack of quality code and other mishaps.

The investigation is done during the sprint, and in the sprint retrospective session, the entire incident management process is under the microscope, including the outcome of the investigation.

What went right or wrong with the acceptance of the incident? Was it the right call, or should the incident have been sent back to L2 support?

Were the Scrum master and product owner informed quickly enough to allow maximum wiggle room in the sprint? Are there any areas for improvement? Was the incident well understood before beginning the development on it?

Were the testers involved when the incident details were briefed by the incident manager? Were the test scripts ready on time? Did the test scripts cover all scenarios?

These are just some of the difficult questions that are addressed during these sprint retrospective sessions. Note that the questions are in relation to the process and the outcome rather than in relation to individuals.

Summary

The ITIL incident management process is the most common support process and it interacts heavily with users, customers, and service providers alike. This chapter provided a brief look into the classic incident management process and further delved into the DevOps adaptation of the process, where incidents come through the pipeline along with the feature development. In addition, knowledge management, the process that fuels the incident management process, was also discussed.

CHAPTER 8

Problem Management Adaptation

Incident management is the first line of defense in providing immediate relief against the disruption of services and eventual downtimes. However, by no means does the incident management process get into the nitty-gritty of putting an end to the cause behind the incidents. Its purpose is to bring the services back up, even if the solution is not a permanent one.

The second ring of process governance ensuring permanence to solutions is the problem management process. This process dives deep into the cause of incidents and follows the problem to its root, ensuring that incidents related to the particular cause do not repeat.

To summarize, the incident management process deals with correction, while the problem management process focuses on prevention.

This chapter provides a brief introduction to the problem management process, the techniques involved, and the typical process, and then moves into how the problem management process can be transformed in a DevOps project.

Introduction to ITIL Problem Management

The problem management process is featured in the ITIL service operations publication and is one of the critical processes needed for services to thrive. Incident management is good, but at the end of the day, the more incidents there are, the more downtime and the greater effort required to bring the service back up. The customer gains nothing from the process, as it's trying to keep the support above water at all times but not taking it to new places. There is a dire need to bring value to services, and value can be brought about only if stability is assured. One of the pillars for ensuring service stability is the problem management process.

207

© Abhinav Krishna Kaiser 2023
A. Krishna Kaiser, *Reinventing ITIL® and DevOps with Digital Transformation*,
https://doi.org/10.1007/978-1-4842-9072-9_8

The problem management process is slightly academic. It does not believe in happenstance and trying to resolve world hunger in one go. There is a definite method to the madness around laying tombstones on top of the problems. I represent the problem management process as the investigation unit of the IT service provider organization. You might have seen the popular TV series *CSI*, where crimes are solved by following leads and finding culprits. The problem management process is the CSI of IT service management, and you can compare incident management to the police squad.

Let's consider an example involving an application that crashes frequently when certain actions are performed simultaneously. An incident is raised. The incident is diagnosed, and the resolution is a complex one. But incident management focuses on helping users move on with their day-to-day activities involving services. Therefore, an incident analyst recommends a workaround so users can perform actions on the application in a sequential manner rather than in parallel. The user's immediate issue is solved, but the impending problem exists. A problem is raised, and an investigation into the problem begins. The problem is recreated, the codebase is examined, and all the relevant logs are studied to debug the underlying cause. The investigation pays off, and the cause is identified and subsequently fixed. All the investigative activities are done under the auspices of problem management, in order to identify the problem and find a permanent solution.

Objectives and Principles

Before you get any further, you need to understand the problem accurately. The ITIL service operations publication defines the problem as the underlying cause of one or more incidents. In simple terms, there are incidents where the fix is yet to be found. The resolution of these incidents is not possible as the root cause of the incident is unknown. This is similar to a doctor prescribing medicines. If the doctor does not know the cause of certain symptoms, the doctor cannot prescribe the right medicine. Likewise, to resolve incidents, the technical resolver groups must know the root cause of the problems. If they do not know the root cause, they start to guess by asking users to restart machines, uninstall and reinstall software, and other hara-kiri that may amount to a waste of time and resources. But, if the principles of problem management were to be applied and the root cause were identified, the solution will be routine.

A problem gets raised when the root cause of an incident is unknown. Or a bunch of incidents with a common thread cannot be resolved, as the underlying root cause is yet to be identified.

Incidents vs. Problems

It is my experience that many IT professionals in the IT service management industry use the terms *incident* and *problem* interchangeably. This does more harm than good, especially when you are working in an organization that takes shape after ITIL and especially if you are preparing for the ITIL foundation exam. This section differentiates the two terms with examples, so as you move forward toward the process and other key terminologies, there shouldn't be any confusion between incidents and problems.

Incidents are raised due to loss or degradation of services. They are raised by users, IT staff, or event management tools. When the incident resolution is not possible, because the underlying root cause is unknown, the IT team will raise a problem. Remember that users and event management tools don't raise problems; generally speaking, they can come only through the incident. However, in a mature IT environment, we can configure event management tools to look for specific patterns of events and raise problems. Let's restrict this discussion to problems derived only from incidents.

Let's consider the example of a software application that crashes when it is initiated. The user raises an incident to fix this issue. The software resolution team tries to start the application in safe mode, uninstalls and reinstalls the application, and finally make changes to the OS registry, to no avail. When all hopes fail, they provide a heads-up to the problem management process to find the root cause and provide a permanent solution.

The problem management process aided by experts in the software architecture group debug the application loading and run a series of tests to find the triggers and sparks for the crash. They find out that the root cause of the crash is a conflict with a hardware device driver. They recommend uninstalling the hardware device driver and updating it with the latest driver. The recommendation works like a charm, and the software application loads nicely without any fuss. This is the problem management process in action, working on iron-legged problems that can cause irreparable damages to the customer organization if they are not dealt with on a timely basis.

Key Terminologies in Problem Management

Problem management digs deep, and the process brings a certain amount of complexity to the table. The complexity includes a few terms that are used quite often during various stages of the process activities. It is key that you understand all this terminology, for work and for the ITIL Foundation exam.

Root Cause

A *root cause* is the fundamental reason for an incident or problem.

Let's say the ATM at your bank does not disburse the money that you requested. The underlying cause or the root cause for the denial of service in this instance is attributed to a network failure in the bank. Likewise, for every incident, there will be a root cause.

Only when you identify the root cause can you resolve the incident. In the ATM instance, unless you know about the network failure, you cannot bring the ATM service back up.

Root-Cause Analysis

Identifying the root cause of an incident is no menial task. At times, the root cause may reveal itself, but other times, it is challenging to identify the root causes of complex incidents. You are required to analyze the root cause by using techniques that commonly fall under *root-cause analysis* (RCA).

Remember that the outcome of an RCA may not always result in the root cause of an incident. In such cases, RCA must be performed using complex techniques and with experts pertaining to related fields of technology and management.

Known Error

When the outcome of the RCA procedure yields results and the root cause is known, it might not be always possible to implement a permanent solution. Instead, temporary fixes, called *workarounds,* are enacted. Such cases where root causes are known along with the workarounds are called *known errors*.

There could be various reasons that solutions cannot be implemented. Commonly, permanent solutions are expensive. Most organizations are price conscious these days and may not approve the excess expenditures. Other reasons could include a lack of experts or people resources to implement the permanent solution or could cite governance or legislation controls that could prevent implementation.

Known Error Database

Known errors are documented and stored in a repository called a *known error database* (KEDB).

The KEDB consists of various known errors, their identified root causes, and the workarounds. The known error records are not permanent members of a KEDB. Known errors will cease to exist in this repository when a permanent solution is implemented.

Workarounds

As mentioned, *workarounds* are fixes that temporarily solve incidents. Each incident could have one or multiple workarounds, but none alleviates the problem permanently, and it may be required to revisit the workaround on a regular basis.

For example, say a printer on your floor is not working and you cannot wait for the technician can get to it. A classic workaround, in this case, is to print from a printer on a different floor. The workaround will solve your problem temporarily by providing a way out, but it may not be a permanent solution as you may find it inconvenient to run down to the next floor every time. Another workaround could be that you don't print the document but instead send the soft copy to the intended recipient.

Permanent Solutions

When the root cause of a problem is known, the follow-up activity in problem management process is to identify a *permanent solution*. This solution permanently resolves the problem, contributes toward a reduction in the incident count, and prevents future outages.

As mentioned, permanent solutions come at a cost, and organizations may not always be willing to shell out the required capital. In such cases, permanent solutions are known but not implemented.

Problem Analysis Techniques

There are a number of ways to investigate a problem. Every problem is unique and may require a different approach altogether to determine the cause of it. My favorite investigative approach is to use common sense and follow the trail until it leads you to the smoking gun—in some ways like Sherlock Holmes conducts his investigation. I don't like to be boxed in with approaches that come attached with a model, such as a theme for investigation; examples include the forensic anthropology used in *Bones* and the mentalism illustrated in the show *The Mentalist*. Yet, it is good to know about the approaches so you can understand the methodology and create your own techniques to solve a problem. This section introduces a few popular techniques used by investigators in the IT industry, most popularly known as *problem managers*.

Brainstorming

Brainstorming that has been used, misused, and underused. It's the power of using our brains to focus on areas of investigation. The brainstorming technique involves focused thinking without any inhibitions. The term *brainstorming* was first made popular by the author Alex Faickney Osborn in the book *Applied Imagination*, published in 1953. Although the methodology around brainstorming existed long before, it was never brought into the limelight as a powerful technique to investigate problems.

Using the brainstorming technique, there are no bad thoughts. Every thought must be weighed, and then a decision must be made. In other words, ideas are not tagged as absurd or made fun of, and everything is accepted, examined, and then acted upon based on the results of the thought. For example, if thinking is a car, it's a car without brakes. You don't want the thinking to stop or be impeded. There must be no action to stop the flow of thoughts. People use the steering wheel to steer their thoughts toward the goal they want to achieve. The more thinking, with the right steering, the closer they get to the destination.

Brainstorming can be done on your own or in a group. The more the merrier, right? Not always. It is possible that clear thoughts in your mind could get unfocused, so group brainstorming must be done with caution and with a process to keep it in a framework. In his book, Osborn says that group brainstorming sessions are more effective than individual ones, as he firmly believed that quantity breeds quality. The assumption is that a greater number of ideas generated, the better the probability of striking gold. If you are planning a group brainstorming session, I recommend following these steps:

1.   You need the right set of people to brainstorm an idea or to investigate the cause of a problem. If you bring like-minded people into a brainstorming session, you are not going to get diverse ideas. Instead, if you bring in a diverse group of people, you get different ideas, all of which are needed to investigate a problem.

2.   Don't bring the group together into the meeting room without preparation. Explain to them in advance the goal of the brainstorming session and what you want to achieve. This agenda helps the group start thinking, even before they set foot into the brainstorming session, and their ideas can be discussed, dissected, and challenged, which is a lot more productive than doing the actual thinking in the session.

3.   In the brainstorming session, restate the agenda and set the rules of engagement. Rules of engagement can be something like this: no ideas are bad, and no ideas should be cast away without examining them. This is an important step to provide a voice to the participants who may sit on the bottom steps of the corporate ladder.

4.   Use a whiteboard to note down every idea. Note an idea, discuss it, and then rate the idea based on its merit. I have used mindmaps (made popular by Tony Buzan) and Kanban dashboards on a whiteboard to visually organize and manage ideas.

5.   As a chairperson of the brainstorming session, you must have a good idea what you are trying to achieve. You must use this knowledge to steer the group toward ideas that matter. In this car without brakes, you are the steering wheel. You need to guide the discussions. Appoint a note-taker to jot down all the ideas for further discussion. Take as many breaks as needed. Our brains work better in short sprints rather than in marathon sessions.

The Five-Why Technique

One of the most commonly used (and misused) techniques in the problem management process is the *five-why technique*. It is used when investigating a problem, specifically during the root-cause determination stage. The technique is so commonly taught and retaught to problem management personnel that it has become a de facto standard in the activity of root-cause analysis.

The five-why technique involves asking the question "why" about the problem at hand five times to arrive at the root cause. It was conceived by Japanese industrialist Sakichi Toyoda, the founder of Toyota Industries in 1930. But it wasn't until the Toyota Production System (TPS) became known that the technique became popular (in the 1970s). The principle relies on being on the ground to find the reasons for something rather than in the comfort of an air conditioner (a "go and see" philosophy).

This technique is popular, partly because it's extremely simple to use and takes a short amount of time to process and execute.

Applying the Five-Why Technique

Let's consider the most common problem in the airline industry. Most airlines have flight delays. Flight delays not only inconvenience passengers but also tarnish the image of flight operators, which works against the optimal use of their assets and leads to disrupting any plans for expansion. In this example, I illustrate a simplistic view of the problem and arrived at the cause of the problem using the five-why technique, as shown in Figure 8-1.

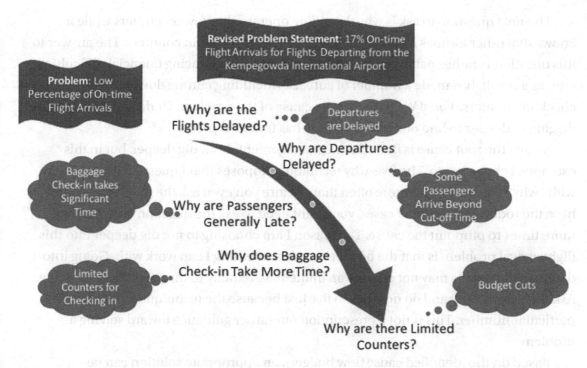

Figure 8-1. *The five-why technique used to determine the root cause of flight delays*

My first step and perhaps the most significant activity is to identify the problem accurately. The problem must be pinned down to its granular details in order to have a better chance at identifying the root cause. The problem is rather simplistic and at a high level: low percentage of on-time flight arrivals for a particular flight operator. Perhaps using the metrics, I should have been more specific with the problem statement: Only 17 percent of arrivals for flights departing from the Kempegowda International Airport are on time. By being specific, you can get on the ground and examine the reasons for the problem.

Using this technique, I question the reason for the problem. Why are flights departing the Kempegowda International Airport late? The immediate answer throws light on the baggage check-in process, which seems to hold up passengers before they arrive at the gate. The airline must wait for those passengers in the queue at the baggage check-in. Thinking through it, the next logical question to ask is why are people spending so much time in the baggage queue? Is this normal for other airlines as well? The answer to this question points toward limited counter space that the airline has set up compared to its competitors, which operate a similar number of flights.

The next question to ask is why the airline operator has fewer counters while it knows that other airlines have a significant number of check-in counters. The answer to this question is rather painful in this example. The airline is facing financial difficulties and, as a result, has made a number of cutbacks including cutting down on the baggage check-in counters. *Voila*! We have the root cause of the problem. Or do we? Why am I not digging in deeper to find out why the airline has financial problems?

Maybe the root cause is financial mismanagement. I can dig deeper, but in this example, I chose not to. The five-why technique proposes that I question the problem with "why" five times, and more often than, before you even ask the fifth "why," you'll have the root cause. In some cases, you might need to ask the question "why" a few more times to pinpoint the cause. The reason I am choosing to not dig deeper into this flight arrival problem is that the budget issue is something I can work with. Going into the financial details may not give me an immediate remedy to the problem I am facing. Ask the whys wisely and do not stick to five just because the technique highlights this particular number. This is not a prescription but rather guidance toward solving a problem.

Based on the identified cause (low budget), an appropriate solution can be conceived. It could be online check-ins with baggage drop-off stations, self-serve baggage check-in counters, or shared resources with other airlines to use common check-in counters for all airlines. The effectiveness of the solution depends on the quality of the root cause. Therefore, it is critical that the root cause is specific enough to offer a full-blown real solution that isn't superficial and molded for the sake of a solution.

Limitations of the Five-Why Technique

While the five-why technique is popular as the model is easy to adapt and simple to use, it begs a question whether this technique can be used to solve problems of higher complexity. Of course, you can further expand on the technique in the flight delay problem if the "why" question gives rise to multiple reasons. You can use multitiered "why" questions to determine the cause of the problem.

The real test of the technique is when the person answering the question does not know the answer. The person might not even know where to look. The technique just asks the question "why" but does not supplement the question with helpful keys to determine the cause. For example, the answer to flight delays may perhaps be the efficiency of people manning the check-in desk. Did the technique attempt to determine whether the reasons could perhaps be any other than those given by the person trying to solve the problem? This is why the five-why technique is limited when there is a complex problem with multiple tentacles. With this, I want to introduce the next problem-solving technique: the Ishikawa diagram.

The Ishikawa Diagram

An Ishikawa diagram is known by multiple names, including a fishbone diagram, a fishikawa diagram, and a herringbone diagram, among others. It consists of a central spine that represents the problem. Several branches jut out of the spine to indicate possible causes. The arrangement of the spine and branches looks like a fishbone (see Figure 8-2).

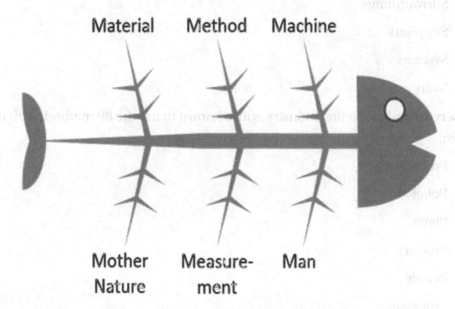

Figure 8-2. *Fishbone diagram (image credit: 4improvement.one)*

The causes are not arbitrary, as discussed in the five-why technique. There is a method to the madness in the Ishikawa process. Each branch is designated to a category, and the thinking behind it is to follow the category to determine the root cause. Figure 8-2 illustrates one of the more popular fishbone models used in the manufacturing industry, called the 6M model. The six cause categories are modeled are as follows:

- Material: Causes related to the material used in the manufacturing process

- Method: The process

- Machine: The actual machinery, technology, and so on

- Mother nature: The environment

- Measurement: The measurement techniques employed in deriving metrics

- Manpower: The people involved

There are other models as well, depending on the industry. For example, the service industry uses a 4S model with these categories:

- Surroundings

- Suppliers

- Systems

- Skills

The service and marketing industry is also known to use the 8P method, with these categories:

- Procedures

- Policies

- Place

- Product

- People

- Processes

- Price

- Promotion

I am most comfortable with the 6M process, so Figure 8-3 uses this model to explain the Ishikawa diagram. However, do not feel you must one of the available models. Come up with your own set of categories to assess the root cause of the problem. These models are just starting points, and this should eventually give way to your own set of categories for the industry, domain, and customers you are involved with.

Using the same example as earlier (the low on-time flight arrival rate) and using the Ishikawa diagram with the 6M categories, Figure 8-3 depicts the possible outcome of the analysis.

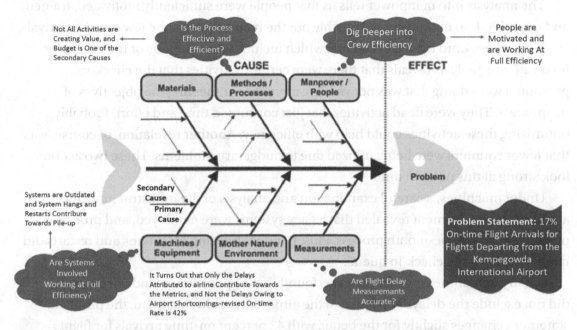

Figure 8-3. *Ishikawa analysis for low on-time flight arrival rate*

In this example, the problem is central to the whole exercise. Under each of the branches, I look at the problem from a different perspective. For this particular example, I find manpower, methods, machines, and measurements to be relevant. Therefore, my analysis surrounds only those categories.

Note   Every problem is unique, so you need to carefully pick and choose the branches to analyze the root cause. Don't feel that you have explore every category. Be judicious and use common sense in identifying the right categories.

When you view the problem from one perspective, say manpower, you can start asking a number of pointed questions to arrive at a root cause:

- Are people sufficiently trained to do their jobs?

- Are people motivated on the job, and are they compensated fairly?

- Are there sufficient people to work the check-in counters?

The answers to these questions will take you closer to finding the root cause. Remember that there is no set formula for probing a problem. You must use logic and work on the ground to understand how things work.

The analysis into manpower tells us that people were sufficiently motivated, trained, and quantified, so manpower is probably not the reason behind the low on-time arrivals.

If you move onto the next category, which includes the methods or the processes involved, the analysis reveals that there were certain activities that the check-in personnel were doing that was not yielding any value or meeting the objectives of the process. They were dead activities that just consumed time and effort. Probably optimizing these activities could help with efficiency. Another revelation, of course, was that fewer counters were being utilized due to budgetary problems. These two actions look strong at this point in time.

Under machines, a careful examination and analysis of the infrastructure and application environment revealed that legacy systems were employed, and processing passengers was not a smooth process. Plus, frequent freezing of systems and restarts did not help reduce the check-in queue.

Finally, under measurements, it was found that 17 percent was indeed faulty. It did not exclude the delays attributed to the airport. By excluding them, the problem statement changes slightly for the better, with 42 percent on-time arrivals for flights departing from the airport at Bangalore.

Now that we have the causes handy, we can get to work identifying necessary solutions. There now exists a single root cause to a problem. However, for problems such as the one considered in this example, it is possible that multiple causes add to the delays, and tweaking various elements could help improve the on-time arrival rate.

The Kepner-Tregoe Method

The Kepner-Tregoe method is yet another popular technique that analyzes problems. It is a problem-solving and decision-making (PSDM) technique that decouples the problem from the decision. This technique was developed by Charles Kepner and Benjamin Tregoe in the 1960s.

There are four steps to the Kepner-Tregoe method:

1. *Situation appraisal*: In the first step, you analyze the situation on the ground. What exactly led to the current situation? At this point in time, you do not identify the problem itself, but simply outline the concerns.

2. *Problem analysis*: During problem analysis, you find the root cause of the problem. You analyze the problem and determine the root cause, possibly using one of the methods discussed earlier.

3. *Decision analysis*: Based on the root cause, you identify various alternatives for resolving the problem. In an unbiased manner, you weigh each alternative to calculate the risks and benefits.

4. *Potential problem analysis*: Against the best alternatives identified in the previous step, you perform further analysis to identify whether there are any regression issues based on the dependencies.

At the end of the four steps, you'll make a decision to go with the best possible alternative identified in the process. This process tries to be unbiased in terms of identifying the approaches for resolving problems and looking at the resolutions objectively. However, some critics rightly say that the decision-makers are always inclined to one side or the other, making it a biased approach after all.

However, the method helps identify options and the associated risks. Wise decision-makers have all the information they need to make the right decision.

A Typical Problem Management Process

The problem management process can be drafted in a number of ways to meet the goals of the problem management process. While ITIL doesn't prescribe how the flow must look, it provides a true north for the process architects to follow. A typical problem management process workflow, with all the bells and whistles, is illustrated in Figure 8-4.

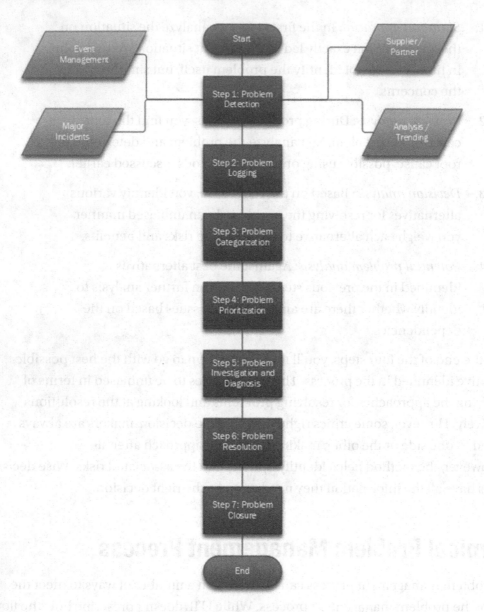

Figure 8-4. *Typical problem management process*

Step 1: Problem Detection

As with the incident management process, problems need to be detected for the process to be triggered. A problem can be identified from any source; it can come as an action item from the customer, a threat notification from regulatory departments, or loopholes identified by hackers. In the problem management lifecycle, I considered the most common triggers for a problem. Remember that the triggers need to be identified beforehand to ensure that the process is well controlled and does not spiral out into directions that were not factored in.

Event Management

These days, event management tools play a handy role in keeping a finger on the pulse and to standardize monitoring and capture events that are of significance to IT service management. We have seen the application of event management tools in the incident management process. In a similar vein, these tools can be programmed to detect problems as well. For example, if a server goes down, an incident ticket is raised. Suppose the same server alternates between being offline and online a preconceived number of times; the tools can be programmed to raise a problem ticket so the problem manager can start investigation-related activities.

With all this said, it is rare to see the event management tools used to raise problem tickets. I have seen such instances with a handful of implementations. Programming problems on automation solutions requires a certain amount of maturity for the service management organization to design, execute, and control.

Major Incidents

The most common source for triggering problems are major incidents. It is a common sight in the process world to see major incidents tagged to problem investigations. Normally, toward the resolution of a major incident, a problem ticket is created by the incident manager. While the major incident resolution brings in a logical closure to the major incident management process, it gives rise to the problem management process to kick-start and initiate investigations.

This is a good practice as major incidents can cause massive damage to clients (financial, productivity, brand image, and so on). It is in the interest of all stakeholders that a problem investigation is performed on the major incident to identify the loopholes and come up with a preventive measure to ensure such outages do not happen in the future.

Partners/Suppliers

We live in a world whereby no single IT service provider organization can afford to provide all IT services based on the supplier's expertise.

Suppliers handle specific areas. Let's say that a particular supplier provides networks, another supplier provides infrastructure, and another supplier manages applications. These suppliers are the best sources for identifying problems in their respective areas, rather than a third party identifying it. Suppliers are one of the main triggers or sources of detecting problems. Suppliers are also referred to as *partners* to make them accountable for the overall delivery of IT services.

Analysis/Trending

Proactive problem management's objective is to forecast future problems and stop them from happening. In the movie *Minority Report*, the aim of the main crime-fighting organization is to stop crimes before they actually take place. This concept of problem management is similar to that movie theme.

How do you forecast what is going to happen in the future? You don't have crystal balls in IT, nor do you have precogs as in the movie. But you do possess historical data. This data can be dissected, and when cross sections are analyzed, you can see into the future.

One of the techniques for doing proactive problem management is to trend the incidents or the common root causes of incidents. This will provide you with insight on what is generally going wrong. If you review these frequent occurrences and devise a way to fix the problem permanently, you will reduce recurring incidents. Along with this, you can reduce the incident count, potential outages, potential penalties, and potential brand image damage.

Another technique is the Pareto principle, whereby you identify the top 20 percent of the causes responsible for 80 percent of the incidents and find a permanent solution for these incidents. If you can do this, you will reduce the incident count by 80 percent.

Step 2: Problem Logging

You need to document detected problems in a formal way to ensure that each problem goes through all the steps in its lifecycle.

Every problem ticket is likely to have all or a subset of the following attributes:

- Problem Number (unique)
- User details
- Problem Summary
- Problem Description
- Problem Category
- Problem Priority
- Incident Reference Number(s)
- Investigation Details
- Resolution/Recovery Details

Event Management

Most modern event management tools can auto-log problems on the ITSM tool. If this capability is not available, the tool will raise alerts in the form of emails to the service desk function. For major incidents, problems are logged by the incident manager or the service desk function, generally toward the end of the incident resolution.

Partners/Suppliers

Suppliers or partners who identify problems either log problem tickets on their own or provide the necessary inputs to the service desk function or the problem manager.

Analysis/Trending

Problem managers who perform the analysis activities raise the problem ticket based on their findings.

Step 3: Problem Categorization

All problems have to be categorized similar to incidents. Categorization will help in assigning the problem tickets to the right resolver groups and in reporting.

Step 4: Problem Prioritization

Some problems are more important than others. They need to work with more focus on the others. How do you differentiate one problem from another? Through assigned priorities. This exercise is similar to incidents.

Similar to the incident priority matrix, a problem priority matrix exists, and a timeline is associated with it to set targets for investigation and resolution. However, in the service industry, problem timelines are not strictly adhered to like with incidents. This is because investigation tends to take longer than expected in the case of complex problems, and generally, there will not be enough resources assigned to problem management specifically but rather shared with incidents and changes. When an incident comes up at the same time as a problem, the incident always takes priority, and resources will always end up falling short on the time needed to investigate problems and find a permanent solution.

Step 5: Problem Investigation and Diagnosis

The step of problem investigation and diagnosis starts with identifying the root cause of the problem. Getting to the root cause of the problem is the biggest challenge in this exercise. A root-cause analysis (RCA) is the output of this step, and it involves various RCA techniques that are employed in getting to the root cause. Five-why analysis, Ishikawa diagram, Pareto analysis, affinity mapping, and hypothesis testing are the popular techniques used. Discussing these techniques is outside the scope of the ITIL foundation examination and hence of this book.

To conduct a thorough investigation into a problem, suitable resources, referred to as *problem analysts,* must be assigned. They are technical experts who have the expertise to delve deeper into the cause of the problem. They are aided by the knowledge management database (KMDB) and the configuration management system (CMS). The KEDB is also referred to when identifying whether similar problems have occurred in the past and what resolution steps were undertaken.

In most cases, the problem analyst tries to recreate the problem to identify the root cause. After identifying the root cause, problem resolutions are developed, preferentially economic solutions.

Step 6: Problem Resolution

In the previous step, the root cause of the problem is identified, and a solution is developed to mitigate the problem. The solution can be either a permanent solution, which is preferable, or a workaround. You should also be aware that the solution implementation may come at a cost. The client might have to invest some capital into resolving problems, maybe adding extra infrastructure, procuring applications, developing connectors between applications, and leasing more bandwidth, among others. So, financial approval from the sponsors will always precede the problem resolution activity. The financial approval is based on the business case that the service provider develops and the return on investment that the resolution brings to the table. For example, if a particular resolution costs a million dollars and can improve the client productivity by 10 percent, the client might be tempted to approve it. On the other hand, for the same million dollars, if the return on investment cannot be quantified, it may not get the nod.

Implementation activities will be carried out through the change management process. The resolution will be submitted to the change manager in the form of a request for change (RFC). The change management process will conduct due diligence like risk and impact analysis to ensure that the resolution does not cause more harm than good and that it does not impact other connected services (regression analysis) or cause outages during business-critical periods. Most solution implementations go into the change advisory board (CAB) approval cycle for further assessments and scrutiny. After getting the okay from all stakeholders, they will be taken up for implementation.

Resolution can also come in the form of a workaround. I discussed workarounds earlier in this chapter. Workarounds must also be reviewed through the change management process.

At the end of the resolution activity, the KEDB will be updated. If a permanent solution is implemented, the KEDB record is archived. If a workaround is implemented, the KEDB record will be updated with the necessary workaround details. In a workaround implementation, it is a good practice to keep the problem record open.

Step 7: Problem Closure

When a permanent solution is implemented, the problem record needs to be updated with the historical data (of the problem), resolution details, and change details; then it is closed with the appropriate status. If a workaround is implemented, you keep the problem record open in an appropriate status to indicate that the problem is temporarily fixed using a workaround. The problem manager is generally responsible for closing all problem records.

Problem Management in DevOps

The problem management process exists to reduce incidents and to ensure that the IT environment is free from anomalies that hold back the system and the services. The process is relevant in an IT services environment powered by ITIL, and a DevOps project is an extension of the ITIL environment. So, it is clear that problem management is here to stay in a DevOps project.

You may think I am contradicting myself based on what I said earlier about DevOps. I mentioned earlier that the goal of DevOps is to deliver quickly and to minimize the number of bugs in the production environment. It is impossible for any methodology to claim that a bug-free system is going to be deployed. If that's the case, there is no room for either the incident or problem management processes. But, bugs are an inherent part of the system. They are like the weeds in your garden. No matter how technologically savvy you are in agriculture, you can never take all the weeds out. The same is true for the bugs in an IT system. They are here to stay and so is problem management to minimize the effects of these bugs.

What Are the Possible Problems in a DevOps Project?

Incidents and problems often look the same in a DevOps project. The speed of delivery is the most important aspect. When incidents flow in, they come in quickly, and they move out quickly as well. The time needed to analyze an incident is kept short to avoid extended downtimes, and this often gives rise to a dilemma of not sharpening the axe before felling the tree.

Of course, there are bugs (and incidents) that crop up, for which the developers may not have the answers. In the interest of moving ahead and reducing the backlog, the developers might put the bug on the backburner, tagging it "unresolvable." These unresolvable defects form the basis for reactive problem management. As the word *reactive* suggests, you react to the problem at hand rather than anticipating it and removing the cause of it before the problem materializes.

The enigma over incidents and problems needs to be reexamined in a DevOps project. In an IT services project, the boundaries are straightforward. Problems are incidents that cannot be resolved permanently or resolved at all without detailed analysis. A post-mortem on major incidents is done on the back of a problem.

Analysis on the incidents can reveal certain interesting aspects such as incidents that have commonalities, often called *repetitive incidents* in ITIL lingo.

In a DevOps project, what can be categorized as problems?

Incidents flow from L2 support to the DevOps team. The DevOps team works on the incident for a reasonable time based on its priority. The planning around working on incidents is taken up the Scrum master and the incident manager. When the developer spends sufficient time on an incident without success, the Scrum master, in consultation with the incident manager, might weigh in on the impact of the incident and workaround if available. Instead of spending excessive time on an incident that does not have a major impact, the Scrum master will make a decision to rebadge the incident as a problem, and the problem goes back into the backlog, only to be picked up in a future sprint. This is one source of problems.

Major incidents are rare in most projects. However, when one does happen, there needs to be a good amount of post-resolution analysis to ensure that major incidents are avoided at all costs. Post-resolution analysis is a necessary evil, and the problem management process is best equipped to deal with it. This is equally applicable to DevOps projects as well.

I started this topic with an axe-sharpening analogy. It is so true that you need to sit back and take a holistic view of the flow of incidents. Only then can you get the true effects of axe sharpening and won't slog away at incidents instead of bringing an end to a bunch of incidents in one swooping move. Analyzing repetitive incidents is a worthy exercise in a DevOps project, and it helps with the stability of the system and helps deal with the problem head-on rather than in a reactive manner, which makes a case for a dedicated role to manage problems.

Making the Case for a Problem Manager

There are discussions on various forums about the relevance of full-blown ITIL in a DevOps world. One of the liabilities according to a certain school of thought is the role of the problem manager. Detractors say that the problem management process is relevant and has value, but having a dedicated role of a problem manager to manage the problems is overkill because the problem manager does not do the heavy lifting that is involved in the analysis of problems and root cause identification. The person merely touches the surface and acts as a record keeper. Well, in my humble opinion, these detractors are wrong. There is considerable value in having a problem manager, and in this section, I hope to prove explain why.

I spoke briefly on reactive problem management in the previous section. The word *reactive* must not be looked at as something to stay away from. There is value in reacting to problems at hand and ensuring that they are resolved quickly. Reactive problem management takes place on two fronts in a DevOps project:

- Defects that cannot be resolved (at least quickly), wherein the impact of the bug is minimal (such as slight misalignment of the footer text). However, these defects must be fixed at point, and sooner than later. Tagging such defects by an appropriate status such as "unresolvable" will provide an opportunity for the planning team (Scrum master) to break down the problem into multiple parts and present them in various sprints for action and closure.

- I presented the case of major incidents in a services project as being appended with a problem ticket to conduct investigations and propose a permanent solution to ensure such major incidents do not happen again. This scope of problem management can be extended to a DevOps project as well. Not only major incidents, there's more coming into the realm of problem management from a DevOps project. DevOps projects are generally anal about defects getting into production. Incidents that are raised against software releases need to be looked at under a microscope. Who best to do this than problem management?

Proactive problem management in DevOps is about analyzing incidents. Incidents are analyzed based on various common factors, such as the nature of the incidents, the configuration item involved, the application features, and so on. This sort of analysis more often than not provides an opportunity to get an overview of incidents. The results are always interesting because you start to find problems in areas where you least expect. As the Pareto principle goes (tailored to ITIL), 80 percent of the problems are caused by 20 percent of the incidents. So, it is important to identify that bugger behind a whole bunch of incidents!

Problems do not cause as many problems as incidents do. Therefore, it is anything but natural to do away with a problem manager, as there isn't much noise around problems. This is how the IT industry operates. The ones who make the most noise get the prize. The problem manager is like a campaign manager, working in the background and drumming up support for your candidate. Thus far, I have established the role of problem management in the overall scheme of things. Having a dedicated problem manager to shepherd the problems to their closure seems to be a logical choice. However, it is also true that with the advancement of DevOps methodologies and catching defects early, defect rates have dropped, and a problem manager being part of the DevOps team seems a luxury rather than a necessity. In Chapter 5, I propose multiple layers of team structures. The DevOps team is dedicated to a single product and shared teams managing multiple DevOps teams. The problem manager can be part of the shared teams and manage problems from multiple DevOps projects if there isn't sufficient load from a single DevOps project.

The DevOps Problem Management Process

The problem management process in a DevOps project is in principle the same as in an ITIL-driven services project. The process, however, is broken into multiple sequential items that are processed in sprints based on their prioritization. A rundown of a problem management process in a DevOps project is in Figure 8-5.

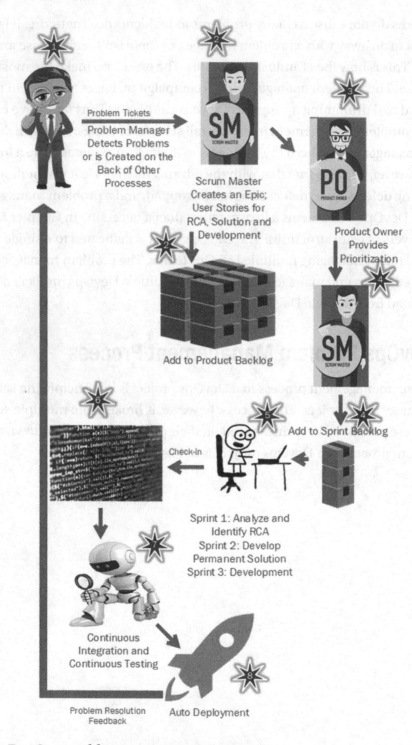

Figure 8-5. *DevOps problem management process*

Step 1: Problem Detection

Incidents are identified while problems are detected. Problems are not obvious; they need to be unearthed based on historic trends or on the back of patterns. The problem detection is primarily entrusted to the problem manager, who is part of the shared team. However, detecting problems is the responsibility of all involved personnel. That means *everybody*. Problems can occur anywhere, be it in the toolsets or infrastructure or the way the Agile implementation is done. After a problem been detected, the problem manager takes ownership of it and analyzes it for its relevance, value, and impact. If it is low on all three counts, the problem manager may close the problems without further action. For problems that rank high on the agreed-on matrix, the problem manager takes them further.

One of the most common ways of identifying problems is through trend analysis. A trend analysis for the past six to twelve months will reveal patterns that can be used to identify the common denominator. A problem ticket is raised against the detected problem. This type of problem management where problems are detected (and rectified) before they grow into major impacting incidents is called *proactive problem management*. The process of detecting and solving problems on the back of a major incident (or coming from other processes) is referred to as *reactive problem management*.

Step 2: Scrum Master Logs the Problem into the Product Backlog

The Scrum master receives the problem ticket and, for every problem ticket, creates an *epic* (a big chunk of work consisting of multiple user stories) on the product backlog with the following user stories:

- Analysis (RCA)

- Solution

- Development

I recommend creating a minimum of three user stories because a problem needs to be analyzed to identify the root cause. Identifying the root cause is potentially time-consuming and can eat away at a developer's time for the entire duration of a sprint. While planning, the Scrum team can sequentially analyze the root cause in Sprint 1, developing a solution based on the identified root cause in Sprint 2, and then develop the solution and test it in Sprint 3. The order cannot change, but the sprint numbers can.

Based on the prioritization, the Scrum team can pick up root-cause analysis in Sprint 2, the solution in Sprint 5, and its development and testing in Sprint 7. The order cannot be turned around; in other words, the solution cannot be developed before the root cause is identified.

Steps 3 and 4: Product Owner Prioritizes the Problem and Adds the User Story to the Sprint Backlog

No surprises here. The product owner is the sole proprietor of the product backlog; they prioritize the epics and user stories. In this case, the product owner has decided to prioritize the problem over all other product backlog items. The user story pertaining to analyzing the root cause (followed by other user stories in subsequent sprints) is added to the sprint backlog.

Step 5: Scrum Team Acts on the Problem

It is okay that the Scrum team, instead of developing and testing the user stories, puts on a Sherlock Holmes hat and investigates the problem. The definition of done in this case is to identify the smoking gun.

When the root cause is identified, the next user story is to develop a permanent solution for the problem based on the root cause. This is prioritized and added to the sprint backlog. Developing a permanent solution can be done by developers, testers, operations, or architects (who sit in the shared teams). During the sprint planning session, the person who is going to derive a solution is identified, and the definition of done is to come up with a solution that plugs the problem.

In the subsequent sprint, the solution is developed and tested if it involves coding. If it involves infrastructure changes, the respective team member gets down to work to implement the recommended solution.

Steps 6, 7, and 8: Continuous Integration, Testing, and Auto-Deployment

If the solution involves coding changes, the changes made to the mainline are fed back into the mainline, the continuous integration and continuous testing processes take over, and the binaries are deployed into environments of choice.

The problem manager is kept in the loop throughout this process. Although this problem manager will have a limited role to play in the process, they will keep monitoring to ensure that the process and deliverables are met as agreed-on. When the solution is successfully developed and implemented, the problem manager marks the problem ticket as successfully implemented.

Summary

ITIL can go deep into the root of the problems, to weed out defects/bugs that can have a long-lasting effect. The problem management process conducts root cause analysis followed by a permanent fix, which potentially prevents a number of incidents. This chapter introduced the problem management process in detail, including some root cause analysis techniques, such as five whys, Ishikawa, and Kepner-Tregoe. It also covered the adaptation in a DevOps project, and the viability of the problem manager role.

CHAPTER 9

Managing Changes in a DevOps Project

They say that change is the only constant. They also say that anything that does not grow withers away. This is true in the software industry. No matter how old the software or the service is, changes happen all the time. No matter how legacy the application is, it still needs to be maintained and updated with the organizational needs.

Changes are inevitable in any industry; therefore, the onus is on management. The question is not whether you make changes but rather how you do so without impacting the product or service negatively.

It is also true that a majority of incidents are caused by mismanaging changes. This is all the more reason that you need to tighten the change management process to increase the overall uptime and reduce the number of outages. This chapter provides the necessary details of the ITIL change management process, including the types that exist and a typical process that is normally employed. Then I move into adapting the change management process into a DevOps project.

To me, a real difference can be made in the way you deliver projects, and the change management process is a major stakeholder in ensuring that the security blanket that it provides protects the service from malicious changes. This is the process that sets the bar for implementing DevOps successfully in organizations; it does this by allowing seamless changes with the least amount of bureaucracy and by providing plenty of support to guard against mishaps. In the ITIL adaption scheme for processes, the change management process will define the way forward.

© Abhinav Krishna Kaiser 2023
A. Krishna Kaiser, *Reinventing ITIL® and DevOps with Digital Transformation*,
https://doi.org/10.1007/978-1-4842-9072-9_9

What Constitutes a Change?

A change can come in many forms. Identifying a change is half the problem, because most organizations fail to define the list of changes as compared to other issues, such as service requests. The big-ticket question is what is a change?

Overview of Resources and Capabilities

Changes in the ITIL framework and changes in the project management framework have different connotations. My focus in this section is ITIL; therefore, the change that I refer to here is the change that comes about for a service. A service is made up of multiple moving parts, and in ITIL they are broadly classified as resources and capabilities. Figure 9-1 shows the resources and capabilities; each item listed is called a *service asset*.

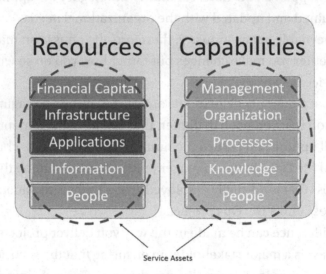

Figure 9-1. *Resources and capabilities of a service*

Note   People are listed under both resources and capabilities, as they directly make up the resources that support and build services, and their capabilities also have a major stake in the quality of their delivery.

The ten service assets listed in Figure 9-1 represent the various moving parts of a service. Changes to any of the ten service assets are likely to have an impact on the service. While some service assets impact services directly, most impact it indirectly. For example, financial capital is a necessity to run services. The lack of it will dwindle the resources that are working to keep the services up and running, and thus it impacts the service. As another example, on the capabilities front, knowledge about the services is like pure gold. If knowledge is well maintained, then resolving incidents and making changes become hassle-free exercises. If the knowledge is all over the place or is not retained, then the real challenges creep in, with longer resolution times and malicious changes. Therefore, it is critical to note that all the service assets have a role to play in the delivery of services.

If changes are made to the service assets, they need to go through the change management process. However, the change management process may not be common for all service assets. For example, making changes to a process may involve a quick conference between the process owner, process manager, business counterparts, and service managers. They sit down, discuss the proposed change, and ratify it if satisfied. The underlying premise is that for each of the service assets, there must be a governance body around them (call it change management or anything else) to ensure that the changes do not negatively impact the services.

Changes come in several layers, such as strategic, tactical, and operational. Strategic and tactical changes are done at a level that's outside the scope of the project, be it an ITIL project or a DevOps project. Only operational changes come go through the change management process, which is discussed in the rest of the chapter.

Change in Scope

In Figure 9-1, the infrastructure and applications are shown in a different shade as the purview of change management comes directly under ITIL. Simply put, in the IT industry, change management refers to making changes to the IT infrastructure and the applications that contribute to the services. In the rest of the chapter and the book, when I refer to change management, I am talking about changes to be done either to infrastructure or to applications.

Note   The official definition of *change* is as follows: "Change is the addition, removal, or modification of anything that could have an effect on IT services."

Even after reading the official change definition, the scope may not spell out everything that you wanted to know. An IT service can spread far and wide, including the suppliers that support the service, the IT professionals who manage it, and the documentation for it. Does changing any of these peripheral components require a change? Yes, but it depends on the agreement between the service provider and customer organization. Managing more items requires more time and resources, which adds up to expenses. If the customer wants to have absolute control over the IT services, then yes, every element that makes up a service must come into the purview of change management. In the real world, this is often not the case, owing to the financials. Many of the indirect components are ignored in the interests of reducing expenses, and some companies find innovative ways of controlling the peripheral objects using standard changes and service requests.

There is much more to change management than adding, removing, and modifying IT services. Take the example of running an ad hoc report. You are not adding, removing, or modifying anything, just reading data from the database. Yet, you possess the power to break systems with the wrong set of queries that search every table, that utilize the infrastructure's resources, and that could potentially cause performance issues to the IT service. In this case, if you bring this through to change management, they can possibly identify the resource-consuming queries and shelve them or schedule them to be run during off-peak hours.

In the ITIL fiefdom, a change is painted as follows:

- Architectural changes to infrastructure and applications

- Additions, deletions, and modifications done to infrastructure CIs

- Additions, deletions, and modifications done to application CIs

- Database schema changes, migrations, and data transformations to data used by services

- Configuration modifications performed on infrastructure and application CIs

The list is not comprehensive, but the underlying idea is that anything that affects running a service is going to change, so it should be brought under the lens of the change management process.

Why Is Change Management Critical?

In Chapter 6, I mentioned that the service asset and configuration management process is critical and is the foundation for the rest of the processes to follow. While configuration management provides the foundation, change management uses the foundational data to make decisions that could potentially break the existing services or could do wonders for the service. The change management process is a governance process and has complete control over what changes can be performed to the services and to the products that make up the service. If you determine your change management process, the service management implementation is bound to mature faster and make way for service improvements quite early in the cycle.

Change management is the sole authority that keeps a close watch on all the changes that are proposed, and after conducting due diligence and ensuring that all concerned parties are happy with the change, it gives the go-ahead for the commencement of the change. This ensures that all the stakeholders know of the change and are given the opportunity to ask questions and oppose it. The process is responsible for bringing in a framework to ensure that changes go through a common pipeline that is governed by a change governing body, called the *change advisory board* (CAB).

The process is that a governing body gives approval for technical teams to carry out the changes. They are a management body; therefore, they do not control the sluice gates if the technical team wants to make changes in a discrete manner. Changes that are done outside the purview of change management are called *unauthorized changes*. Such changes hurt organizations, and service management generally loses control of their services because of such irresponsible actions by the technical teams. To state an example, an unauthorized change does not lead to changes to the content management database (CMDB). So, if an application is installed without going through the change management process, the application CI does not get registered in the CMDB. In the future, when an incident is raised against the data coming out of the installed application, the application support teams refer to CMDB and become perplexed because there is nothing to troubleshoot. They need to later dig into the server to check what exists, and eventually, the overall diagnosis and troubleshooting take a lot more effort, leading to extended downtimes and perhaps penalties. All such unwanted and unnecessary outcomes are the result of unauthorized changes. Therefore, it is critically important for the change management process to spread awareness on making the changes the right way and keeping a tight leash overall services in scope. One of the ways that the process keeps a watch over unauthorized changes is through the service asset and configuration management process audits, which are responsible for identifying such discrete changes. In the DevOps change management process, I introduce a technical way to keep a close watch on the aspects of changes to the services and products.

A major mistake that most ITIL implementers make is to prioritize the design and implementation of the incident management process over the change management process. It's true that a process must handle downtimes and degradations, but it is a whole lot more important to keep sentries at the door of services to allow only the authorized ones through. This blip of prioritizing the wrong process places many ITIL projects on a path of constant firefighting even after months and years after the completion of the implementation. My advice is simple. Put a change management process in place to keep track of all the processes. This process may not be a full-fledged one but rather something like its skeletal cousin that can help prevent unauthorized changes. Once a full-blown incident management process is designed and implemented, get to work bolstering the change management process.

Objectives and Scope of ITIL Change Management

The change management process is one of the governances put in place in the ITIL service management framework. It is a process that controls the changes that go into the IT environment. It is a process that acts as a gatekeeper, vetting, analyzing, and letting through only qualified changes.

According to ITIL, the official definition of *change management* is that it controls the lifecycle of all changes, enabling beneficial changes to be made with minimum service disruption. This is change management in a nutshell: ensure only beneficial changes go through, remove the wheat from the chaff, and ensure that if anything were to go wrong, the risks are well understood, mitigated, and prepared for with minimal disruption.

To expand on this, the way this process works is somewhat like the changes that are funneled through the change management process. Only the changes that pass all the criteria set forth, that are of good quality, and that are deemed beneficial to customers or service providers, in general, are approved for implementation. You should also know that the buck stops with change management for providing approvals. Change implementation is managed through the release and deployment management process, which works in tight integration with the change management process. To reiterate, change management is accountable for providing approvals, and the release and deployment management process is accountable for implementation and post-implementation activities.

Digging deeper into change management, the output, or the objectives, of change management are as follows:

- Respond to the customer's ever-changing needs (technology upgrades and new business requirements) by ensuring that value is created

- Align IT services with business services when changes are planned and implemented

- Ensure all changes are recorded, analyzed, and evaluated by the process

- Ensure only authorized changes are allowed to be prioritized, planned, tested, and implemented in a controlled manner

- Ensure changes to configuration items are recorded in the configuration management system

- Ensure business risks are well understood and mitigated for all changes

Types of Changes

One size does not fit all the changes that happen in services. They come in all shapes and sizes. Therefore, you cannot use the same yardstick for all changes. You need a different set of protocols, policies, and processes to handle various types of changes. Say, for example, you trip over a water pipe and hurt your shoulder. You go to the hospital, and a doctor tends to you and does what is necessary with minimum fuss. Instead, if you were in a car wreck that required stitching you up after and putting some dislodged organs back in their place, this process will require an operation, surgeons, an anesthesiologist, and nurses, among others to be present to ensure you survive and the operation is a success.

Between the two instances, the processes carried out is expectedly different, as one instance requires a host of professionals, utmost care, and some amount of planning, while the other can be done when needed with a basic medical skillset. For the patient who hurt their shoulder, you don't need to assemble surgeons and others. Likewise, in change management, some changes need to be dealt with proper attention, planning, and care, while others can be carried out with minimum scrutiny.

In ITIL, there are three major types of changes:

- Normal changes

- Emergency changes

- Standard changes

For your organization, you can define as many types of changes as you need. ITIL is not prescriptive, so the types of changes are served at best as a guideline. I once worked for an organization that had a fourth type, called an *urgent change,* that was placed between a normal and emergency change.

Type 1: Normal Changes

Let's say that a patient has a heart problem, and they need to have open-heart surgery. The doctors and surgeons involved carefully and meticulously make all the plans, reserve the facilities, and then carry out the procedure. These are planned surgeries, and in the change management world, such changes that are planned in advance are called *normal changes.*

Most changes in any organization are normal changes, as no organization wants to make changes without proper plans in place. Such changes are often lengthy because of the planning sessions, stakeholder visibility, and approvals, and to ensure that all the dependencies are managed.

Normal changes are generally associated with all the bells and whistles of the change management process and are often well analyzed, tested, mitigated, and verified. The maturity of an organization's change management process is often measured through the normal change process and the metrics and KPIs associated with it. Examples of normal changes include an application refresh to a newer version, a server migration from in-house to a cloud service provider, and the decommissioning of mainframe applications and servers.

Type 2: Emergency Changes

During REM sleep, a person clutches their chest in pain and starts to sweat. An ambulance is called, and they are transported swiftly to a nearby hospital. The doctors diagnose a series of heart attacks that were caused because of a blockage. They don't have time to plan the surgery but rather do it right away so the patient will survive. So, with minimum planning, they carry out the surgery. Such changes that are done during firefighting exercises are called *emergency changes* in the change management process.

Emergency changes are necessary to urgently fix an ongoing issue or a crisis. These changes are mostly carried out as a resolution to a major incident. The nature of such changes requires swift action, whether it is getting the necessary approvals or the testing that is involved. Generally, emergency changes are not thoroughly pretested, as the time availability is minimal. In some cases, they may go through without any testing, although this is not recommended, even for an emergency change.

The success of emergency changes reflects the agility of an organization and the change management process to address disruptions in a time-constrained environment and to come out unscathed in the eyes of the customers and their competition. Emergency change management supports the incident management process in the resolution of incidents, especially major ones. Emergency changes are generally frowned upon and are not preferred. The number of such changes in an organization reflects poorly on the organization's stability of the services it offers.

Examples of emergency changes are the replacement of hardware infrastructure and restoring customer data from backup volumes.

Type 3: Standard Changes

A patient with failed kidneys gets dialysis multiple times a week. The process for carrying out a dialysis procedure is well known and rarely fails. Most patients set up dialysis treatments at home and do them fairly regularly. The risks involved are low, and if something goes wrong, the impact is on the lower end of the spectrum as there are multiple workarounds. Such changes for IT services that pose no danger to services and are low key are referred to as *standard changes*.

Standard changes are normal changes that are low risk and low impact in nature. Standard changes are at the discretion of the service provider and customer organizations.

Any organization will have a good chunk of low-risk and low-impact changes. In my estimate, it should run up to 50 percent of the overall changes. The service provider's responsibility to deliver Agile change management depends on their ability to identify standard changes from the normal change list and obtain the necessary approvals to standardize them.

Standard changes have distinct advantages and create value for customers. They follow a process that is less stringent and is free from multiple approvals and lead times that are often associated with normal changes. This provides the service provider with the arsenal needed to implement changes on the fly, which increases productivity and helps deliver better value to the customers.

Examples of standard changes include minor patch upgrades, database reindexing, and blacklisting IPs on firewalls.

ITIL Change Management Process

Of the three types of changes (normal, emergency, and standard), the normal change process is elaborate, lengthy, and contains the most elements of the change management process. Figure 9-2 indicates a typical workflow for the normal change management process.

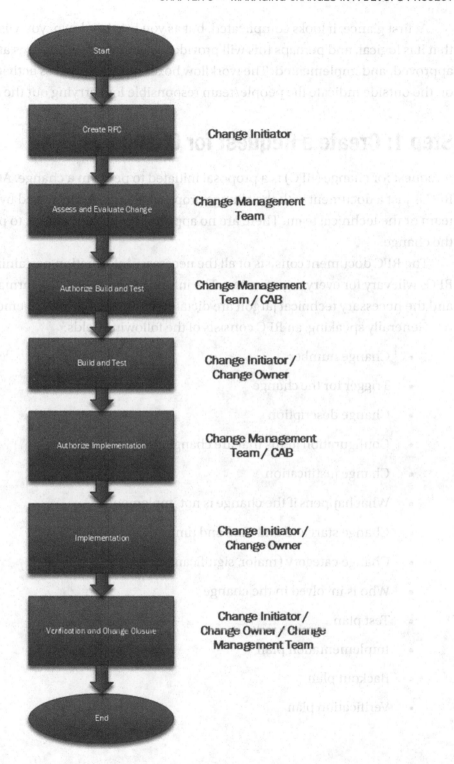

Figure 9-2. *ITIL change management process for normal changes*

At first glance, it looks complicated, but as you break it down, you will understand that it is logical, and perhaps this will provide insight into how changes are recorded, approved, and implemented. The workflow boxes indicate process activities, and the text on the outside indicate the people/team responsible for carrying out the activity.

Step 1: Create a Request for Change

A request for change (RFC) is a proposal initiated to perform a change. At this stage, the RFC is just a document with the change proposal. It is generally raised by the customer team or the technical team. There are no approvals or authorizations to perform the change.

The RFC document consists of all the necessary information pertaining to a change. RFCs will vary for every organization. The information needed, the format, the depth, and the necessary technical jargon are dictated by the change management policy.

Generally speaking, an RFC consists of the following fields:

- Change number

- Trigger for the change

- Change description

- Configuration items that are changing

- Change justification

- What happens if the change is not implemented

- Change start and end date and time

- Change category (major, significant, minor)

- Who is involved in the change

- Test plan

- Implementation plan

- Backout plan

- Verification plan

In most ITIL change management implementations, the RFC is directly available on IT service management tools such as ServiceNow and BMC Remedy. The details required are collected using web forms. A few years back, before ITSM tools were used, RFCs were presented in the form of Microsoft Excel templates. IT stakeholders used the copies of the template to populate and send RFCs to change managers for processing and approval. This process was rather cumbersome, as it was manual and was not governed using a system that applied the same yardstick for all change requesters. Change management has come a long way with the application of digital technology.

Step 2: Assess and Evaluate the Change

The RFC is analyzed and evaluated for risk, impact, and conflicts. The change management team is responsible for performing the assessment. They typically understand the change details, check whether the right stakeholders are indeed carrying out the change, and check for conflicts with connected systems and related changes going in during the same change window, among other conflict criteria. When the change is free of conflicts and is fully scoped and documented, it is scheduled to be presented in the CAB meeting.

In this activity, the role of the change manager is critical, as the change manager alone would have visibility across the organization's changes and is in the best position to identify conflicts, if any arise. You can think of change managers as the first line of defense against potential malicious changes.

I worked as an enterprise change manager at one stage in my career. The role was daunting, and knowing that the entire billion-dollar organization depended on my foresight and analysis was a scary thought. It was a challenging role that I enjoyed during my heyday in operations.

Step 3: Authorize the Build and Test It

The change manager calls for a CAB meeting of all stakeholders, from the technical and business lines in the organization.

In the CAB meeting, the change manager leads the meeting and presents the change. The CAB provides its approval for building and testing the change. The forum provides authorization for developing the change, and this is the most critical approval in the change management process.

Change Advisory Board

The CAB exists to support the change management team and to make decisions on approving or rejecting changes. To state it simply, it can be described as an extension of the change management role, and it exists to ensure that the proposed changes are nondisruptive, scheduled to minimize conflicts, prioritized based on risk and impact, and analyzed for every possible outcome to the hilt.

In an organization, you can have multiple CABs to support change management. A typical example would be a change being represented in an infrastructure CAB before it goes into the enterprise CAB and perhaps followed by a global CAB. The essence of having a CAB is important, not the way it gets implemented.

It is critical for the change owner to present the complete change to the CAB, with all the possible details. This will help the CAB decide on authorization to proceed with it. The CAB has the authority to ask for additional information to be gained, additional tests to be conducted and presented to them, and changes to be rescheduled. In some cases, the CAB can reduce the scope of the change to ensure minimal impact for business and technical reasons.

Composition of the Change Advisory Board

The CAB consists of stakeholders from the business as well as from service delivery. It can also include suppliers, legal experts, business relationship managers, and other stakeholders as identified by the chairperson.

CABs are dynamic. They could be different for every change that comes up for discussion. For a particular change, you may have Supplier A, a network manager, an exchange manager, and IT security. For another change in the same CAB meeting, you may have Supplier B, an application delivery head, and the SAP manager as CAB members.

Some organizations might insist on a set of permanent members of the CAB who sit in on all proposed changes, during every single CAB, and additional approvers (dynamic) would come and go as necessary.

No matter who sits on the CAB as an approver, the change manager, who is responsible for all the change management activities, is the chairperson of the meeting and decides on CAB members, on the changes that are represented on the CAB, and on the final decision of the CAB.

These are potential CAB members:

- Change manager as chairperson

- Customers

- Suppliers

- IT security

- Service owners

- Business relationship managers

- Application delivery managers

- Operations managers

- Technical subject-matter experts

- Facilities managers

- Legal representation

Emergency Change Advisory Board

Emergency changes require urgent attention and quick decisions. A CAB will not work for assessing emergency changes. These changes may happen in the middle of the night and require people to spring into decision-making mode to approve or reject changes.

The need of the hour to help change management decide on approvals is the emergency change advisory board (ECAB). The need for emergency changes pops up through incidents. It is possible that carrying out an emergency change (unsuccessfully) could impact the service more than the incident itself. So, in all necessity, there is a need for a few extra pairs of eyes to look at the proposed emergency change and provide the approval in the most awkward hours of the night (or day).

In most cases, a change ticket will not be created when approvals are sought. Change documentation may be done retrospectively for emergency changes. So, it is imperative that emergency changes are approved based on what is heard and what was relayed.

An ECAB is comprised of key members who provide their decision on the proposed change. ECABs mostly happen over a phone line, and it's extremely unlikely that there would be the luxury of members sitting across from one another. In some instances, the ECAB members may provide their approval individually but not while they sit in a gathering. Individual responses are collected, and the change manager uses wisdom in providing a direction for emergency changes.

Note   The changes that can come to an ECAB have specific, predefined criteria attached to them, such as a major incident requires executing a change for a fix that might have a significant impact on the organization or its customers.

Not all emergency changes call for an ECAB. Most of these are approved directly by the change manager if the ECAB rights are delegated. The critical ones, where entire enterprises could possibly be negatively impacted, would call for an ECAB to make decisions. The emergency change management process should not be exploited to push nonemergency changes under the guise of emergency changes.

It is possible that ECABs could ask service delivery teams to convert an emergency change to a normal change if a workaround exists to keep the service running. An example could be a database containing customer information that has gone corrupt and the database team wants to restore data from backup tapes. They want to do it as an emergency change to ensure that the customer's data are present before the customer's business starts in the morning. An RFC for performing an emergency change is raised. An ECAB is convened, and approvals are sought. Change documentation may be done retrospectively. The database team restores the customer's data from the backup tapes, and the emergency change is a success. During the business hours, the change document is created with all the bells and whistles, and it goes through the entire cycle of obtaining approvals for visibility and to keep other stakeholders who were not involved in the ECAB process informed.

There is a specific place for ECABs, and they have a specific job to do. This process must not be abused with trivial emergency changes knocking on the doors of ECAB. It dilutes the process and forces the ECAB members to lose focus on what really requires their attention.

Standard Change Advisory Board

The standard change advisory board (SCAB) is my own making; you will not hear or read about it elsewhere. A SCAB is a type of advisory panel that makes decisions on whether certain changes can be standardized. It is not a panel that works in the operations layers or service management but rather in the tactical realm.

The SCAB's prime objective is to ensure that the change presented to the board for standardization presents no major business impact if things were to go south; it also ensures that the possibility of things going wrong is minimal. Essentially, the SCAB is giving the technical team a free pass to carry out the standard change as per the agreed-on triggers with minimal external supervision. Therefore, it is important that the makeup of the SCAB consists of people who understand their areas very well and the associated business impacts.

Step 4: Build and Test

The build and test process, which includes software development, unit testing, system integration testing, and user acceptance testing, is not part of the change management process. I include it under the change management process to provide continuity in the process activities. These activities belong to the release and deployment process, which is discussed in Chapter 10.

Step 5: Authorize the Implementation

The test results are presented to the change governance body, meaning change management and the CAB. Based on the results, the change management team provides the authorization to implement the change in the production environment.

This is yet another important activity, as all the identified testing activities must be completed successfully before the change is allowed to be implemented into the production environment.

Step 6: Implement and Verify

The implementation and verification process is not part of the change management process per se. Like the build and test activity, this one comes under the release and deployment management process.

In this activity, the technical team will deploy the change in the production environment during the approved change window and perform post-implementation verification to ensure that the change is successful. If the change is not successful, it will be rolled back to the previous state if possible.

Step 7: Review and Close the Change

A post-implementation review (PIR) is conducted to ensure that the change has met its objectives. During this review, checks are performed to identify whether there were any unintended side effects. There are lessons to be learned from changes. If there are any such candidates, they are fed into the knowledge management database (KMDB).

After the successful completion of the PIR, the change ticket is closed with an appropriate status, such as implemented successfully, change rolled back, change caused incident, or change implemented beyond the window.

The responsibility for carrying out this activity generally falls to the change management team, but some organizations have the change owners and change initiators close the change with the correct status.

How Are DevOps Changes Different from ITIL Changes?

When I worked as an enterprise change manager, I often got feedback from various delivery teams and business teams stating that the process was rigid, and they had to plan at least a few months earlier for major changes. When the execution of change approvals started, the number of stakeholder identification and approvals was cumbersome. Some even shared with me they decided to forego certain changes because of the lack of time and the enormity of the bureaucracy that was instilled in the process. I was managing changes for one of Australia's biggest retail outlets, and with a number of moving parts including presence of legacy applications and the lack of a proper CMDB, the change management process indeed asked for good amount of lead time for the analysis to be completed before the change went in for approvals, and it had multiple approval stages because we did not have a matrix (usually generated through CMDB) to identify the right stakeholders.

This was a pure service management project with no principles of DevOps inculcated in it. Hypothetically speaking, if I were asked to redesign the change management project as the retail organization decided to jump fully into the Agile and DevOps world, I still would not compromise on any of the change management principles. There is nothing wrong with them; there is a reason why certain principles exist, like having a CAB look at the major changes and providing lead time before a change can be executed. What needs to be stronger, however, is the enablement of accurate information through a healthy CMDB and the use of common sense and logic to cut down on unnecessary bureaucracies. Changes are in fact one of the main drivers for DevOps. Changes are good. The Agile methodology embraces changes and does not shy away from it. The change management in DevOps should be a steering process more than a governance process. It must help steer the entire DevOps boat through automation, simplification, and common sense.

The Perceived Problem with ITIL Change Management

At the core, the ITIL change management process is designed to manage complex changes. It calls for all the bells and whistles in terms of governing changes, from planning to ensuring minimal risks while making a change. The underlying unstated motto is maximum and effective governance with minimal risk appetite. However, the ITIL process also tries to be nonprescriptive in suggesting that the organization implementing the process can decide on its risk appetite and the level of governance scrutiny over the changes.

Organizations that tend to go by the book prefer to take a risk-averse approach and bring in all the changes under the same umbrella (following the same process for data center migrations and periodic security updates on a server). This is, in fact, a good approach for an organization that has stepped into the ITIL world. But as companies mature, they must diversify and put changes of different magnitudes and impact into different silos, with a different governance structure. This is frequently missed in most organizations today. Therefore, there is a sense of antipathy toward the change management process as a whole.

Change managers and people governing changes are considered people who are against innovation, blockers of improvements, and bureaucratic and traditional by mindset.

The ITIL change management process is believed to be a sequential process, as you have a set process where certain activities have to be complete before you can embark on the next set of activities. The sequential nature is in stark contrast to what we are trying to achieve today, which is to develop and progress through iterative changes. Yes, the change management process is sequential. You cannot analyze a change if the change performed is not fully documented along with the risks it introduces. A decision on whether a change should go through cannot be made unless all the ducks are in a row.

There is a reason for change management's sequential nature. How can you add a roof to your building if the foundation and the pillars are not erected? It's a fool's dream to make changes either with no governance or by doing activities in parallel. This is where applying DevOps methodologies bring the focus required to better the process toward progression and agility.

DevOps to the Rescue

When you are faced with a problem that you address from a unilateral perspective (such as change management being sequential and DevOps being iterative), the solution can be evasive. What you need to do is think outside the box or look at the problem from a different perspective. Don't concentrate on the solution to a problem but rather take a step or two back and determine the objectives that you want to achieve. Find a solution to meeting the objectives rather than the problem itself.

The approach DevOps has adopted is to make frequent changes with minimal governance. If something goes wrong (even terribly), the impact will still be manageable, and rolling back will be brisk, as the rollback too will be quite straightforward (given that the change is a small one). When you do such multiple changes on the back of one another, you are managing the risk effectively, and the combination of the multiple small changes is equivalent to a decent-sized change (or even a major one). And you are able to deliver changes with (almost) no lead time and with minimal governance and manage risks that come as a result of its failure.

DevOps changes the nature of change management from being sequential to iterative. Within iterations, change management is still sequential, but because of the scale of the change, its sequentially does not become bothersome.

DevOps can be applied to projects that are built in an iterative model alone. For example, data center migrations or nonsoftware projects may find it difficult to follow the DevOps iterative approach to change management.

Project Change Management

Earlier in this chapter, I introduced the three types of changes in the ITIL world. When you look beyond ITIL and service management, there are multiple types of change management. I am not referring to the strategic, tactical, and operational changes. In project management, we refer to change management as *change control*, where changes pertaining to the triple constraints (namely, scope, cost, and schedule) come under the purview of the change management process. In fact, it is considered that quality is the fourth constraint, and this too comes under change management's purview.

Any changes to scope, cost, time, and quality go through the process of change control. It is a fairly bureaucratic and time-consuming process that considers changes to all aspects and measures the other constraints based on the change. This is a fairly common process that is implemented and practiced religiously in projects that follow the waterfall model of project management.

In the Agile world, although some projects do maintain this process and practice, I do not see its value. As the foundation of Agile project management stands on being Agile and embracing changes, keeping a change management process to manage the constraints is hypocritical. Let's say the process exists in an Agile project, and considering that changes are fairly common, at the beginning of every sprint, you might expect a formal change control process to kick in and sort out the impacts to other constraints. But to what effect? It is going to change again anyway. You are going to do this all over before the next sprint begins. The effort that goes into managing the changes will probably be a good percentage of the overall project management efforts, which is a waste.

But then, how do we manage projects when we have no control over the changes that are flowing in? The planning of projects is done at a fairly high level, and the actual planning of development is done during Agile release trains (ARTs) if SAFe is the Agile framework or at a sprint level for a Scrum-based approach. At the ART or sprint level, we know exactly what we are trying to achieve, and all the planning is done during the sprint planning session. The quadruple constraints are managed in the following manner:

- *Scope*: The scope of a sprint is managed by the product owner, who is preferably from the client organization, and they identify the set of user stories that will be acted upon during a particular sprint. This is a classic example of the client having complete control of the scope and cherry-picking the functionalities that need to be developed.

- In ART, multiple product owners and relevant stakeholders are involved during the program increment (PI) planning session held over two days. During the planning session, the set of functionalities that are to be developed over the next ten weeks are charted with ample wiggle room for changes during this period.

- *Cost*: The costing model for an Agile project has been a discussion that has sparked multiple conferences around the world as well as garnered energy and enthusiasm in digital and physical forums. The question is, if you are not clear about the scope, then how do you set a budget and track costs? Since the scope is a moving target, the costs too will start to shift right, making it impossible to manage. While scope being moved repeatedly is okay with most organizations, when it comes to finances, the freedom is measured differently. Organizations make yearly budgets and don't like the accounts to swing too far toward the red, and it is believed that Agile projects can completely blindside financial aspects.

- Models for budgeting and accounting projects can be created in a number of ways. Any project can be dissected into logical phases to track and manage discrete bodies of activities. We generally don't start with sprints from day 1, as there are usually project inception and road map planning phases that precede development and testing. Resource allocations follow the pattern of project phases with business analysts, architects, and environment engineers preceding the development team in projects. Figure 9-3 shows the IBM Rational Unified Process indicating the various phases of a project and the allocation of resources against each phase.

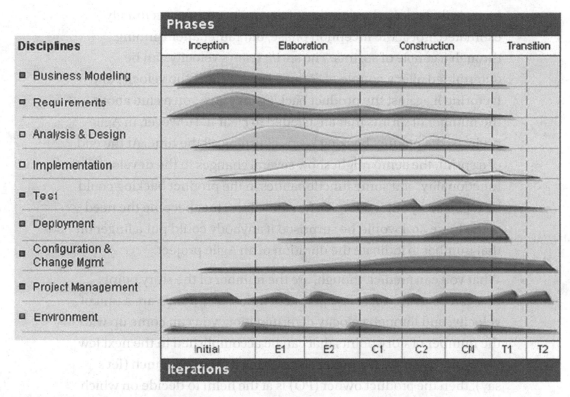

Figure 9-3. *Resource allocation in a project (image credit: ibm.com)*

- For resources that sit outside the sprint, based on the resource allocations, budgeting and costing can be done in a fairly direct manner. It gets easier for teams in sprints. A sprint is made up of cross-functional resources, and the sprint makeup does not normally alter through the course of a project. Therefore, the cost of resources for each sprint is a finite number, and multiplying this by the number of sprints gives a fairly accurate cost of the developing and testing efforts.

- *Schedule*: A waterfall project is a sequence of activities where the schedule is the direct result of all the sequential activities. The schedule is more likely to be extended than the scope. If more money is pumped in, the schedule can be squeezed by bringing in additional resources. In a lot of ways, in Agile project management, similarities exist in how the schedule can be managed through scope and costing. In a similar vein, scope and costs can be managed by managing the other two constraints.

- In an Agile project, the duration of the project can be accurately estimated, not at the inception phase, but rather after running through a couple of sprints. The sprint team's velocity can be determined after a couple of sprints. Determining the velocity and factoring it against the product backlog may give you a clue about the number of sprints that are needed to clear it. However, in Agile projects, the product backlog keeps churning all the time. At the end of a sprint, the demo might show several changes to the developed functionality, and some functionalities in the product backlog could be replaced by other complex functionalities that become the need of the hour. So, I would be surprised if anybody could put a finger on that number to indicate the duration of an Agile project.

- What you can predict, though, are the number of the story points that can be delivered over a period of time. Story points are a unit of velocity, and through velocity determination, you can come up with the number of story points that can be accomplished in the next few weeks and months. If a project is realizing a product launch (let's say), then the product owner (PO) is at the helm to decide on which user stories from the product backlog make it to the sprint backlog. The PO has been intimately aware of the velocity and can make calls to move priority items into a sprint.

- *Quality*: Quality, the fourth constraint, is a critical aspect of any project. It has a direct correlation to the cost of the project, as the costs tend to increase as you try to increase quality. Likewise, the schedule of a project tends to get extended when a high benchmark is set in terms of the quality to be achieved.

With DevOps coming into play, the game has changed. It is no longer just the project management aspects that alter the quality landscape. DevOps pipelines can ensure that the right quality is maintained in the software based on the set expectations. The best part is that the pipelines have to be set up once (with minor tweaks in between, of course), and the software can be run against the test scripts in an automated manner as many times as needed without requiring precious human resources. This setup creates a strong backbone to projects so you need not worry too much about quality pushing the schedule ahead or exceeding the budget. As long as the quality is well thought through and test scenarios and scripts target the heart of user stories, the quality of the software can stand on its own, even amid the ruins.

Risk Mitigation Strategies

The change management process exists to minimize the risks of untoward changes going into the system and to make the stakeholders aware of the possible risks by going through with the change so that the stakeholders can use their discretionary powers to either allow or deny the change. That said, the change management process prefers to go with approaches that are less risky.

DevOps is just not a methodology that automates everything and quickens the software delivery lifecycle. There is more to it than the general DevOps-aware public knows. One of the main tenets of DevOps is to uphold the quality of software, and the quality directly correlates to the risk each change imposes. The lower the quality, the higher the number of risks, and vice versa. Not only in the software industry but in all industries, the lack of quality is one of the top-rated risks, but by using DevOps methodologies and processes, organizations can ensure that high quality becomes a hygiene factor rather than something that they strive to achieve.

Auto-Deployment and Auto-Checks

Automation kills two birds with a single bullet. The first and fairly obvious one is that automation is far more effective than humans, and productivity is bound to increase, as the lead time from one activity to another is typically nonexistent. The second point I am making in this section is that automation eliminates human error.

Humans are imperfect; we have moods and emotions and are open to distractions. The activities we perform in the software delivery lifecycle are open to errors, even if it is a simple task of copying files from one location to another. Simply put, humans cannot be trusted to carry out work without errors because of carelessness, confusion, or ignorance. These shortcomings can be mitigated by asking systems to do this work, and if the design of automation is perfect (which is a one-time activity), then the machines can carry out the job entrusted to them error-free.

261

Automation does have its drawbacks. It does not have its own intelligence (duh!), and the activities that it can perform are merely repetitive ones that we have identified, designed, and implemented into it. These are some of the repetitive activities in a software delivery lifecycle:

1. Code review

2. Code build

3. Artifact storage

4. Artifact retrieval

5. Testing (all types including acceptance)

6. Defect logging

7. Deployment

8. Reporting

As discussed earlier, the quality of the software is greatly enhanced by applying automation with the right rigor, which correlates with various testing activities. However, what goes unnoticed is the risk mitigation through the other automation that we achieve, primarily in the areas of code reviews and deployments.

Software projects can reduce risks (and make change management happy) by employing automation to the fullest extent. In my experience, apart from the defects, manual deployments on the production environments gave rise to a number of failed changes, which can be easily mitigated through automating deployment by using tools such Ansible and Puppet. The automation design around deployments is straightforward and simple compared to the automation around testing, so projects must ensure that all their deployments happen automatically, leaving no leeway for human errors to creep in.

Static and dynamic code reviews give insight into the health of the code and the binary. By automating code reviews using tools such as SonarQube and Crucible, any risks emanating based on unhealthy coding practices and faulty binaries can be mitigated through a simple integration of the toolsets into the DevOps pipelines.

DevOps Change Management Process

I have heard from quite a few hard-core DevOps proponents that there is no room for the change management process in a DevOps-driven project. They say that things move way too fast for any approvals and bureaucracies to creep in. When questioned on the risks it imposes and the lack of transparency, I was told that the magnitude of changes was so small that most times even if things were to go south, they could fix it by any means necessary as long as they didn't have to report to any governance bodies. This answer did not bode well with me. Although I am a big advocate of moving to DevOps, implementing without a governance body, especially without a change management process in place, is a disaster in the making. This particular incident was one of the reasons for the existence of this book.

Earlier in this chapter, I introduced the ITIL change management process, which had at least a couple of "bureaucratic" blocks (if I may say so) that required authorization before moving forward. The rest of the activities mentioned in it were logical for any project in terms of coding, testing, and implementation. The ITIL change management process has been proven time and again to be effective against malicious changes, so my effort here is to incorporate the process in a DevOps project without sacrificing the process objectives and, at the same time, not introducing hurdles in the DevOps way of working.

In Chapter 1, I introduced the two main processes of DevOps that are leveraged to provide end-to-end delivery of software from the coders' desk to the production boxes: continuous delivery and continuous deployment. The change management process is adapted differently for each of the processes.

Change Management Adaption for Continuous Delivery

Typically in projects governed by ITIL change management, technical teams develop and test all their wares before approaching the change management process for approval. As the ITIL change management process recommends a two-step approval and authorization, first from the CAB and later from the change management team, the process is looked at as hindering the good work done by the technical teams and as obstructing the complete value by implementing it as soon as possible. This is a criticism from the ignorant, but when we try to adapt the same change management process in a DevOps project, it is important to emphasize the activities that need to be done even before the first line of code is written.

The change management process adaption for continuous delivery is indicated in Figure 9-4.

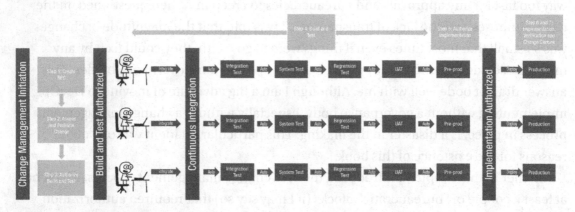

Figure 9-4. *Change management adaption for continuous delivery*

Continuous delivery is a development and deployment process where all the development and testing activities are automated, except for the deployment to production. The deployment to production requires a manual trigger for the binary to hit the production boxes.

Steps 1, 2, and 3: Change Initiation

The process of continuous integration, where coders check in their code frequently, followed by automatic build, review, and the test, should not and does not change. However, as indicated earlier, change management wants to know what you are doing before you start doing it.

Before the coding begins and well after the requirements are documented and agreed on and designs and blueprints are drawn up on paper, the change management process must be initiated. Initiation of the process begins by raising a request for change (RFC), indicating that you intend to make changes to the existing production environment. The RFC is analyzed by the change management experts and the relevant stakeholders, and the members of the change advisory board are identified. The CAB is convened, and the owner of the change is summoned to the forum to present the change and answer all the questions the CAB members might have. The CAB will provide its approval when the change owner convinces them of the change's value, along with the risks identified and its mitigation actions.

Step 4: Build and Test

After the CAB approval/authorization, the build and test activities can start; this is continuous integration. The continuous delivery process ensures that the coding and testing of the package are done at a level that the binary can be deployed at any time, meaning it is ready from a quality standpoint. The activities surrounding build and test in the change management process are correlated to Step 4.

Step 5: Deployment Authorization

When the binaries are ready to be deployed, meaning the coding and testing activities for the scoped set of requirements are completed, the change owner goes back to the change management team, indicating that the binary is ready to be moved into production. The change management team carries out some basic checks to ensure that the scope of the binary is as agreed on in the RFC and that the timelines for deployment are acceptable to all stakeholders. When all checks come out okay, they give their authorization for implementation, as indicated in Step 5.

Steps 6 and 7: Deployment and Verification

The binary is deployed to production during the agreed upon change window. Smoke tests and other verifications (post-implementation review) are done as part of ensuring that the change is a success. Once it is deemed successful, the change ticket is marked up as a success and the ticket is closed. These actions are indicated in Steps 6 and 7 in the change management process.

Continuous Delivery for Maximum Change Governance

The continuous delivery process is perhaps what the change governance prefers, as the process ensures that the production systems are untouched unless the proposed changes are tabled back to the change management team. This ensures that the deployments to production are governed closely, and this provides a sense of control for the change management governance teams.

Continuous delivery is a good process for most organizations, as they are able to draw a good balance between control and automation. The productivity is unaffected as the entire chain of development and testing activities is running smoothly on the back of automation; during deployment, governance comes into play to decide on further courses of action.

Change Management Adaption for Continuous Deployment

Continuous deployment is the big brother of continuous delivery. It is a lot older and more mature and prefers to take an automated approach. There is no manual trigger for binaries to move into deployment. As soon as a piece of code is developed and tested satisfactorily (as determined by machines), it gets deployed onto the production boxes automatically. There is a pause to see whether everything is okay because the changes being done are minute and chances are such that nobody will even notice them. It is a like an army of ants moving sugar crystals one at a time to its home, and over a period of time, a sack of sugar that was brimming is now only half full. The movement happened over a long period of time, continuously, and since the volume of the movement was so low, nobody even noticed it. After a couple of months, though, the change is visible to the naked eye. Likewise, continuous deployment changes happen in minute batches, and the collective set (say around 10,000) might represent a change that a project employing continuous delivery opts as a change.

Although most organizations feel trepidation about continuous deployment, it is not risky in the sense that it might break systems or it is an accident waiting to happen (because of a lack of governance). It is similar to a jigsaw puzzle being constructed, one piece at a time, and over a period of time, the picture comes together. If one of the pieces don't fit into a particular groove, no problem; it is pulled out and adjustments are made.

In Chapter 1, I explained continuous deployment in detail. Figure 9-5 is similar to the ITIL change management process. You can still apply and adapt the ITIL change management process for the continuous deployment process. But how can you govern when everything is automated? Everything is automated after the development starts, but there's a whole lot of open space before and after.

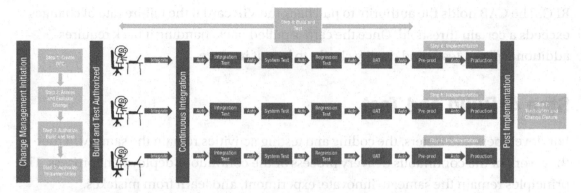

Figure 9-5. *Change adaption for continuous deployment*

At the outset, when you compare the change management adaption for continuous delivery and the change management adaption for continuous deployment, they look similar. But there is some shuffling of the change management process to fit the automated nature of the continuous deployment process.

Steps 1, 2, 3, and 5: Change Initiation and Authorization to Deploy

The change initiation steps of a creating an RFC and running through the CAB is similar to the continuous delivery process. The rules remain the same; there is no coding and testing to be done unless the CAB gives their go-ahead. But there is a difference in what you seek from the CAB.

When the change owner presents the change in the CAB, the change owner proposes that the CAB provides not only the approval for coding and testing but also the authorization to implement the binaries when they are deemed successful, generally multiple times a day. The change owner has to convince the CAB that the quality will not be compromised by sharing the DevOps pipelines strategies, plans, and various checks and balances put in place. This change presentation will be a lot more rigorous than the one faced for the continuous delivery process.

The CAB will provide its approval only if it thinks the pipeline that has been constructed meets all the quality standards put forth and does not come in the way of accepting more risk than necessary. Yes, once the approval and authorization are obtained, the change owner gets a VIP card to the production systems that lets them deploy as many changes as needed during the duration of the change, as specified in the

RFC. The CAB holds the authority to pull back the VIP card if the failure rate of changes exceeds a certain threshold. Once the card is pulled back, handing it back requires additional plans, tests, and quality checks to be put in place.

Step 4: Build and Test

For developers and testers, the coding and testing activities remain the same, whether they work in the continuous delivery process or the continuous deployment process. The principles remain the same: to innovate, experiment, and learn from mistakes.

Step 6: Deployment to Production

In Figure 9-5, you will notice multiple steps as the deployments happen multiple times. The DevOps pipeline is built in such a manner that if the checked-in code is successfully built and satisfactorily tested across all the various designed tests, the binary gets deployed into production automatically.

If any of the tests were to fail, then the binary would not get promoted to production, but rather a defect would be raised for the developer to fix and rebuild the code. This is a powerful way of ensuring that the quality is not compromised even in the wake of full automation; it's a hands-off approach. These quality parameters have to be built into continuous integration orchestration systems such as Jenkins and Bamboo.

Step 7: Change Verification and Closure

When binaries are deployed into production, the verification activities (smoke tests) are automated as well. The automation ensures that the deployed binary is working the way it should, and any anomalies should trigger an automatic rollback of the deployed binary.

The change closure happens when all the objectives of the change are met. The change management team will dive deep to identify what changes have been done and whether there is scope creep. In cases where scope creep is identified, the change owner is reprimanded, and the opportunity to leverage continuous deployment (VIP card) is not entertained in the near future.

Maximum Agility with Standard Changes

There's another way of achieving flexibility and agility in the world of governance in service management: standard changes. Standard changes are preapproved to be executed during certain scenarios. The changes that are categorized as standard usually don't bring down entire systems or cause fatal damages; they are low risk and low impact. Most important, these changes are documented with specific procedures.

It is believed that the maturity of the service management process of organizations offering services can be determined based on the number of standard changes in the system. That's true, as standard changes present a system to segregate difficult changes from the usual ones. The commonly performed changes are like a well-oiled machine. It operates smoothly and can be relied upon in most circumstances. Around 60 percent to 70 percent of the changes in any organization are common, repeatable, and straightforward. If all these changes are standardized, imagine the number of approvals that don't have to be sought and the number of meetings, telephone calls, and waiting around that can be skipped.

The advantage with standard changes is such that in most situations, it can be done on the back of any defined trigger. When a team wants to perform a standard change, they don't have to go to the change management team or to the CAB to present their change. They simply log a standard change in the system (yes, records are an absolute necessity), and then they can carry it out. Once it is successfully implemented (which is expected), the change is closed. *Voila*! There's no need to do a post-implementation review.

Examples of standard changes can be anything and everything under the IT sun that are repetitive in nature and do not pose major risks. That sounds like every single deployment you do under DevOps, doesn't it? Do you now see the connection between standard changes and DevOps? Typical examples include installing security patches on operating systems, running batch jobs, and performing nonintrusive backups.

Championing Standard Changes

I started my career as a service management consultant, and over the years, I earned the reputation of creating value for my clients through my designs and improvements. Implementing standard changes was one of my secret weapons. These are the first things I look at during an assessment:

- Does a robust change management process exist?

- Are there provisions for standard changes?

- How many changes are implemented as standard changes?

- Are standard changes monitored and audited regularly?

Standard changes are the low-hanging value creation fruit for clients. Most service management experts and consultants have yet to come to grips with them, and that hurts their clients' chances of making a difference through service management.

When I worked as an enterprise change manager for a retail organization in Sydney, Australia, I noticed that the organization did not have an active standard change process. A team of change managers reviewed and processed anywhere between 150 to 200 changes each day. They knew the changes so well that by reading the change summary, they would just scroll down to where the approval task became visible and hit Approve. What struck me first was why this human effort was even required as it amounted to a process to be followed rather than any visible value through the additional pair of eyes.

I got down to work by pulling data for the past couple of years and identifying such changes that could potentially be categorized as standard changes. I did some arithmetic and some guesswork to crunch some numbers, and according to my analysis, the organization could save efforts anywhere between 25 hours and 40 hours every single day. I considered modest numbers for my calculations, and this was the minimum savings that the organization could do. Considering 200 hours of weekly savings, and the average wages for a week typically in Australia is about $2,500 ($12,500 for the 200 hours saved). This saving translates to a monthly savings of around $60,000 ($12,500 X 4 weeks). Out of nowhere, the company could save over half a million every year, and they jumped onto it, not without a number of warnings from the company old-timers.

I managed to convert about 60 percent of the overall changes into standard changes within four months, and the benefits of showcased the power of Agile and DevOps. A number of businesspeople in this organization were relieved not to have to worry about getting approvals for all their changes. The best part was that they didn't have to bundle their changes into releases, so the changes went quickly to production and provided maximum benefit to the business.

Process for Identifying and Managing Standard Changes

There is no guideline or typical process in the ITIL publication to identify and manage standard changes. I believe the reason could be that standard changes are viewed as a mature service management element and the ITIL publication has provided guidance on processes and procedures around generic service management processes only.

I devised the process that I present in this section, and it has been implemented across organizations with excellent results.

In this process, Steps 1 through 4 are employed sequentially for identifying standard changes, and Steps 5 and 6 are independent activities for managing standard changes and are not carried out in any sequence. In fact, Steps 5 and 6 are processes on their own. (I provide a glimpse of how the process activities can be designed under the process steps.)

Figure 9-6 illustrates a process for identifying and managing standard changes.

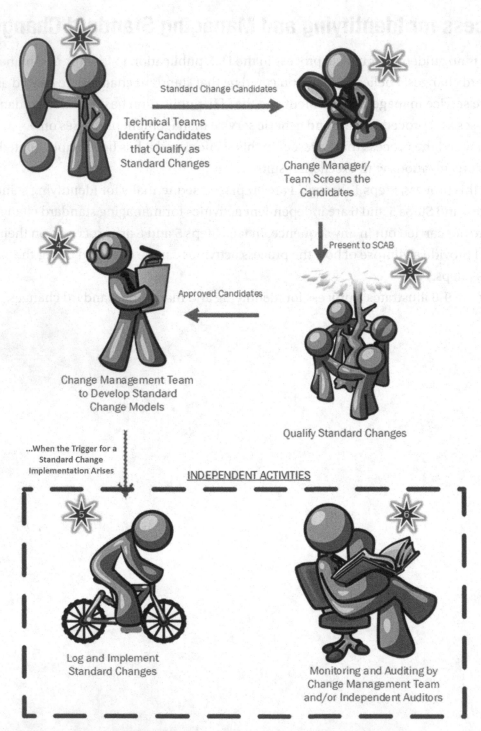

Standard Change Candidates

Technical Teams
Identify Candidates
that Qualify as
Standard Changes

Change Manager/
Team Screens the
Candidates

Present to SCAB

Approved Candidates

Change Management Team
to Develop Standard
Change Models

Qualify Standard Changes

...When the Trigger for a
Standard Change
Implementation Arises

INDEPENDENT ACTIVITIES

Log and Implement
Standard Changes

Monitoring and Auditing by
Change Management Team
and/or Independent Auditors

Figure 9-6. *A process for identifying and managing standard changes*

Step 1: Identify Standard Changes

The best teams or people to identify standard changes are technical teams themselves. They best know their line of work and the changes they have been carrying out for days, months, and years. They are in a great position to qualify those changes that are of low impact, that are low risk, and that are carried out multiple times in a given period. For example, if there was a super-simple change that gets carried out, maybe once every two years, then there is no point in standardizing it as the effort required to standardize it is far greater than implementing the change through the normal change process.

The process for nominating candidates can be done in a number of ways. The simplest one is to manage a Microsoft Excel template that asks for qualifying details to be filled out, such as the following:

- Summary of the change

- Justification on low impact

- Justification on row risk

- Number of times the change might be implemented in a given period, say a quarter

- Trigger for the change (under what circumstances will it be implemented)

- Document the steps were taken to implement the change

In some of my implementations, I did not use Microsoft Excel but instead used the change management module in the service management tool to obtain the candidates. In these implementations, technical teams have to create a new change (just as they would as any other change), but they select a particular type of a change (called a *standard change qualification*). This type of a change request will come ordained with a template for capturing all the necessary details. Once they click Submit, a change ticket number is generated, and the change ticket's workflow is designed to move the change ticket to the change management team's queue.

Step 2: Screen the Candidates

The change management team typically receives a number of candidates for standard changes. In fact, it is my experience that technical teams dump their entire list of changes in the qualification list for standard changes because they typically wouldn't prefer to work with normal changes, and standard changes make their life a lot easier.

The change management team vets the changes and the justifications and cross-checks from their records the number of times certain changes have been done in the past and their outcomes. If a simple change with low impact and risk was screwed up once before, the change management team would probably reject such a standard change candidate up until the point that such changes are implemented successfully at least a few consecutive times.

The vetting generally includes plenty of phone calls and conference calls with the technical teams to understand the change (if needed), and the extensive analysis is done. The intent is to ensure that only good changes are represented in the SCAB, and the chaff gets removed during this step.

Step 3: SCAB to Qualify Standard Changes

The SCAB is a virtual committee that I conceived of (you will not find it in ITIL publication or elsewhere). It consists of the set of (wise) people who get to decide which change candidates can be standardized and which should remain as normal. The board members are picked to cover all areas of IT to provide a full 360-degree dimension for the decision-making. I include the heads of infrastructure, the cloud, networks, applications, and databases represented on the SCAB. This provides good coverage across IT.

The SCAB is built along the same lines as the CAB. The CAB is more dynamic in nature, with its members differing based on the specific changes that get presented. However, the design of SCAB is to have a standard (static) set of members who collectively make decisions about standardizing changes.

A representative from the technical team is asked to present the change, explain justifications for why the change can be standardized, and answer all questions posed by the SCAB satisfactorily to have a change standardized. In my experience, at times, the SCAB just looks at a certain change and says, "Yeah, that's a standard change." The team's representative, although present, will be happy to get clearance with minimum work.

Step 4: Develop Change Models for Standard Changes

When the standard changes are approved by the SCAB, the change management team gets to work developing change models for the changes that are standardized.

A *change model* is a way of predefining the steps that should be taken to handle a particular type of change in an agreed upon way, according to the ITIL service transition publication.

During this step, a standard change template is created for a particular change (say running batch jobs), and workflows are created for, say, activity 1 to log the details of the batch, activity 2 to vet, activity 3 to program the batches, activity 4 to run the batches (automatically), and activity 5 to verify.

The activities defined for a batch job run are different compared to a database reindexing. A different set of activities is loaded in this workflow.

So, for every single standard change that's approved, the change management team has to develop change models individually, which is time-consuming. But, it's a one-time activity. Do it once, run it a zillion times!

With this step, the process for standardizing changes ends. Steps 5 and 6 are independent activities that can be carried out any time after changes have been standardized.

Step 5: Implement Standard Changes

The change management team informs the technical teams that the standardized change models are available on the change module of the service management tool for their perusal. The next time, when the situation arises to implement a change that is already standardized, the technical team creates a change ticket based on the standard change model for that particular change. The workflows are laid out beautifully for them to follow and carry out their change. An important thing to note is that the technical team can carry out a standard change only when the circumstance (trigger) presents itself.

For example, the SCAB, while standardizing changes, can impose constraints such as "For this particular standard change involving file backup, it can be done only during the following hours: 0000hrs to 0400 hrs." So, the technical team must comply and carry out the standard change only during the window. This is just one example of a constraint; there could be many others that the SCAB could impose.

All standard changes must be closed, and the closure of the standard change is the final task in the workflow. This is one of the areas where I find most teams lacking. Teams are good creating changes and carrying out workflow tasks until they hit the implementation stage. Once a change is implemented, they forget all about the closure as they get consumed in other technical stuff.

Step 6: Monitoring and Auditing Standard Changes

Some critics of standard changes feel that they are free tickets to technical teams to do as they please. They can do anything and everything.

It is true that technical teams can do anything and everything because they have all the access they need. But why restrict this criticism to standard changes alone? Teams can make changes even without a change in place (referred to as *unauthorized changes*).

So, how do we make sure technical teams don't abuse their power?

There are multiple ways to do this. In one of my implementations, I leveraged the monitoring tools and the CMDB with some automation conjoining the two to identify unauthorized changes. The monitoring tools keep an eye on the components and services that come under its scope and on a regular basis compare the monitoring elements with the CMDB's classes and attributes. The tools do a cross-sweep across the changes registered in the system, with a similar change window as the anomalies are identified. If a change ticket is present and is in the correct state with all the requisite approvals (for a normal change), then the anomaly is closed down. Otherwise, an anomaly flag is raised, and the change management team is alerted. The change management team will further work with the teams to identify the problem and work through it. Once done, they close the alert to logically close the flag.

This change monitoring solution was extremely effective in combating unauthorized changes more than identifying noncompliance on the standard changes. Therefore, the second part of this step is to conduct logical audits on the standard changes.

I recommend a monthly audit schedule by the change management team to audit the standard changes. Or you might do this more frequently, depending on the number of standard changes. If there are provisions or mandates to have an independent auditor perform audits on standard changes, they normally do it either once every six months or once a year.

Auditing standard changes is simple enough. Pull all the standard changes implemented during a period. Identify a sample set. Note the constraints, triggers, and documented steps for implementing standard changes. On the standard change tickets, check whether they meet all the requirements. There are a number of audit tools available, or a simple Excel spreadsheet will do. The audit process is a separate process by itself, but for standard changes and in the context of DevOps, it can be simplified to include only the items that matter.

Summary

This chapter looked at how changes are handled in a DevOps project. Change management in ITIL is traditionally bureaucratic, with lots of planning ahead of time and a number of approvals to go with it. DevOps, on the other hand, is rapid and there is no time for such approval processes. In this scenario, the topic of change not only needs to adapt but must transform to become Agile and accepting of dynamic changes. The changes that can be brought about to the change management process, especially empowering the teams through standard changes, form the bulk of the DevOps adaptation.

CHAPTER 10

Release Management in DevOps

We have come to the end of transforming ITIL processes into DevOps projects. Release management is the final (major) process that needs to be adapted to the Agile way of developing and promoting deployments into various environments.

The release management process is an inherent part of service management and software development. It has stood the test of time over the years and has changed rapidly as technologies have evolved and practices have transformed. Release management must deal with an influx of automation, the flair of collaboration, and the management abilities needed to see releases through.

This chapter jumps into the ITIL release (and deployment) management process and provides an overview of the process for managing releases. It then covers the DevOps way of understanding release management and proposes a DevOps adaptation of the ITIL release (and deployment) management process.

Change Management vs. Release Management

Change management is responsible for obtaining all approvals and authorizations from relevant stakeholders and for controlling what changes go in. The *release management* process, on the other hand, deals with the management of technicalities of the changes. For example, let's say that a change has been raised to deploy a new software version. The change management process exists to put the change in front of the jury (CAB) and obtain approvals and authorizations so that the change can be deployed seamlessly. The release management process manages the requirement gathering, coding, testing, and deployment activities of this change.

© Abhinav Krishna Kaiser 2023
A. Krishna Kaiser, *Reinventing ITIL® and DevOps with Digital Transformation*,
https://doi.org/10.1007/978-1-4842-9072-9_10

The two processes work together, exchanging information from related activities in the processes. This is illustrated in Figure 10-1.

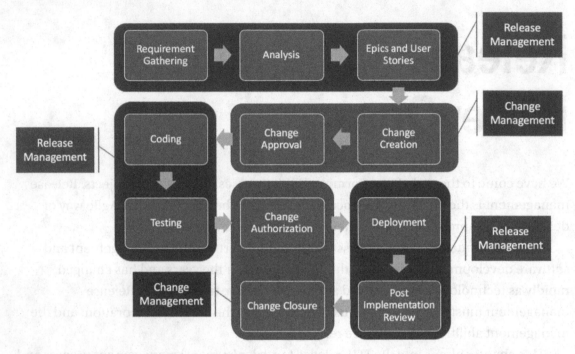

Figure 10-1. *The overlap between the change and release management processes*

In Figure 10-1, setting the scope, creating a plan, and gathering the requirements all come under the auspices of release management. Once there is a plan in place, including the known dependencies and impacts, the change management people do their bit of formal vetting and approval, before giving the go-ahead to begin development.

The change management approval process is necessary before the development begins because of two reasons:

- It ensures that the efforts that go into development and testing are not wasted if change management decides not to approve the changes.

- If there are modifications to the solution proposed by the CAB, then rework can be avoided.

The release management process manages the overall planning, building, testing, and deployment portions of the project. However, after the tests have concluded, the release status is back in change management's court. Change management's authorization is a necessary step to ensure that all the entry criteria for deployment have been met. It also provides oversight before changes to production are set to begin.

The deployment and post-implementation review activities are owned by the release management process, and the results are duly reported to change management for change closures with the appropriate status.

In this sample process, the release ping-pongs between the release and change management processes at least six times. The more exchanges there are, the better the process is for ensuring the quality of governance and sharing accountabilities.

It is also true that some of the activities that originally showed up during the change management process (such as deployment and post-implementation review) actually belong in the release management process. This was intentionally done to ensure the continuity of defining the change management process.

Release Management vs. Release and Deployment Management

In ITIL v3, the process pertaining to releases is called *release and deployment management*. There is no release management process in ITIL today. In the software development lifecycle, we use the term *release management*, and a process is associated with it. So, the question to ask is, what is the difference between release management and the release and deployment management processes?

There is absolutely no difference between the two processes. The ITIL process looks at a process from a service provider's perspective, and the software development's process gives it a development team's touch. So, whenever I refer to release management, I am also referring to the release and deployment management process. They are one and the same.

In fact, in the previous ITIL version, ITIL v2, the release and deployment management process was referred to as the *release management process*. Only in v3 (2007) did the process get coined the release and deployment management process.

The Basics of a Release

The release management process is a vast process that includes everything from requirements gathering to the nuances of planning, building, testing, and deploying. The entire project gets played out within the realm of the release. Therefore, it is key that the process is understood, precisely planned, and executed with razor-sharp precision.

This section introduces certain fundamentals of the release management process that are common across the ITIL and software development areas.

Release Units

A *release unit* is the combined set of items (configuration items, software files, and so on) that are released together into the live environment to implement a certain change ticket or multiple change tickets. The crux of the release unit lies in the grouping that is deployed as one unit.

Figure 10-2 shows an example of a release unit.

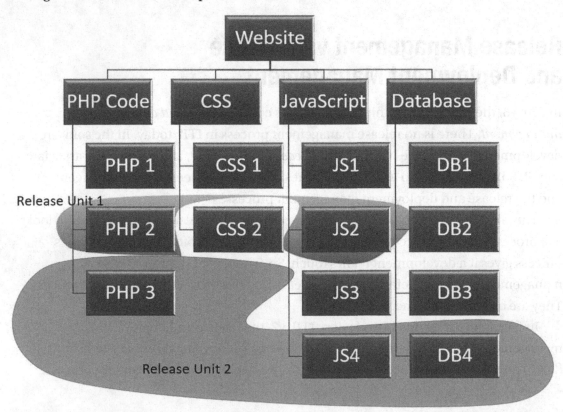

Figure 10-2. *Release units for a website*

Figure 10-2 indicates the various components of a website that are under the scope of release management. On this website, there are PHP, CSS, JavaScript, and database components. Under PHP, there are three files that make up the PHP code for the website. Likewise, for CSS, there are two files, and JavaScript has four files. Also, there are four databases storing the website's data.

Figure 10-2 highlights some boxes as Release Unit 1 and Release Unit 2. A particular functionality is being delivered by making changes to the files PHP2 and JS2, and together, the grouping is referred to as a *release unit*. This grouping is because the functionality is delivered together from both the files. Without the JS2 file, the PHP2 file alone cannot deliver the required changes. Likewise, the JS2 file cannot do the job alone. Therefore, the files PHP2 and JS2 are grouped together as a release unit.

The next release unit, Release Unit 2, is a bit more complex at the outset. It requires changes to the PHP3 and JS4 files and to the DB4 database. Just as in Release Unit 1, all three need to be deployed together to be able to deliver the required changes. Therefore, they are grouped as a release unit, united by a common release unit number, Release Unit 2.

Release Packages

A *release package* is a combination of one or more release units that will be deployed together as a single release. In Figure 10-2, let's say Release Units 1 and 2 are slated to be released under a single umbrella. This would constitute a release package.

A release package is not merely a grouping of release units to be released in one window. During its planning stages, the release package has to consider the effects of certain release units being together, especially if there is a strong dependency and high business impact between each other. The next steps for a release package planning are to ensure that sufficient resources are available to build, test, and deploy the release and to see whether sufficient infrastructure resources are available for accepting the new release packages. There could be many such considerations that determine how you will plan and execute a release package.

There is more to a release package than the release units. The associated deliverables, such as documentation, training, and compliance set, also make up the release package.

It is also important to note that release packages are uniquely identified with release numbers. The decisions for numbering are documented in the release policy, which states the manner in which release numbering takes place and sets the rules for other release-related decisions.

Types of Releases

The release policy defines the types of releases in an organization and at a project level. The distinction for differing types of releases is based on the complexity of the release, the schedule it maintains, and its associated business impact. Some organizations may decide to do a release every week with some minor updates and then, at the end of the month, plan for some serious packages to make their way into production. The release policy can state what constitutes a major release, a minor release, and even types of releases. I know of an organization that used to have medium and urgent releases. They may not find their way into ITIL, but nonetheless, if the organization finds them relevant, then that's all the more reason to keep them and define a number of types as necessary.

According to the ITIL publication, there are three types of releases, covered in the following sections.

Major Releases

Major upgrades to software generally come under *major releases*. The business impact of major releases can be anywhere between high and critical. This type of a release is the mother of all releases and takes priority over any minor releases happening around the same time. A number of resources are usually dedicated to the building and executing of a release, and from a compliance angle, all the hawks should watch it with extra attention.

In my experience, major releases are far and few between. In most cases, they are done on an ad hoc basis, with some organizations deploying at least four major releases in a year. For example, you might notice the updates being applied to the Windows operating system. Some changes are quick and may not even demand a restart. However, additions, modifications, or the removal of integral features happen on the back of major releases that could require several minutes of installation followed by multiple restarts.

Minor Releases

As the word *minor* suggests, *minor releases* include release units that are small and do not usually bring down the business if the release goes south.

Minor releases are usually carried out on a weekly basis or monthly. It all depends on the number of changes and the number of resources available to work on them.

Emergency Releases

Emergency releases are the planning and execution counterparts of the emergency changes. They come into play on the back of an emergency change and are deployed (usually) to fix an incident and to avert any negative business impact.

The number of emergency releases reflects negatively on the organization and the project. Therefore, this is a type of release that's not preferred or planned but rather is imposed by a turn of events. It is also not uncommon that the release policy allows emergency changes to be helicoptered in only between releases, say between two minor releases.

Early Life Support

Early life support is one of the key lifecycle stages in the ITIL service transition phase. In non-DevOps projects, the team that supports the services is different from the team that builds it. The gap between the two teams is bridged through a temporary phase of overlap right after the deployment is done.

The build team provides support right after deployment, and the support team usually supports them. So, when incidents happen, the build team is ready with the fixes right away because they know the product in detail. At the same time, the support team that's monitoring them will get a chance to learn. Since the support is provided during the first few weeks after deployment, it is referred to as *early life support*. Some organizations refer to it as a *hypercare period,* where the best resources are tasked with providing support during the product's initial days.

Generally speaking, during early life support, the SLA does not kick in nor does any of the other parameters that are used for measuring the level of service.

Early life support is completely eliminated in DevOps projects, as the team that builds and the team that supports are one and the same, and therefore having a hypercare period isn't relevant. Or in other words, the product that's being serviced is always in hypercare support, meaning that it gets the best support possible during its lifecycle.

Deployment Options

When the software is ready to be deployed, you can deploy it directly across all the target devices in parallel or do it in pieces. Based on these strategies, the ITIL service transition publication talks about two basic types of deployment options.

- Big Bang option
- Phased approach

Figure 10-3 illustrates both approaches.

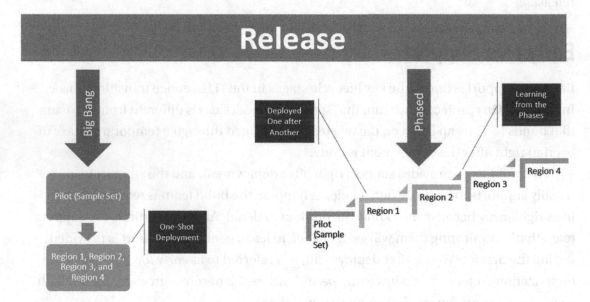

Figure 10-3. Big Bang and phased deployment options

The Big Bang Option

The Big Bang option is derived from the Big Bang theory, which states how the universe came into being from a single, super force. Likewise, when software is deployed, it is deployed to everything that's under the scope at the same moment. In other words, all users get to experience the software (or the trauma of deployment) at the same time. This type of deployment is referred to as *Big Bang deployment*. It is also called *parallel deployment*. In Figure 10-2, after a pilot deployment to a sample set of users, the release package is deployed to Regions 1, 2, 3, and 4 at the same time.

The upside is that all users will be in a position to enjoy the upgraded services at the same time, and the service provider can claim to be consistent with its services. This is generally preceded by a pilot (or multiple pilots) to ensure that the software does work. When the pilot is deemed successful, a time is set, and the users are made aware, and then the entire scope of the targeted system will receive the release package.

The Big Bang option is almost never considered in these modern times. You might have noticed that releases happen to certain smaller regions first (pilot) followed by, say, the United States. iOS updates are known to follow this pattern. The downside of deploying to everyone at once is pretty significant. Any mistake will result in a disaster, and the negative business impact that follows will be unbearable. Therefore, no organization likes to take chances by pushing everything out worldwide in one go.

The Phased Approach

The alternative to the Big Bang option is to deploy in a phased manner. In Figure 10-3, an initial pilot to a sample set of users is followed by a phased deployment to Region 1 first, followed by Regions 2, 3, and 4. It is okay for the deployments to have weeks and months between them to allow for the learning to sink in and corrective actions to be implemented before the following release. This is the biggest advantage of a phased approach. Organizations can manage their risks and target their audience based on various parameters. For example, say an organization wants to deploy packages during usual downtimes in different regions of the world. This may be the Diwali season in India, Christmas in the United Kingdom, and Rosh Hashanah in Israel.

I don't see any obvious downsides to the phased approach except that it requires a lot of continued planning and differences in release version between users, so this may end up being a support challenge. But there are a number of ways to mitigate this.

There are multiple variations of phased approaches that can be conceived apart from the geographical deployments described earlier:

- Different features are deployed separately, so users can enjoy certain features first.

- All users face downtime at the same time, although the deployment happens in phases. This usually refers to a deployment taking place on the tail of a previous one.

- A combination of geographical deployments, feature-wise deployments, and downtime for all.

The Four Phases of Release Management

Release and deployment management has four major activities, or *phases*:

- Release and deployment planning

- Release build and test

- Deployment

- Review and close

Release and Deployment Planning

A good amount of planning has to go into release activities. A good plan is half the job. To ensure that the release is successful, it is critical that the architects and other experts brainstorm various possibilities, risks, and mitigations.

Before the plan gets underway, change management typically provides approval to start the planning process. However, in practice, the approval to create release and deployment plans is provided from a different body, such as a transition management group or a group that governs the projects that are chartered. In principle, these bodies govern the changes made to the system, and this can be the equivalent of change management authorization to create release and deployment management plans (part of the transition plan in the transition planning and support process).

Release Build and Test

The release and deployment plans are submitted to the CAB. The plans are dissected from every possible angle to identify loopholes and vulnerabilities. Upon successfully passing the CAB and change management scrutiny, the authorization to build and test the change is provided.

Building a change amounts to developing the code, getting hardware ready, or addressing the prerequisites for building the change.

There are various types of testing. The most popular ones are unit tests (UTs), where individual components of a change are tested in isolation. Upon successful testing, the individual components are conjoined, and a system integration test (SIT) is performed.

After a test successfully passes, users are asked to test the function in the user's environment to check whether the change meets the requirements that are needed. This is called *user acceptance testing* (UAT). The testing is deemed complete after the user provides the okay that all elements of the change meet the requirements and are good to proceed.

The definitive media library (DML) is a repository where all the original code, software licenses, and other software components are stored, physically and logically.

When release and deployment management provides ample proof that the testing has been successful, change management provides authorization to store the code/software in the DML (discussed in Chapter 6).

Deployment

The results of release and deployment testing are brought before the CAB once again, and the results are vetted for possible complications and unseen bugs. When the CAB and change management team are happy with what they see, they authorize the change for deployment during the planned change window.

Deployment is a common term for implementation. It could include retiring services or transferring services to another service provider as well. For simplicity, I'll just refer to it as deployment.

Deploying release packages is a specialized skill and calls for the alignment of a number of parameters. There are a number of approaches to the release package. The Big Bang approach is used when all the CIs are targeted to receive the package at the same time. Say there are 10,000 workstations that need to get a security patch. All 10,000 systems will receive the release package during the same window.

This method is rarely employed, as it has the ability to choke the network. And, if there are any mishaps, all the targeted systems could be affected, causing severe damage to the customers. The most popular approach is a phased one, where the release is staggered through multiple phases to minimize complications and avoid network choke. In the same example involving 10,000 systems, it could be phased to target 1,000 systems a day and to run the entire release cycle for ten days.

Review and Close

After deployment, the release and deployment management process conducts a review (post-implementation review) to check the performance of the release and assess the targets achieved. Lessons learned are documented in the KMDB. The release is closed after the review.

Releases in DevOps

The release management phase discussed earlier in this chapter is highly sequential in nature. Its sequential nature is the backbone of the waterfall model of project management. Agile is iterative in nature, and so is DevOps. So, can the sequential release management process be compatible with the iterative DevOps model?

Yes! Release management is sequential in nature. It waits for one activity to complete before the next kicks in. I am referring to some of the high-level activities such as planning and deployment. Unless planning is complete (consider a roadmap), development cannot begin. Unless testing is complete, it should not be deployed. Therefore, it is fair to assume that the sequential nature of release management is best handled the way it is designed. But it is also possible to make it a whole lot more Agile and give it a hint of "go-with-the-flow" flavor.

Sequential and Iterative Nature of the Process

Figure 10-4 illustrates the release management process's iterative and sequential phases.

The release and deployment planning was considered to be a detailed exercise that spelled out all nuts and bolts of the release, including the date and owner. With the advent of Agile, the planning bit of the exercise was simplified, with more importance given to the subset of requirements in development. In addition, a roadmap was created by the strategists in the organization. The planning exercise is an iterative process where the immediate bits of the puzzle are determined, and once it is close to being delivered, the next bit is brainstormed and planned. This way, the planned items more often meet the deadlines assigned to them and make sense, instead of a whole bunch of missed timelines and detailed explanations and root causes for the misses. In effect, the planning phase that used to be highly sequential is now carried out in a highly iterative manner.

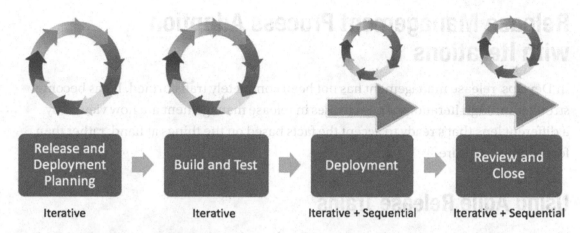

Release and Deployment Planning	Build and Test	Deployment	Review and Close
Iterative	Iterative	Iterative + Sequential	Iterative + Sequential

Figure 10-4. *Release management iterative and sequential components*

The next phase consists of the build and test activities. These activities are technical in nature. Chapter 1 explains how the continuous delivery phase is built, which is iterative as well.

When the product is built and tested, it is time to deploy it. In continuous delivery, the objective is to keep the package deployable at all times. Therefore, when you implement continuous delivery, the deployment phase becomes sequential as the build and test activities need to be complete, and a suitable window needs to be identified for the deployment to happen.

Let's say you are going in with a continuous deployment type of delivery, where every time a piece of code gets checked in, it gets tested automatically, and if it meets all the set criteria, it gets deployed automatically. In such instances, the deployment piece does not wait for a precondition but rather goes with the flow (the flow being the test criteria being met and the coding and testing taking place in iterations). So, the deployment phase too becomes iterative in nature.

Finally, the review and close phase follows the previous deployment phase. If the deployment phase is sequential, the review and close phase takes on a sequential tone (and likewise for an iterative nature).

Release Management Process Adaption with Iterations

In DevOps, release management has not been completely transformed. It has become stronger through iterations. The activities in release management are now viewed by a different lens that's ready to accept the facts based on the things at hand, rather than foretelling the future.

Using Agile Release Trains

The range of planning that we have started to do under releases is not limited to a sprint alone, which is the Agile/Scrum way of working. However, using the SAFe framework and applying release management to Agile release trains (ART) gives us a steady plan for the upcoming ten to twelve weeks. The entire ART represents a release with software packages pouring in every couple of weeks at the end of each sprint. When we put the sprints together along with their outcomes, the end product is the release package.

Applying Release Management to Continuous Deployment

In the DevOps world, the release management process can be adapted depending on the kind of process (continuous delivery or continuous deployment) you leverage. Let's say that you plan to employ continuous deployment where every time a package is tested successfully, it gets deployed automatically. Release management's role here is to ensure that the path to production is stable, relevant, and consistent.

The release management process will have a lot of planning and execution during the initial two phases rather than the final two phases. Still, if a faulty package makes its way to the production, the ball falls back into the release management's court to fix the pipeline and the associated factors that make the pipeline work (such as testing scenarios, scripts, and so on). Also, release management has to identify multiple release windows for the deployments to take place because the possibility of deployments happening multiple times a day is routine in a continuous deployment process.

Applying Release Management to Continuous Delivery

In continuous delivery, however, saneness can be maintained to a certain extent. The release management process becomes bimodal, with release planning and builds/tests using the iteration model and deployments and reviews taking the traditional sequential approach.

The plan for continuous delivery works well with ART, with the planning exercise being done once every 12 weeks and refined as the sprints go along. The sprints are executed in iterations with the software packages, getting them to a state of readiness but not getting deployed. When all the pieces of the release are developed and integrated, the deployment happens (sequentially) followed by a review of the release.

Most organizations tend to go with this approach, mainly because it gives people in charge a sense of control. Since continuous delivery still commands a manual trigger before deployment, the decision-makers feel comfortable in opting for a process that not only accelerates production but also awaits a formal order before hitting production.

Maturity is leading the way toward continuous deployment. The decision-makers, after a few releases, will realize that their decisions have always been backed by the figures, that the releases put forth in front of them have always been good for production, and that their decisions have become just a formality. So, the end game will always be with continuous deployment.

Expectations from Release Management

Every process has to meet certain objectives to justify its existence. Incident management exists to reduce downtime and to restore service as soon as possible. Change management is implemented to control the production environment from malicious changes. Likewise, at a high level, release management exists to ensure that releases are deployed successfully in the targeted environment.

In DevOps, the processes don't get away with such simple objectives. There's always more to the story, such as productivity, effectiveness, efficiency, and automation.

The DevOps release management process's expectations are multifold. We are not happy with just successful deliveries; we need them faster, and the process for delivering must be consistent and not two-paced.

Since there is potential to make hundreds of changes in a day, it is critical for the release management process to provide strong auditing capabilities. Most important, we need to trace the feature changes back to their requirements in a straightforward manner.

Where there is DevOps, there's automation. Release management in DevOps must be automated to a greater extent than before and that's one of the key expectations from the process. Automation ensures a systematic execution of work processes, an avoidance of defects owing to human errors, and consistency in delivery.

Blue-Green Deployment

Seeking downtime for releases is a thing of the past. In DevOps projects, carrying out deployments without downtime is the norm, and release management must do this at a minimum. There are a number of ways the process could achieve this. One such example is the *blue-green deployment* approach, whereby two environments run in parallel (each of the environments is designated with the color blue or green).

Figure 10-5 illustrates blue-green deployment approach. We have two parallel environments, designated as blue and green. The environments are identical; however, one of them is active and the other passive. In this example, let's say that the blue environment is active and the green one is passive. This refers to the load balancer routing all the user requests only to the blue environment and not to the green environment.

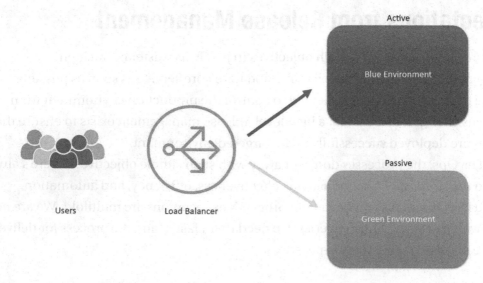

Figure 10-5. *Blue-green deployment*

Let's say that we have a release on hand that requires mandatory downtime to install and configure packages, followed by elongated sanity reviews. In this scenario, the passive node (green) is deployed first. As there are no user requests being routed, there is no question of seeking downtime. The users continue to operate normally in the blue environment. When the deployment is successful and the environment is production ready, the load balancer routes all the user requests to the green environment. While users are busy operating in the green environment, the blue environment goes down, gets deployed, and becomes production ready. The load balancer can either be set back to blue or be shared between green and blue; this is a decision of the architects. *Voila*! Both environments have been deployed with packages that required downtime, but the users never felt the effects of the downtime.

The Scope of Release Management

The scope of release management based on the activities we discussed falls across the software development and software support teams. Because of the overlap, the process has traditionally lacked ownership where one entity throws it back to the other, stating various reasons for complications. For example, during the time of deployment into production, where production is owned by the support team, the development team takes their hands off the deployment and related configuration settings. This will, in turn, become a support issue. But the support team is rather clueless, and they need the help of the development team to set the right configurations. The only way out is that the two teams work together to move past the obstacles and to make the release a success.

Enter DevOps! The reason that DevOps adapts so easily with the release management process is that it has already solved the unending problem involving collaboration and cooperation between the development and support teams. Under the DevOps umbrella, both teams are placed on the same team, and they don't have a choice but to work as a team. Either both fail or both succeed. The obvious sane choice would be to cooperate and see through the deployment and the acceptance parameters of the release.

As per the Agile and DevOps principles, the entire ownership of the release will lie with the team, as they are self-supervised, although we have a formal release manager still in existence to give the release a touch of what the customer is thinking. With the entire team working toward the release's success, the argument about whether development or support is taking the ownership of the release is put to rest.

Automation of Release Management

The release management process as defined in ITIL is solid and mature. I don't see any need for it to be altered or adapted for a DevOps project (in terms of the process activities). However, what you can still do is make it more efficient by using the power of technology to automate certain aspects of release management.

Of the four phases of release management, at least two can be automated: release build and test, and deployment. The majority of the time of a release is taken up during these two phases, and it absolutely hits a home run with the automation running against activities that are designed to eat up most of the release time. Another important concept in deployment is a rollback plan. This plan is used when the deployment fails and needs to be recovered and restored to the previous state. Automatic rollback is achievable using tools such as Ansible and Puppet, and it can help to restore the original build and configuration efficiently.

The automation for releases is done on the pipelines that are built on release orchestration tools, such as Jenkins and Urban Code. I touched upon the pipelines in the initial chapters that form the basis for building and implementing continuous delivery and continuous deployment. The pipelines define the various stages of software development and testing that make the software acceptable to end users. The pipeline ensures the developers and testers spend their efforts doing what they do best—coding and writing scripts. The execution of these activities such as software build and testing is taken care of by the orchestration tools. The results are duly updated, and the defects are logged in the designated project management tool.

To state an example of the kind of efforts that can be saved through automation, consider this: every time you make a change to a functionality, there is a need for the regression issues to be tested. Testers spend a good amount of effort testing for regression defects every time the changes are put back into the development and testing environments. The time taken to test regression issues forms a major portion of the overall testing efforts. You can automate regression testing, and every time a new check-in happens, the testers don't have to fret anymore. The machines take over automatically by checking all scenarios of regression and reporting on the status. If there are any defects, the orchestration tools generally have the privileges to log defects automatically based on the result of the regression run. Just merely logging defects saves testers tons of time that they can use to write more scenarios and automation scripts to make the testing process more accurate and intensive. Before the time of automation, all the efforts going toward test execution and defect logging were wastes of time that were effectively discarded.

The automation of release management activities is not restricted to testing alone. The version control system that is part of comprehensive configuration management (CCM) is a major catalyst for making automation work smoothly. Imagine working on automation without a single source of truth. It's like an airplane trying to land on a runway without runway lights. There is no reference point for the plane to land, and similarly, the coding, testing, and automation activities designed around the activity fail without the integration of CCM and automation.

The DevOps Release Management Team

I made it pretty clear that the ITIL release management process is good as is with some iterations plugged in. The process is good; however, the people who run the process in a typical service management project may not be as lucky. The release management teams that are responsible for driving the process from the planning sessions until the closure of releases are no longer needed. Am I crazy to suggest that we have the process but not the people who run it?

Remember that the objective of DevOps is to ensure that productivity increases and that no humans are needed for repetitive activities. The release management process falls into the direct firing line of the DevOps objectives, and this has consumed the team that runs the process. Yes, the reasons are obvious: the majority (or all) of the build, test, and deployment activities are done by machines. These two activities account for more than 70 percent of the overall release management activities. So, automation has simply killed the release management team! Yes, that is indeed true, but what about the remaining phases, like planning, reviews, and closure? You certainly can't ask the machines to do these too. Definitely not—at least not the planning phase because of the human's cognitive powers, which cannot be matched by the machines (yet).

Then who is going to carry out the human part of the release management process? We explore this further in the next section.

Before you embark on specific roles, you should be wary that DevOps teams are made up of two sets of broad roles that people play. There are developers, and then there are operations. The way they communicate or the terminologies they use is not even the same. When an operations person talks about a service, that person basically means the service you are offering. The same service is also a product that is being developed. But the developer might not call it a service but rather refer to it as software or a system.

That's not the only difference. Even the tools they typically use are different from one another. The development team uses a tool such as Jira for managing its product backlog, while the operations team uses a tool such as ServiceNow. So, the lack of a single source of truth might lead to more differences.

This is precisely why release management is handy and provides the common understanding between the two teams. The teams can understand each other because they stretch across both sets of roles and people. This helps the overall DevOps teamwork and collaborate for the betterment of the project.

Release Management Team Structure

In DevOps projects, having a release management team is a luxury, given that the entire focus is on optimization and there are fewer human hands to work on repetitive actions. However, in the industry, many DevOps projects still leverage release management teams to make releases work. The structure, however, differs from one organization to another. Let's explore some common ones.

Separate Release Management Team

This is the traditional approach where a separate release management process exists to take care of releases. The release management team is generally governed by a separate release management practice that ensures that common release management practices are followed across all projects under their control. So, in a way, there is an amount of standardization they bring to the table.

Having additional hands to work on releases is a godsend, especially if the release management teams start working with the team rather than acting as stage gatekeepers. However, since the release management team gets helicoptered into projects, their intimacy with the ground situation, solution, and customer expectations can be lacking in some ways. Also, this option costs more and affects the cost of delivery.

Release Management by the Delivery Team

The delivery teams (development) can run the management of releases. This is helpful because of their closeness to the development and their intimacy with the requirements and customers. Organizations that cannot afford to invest in separate teams go for this approach.

On the downside, such a release management team could end up playing both sides, development and release management. Unfortunately, the conflicts of interest will be written all over the decisions made. This option is generally implemented only when there are limited finances, and I do not recommend it.

Release Management by the Operations Team

In contrast, you could have the operations team working on the releases. They are close to the production and the users, so they make a good choice for managing releases, right?

Not really. Like the separate release management team, they end up being on the outside of the solution and could end up not knowing what the customer wants. But wait—in a DevOps team, the operations team works closely with the development team. So, they are close to the solution. Yes, that is true, and therefore they make the second best choice for a release management team. You might be thinking about the best choice, though. The next section introduces the best option for a release management team.

Welcome Release Manager, the Role for All Seasons

You can probably guess that a release manager is somebody who manages releases! This is a simplistic definition of a release manager and does not emphasize the value of the position. Yes, in an ideal sense, the release manager is in charge of managing releases and ensures that the releases flow as per the design, with no anomalies. The release manager also makes judgment calls on the contents of a release, sets deployment parameters, and manages stakeholders.

However, there is more to a release manager than this definition. Remember the picture from Chapter 1 that illustrated the actual distance between the development and operations teams in a traditional project? See Figure 10-6.

Figure 10-6. *Cloud of uncertainty in a traditional project*

Chapter 1 also states that, through the merger of the development and operations teams, you are breaking down the barriers, and the teams don't have to be on either end of the cliff. Rather, they can come together and work as one. This is the premise for making DevOps work.

However, how do you bring the two teams together? Where's the bridge? See Figure 10-7.

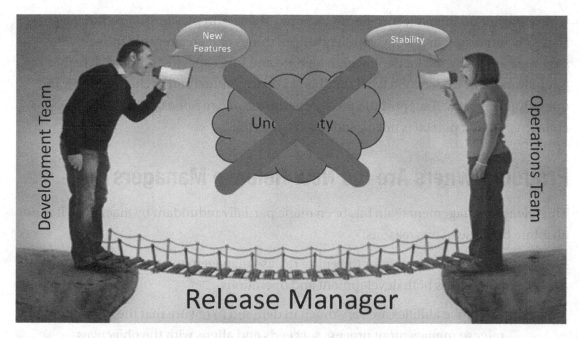

Figure 10-7. *Bridge between development and operations teams*

The bridge between the teams is the release manager. Release management's scope starts with the business analyst, runs through the development team, and ends with the operations team. So, in effect, release management cuts through multiple teams and brings all the involved teams to the table to get the job done. The person who manages the releases, the release manager, is at the forefront of releases—understanding requirements, planning for its execution, running the code builds and tests, deploying them onto target locations, and finally carrying out the checks and balances to put a logical closure to the release. Throughout the lifecycle of release management, the release manager will have brought multiple teams to the same table, challenged the teams to work together to achieve what is needed, and built a bridge between the development and operations teams, as illustrated in Figure 10-7. When there is a bridge, there is a certainty because the teams don't have to yell to make themselves heard but rather can cross over to the other side and work shoulder to shoulder to ease the workload.

The bridge between the teams would not be possible if not for the release manager. Yes, the management bit is what the person does as a hygiene factor, but building the bridge will actually get the job done with minimal controversies, conflicts, and escalations. There is nobody else on the DevOps team whose influence has such a wide span across the project. Take, for example, the Scrum master. The Scrum master is merely interested in the development side of things and ensures that the software packages are delivered for deployment on time and in an effective manner. Whether the operations team understood what they had to do to conduct sanity checks or how the operations teams will support the product in the future are none of the Scrum master's concerns, so that person is not a good fit to be a bridge!

Product Owners Are the New Release Managers

The release management team has been made partially redundant by machines. It is not absolute because of two reasons:

- You need an owner for the entire release management process that cuts across both development and operations.

- Cognitive abilities are very much in demand to ensure that the release management process succeeds and aligns with the objectives set forth.

The person who manages the entire release from end to end is the release manager and is still necessary. However, the release management role went from being a full-time position to a part-time one (statistically speaking), mainly because of the diminished work (thanks to automation). Capable release managers are:

- Well aware of the customer landscape, the requirements, and to an extent the business priorities

- Fully involved in the development and deployment processes

- Knowledgeable of operations and their acceptance criteria

The person who could do all this in the past was the product owner (PO), and thus that person is a favorite choice for a part-time release manager. POs are an adequate choice mainly because of their closeness to the business and to the development and operations teams. The person was like a bridge between the two entities and was expected to keep the boat going in the most turbulent conditions.

Product owners are indeed the best people to plan considering that they had a first-hand knowledge of the priorities of the user stories in the product backlog. This gave them a clear advantage to pick and choose what went into a release, considering that we were not operating in a continuous deployment mode. Clubbing user stories for a particular release is rather a hard task considering the dependencies that exist between them, and the PO can definitely make it look easy.

The PO is expected to be part of the sprint and carries out the role in terms of clarifying requirements. Combining this with the control over how the code flows and the quality that gets embedded gives this person the authority, flexibility, and freedom to spin the yarn the way they want. On the flipside, however, the entire responsibility for the release and the customer expectations lie heavily with the PO, making this person seem like a single point of failure. This is why you need to have powerful and robust governance in place to support the product owner to become successful. I can't comment enough on the importance of a governance body to steer the decisions and directions. The PO is only human and can take a wrong step once in a while. If the governance body is there to support the PO, the product owner is stronger, and the product and the release have no other alternative but to become a roaring success.

Summary

Release management in ITIL is fairly straightforward and looks into the nitty-gritty of getting releases into production. It is tightly coupled with the change management process. When this process is overlaid with DevOps, it takes on a deeper hue. The process gets into multiple layers of activities, including automation, which is the desired state in DevOps. Release management in DevOps is a field in itself because of the synchronization it needs between various parties using the same DevOps pipelines to release into lower environments to begin with and into production. The chapter also recommended that the role of a release manager in a DevOps project ideally be played by the product owner.

PART II

DevOps to Digital Transformation

CHAPTER 11

Digital Transformation: The Driver of Business Success

We knew 20 years back that IT had become an integral part of organizations. We knew that the business was the primary driver and IT supported it. Back then, what we did not know is how IT would not only become an integral part of a business but also determine a business' success (or failure). The word IT became too generic and antiquated. Today we simply call it *digital*.

There is a lot more to digital than just IT. For starters, IT followed the business and was subservient. Digital is seen as a driver for the business to flourish—it takes the business to greater heights. This, in turn, has made digital and business inseparable. While the term digital evolved from IT, it added a number of dimensions that were never thought of as IT. Channels such as social media, email marketing, websites, and mobile applications have become synonymous with all things digital. The traditional IT that consisted of servers, routers, and other infrastructure fall under cloud technology in today's digital world.

DevOps and Beyond

Every decade or, in today's terms, every five-year period, there are certain themes of transformation. It's like fashion trends that come and go, transformation too, is in the mold of seasonal theses.

© Abhinav Krishna Kaiser 2023
A. Krishna Kaiser, *Reinventing ITIL® and DevOps with Digital Transformation*,
https://doi.org/10.1007/978-1-4842-9072-9_11

The 70s was the period when modern programming languages like Pascal and C were born. With C, came the UNIX operating system. Object-oriented programming was the toast of the programming world in the 80s. ITIL too made its entry during this era. The 90s was the Internet period, where access to the Internet and web-based programming languages like Java, HTML, and JavaScript gained popularity. During the 2000s, ITIL gained traction and so did the roots of the Agile framework. But it wasn't until the 2010s that Agile got its due recognition.

DevOps started as a conference during this time, but became a *thing* around 2015. The DevOps methodology did not exist as a standalone idea, but rather brought Agile, ITIL, and automation under a single umbrella. Its inclusivity rather than exclusivity made it attractive to the majority of industry players who had *something* already in place. While it brought Agile under its wings for its *Dev* activities, the *Ops* was strengthened with ITIL. A product's development and maintenance came under a single structure, and the synergy reaped several benefits, which I discussed in the first half of this book.

A product's rapid development was achieved through DevOps, reducing cycle time of individual feature development and as well providing the ability to deploy selective features with feedback mechanisms. The support structure was strengthened with its unified teams, thus reducing the downtime and increasing customer satisfaction.

With the advent of all things digital, there was a need for all-round development to gain further benefits. The amalgamation of IT and business started with Agile and became stronger under DevOps. The next step was to tie it up further. DevOps was good until a certain point, but it wasn't holistic. It brought benefits, but the benefits were limited to a product's development and operations. The other aspects of customer satisfaction, delving into business problems, were outside the agenda. Thus came a bigger, more inclusive umbrella that didn't have any boundaries. This movement focused on the subject rather than the object.

The digital transformation movement succeeded DevOps. It became more inclusive than DevOps ever was. Organizations could pull various rabbits out of their hats and bring them under the digital transformation umbrella as long as they served a purpose and solved a problem.

Figure 11-1 illustrates the digital transformation space. It includes a number of current technology and management trends that are poised for the future. This list is by no means comprehensive. More importantly, inclusions grow by the day. In Figure 11-1, you will find DevOps, IoT, machine learning, and a whole lot of transformative areas.

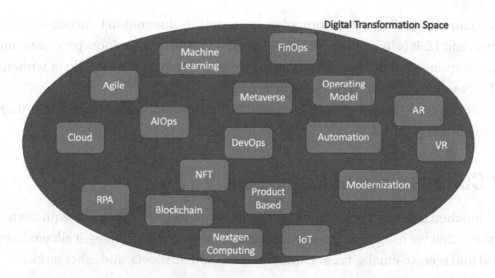

Figure 11-1. *Digital transformation space*

To jump onto the digital transformation bandwagon, an organization need not start making plans to do all the things listed in Figure 11-1. The digital transformation space is a superset and contains transformations across various areas, technologies, management methodologies, and so on. So, an organization intending to get in on the journey should judiciously pick what is relevant and plan for it meticulously.

In this list, you will also find DevOps, which indicates that DevOps is one of the various transformation elements that fall under the digital transformation umbrella. So while we moved the ITIL bar in the direction of DevOps in the first part of the book, the focus in this chapter is to move further outwards, toward the digital transformation space.

The World of Digital Transformation

With digital becoming a vital, unsubstituted component of business, something was needed to shake off the traditional practices that were rigidly set in. Bringing in digital was going to disrupt the status quo; it was going to redefine the postulates of IT. Change is never easy, especially when the change was going to sweep every person off the business floor. Life in IT was never going to be the same. Welcome to digital transformation!

You can look at digital transformation as a seamless integration between the business and IT. It is like a piece of cloth weaved with yarns of business processes and digital components. The cloth gets its form from the business and IT (with or without equal measure). They simply become inseparable.

While the components of digital transformation are established in principle, there is more to the story. Why does digital transformation arise to begin with?

The Curious Case of Magic Link

Sony launched a personal communicator device back in 1994. This is the equivalent of the tablets that we use today. It was an advanced device for the times—it allowed users to send and receive emails, fax documents, create spreadsheets, and other tasks.

Figure 11-2. Sony Magic Link (credit: https://en.wikipedia.org/wiki/Magic_Link#/media/File:SonyMagicLink.jpg)

The technology was beyond anything at the time. Its design and conception made Sony the leaders in this space. It impressed the geeks and technology freaks alike. But the common folk didn't bother. Why? It didn't really solve the problems that they were facing. The general population didn't need to send emails on the go, or carry out computing actions remotely—they wouldn't for another decade. As Tony Fadell, the creator of Magic Link puts it, most people did not understand what the device did. The device became a luxury toy for rich nerds. The Magic Link device was built to solve problems that did not yet exist. This was the primary reason for its colossal failure.

What About Google Glass?

One of the most anticipated products in recent history was Google Glass, shown in Figure 11-3. One critic compared it to tablet devices and predicted a market creation for the smart eyewear. The hype was such that it was linked to the likes of the *Mission Impossible* movie, in which Tom Cruise reads the message and flicks it away before it could *self-destruct*.

Google Glass turned out to be a massive failure. The device did not find sufficient takers and the interest waned away too soon. Reasons are multi-fold.

For starters, the product manufacturers did not define the problems that Google Glass was going to solve. They could have defined and validated a set of use cases where the product would be used and marketed it accordingly. But that didn't happen.

Groups of users started to define its application after its release. While a group argued that it represented a new fashion statement that demarcated the tech savvy from the rest, the other group looked for the utilities such as GPS functionality and to act as a device that doubled up as a mobile entertainment station. Its camera feature made the device socially unacceptable to worn in public—who wants to converse or be around people who may be recording everything in sight?

The fundamental issue was that Google Glass did not provide value to users. It just did not solve any problems nor did it benefit users in carrying out tasks. The company had to identify potential type of users and specific use cases. Had they done a good job of doing this, I doubt if Google Glass would have seen the day.

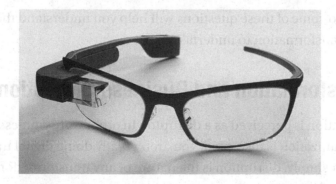

Figure 11-3. *Google Glass (credit:* `https://commons.wikimedia.org/wiki/File:Google_Glass_with_frame.jpg)`

At the time of this writing, Google has indicated at their developer conference that a new avatar of Google Glass that would allow for live translation and transliteration of speech to text. This, in my opinion, is a good start that defines a use case and solves a real problem that we all face when traveling to countries where we do not speak the language.

The Right Questions to Ask

Technology and futuristic processes do not dictate the direction and journey of digital transformation. The problems solved or the opportunities created by a digital transformation program matter, even if they leverage technologies involving on-premises servers and methodology such as waterfall led project delivery. The question is not about what you are leveraging or how you are achieving it, but why you are carrying out a digital transformation exercise.

- What are the problems and opportunities that are you trying to solve by going digital?

- Are you reducing the spend on operations?

- Are you increasing the throughput?

- Are you considerably increasing the quality of the product?

- Are you improving the image of the company?

The answers to some of these questions will help you understand the need and extent of digital transformation to undertake.

Digital Transformation and Business Disruption

Digital transformation is perceived as a disruptor. In other words, unless the ways of working of an organization is disrupted, you aren't really doing digital transformation in principle. To put it simply, disruption is the nature of any transformation business, but it isn't a necessary evil.

Look at digital transformation as doing the same set of business processes using digital means, which mostly means sets of applications and toolsets. By introducing digital means, there is a good possibility that the business will have to transform (some) their ways of working (process or sub-process level). The change effected by the digital tools for the business is generally pinned as an unwelcome disruption. Why? Because the thought process is that the business process should dictate how the tools are to be set up and not the other way around.

Any time the new makes way for the old, there will be changes all around. Even if the change is more efficient, it is considered disruptive. What is important in most such cases is for the employees or the people involved to have an open mind to embrace change. An open mindset will help disruption no longer be perceived negatively, but objectively. This will help employees see the positive side of disruption and its potential impact.

Consider the taxi business. Taxis were hailed on the street, and this was a norm that the passengers and taxi drivers accepted. This method had its own set of issues where passengers had to visually locate empty taxis and hire them. The taxi drivers too faced uncertain times trying to find a passengers mid-street. Then came the next level of convenience with call taxis. Passengers had the luxury of ringing a central number and the taxi would arrive at their doorstep. This was much better for both the parties, as a level of certainty and convenience was brought into the process.

When Uber created app-based taxi hailing, the business went through the roof. Such was the disruption that not only the middlemen were made redundant but the fleet of taxis multiplied overnight. Anybody with a car willing to ferry people around could become a taxi driver, and passengers could book at a taxi with their fingertips. What's more, they could even track the taxi as it arrived. Yes, passengers benefited the most from this disruption. The days of uncertainty were long behind them. It also generated employment for a number of drivers who could also drive part time. On the flipside, the taxi companies that received calls and dispatched taxis went out of business. The *original* taxi drivers probably lost some of their business to Uber drivers. Harking back to the mindset—a passenger with an open mind can benefit multi-fold by adapting to the new ways of working.

Another aspect of digital transformation is that it does not change your core business. For instance, the taxi business is always about ferrying people from point A to point B. If the strategy of the business is reinvented around the digital transformation aspects, more often than not, business leaders will end up pivoting and moving in various directions, only to lose sight of the goal and be stranded midway to where their business goals are.

Business Disruption 101

A new technology in town or a new offering does not induce disruption. At the most, it brings in another player with services and products to offer, and further competition. So, the golden question is—what qualifies as a business disruption?

A business exists because it can generate value for its customers and is able to market it to its customer segment. In return, the business gets fairly remunerated. Borrowing the concept of a business model from Mark W. Johnson, Clayton M. Christensen, and Henning Kagermann (*Reinventing your Business Model,* Harvard Business Review), a business model consists of four elements:

- Customer value proposition
- Profit formula
- Key resources
- Key processes

The most important of the four elements is the customer value proposition, which is perhaps equivalent to the other three put together. Let's look at the four elements from a digital transformation angle.

Customer Value Proposition

Customer value proposition, simply put, is the value created by the business for the customer. The value created for the customer must simply outclass whatever was in existence. The change that comes about should be so different that the change must create a different level of value from the start.

Take the example of a traditional hotel versus Airbnb. While traditional hotels offered rooms with certain expectations of a hotel room and amenities, Airbnb jumped into the ring, targeting perhaps the same set of customers but providing value that was dramatically different. For starters, Airbnb rentals were economic and tourists could experience staying at local places that were not exactly commercial. Staying at actual residences brought the kind of comfort that made them feel at home and unrestricted.

Profit Formula

Businesses exist to make profits. The value created for the customer comes at a cost. The profit formula is the financial planning that the business need to have in place to make profits while delivering value to customers. The balance is quite fine—as the business tries to up the profits, it could come at the cost of value. As the value proposition goes down, there is a good probability that either the customers will move to a different business or a new competitor with better a profit formula could move in.

Consider the example of Tata Nano, a car introduced in India for about $2,500. While it is not easy to manufacture a car at that price, Rata Tata, the chairman of the Tata Group, had to find a way to make it happen. With large sales, even a small profit per car can lead to large profits. The trick was to find the equilibrium between sourcing the parts, labor, and manufacturing economically and yet maintaining a minimum quality and acceptable look.

Key Resources and Processes

Identifying value proposition is one thing, but putting it into action is a completely different art. To realize value proposition, the business requires people, processes, raw material, and machines, among other things.

In the MP3 player segment, iPod is a leader and has been since it was launched in 2001. Interestingly enough, Apple did not invent the MP3 player. They existed long before, and were commercial since the 1990s. Elger Labs introduced an MP3 player with 32MB, but the product was mostly immobile. Personal Jukebox, with a whopping 4.8GB of storage, was introduced the following year. That player was bulky and expensive, at $800. There were a few other players who came out with MP3 players before the iPod was introduced. How is it that the iPod went on to become a success, while the others languished?

The combination of people, technologies, partners, and processes that came together in the making of iPod made it an instant success. Tony Fadell of Magic Link fame was hired to run the iPod division. His prior experience at General Magic and Philips helped accelerate the product development. He brought in other experts who he knew personally. Steve Jobs overlooked the aesthetics and design. A number of products in the iPod were outsourced from other partners and the product became an overnight success. It sold at $400 with 5GB storage, and it wasn't top of the line configuration. Its design, aesthetics, and size had the right set of ingredients for customers. The individual elements like the Toshiba hard drive, Portal Player that designed the operating system, Tony Fadell, Steve Jobs, and other individual elements that came together are the key resources and processes that were responsible for creating value. While there were other giants in the market, they couldn't compete as the coming together of iPod had captured the market. For others to take over the market, it required something dramatic to displace iPod, which was nearly impossible, even today. Microsoft's Zune MP3 player tried to compete in the market with top of the line products and similar or better configuration. Yet, the market for MP3 players is unequivocally dominated by Apple. With mobile phones gaining in storage, big batteries and multi-threading, the end of iPods did not come from a competitor but another device that could multi-task. Apple officially discontinued their iPod line on May 10, 2022 (`https://www.apple.com/newsroom/2022/05/the-music-lives-on/`).

Does the Disruption Have to Be Big Bang?

Yes, transformation often implies a massive makeover, but it doesn't have to be done all at once. A Big Bang approach does not gel well for organizations that have a long history of legacy processes and employees who have aged along with them. The plan is to change to transformative ways of working, and in incremental approach serves just as well.

Consider the example in Figure 11-4. It showcases a series of improvements done over a period of time.

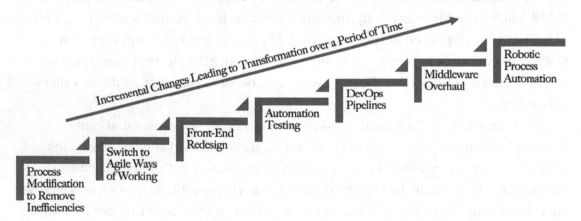

Figure 11-4. *Incremental improvements on a modernization journey*

In this instance, first you modify the processes to remove inefficiencies like reducing the hops, retaining only the activities that have bearing on KPIs and bringing clarity to people on their roles and responsibilities. Next up, once the path is ripe for Agile implementation, you bring in the coaches for a few months of Agile training and coaching. Replacing legacy systems is not straightforward. You wouldn't really have a good handle on all the integrations and the various dependencies with other systems. The best way to modernize is to break them down into smaller chunks and modernize them one after another. In any application, the frontend plays a significant role in enhancing user experience. It is also the least risky option on the modernizing journey. The next step in the transformation is identified as the frontend redesign. Likewise, the company will embark on a series of improvements, like automation testing and introducing DevOps pipelines, among others. At the end of a series of improvements, the company would have realized the transformation journey without really shaking the tree with rigor. The incremental approach to digital transformation is perhaps the path of least resistance and goes well with carrying out improvements, observing the outcome, and moving onto the next step.

A few things to note. While I have showcased this example of digital transformation as a sequential activity, this may not be the case in every journey. For example, the company could decide to carry out automation testing and DevOps pipelines in parallel. There is plenty of synergy between the two activities and doing it in parallel will be a win-win scenario. Most importantly, digital transformation needs to be seen as a journey and not as a destination. No organization can ever claim to have digitally transformed and stop at that. The journey is ongoing and, with the right set of transformation consultants, there are always ways and means to reach the next level of digital transformation.

Is Virtual the Assumed Goal?

Digital transformation involves leveraging technology and digital toolsets in business. The Uber example in the last section detailed how physical taxi hailing was replaced with an application. So, the question to ask is if digital transformation's objective is to move all things to the digital world? Like for example, replacing paperback books with ebooks and diaries with e-journals.

Not quite everywhere! There could be instances where digital makes everything virtual, like the business of video renting that has gone to the likes to Netflix, meaning, no more brick and mortar stores.

There are certain businesses that would be better served if a combination of virtual and physical was employed. This hybrid model is a powerful strategy where touch and feel or emotional connections have a bearing on buying decisions.

Take for example Max Fashion, a budget clothing store in India. Their entire wardrobe is available online. They have multi-storey physical stores too. Some people like to shop for clothes in person, and as they enter the store, there are people wandering about in the aisles carrying around an Android tab. They get the customer's phone number and check on the app to see if there are personalized offers available. As they help with the physical shopping experience, if customers are unable to find their fit, the agents with tabs provide the option to order online. Customers can also try the clothes on in the physical store and order everything online at a special discount. The fashion company is engaging with the customer physically to feel and try their choices, and the limitations of physical space are made up by online ordering at the stores with a special discount. It's actually a wonderful idea for somebody who loves physical shopping but dreads carrying around bags as they move from one shop to another.

This concept applies to all consumer products. Seeing a live product and seeing it on the screen is not the same experience. The premium feel, the 3D spatial view, and the pleasant odors can only be experienced first-hand, and not through customer feedback in brick and mortar stores. This is an opportunity for retailers to combine the best of the physical and digital worlds and maximize sales and profits.

Finding Synergy with Partner Organizations

As much as the current generation is digital, it is equally made of partnerships as well. Many businesses have moved toward their respective niches and the scenario calls for them to come together to innovate and co-create value for customers. In other words, value creation is no longer the enterprise of a single organization. It just cannot be achieved. You need the expertise of design, software, hardware, UI/UX, branding, and a host of other factors to come under a single roof to create synergy for value to take shape. Not only value—for digital transformation to make sense, it must be significant value justifying the cost and benefits.

Apple is perhaps the only company that tries to make everything in-house, but that did not happen overnight. As I discussed earlier, iPods were made with the help of other businesses. Likewise, all their products had outside help. Over time, Apple has invested in these companies or acquired the necessary resources. Yet, they still have to maintain partnerships to stay relevant. Say for example, they have partnerships with Microsoft to offer Office and other products, distributor networks (like AT&T and iPlanet) for sales, the Foxconn Technology Group for manufacturing, and Qualcomm for mobile 3G/4G/5G chips.

Some businesses find it enticing to acquire startups that show promise of innovativeness. Acquisition is a business decision, but what happens after the fact is important. If the startups are integrated with the parent organization, the innovative culture for which the startup was acquired will start to diminish and the talent will start to look for another startup. Businesses must resist the urge to amalgamate startups but rather allow them to operate independently and flourish. This may be true for organizations that are non-startups as well.

Key Focus Areas

Digital transformation is inclusive of all things that accelerate an organization toward digital ways of working—it comes through various management, technological, and leadership changes.

We can identify a few areas that lay the foundation for a successful digital transformation. The areas play a significant role in shaping the digital transformation toward a successful implementation. Customers, value, innovation, and data are the pillars that need to be closely examined during any digital transformation exercise. These key focus areas are shown in Figure 11-5.

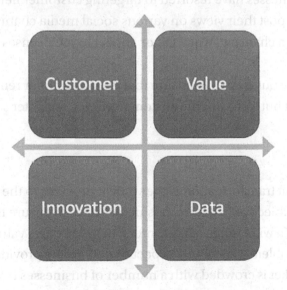

Figure 11-5. *Key focus areas of digital transformation*

Customers

There was a time when customers were seen as the people with purses and the marketing strategy revolved around influencing them to make a *buy* decision. That was simple enough! While the world has gotten flatter, there is an inherent change that has come about with customers. They don't see themselves as an individual entity that makes up an independent decision. Yes, the decision could have other stakeholders weighing in on the options. But the most important characteristic that influences customers' decisions today is feedback from other customers.

Amazon and other online shopping channels display customer feedback ratings next to the products they sell. Products with higher ratings and volume sales often attract buyers. There was a time when full-page ads on magazines and newspapers used to sway customers. My personal buying behavior is to scout the ratings across various channels before making a decision. Yes, I know that some of these ratings can be fudged by the lure of a gift or cashback, but when you see volume sales coupled with high ratings, it is hard to go wrong.

Customers are no longer the target in the digital age—instead, it is customer networks that businesses should target. The power of networks through various social media channels can make or break product success. Ultimately it is the product value, quality, and other features that defines its success. And yet, without the customer networks playing a significant role, even the best products may go unnoticed.

A number of businesses have resorted to targeting customer networks by encouraging users to post their views on various social media channels. Some may lure buyers with a chance to win a gift or appeal to their senses by including personalized notes.

The onus is on the businesses to ensure that every customer remains satisfied, not only with the product but also with the customer service and after sales services.

Value

The lifeblood of digital transformation is the value it provides to the customers. Although value perception is subjective in nature, businesses have to ensure that the product/service offered meets a wide range of customers. In today's age, value proposition remaining still is a problem. Customers expect that the value provided will improve over time, as the market is crowded with a number of businesses that provide similar products.

Take for example Microsoft Office 365. Although the product does not realistically have any competitors, it improves on a regular basis. There are regular changes being done, and most importantly, communicated to customers. This is done to ensure that the interest in the product remains fresh, and to ensure that no competitors crop up by offering similar products. An ever-changing product is the best way to ensure businesses remain ahead in the market.

It is therefore important for businesses to remain on the lookout for making positive changes to their offerings by piggybacking on the various digital transformation exercises that can take their offerings to newer heights, most importantly ahead of their competitors.

Staying with Microsoft Office 365, their MS Office product was doing just fine. It was the market leader. Yet, they decided to move to a subscription-based SaaS service. The reason was twofold—the market was moving toward reducing capital expenditure and converting them into small chunks paid over a period of time. The subscription model fits this market well. Secondly, the subscription model helped Microsoft generate a constant revenue source, which turned out to be more profitable than software sales. As a collateral benefit, the company could contain the piracy levels as well with the SaaS model.

Innovation

Ensuring that value remains fresh, enhancing and engaging requires a good innovation engine. Businesses that innovate rather than simply deliver often excel in their value proposition and are also found to be well ahead of the curve.

There was a time, about 12 to 15 years back, when organizations had innovation departments. The team consisted of a handful of niche domain and technology experts, and their job was to innovate. Organizations that had an overall employee strength of 100,000 or more had innovation teams that were in the low double digits. While this small percentage of employees innovated, the rest of the workforce carried out mundane activities to keep the lights going. What a shameful existence of an organization we would say, but this was the norm with most organizations during those days. Innovation required experimentation. A majority of these experiments failed. Organizations needed an appetite to fail to innovate faster. Sadly, most didn't.

The ones that did roared ahead, like the Apples and Googles of the world. Do you know how many different services Google has introduced over time? Plenty. Who's counting? Do you remember the likes of Picasa and more recently, Hangouts? Yes, they have been discontinued. Head over to the Wikipedia page at `https://en.wikipedia.org/wiki/List_of_Google_products` to see the various products that the company introduced and discontinued over the years. These discontinued products did not succeed. Unless you try something, there is no way of finding out if it is going to be a winner. Google is a market leader in a number of areas—be it Internet search, ads, and their email engine. They have become the de facto name in our households because they innovate like crazy. Organizations that want to succeed have to build an appetite to fail. As Einstein said, "Anyone who has never made a mistake has never tried anything new." And Thomas Edison said, "I have never failed. I've just found 10,000 ways that won't work."

A framework that fits like a glove when it comes to supporting experimentation is DevOps. With DevOps, the onus is to build a system that provides an ideal platform for experimentation. The platform gives you rapid feedback when something does not go according to plan. This helps ensure that when you fail, you fail fast and you can pick right back up and start a new experiment.

We also have techniques like A/B testing today that allow you to test in real time and not commit to one direction or another. A/B testing is a live experiment that businesses can do with their products. Instead of launching their product using the Big Bang approach, they can release products to a small group of customers and solicit feedback. Based on the feedback, they can either roll it out to the rest of their customer group or simply roll it back. Many banking organizations launch their Internet banking applications in this manner. They give users the option to switch to the new application. And users who switch can either stay with the new application or switch back depending on their experience and comfort levels. This helps the banking organizations gauge the acceptance rate in real time, and without having to risk their reputation and deal with acrimony from their customers. Microsoft also back-launched their Outlook application for Macs with an option for users to switch back to the legacy mode.

Another technique that is in vogue is using the minimum viable product (MVP) approach. Instead of developing an entire product, you develop a minimum version of it that has limited functionalities. By releasing a MVP product, your customers can provide feedback on a product that is likely to be launched in the future. The feedback is invaluable because it sets the right direction for the organization from the product perspective, and the chances of them being wrong about its direction is minimum if not nil.

Data

Data is key to making good decisions. Good decisions chart the way for an organization's success. The problem with data is that it's in abundance. When I created my first website in 2003, I leveraged a third-party website called Site Meter to get an understanding of how many users were visiting my website daily and where they were from. These were the only things that I needed to know, and they met my needs back then. Today I use Google Analytics, which is multiple hundred fold of my Site Meter experience. I know the behavior and interests of my visitors, their past visits to other websites, and more. Simply put, there is so much data around us; the onus is on carefully handpicking the data that is useful and discarding the rest.

Data is on the overload in every area today. The key to success is to rely on data that matters. Following the wrong sets of data points is likely to be disastrous. For example, if I want to know what my users are saying about a new product that I launched, I must rely on AI analytics tools that scour the various social media channels. The reason to use AI is to understand the emotion behind the feedback. For example, if somebody says, "This product is bad boy!," the bad might indicate appealing. Or if somebody posts, "Not bad at all." You want the AI analytics engine to understand the context before providing results to the product manufacturer.

The next set of data engines that drive digital transformation are predictions. Companies rely on predictions to make decisions about their products. The data obtained is generally passed through an AI engine that can predict the next course of action. Downstream petroleum companies rely on predictors for setting the price of gas based on their competitors. They want to price it right to attract customers and not drive away customers by costly gas or lose profits by selling too cheap. I worked part time at a gas station and the man who owned it used to drive around the neighborhood to find out the gas prices in other stations. Those days are over. In the digital age, data is available instantly, and the predictions are also based on scientific calculations rather than gut feelings. That being said, data-based decisions alone are like taking a safe conservative measure. At times, going with your gut defines the quality of leadership and makes a difference in companies' fortunes.

While much of the data is available for free on various channels, there is room for data obtained from surveys as well. If you are releasing a new product, the only way to understand what customers really want is to post a survey and use the survey results to choose the direction.

Balancing All Things Digital

Digital transformation promotes dynamism, rapid feedback mechanisms, state-of-the-art technologies, and staying ahead of curve. There is also some caution that needs to be thrown to the wind. As they say in the game of any sport, offense and defense must strike a balance. In digital transformation, this too is the case. These are the digital balances depicted in Figure 11-6. There are several areas in digital transformation that need to be balanced. I identified the top three that require attention at all stages of digital transformation.

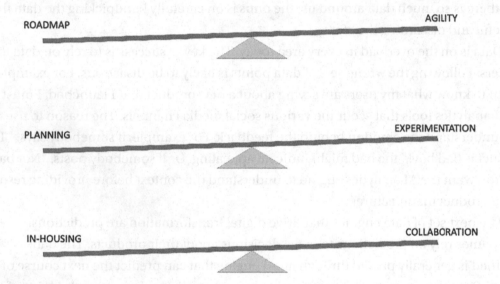

Figure 11-6. *The digital balance*

Roadmap vs. Agility

Digital transformation is generally a program that runs for multiple years. Rather, let me say that digital transformation is a journey, so it can be ongoing in a true sense. While it is a long-term plan, there are best practices that are being shaped frequently, new technology implementations are evolving, and market demands change daily. In this environment, it is expected that the digital transformation be nimble and agile, and is able to take shape as the market swings. But does it mean that a digital transformation plan takes shape and turns when required?

Digital transformation journeys must indeed have a roadmap defined. It must define the outcomes to be achieved and the metrics that will determine success. The roadmap can be developed for the length of time where visibility exists. The balance however is that the roadmap must provide sufficient fissures for the plan to change/pivot on a different axis when needed. The roadmap essentially provides a robust backbone for carrying out the digital transformation and the agility of such a roadmap will ensure that the organization is always traveling alongside market conditions.

Planning vs. Experimentation

Planning is important. A good, sound plan will win the day. But on the flipside, a plan that requires microscopic details takes time to formulate. Such a plan is still good, but in the current market where competition is cut-throat, taking a lot of time to plan is problematic.

Unless the plan is sound, the outcome may be like shooting in the dark. Companies either come out on top, or they lose out completely if they go in without a balance. What is the balance to strike?

Organizations must make room for experimentation and Agile ways of working where a minimal viable product is rolled out before the entire set of features are developed. This is a balanced way of approaching digital transformation. Therefore, organizations must engage in experimentation along with planning.

The plan needs to be minimal, leaving space for it to pivot as needed. It must have sufficient line items to account for the various possibilities and intended direction to move into. It must experiment with ideas in a minimalistic way, and not as a Big Bang. By combining minimalistic planning and sensible experimentation, it is likely that the company will come out on top if the experiments succeed; the company will not be left too far behind if the experiments fail.

Operating systems like macOs and Windows release Alpha and Beta versions before the full launch. Most of the time, these versions may not carry the entire functionality list. Volunteers and enthusiasts who engage with these versions provide feedback, which is rapidly incorporated into the complete version. If they had engaged in complete testing by their in-house teams, not only would have they have delayed the final release but also not created keen interest among the users through the Alpha and Beta versions.

In-Housing vs. Collaboration

It is a great achievement and a moment of pride for organizations to build products indigenously. Not only will their costs be contained, but the knowledge and experience of building a product will remain within the organization. But at what cost?

Doing everything in a single organization is possible but gaining expertise in all the associated fields is unlikely. There are companies that focus solely on certain areas of technology and leveraging these companies will help the organization accelerate their digital transformation journey. The benefits and drawbacks of outsourcing versus insourcing in the context of digital transformation and acceleration reveal that organizations find lots of positives in outsourcing/engaging partners rather than doing everything in-house.

When organizations collaborate intelligently with their partners, they can achieve intended outcomes and, at the same time, find ways to retain the experience and knowledge within it. In my view, host organizations must play integrator and key governance roles and collaborate with partners who have respective expertise. This ensures a good mix of in-house leadership and technical expertise from partner organizations. A good case management system and process ensures that the experience gained, and the case studies designed, will not be lost to the outsourcing business.

Summary

This chapter introduced the concept of digital transformation and explained how it is different compared to DevOps. Several real-life examples were discussed during the course of the chapter to highlight the journey that you have undertaken thus far. The chapter also discussed the various elements to focus on during any digital transformation exercise.

CHAPTER 12

The Digital Transformation Framework

Organizations and consultants can talk about digital transformation and they can say that they are implementing it. But what they cannot accurately do is define the complete scope of digital transformation. Nobody has defined its scope comprehensively, and it will not be done for years to come. And, it's completely okay because the scope should be seen through the eyes of the product or the program that is undergoing digital transformation.

Even though the contour of digital transformation is vast, ambiguous to an extent and unknown for the most part, it still requires a guide, a structure to support it. A framework for digital transformation is the need of the hour to build it from the ground up and to be certain that it stands the test of time.

A framework for any other discipline needs to be somewhat prescriptive, a structure that defines the various layers and the various processes, procedures, and other activities that are deemed necessary. Digital transformation is unlike any other, and a typical framework will not do. What it requires is a vehicle that can drive the transformation through the rough tides and yet give plenty of room to maneuver, to call its own shots and provide the crosshairs for meeting the intended outcomes. I call it the *battle tank framework*.

The Battle Tank Framework

A battle tank is an effective fighting weapon in surface warfare. The fighting vehicle can move fast, maneuver across terrains, fire accurately at the target, and has a thick armor to withstand brutal attacks.

© Abhinav Krishna Kaiser 2023
A. Krishna Kaiser, *Reinventing ITIL® and DevOps with Digital Transformation*,
https://doi.org/10.1007/978-1-4842-9072-9_12

There are a lot of similarities between a battle tank and digital transformation. A digital transformation exercise has to be done swiftly to gain the full benefit. Most of the time, we know where we want to end up, but the path to it may be a rocky one, and the exercise must have the rigor to withstand the unknowns. This requires a framework that helps digital transformation reach the intended goals and guard it from the risks, issues, and unknowns. Hence the battle tank framework for digital transformation as featured in Figure 12-1.

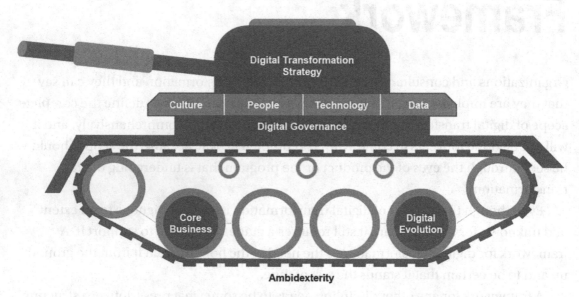

Figure 12-1. *Battle tank framework for digital transformation*

The digital transformation strategy sits at the top, where the hatch of a tank opens up. The vision for conducting any digital transformation exercise must be set by the senior leadership as executive sponsor, and only with their buy-in will the exercise have the required funding and the support of all the people involved.

Most of the offensive action happens in the turret. It is loaded with a main gun and the turret can rotate it to the direction of choice. In the framework, consisting of the turret are four critical elements that drive the transformation—culture, people, technology, and data.

The hull is the main body of the tank and it provides support for the turret to sit. Digital governance in the framework takes this place, which is the backbone for successfully running digital transformation exercises.

There are a number of wheels in a tank; the bigger the size, more the wheels. The main wheels are called bogies, and a chain runs around them to reduce the ground pressure and prevent it from sinking when the surface is soft. The set of wheels and the chain is together called a track, meaning the tank has its own steel road surface. For digital transformation to succeed, it requires the business to focus on its core offering on one end, and to apply the digital evolution acceleration from the other. Ambidexterity is a fine balance between innovation and fully leveraging the expertise on hand, and with it in conjunction with the two wheels makes for a perfect digital transformation track.

The Digital Transformation Strategy

Putting a strategy together to go digital is not a set template. Businesses cannot follow a rule book and meet their digital goals. Every business is different, its model and digital maturity is at varying stages. Many businesses want to go digital, and their main objective or motivation to do so is to remain relevant. In other words, they believe that their business may not exist if they don't go digital. Think, for example, about a bank that has a rich history of multiple decades. As newer banks go online, traditional banks will be forced to digitize. What they do in such cases of existential threat will chart the course of such traditional institutions.

So, the million-dollar question of strategizing has to be done at a business level.

It is true that startups or small businesses find it easier to get on a journey of digital transformation than a company that's been in traditional business for over a 50 years with multiple lines of businesses. A smaller company will find it easy to start making changes, and pivot if something doesn't feel right. It is not easy for traditional businesses to pivot because the company carries inertia, comfortable ways of working and the people showing aversion to change. On the flipside, a startup company will not carry the memory of what has always been done, and can turn in the direction of reason as and when they see fit. Their limitation generally sticks up with the financial resources, which is generally manageable for traditional businesses that have stood the test of time.

With the threat hanging over the business's head, traditional businesses jump into the puddle of digital transformation. They swiftly put together where they want to go, trying to emulate other businesses, getting the resources onboarded or contracting them out to a partner. If the strategy fails, the business will find itself in a teetering situation having to bear the financial losses, answer to their shareholders, and most importantly face the inevitability of being wiped out. Although the threat is huge, the response need not be of a similar magnitude. Earlier in the book, I compared the Big Bang and incremental approach to digital transformation. An incremental approach is better, as it gives businesses enough time to explore the possibilities and pivot as needed during the digital transformation journey. Instead of digitizing, think of the customer journey, the supply chain, the processes and technologies employed, and find opportunities to improve aspects that impact the customer one step at a time. Measure the current state, make a change, and remeasure. Metrics will tell you if you are going in the right direction. Continue the efforts bit by bit until you reach where you want to be (the irony is that digital transformation is a journey and not a destination).

The progress made may not compare a successful outcome of a Big Bang approach, but it definitely favors the odds of a success, especially for a business facing existential threats.

Figure 12-2 shows a roadmap to achieve digital transformation. The roadmap takes into consideration a logical, sensible, and least risky path to get on the route toward digital transformation. Of course, since we are considering taking the least amount of risk, the progress may not be swift and the transformation will not be achieved overnight. This is the reason that I call this *a* roadmap and not *the* roadmap to digital transformation.

While Figure 12-2 represents five steps, it is not a sequential process. Based on the context and circumstance, it is not uncommon for multiple steps to run together. The steps do not run in one sweeping motion but rather are iterative. In fact, it is recommended that the digital transformation exercise be run in an iterative manner, learning and adapting based on the previous cycles.

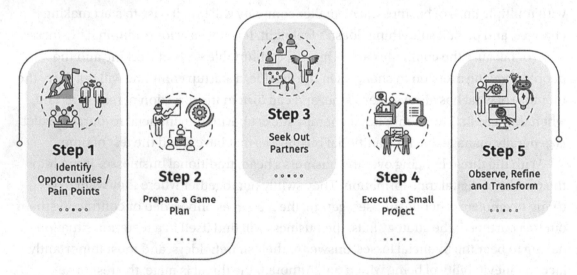

Figure 12-2. *A strategy roadmap for digital transformation*

Before you embark on digital transformation journey, there is a Step 0 as well. The people transformation step. Unless the people who are going to be a part of the transformation journey have a transformative mindset, no matter the best of processes you design and implement, none of it is going to work. You can't force people to transform, and you will not be able to impose new ways of working to people with a mindset that's blocked to accepting changes. Organizational change management (OCM) is good in theory but in reality, you need the right kind of people to take the journey with you.

In the new ways of working, processes are not the king. Knowing what to do and at what point in time is not going to get the results in a transformative environment. People who are going to be on this journey have to value relationships, as sharing responsibilities is not through RACI but through the context. I am also not alluding to a zero conflict environment. There will be conflicts. There will be various challenges along the way. With the right people, dealing with challenges and conflicts will remain constructive.

Step 1: Identify Opportunities/Pain Points

Transformation is an exercise that is conceived by the need to reach new heights or when a pain is too unbearable to withstand. This is not cheap, so the desire for a shiny new thing will not drive the need, but rather a strong desire to get ahead of competitors or an even a stronger necessity to survive.

At the center of any digital transformation exercise is the question *why*. Why does an organization want to spend a significant amount of time and effort to transform from the present way to something else? It can be as simple as for productivity increase or to capture a segment of a market through a new offering. Every organization, in every sector, will have a specific reason for undertaking the journey. And once they do, more often than not, digital transformation will remain a journey and never a destination. As an organization reaches a new level of transformation, there will always be something shinier that has additional benefits, and naturally, having tasted success, the organization will be inclined to push the accelerator toward the next destination. Recall Figure 1-3 in Chapter 1, where an elephant is depicted with the superset of all DevOps activities. Digital transformation is a lot bigger, this time it will be a big blue whale with the world of opportunities for the organization to take the plunge.

Identifying transformation avenues requires data points, and lots of it. Usually, a single set of data might tell one side of the story. So, it becomes key to cross-reference the findings with additional data points and iterate.

A popular technique to determine the ins and outs of an organization's ways of working is by conducting assessments. This can be done by conducting workshops with key stakeholders, asking them relevant questions that point toward what is being sought. The first nut to crack is to identify the right set of people who need to be interviewed. Talking to too many people might enrich the data with multiple data points, but it may also muddle and confuse the findings. So, it is important for the assessor/transformation consultant to understand the organization structure and their roles and responsibilities before carefully selecting the people who are going to serve as data sources.

Every person who the assessor talks to will have a story to tell, and more often than not, it will differ from the next person. Everybody has a perspective, and all perspectives of curated list of stakeholders are important, even if they contradict with others. The assessor can always revisit some of the conversations to clarify certain aspects with the stakeholders, but should bring in enough data to tie the answers together and stitch together a story that gives a true picture of on-the-ground situation.

The other data point that is dispossessed of perspectives/opinions is that the data is pulled from tools. There is a lot of data that you can gather from monitoring tools, logs, value stream tools, and testing tools, among others. The data may be raw but there are hidden gems that tell a story. For example, the data obtained from a testing tool will give the data points around the quality of the product while it is in development. Does the development team get it right when they develop it the first time? How quickly are they able to rectify bugs? A straight reading of the data might give us a direction on the effectiveness of the developers to do it right the first time. But couple this with the organization's culture and the intent to experiment and *fail fast*, and the testing data will point toward a different story line.

The next pitfall is understanding the problem. Sometimes, even with all the data that is available, the issue at hand might still not be fully understood. We may end up solving a non-existent problem unless the problem is rephrased and parroted back to the customer stakeholders. This solves two issue: the first and straightforward issue is that the customer may agree with your understanding of the problem, or they may request changes to the problem statement. Second and most important is that reading the problem statement from a different perspective may get the customer to think and validate if the problem really exists as it was projected. The very well understood problem statement by the customer organization may just receive a jolt when reading it from a different perspective, and this could essentially get them thinking and moving toward the right problem statement.

Even if it is sounds repetitive, the problem statement should be rephrased in your own words. A number of transformation consultants use the same problem statement phrases as stated by the customer in order to display their understanding of the customer problem accurately. This is counterproductive and any smart stakeholder in the customer organization will be able to see through it. From the customer standpoint, stating the right challenges solve half the problem.

Step 2: Prepare a Game Plan

Planning is hard work when it comes to digital transformation because we can hardly see how the pieces will fall once we get going with the digital transformational activities. Therefore, it is recommended that the plan be nimble, and be able to pivot to different directions as needed.

For a plan to come through, some necessities such as the funding that is available, the leadership support and the goals to achieve must be well known.

Funding

Digital transformation is anything but cheap. If an organization believes that they can get onboarded on a digital transformation journey by using the spare time of people and available resources, they probably have no clue what they are doing. At best, they are embarking on a journey of improvements. Transformation requires funding because it tries to flip the nature of working, and for anything of such nature, money is essential.

There are ways in which smart CEOs can find the money—one of the popular methods these days is through self-funding. Identifying areas of transformation within a value stream or department of an organization and calculating the return of investment over a period of time is a good way to justify spending on digital transformation. For example, if an organization intends to carry out all of its business processes sans people through the employment of robotic process automation, the initial investment is likely to be steep. The learning stages will require effort by people. But when the processes start to function, they essentially free up people's effort, which saves on operational expenses that can be leveraged elsewhere. More importantly, these bots can function around the clock—imagine the efficiency an organization can expect. If implemented right, this solution is bound to make the organization more profitable over a period of time. The funding for this exercise was essentially internal and the benefits realized had a telling effect on company's financial reports, quality of work, and possibly turnaround time.

Senior Management Support

This exercise requires senior management backing, specifically it will be effective if the CEO champions the cause. You need the full support of senior leadership by actively contributing as a member of the digital transformation's steering board and providing direction on strategy. This begins with the allocation of the necessary funds to run and maintain the program.

The vision behind the transformation must be spelt out, including what needs to be done too be accompanied and it must be made clear to all senior leadership and the rest of the organization that this program is high on the priority list. Unless you have the complete backing of the CEO/CXO and senior leadership behind the digital transformation, the program's full potential and its distance to go the entire distance is unlikely.

A smart leader builds a governance structure to give complete visibility of the digital transformation progress without micromanaging the work on the ground. And yet, when the time calls for intervention, they put themselves in a position to steer the team in the right direction.

Goals and Metrics

Absolute targets have to be set. Instead of saying that you will improve revenue by 20 percent YoY, the target must say that the revenue to be achieved is $506 million. All areas that are touched by digital transformation must be accounted for—be it performance, quality, new business, customer experience, among others.

The next secret to setting goals for the digital transformation exercise is to set higher goals and secret stretch goals. The age of conservatism is long over, and with digital transformation, the belief is that anything is possible. So, steep goals come with the territory. The numbers need not be arbitrary. Multiple models can be drawn to come up with targets. Comparing goals of other organizations' capabilities and setting goals to mimic them is also a decent start.

How do you know if you are transforming? Measurements. Identify all the metrics that will be used during the course of the program to get real time/near real time data and understand the progress made. Even if it means spending more to get the tool licenses just to report on the metrics, it is a worthy investment. The more metrics you have, the better it is for the CEO and senior leadership to notice and make decisions to refine, adapt, and pivot.

Step 3: Seek Out Partners

This is a connected world—more so from a digital transformation sense. If organizations need to embark on digital transformation journeys, they need partners. If they think they can do everything in-house, they should read the Dell Digital Transformation Index, where one of the top barriers to digital transformation is the lack of the expertise and skills in-house. Yes, organizations need to think beyond conservatism and beyond doing everything if they are serious about digital transformation.

Technology is available at one's fingertips for a certain cost. Acquiring technology is the easy part. What matters are the skill and expertise to put it to use. An organization that tends to buy technology and start to begin hiring people to use it will be left behind in this fast paced digital world. Imagine an organization having to hire all the required skillsets, figuring out how they can work together, and then coming together to do whatever they set out to do. Sounds like climbing Mt. Everest for the first time! On the flipside, imagine engaging multiple partners who have expertise on their respective areas, including an integrator, and giving them the laundry list of what you need and watching them deliver is more sane and practical.

There was a time when concepts, practices, and case studies were walled in. With the world opening up, and open source leading the way, digital transformation practices have to be open to borrowing ideas of what worked well for other organizations, sharing their own experiences in conferences and other forums, and passing the baton. Case studies therefore are not limited to certain organization, but to the digital ecosystem that exists with like-minded companies.

Key Ingredient for Partnerships to Work

For digital transformation to succeed, partners have to work in unison to understand customer expectations and deliver what they need rather than what they ask for. This is not possible by merely dividing and conquering work, but rather applying themselves to the digital culture (transparency, innovativeness, trustworthy, shared responsibilities, and so on) that acts as a differentiator between success and failure.

While the partners in the customer ecosystem work together for the success of the customer, the human-centric design principles must be applied unequivocally. Suppose a need surfaces which requires a solution. There are multiple ways of looking at it, a cost-effective solution, a technology approach based on what is implemented in the organization, or a solution that considers what adds the most value to people using it. Remember that most of the digital transformation aspects are not carried out for backend processing activities but rather for the people to use, and make full benefit of the digital technologies in achieving their objectives. Therefore, the digital transformation design and implementation must consider the human-centric approach, which should be a part of the ecosystem supported by all the involved partners.

I will talk about digital culture in detail later in this chapter. If partnerships have to work, the digital culture has to be the norm. Unless partners trust each other and share knowledge and information openly, they will not be in a position to deliver the best possible results for the customer. Even if two competitor organizations work in the customer ecosystem as partners, they must keep their differences and doubts aside and do what is best for the customer.

Responsibilities and Contracts

Partners working collaboratively and trusting each other is good and preferred. But beneath the surface, they are part of different organizations. Every organization has a contract of its own, commercials mapped to the scope and delivery. So, the work to be carried out by each of the partners must be written down unambiguously. A RACI chart must be developed that covers all the partners, so there is absolute clarity on the role played by each of the parties and the extent to which they can go.

Furthermore, each of the partners bring in their set of intellectual properties and proprietary solutions. These must be protected most importantly. Working for the customer should not be the invitation for possible infringement of copyrighted, patented, and contracted properties. Each of the partners has to bring in their own measures to make sure that their properties are well protected, away from prying eyes.

Step 4: Execute a Small Project

There are a few variations of how a digital transformation implementation can be carried out. You can make massive changes across the organization, or you can make one change in one value stream and then move to the other changes in a phased manner. Using a Big Bang approach will get immediate results and when pressed against time, is the best option. However, the disadvantages are great. If the transformation does not provide the intended outcome, then all the effort, money, and time spent doing it is wasted. You win all or nothing.

A phased approach is good, but the success rate is either complete or nil for the identified value stream. A value stream (discussed in detail in Chapter 15) is a part of the organization's structure that goes through the transformation cycle rather than the entire organization.

With digital transformations, it's not wise to be conservative because conservativeness and experimentation do not necessarily go hand in hand. If you go aggressive, then there are potential for massive failures. To strike a balance, identify a small but relevant portion of the organization that is a good representation of the entire organization. Then carry out the digital transformation exercises and go through the motions in this part of the organization. If success follows, you know that the direction of transformation is right, and you can possibly apply it to the rest of the organization (using the Big Bang approach). If it fails, you'll need to go back to the drawing board and analyze the causes for the failure and come up with a new action plan. This approach of transforming a small chunk of an organization is called a *lighthouse project* or a *minimum viable product* (MVP). You continue to run lighthouse projects until you succeed, and until you can replicate it in the broader organization.

When the lighthouse project is successful, how do you implement it in the rest of the organization? Providing the processes, architectures, and related documentation to each of the value streams and asking them to get it implemented is an option but not ideal. When it comes to digital transformation, you want the same group to be involved in implementation across the organization to ensure standardization and swift measures, to enable learning, and to apply past experiences.

My recommendation to implement digital transformation measures is to build an enablement team. This team is responsible for implementation across the organization. It consists of all the necessary people with the skills needed for implementation. In fact, this team is enabled with high caliber resources who are champions in their respective areas. You need your A team, and the digital transformation enablement team should be top notch.

This is a temporary team. The team exists to implement the digital transformation controls across the organization. Once they complete their mandate, the team is dispersed.

Step 5: Observe, Refine, and Transform

The process of reflecting, modifying, and seeing the transformation in action is the final step in the digital transformation plan—observe, refine, and transform. This step is the most valuable step because it provides the input to ensure the digital transformation's success. Up until now, you did what you thought was the best, but this step is all about measurements, observations, and corrections. Figure 12-3 illustrates the observe, refine, and transform approach.

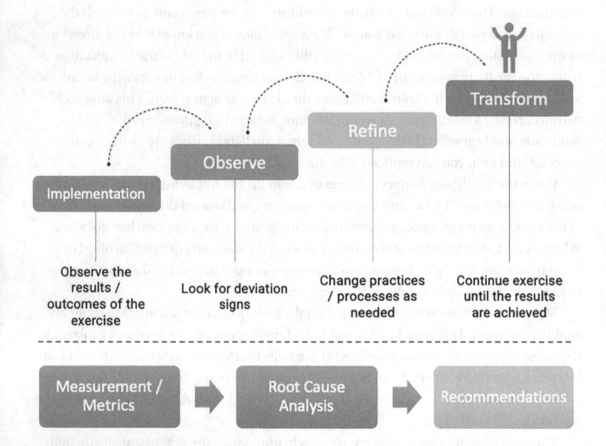

Figure 12-3. *Observe, refine, and transform*

There is plenty to learn about the digital transformation exercise in every implementation you do. The same processes might work like magic in one organization and fail terribly in the next. The rationale therefore is to pick the horses for the courses, and to understand that one size does not fit all. That said, you still go with a hunch and implement the controls that you think work well in an organization—like cookie cutter kind of practices. At first, you expect it to fail, it would surprise you if it does. Then when it fails, the learnings will help you understand a whole lot more about the organization. The changes that you make are invaluable, and to a certain degree, you know that it will work.

The general argument that I hear is about the learning. They say that learning should be a part of the process anyway, and this is something that should happen even during the implementation activities. So true! However, there is a difference between being in the ring and learning from experience and sitting outside and learning about the fate of the outcomes The structure you build to learn while sitting outside is precious in terms of getting the feedback and enacting the next set of changes.

The observe, refine, and transform process works in three tiers:

- Measurements and metrics

- Root cause analysis

- Recommendations

Measurements and Metrics

When the digital transformation processes, practices, and controls are defined and implemented, metrics too are identified along with the threshold to deem a certain control as successful. For example, if automation testing is a digital transformation control, then the metric would be test coverage and automating 90 percent of all the functionalities as a possible threshold. When implemented, the test coverage metric would be measured and if it falls beyond 90 percent, then this control is marked a success. Otherwise, it's a failure. This is a straightforward example that I have quoted, but generally there would be multiple criteria that make up the success factor.

The example with automation testing is quantitative in nature—which is the easier bit of measuring. What about something that cannot be directly measured? A new interactive voice response (IVR) system can be measured quantitatively by the time it takes for calls to be routed and the number of customers who hang up before talking to an agent. To understand the customer experience of the new IVR system, a survey can be rolled out at the end of the call. The customer provides a response, and this response is subjective. Here too you can ask customers to rate on a scale of 1-5 and provide opportunities to add comments about their experiences, which is qualitative feedback. Both sets of feedback are important for understanding the impact of digital transformation and for identifying positive changes/improvements.

Root Cause Analysis

Following the measurements and feedback received from various channels, the data (qualitative and quantitative) is analyzed. The quantitative data analysis follows various techniques, like regression analysis, factor analysis, and trend analysis, among others. The output of the analysis suggests the success or failure based on the threshold that has been agreed.

For qualitative feedback, the data needs to be manually sorted and grouped, and the outliers must be discarded. You will have data on the table that is trying to tell you something about the digital transformation adventure.

Looking at data at face value may be of some use, but the real deal is with the *why*. Why do customers like to purchase laptops but not tablets from our portal? A root cause analysis may point to the rate differentials with the competitor portals.

There are multiple tools available, like Ishigawa and Five Why techniques, to conduct root cause analysis. It is a key step that will help you root out the problem, and point you toward identifying permanent solutions that will put you on the path of digital transformation success.

Recommendations

With the root cause of the control's sub-par performance known, the next logical step is to put together actions that will take the measurements beyond the identified threshold. Transformation consultants who are behind the definition of the digital transformation controls can put together a set of actions/recommendations that can move the needle in the right direction.

These recommendations are implemented. The cycle of observe, refine, and transform is repeated until you achieve the intended outcomes. It is an iterative process, and the more cycles, the better. This is empirical data that you can derive from the process, which helps shape the digital transformation controls to the organization and its culture.

Culture and Digital Culture

Culture is broadly defined as the way of life—such as people's behavior, beliefs, values, and traits. Retrofitting the definition in the digital transformation ecosystem, it points to the ways of working, the mindset of people, their risk appetites, and working relationships with other stakeholders, among others.

Culture in IT came into the mainstream during the DevOps era. While the popular belief pointed to CI-CD pipelines at the utterance of the DevOps word, purists referred to DevOps as a cultural change. The origins may have started with the mindset of accepting shared responsibility as the entire team. Further, DevOps is big on experimentation and that required a specific kind of mindset, which assimilated into the culture angle.

Digital transformation draws heavily from DevOps on the cultural aspects. A number of cultural aspects that were desired in DevOps methodology are more pronounced in digital transformation. This new culture these days is referred to as a *digital culture.*

This is a growing field, as demonstrated in the previous chapter. Therefore, the elements that make up the culture will evolve as time passes and when case studies reveal new information. So, in essence, the culture that you are looking at is more fluid/ dynamic in nature, rather a set of values and principles to live by. It's important to note that at the very outset, as the cultural quotient changes by the day, the people who are part of the digital transformation equation should most necessarily have a growth mindset that will allow them to adapt to the changing ways of working when it changes.

Carol Dweck, American psychologist, is widely associated with the growth mindset studies. In her book, *Mindset: The New Psychology of Success,* she sets aside people with a mindset to learn new talents through hard work, strategy, and learning from others as having a growth mindset. On the other side of the spectrum, you have a fixed mindset— people who have strong beliefs that talent is innate, and either people are born with talent or without. So, the idea that working hard or strategizing cannot make a not-so-smart person smart is the fixed mindset DNA. As the DNA of digital transformation thrives on experimenting, learning, and not getting too comfortable with set ways of working, from the lingo of Carol Dweck, people with a growth mindset will find a natural calling in organizations that are on a digital transformation journey, which you should consider to be a majority of the organizations in the next three to five years.

There are several aspects of culture that are desired in digital transformation. There are five principal elements that make up digital culture, as represented in Figure 12-4. They are as follows:

- Innovative

- Openness

- Collaborative

- Entrepreneurial

- Customer centric

Innovative

Experiment to create
value and stay relevant

Customer Centric

Revolve decisions
around customer
wants and needs

Openness

Transparency in the
system

Collaborative

Work as one-unit and
shared responsibility

Entrepreneurial

Take risks and
innovate

Figure 12-4. *Elements of digital culture*

Innovative

DevOps promotes experimentation. It builds an ecosystem to thrive, and for the teams to experiment and innovate. If they end up failing, they fail fast so they can start on the next set of experiments. Only through an environment where experimentation is encouraged, a culture of innovation can bloom. Unless organizations innovate, their fates are in the hands of other organizations that are willing to hedge their bets on the next big thing.

Case in point is Nokia, which stuck to their guns with phones with buttons or a resistive touchscreen with a stylus (Nokia 5800). Before they could blink, the market and their loyal fanbase had shifted to capacitive touchscreen phones with play stores hosting a repository of apps through an ecosystem of app developers. Even after the Microsoft acquisition and their introduction to touchscreen phones, the market would not move back in their favor. They became a classic case of the perils of non-innovativeness. Kodak is another example. Their strong bond with touch-and-feel photography dug their grave. As the world went toward digital photography, Kodak argued that people loved and adored photographs on paper rather than on a monitor. As Fuji brought in its digital cameras, instead of following suit, Kodak stood firm by engaging in debates over real photography versus digital photography. Their sales tanked, their stock price avalanched, and the company went into bankruptcy.

For organizations to survive the next half decade, they must launch new products and offerings that are unique, add value to customers, not be easily replicable by competitors. To make it happen, a culture of innovation must run deep in the organization, and the people who are part of the journey (with growth mindset) must be curated carefully.

Some red flags to beware of:

- Teams saying that they are comfortable with a particular way of working because they know it works rather than trying a new method to see if it works.

- Teams fearing to fail rather than to learn from failures.

- Detailed planning and ensuring certainty over showing flexibility to improvise.

- Forming multiple teams to perform respective sets of activities and objectives rather than bringing together teams with a common objective.

Efforts must be made to ensure that an environment of innovation in inbred in the organization. This is possible if there is overwhelming senior leadership support, followed by the practice of keeping teams accountable rather than individuals. People who work in fear of failure will not innovate. Innovation comes through the right set of people and in an ecosystem that allows team members to experiment, fail, and take risks.

Openness

A major support system for innovation to breed in an organization is through transparency. The information pertaining to work should be available to all team members, whether it is good news or bad. In DevOps, we follow a principle of sharing all project related information on a medium that is accessible to all team members. The idea is to ensure that the information shared will help team members make decisions in terms of the product development and roadmap. For example, a bug found in the functional testing process should be broadcasted to all team members even if they have not particularly worked on the related feature. This information will help them identify dependencies if any and decide on the future course of action.

Open communication should be a norm and should be promoted steadfastly by the senior leadership teams. Team members should be able to openly express their views without fearing judgement by peers and managers. The office environment should be psychologically safe, which in turn helps generate views (for and against), and importantly ideas that can potentially take the company to the next level. This has further collateral benefits such as strengthening teamwork and enhancing trust in the system and the leadership. Good ideas, interesting views, and good work by team members should be recognized appropriately, which will further encourage them to open up.

Making openness a part of the culture is not as easy as documenting it in a policy document. Leaders must walk the talk in opening up about the company and its decisions, and encourage team members to share their thoughts. This can be further facilitated by setting up various forums that allow team members to exchange their views. It need not be a team meeting or any other meetings in a different name—an online forum or a group chat will do just as good.

Collaborative

You can call collaboration the conjoined twin of openness. Both are joined at the hip, because as you start to promote one, the other benefits automatically. While openness makes communication free and without bias, collaboration leverages the open communication for team members to work together to deliver digital transformation (or anything else that is being worked on). Collaboration could be between team members, different teams, or even different organizations working for the benefit of a customer.

Collaboration like openness will help build trust with the team and with the system in place. The teams will find it a lot easier to work with each other, respect each other, and show compassion. When collaboration in the team increases, the productivity takes a boost.

A definite way to foster collaboration is to break down silos. The moment you build silos, people get bottled in, and the sense of possession is for those within this silo. When silos are shattered, team members feel that they belong to the same community of work product that's getting delivered. This will help them communicate openly and work freely with each other as long as the organization plays fair by rewarding the deservers and by following blamelessness. The goals laid out by managers should be measured for teams rather than individuals, this will promote team working over individual contributions.

Looking at the other side of the pyramid, the leadership must be appraised (at least partly) based on the feedback by the team members. Many organizations follow this culture where leaders are rated by their peers, team members, customers, and other stakeholders. This system is often referred to as 360-degree feedback. It is a good system to get the feedback not only from their managers but also to get a sense of what other stakeholders and team members feel about their performance. Care should be taken to ensure that sufficient number of people provide feedback in each of the categories to allow normalization of feedback rather than deviant ones.

Entrepreneurial

Entrepreneurs are a rare breed. It all starts with an idea which is cultivated, socialized, invested, and finally developed. Whether the product makes it big or not is not certain. In 2021, 90 percent of the startups failed within five years of inception. This is not an encouraging tale but the fact remains that there are more startups every year compared to the previous year. What does that say about the entrepreneurs behind it? Plenty!

Entrepreneurial character is a must-have for the digital culture to thrive. Entrepreneurs exist because they innovate, and we have discussed earlier about innovation being one of the driving forces of the digital culture. They innovate because they are willing to take risks. While they hate failing, it does not deter them from finding the fastest way to innovate and fail.

Entrepreneurs have a big asset that makes them what they are—apart from their risk taking attitude. They start companies because of their positive attitude. They always see light at the end of the tunnel no matter how deep and far it digs in. You might have probably heard of KFC founder Colonel Sanders' story. At 65 years, he had a monthly social security check of $105 to live on. He had experience selling chicken dishes at a younger age, and he wanted to sell his fried chicken recipe to willing restaurants who were ready to team up with him. His proposal was rejected 1,009 times before getting accepted, and this was at a ripe age of 65 years. How many of us would give up after 25 rejections? His positive mental attitude helped create what we know today as Kentucky Fried Chicken, which is a global conglomerate with revenue earnings nearing $30 billion mark in 2020.

Entrepreneurs and their positivity do not only make them successful, but it rubs off on others who work with them. Imagine companies having people with such a mindset, and the various opportunities for innovation, experimentation, and ideation! A psychologically safe environment with no fear of judgment will foster positivity.

Entrepreneurs are intrinsically motivated. They find sufficient reasons to do what they venture into. This quality, when imbibed in digital transformations, helps organizations self-manage teams and team members.

When it comes to a team of motivated individuals with ideas, thoughts, and differing views, there comes a point where the person who can rationalize well wins the day. This requires the power of persuasion, which buttresses their solutions and viewpoints. Remember that entrepreneurs are always in a situation to find new investors, and to do that, they must convince others that the idea is a good one. In digital transformation too, there will be multiple ideas floating around, and differing views coming from all corners. Persuasion skills in this context are an asset.

Customer Centric

Gartner's definition of customer centricity is as follows:

> Customer centricity is the ability of people in an organization to understand customers' situations, perceptions, and expectations. Customer centricity demands that the customer is the focal point of all decisions related to delivering products, services and experiences to create customer satisfaction, loyalty and advocacy.

Let's get it real. There is no business without customers. Unless a customer gets into the act of buying products or services, the company that is offering them ceases to exist. So, it is a rational thought to keep customers at the center of the universe and give them what they need.

If you are going to spend an hour of your busy day watching a TV show, and if Netflix cannot produce a show that piques your interest, then as a customer you have the right to go elsewhere. There is nothing that Netflix can do to hold onto you, and make you pay for their services if you don't like what they have to offer. The only way that Netflix can make customers continue paying for their subscription is to produce shows that intrigue interest, are of high production quality, and most importantly, are entertaining. This is the prime reason that Netflix launches new shows and movies on a regular basis. There are keeping customers at the center of their business and producing entertainment that is suitable to them.

Organizations must ensure that they are not internally focused. You find a lot of companies doing this—going through organization changes, making changes to their offerings, changing their policies and a whole lot of other stuff without bothering to see what the customer is doing all this time, and how these changes affect the customer. Any change that is done internally must have a bearing on the customer. Even an organization change that's a purely internal matter should be done to better serve customers, and to better prepare for what customer's future needs.

Digital culture centers around the customer. Those who get this right are well placed on the path that takes them more or less where they want to be. In this quickly changing world, it is important for companies to know what their customers are thinking, what the customer's needs are, and how they feel about their products. No transaction with the customer is an one-time affair. Feedback is key. Feedback is the data that aids companies shape their products and services to get more customers and repeat business. Soliciting feedback may not be as straightforward as it used to be once upon a time. A survey or a phone call won't cut the mustard. The real feedback to obtain is from various social media channels. Organizations should employ the machines (read artificial intelligence) to scour the various social media channels to read the pulse of customers.

Customers generally don't trust companies to do what is in the customers' interests. They know that companies are self-serving and exist for their own benefit. Organizations must go the extra mile to earn the trust of customers. How do they do it? Every sector is different and earning trust is an art that takes time to master. In the food delivery business, Swiggy, a popular food delivery service, doesn't ask too many questions or interrogate customers when they complain about missing food items. Refunds or missing deliveries are provided immediately. This gesture ensures the customer that Swiggy does right by them, and the money they pay is worth it. Just for comparison, the food prices at Swiggy are at least 30 percent more than what you get at the restaurant. Yet, knowingly paying more is not a problem when you know that the food you seek will be delivered (mostly) on time, and that customer service is there to serve you when necessary.

People

While businesses disrupt, processes overhaul, and technologies upgrade or switchover, there is a common thread that powers all other parts of the digital transformation—the *people*. Digital transformation is not about technology, it is the people who are affected, and who are expected to take the digital transformation forward. And yet, people powering digital transformations is often assumed or taken for granted. Digital transformations that don't consider the people aspects tend to fail.

The whole intent of digital transformation is to bring about massive changes in a short span of time to allow companies a first mover advantage. However, people can be a bottleneck if they are assumed to move with lightning speed. One cannot expect somebody who has played a particular role for a decade to do something else the next day. While attitude is one part of the equation, training and expertise challenges are also not easily surmountable.

The Coca-Cola Case Study

A case study published by McKinsey shares the story of people transformation at the Coca-Cola company. McKinsey's discovery process identified that about 60 percent of the workforce had to change their roles before 2030. This is a company that is close to 100,000 strong worldwide and we are talking about 60,000 of them changing their roles, which includes re-training on digital skills. Training commenced last year, and in the first year, 500 people were trained on digital skills and an additional 4,000 people are being trained. Putting together a digital academy and putting people through the churner is a massive program that costs a lot of money. and The company expects the digital graduates to deliver, but not everybody will come out on top. This is a massive risk that organizations have to take head-on. One might say, why not cut ties with the existing employees and hire digitally skilled employees? The problem with this approach is simply this—new folks will not have the specific business and domain knowledge to run the business. While they may do digital things well, business too needs to be run, and for that, experience counts. Hiring new people is not ruled out, but it will not be done on the same scale as the ones that go through the retraining process. For the record,

McKinsey reported that the freshly trained graduates have helped the company develop new approaches to automation and analytics, which has led to a productivity increase of 20 percent.

The Psychological Effect of Change

Numbers tell you only one part of the story. What they don't report is the mental state of the people. Borrowing Elisabeth Kubler-Ross' five stages of grief model, when asked to learn a new skill or change their role, people are in shock and confused about the mess that is in front of them. Over time, they get angry at the prospect of going back to school and doing something new. As the anger simmers, they bring out their connections within the organization to see a way out of the inevitable change. With change staring them in their face, they can go into depression. Finally, when the writing is on the wall bold and big, they accept their fate and jump on the bandwagon. These stages cannot be plotted against a project management plan, and they take time. Most organizations employ change management experts to deal with people and help out during the entire process.

There is no easy way out. Organizations have to find a way out to identify people with a growth mindset and start putting them through pilot and initial batches.

Fear of Automation

With automation taking precedence over manual activities, people see themselves as becoming redundant. This assumption may not be entirely false, but there is an opportunity or silver lining with the rise of automation.

Automation is heavily employed where there are opportunities of manual activities that do not require human intelligence. I use the word heavily and not a blanket statement because artificial intelligence can mimic human cognition and actions to a good effect if it's implemented well. While automation replaces human tasks such as running batch jobs, publishing reports, restarting services, and other mundane tasks, the human effort required for operational tasks has significantly decreased. This, however, has not led to loss of jobs in a number of sectors where the people getting replaced have showcased a growth mindset. People with business experience are priceless, and letting them go is a waste of assets. Grooming new people on business knowledge takes time and effort. As employees become redundant due to automation, people have found new avenues and have begun working in new roles. Essentially, this serves two purposes:

- People are moving to newer roles as an outcome of digital skills they acquire.

- People are carrying out tasks that are at a higher level of complexity, which require human cognizance, challenging them and keeping them interested in their new roles.

Most people naturally prefer to work in a challenging environment, and automation has nudged them toward learning new areas of study and has pushed them toward becoming better creators.

Automation has not made people redundant. In fact, automation has made people more relevant in the digital scheme of things. It has given some employees new inspiration to learn new skills and perform meaningful tasks. Over time, the new skills they acquire will get automated too, and they will have to rinse and repeat the entire process. It can be a fun process as long as they have the right mindset.

Chapter 13 delves deeper into the people and leadership aspects.

Technology

Technology is the reason that digital transformation came into existence, and yet, it is a byproduct of everything else that we do, like operating models, process methodologies, and culture, among others. We know for a fact that anything that we can imagine, we can realize using technology.

It goes without saying that technology is an integral part of any digital transformation exercise and one of the potent skills that sets leaders apart from the rest. Together with culture, people, and data, it makes for a delectable solution that can take problems head-on. The art of digital transformation is to use it suitably and craft it for specific purposes and accelerators.

The L'Oréal Case Study

With the pandemic raging across countries, there was one company that was sitting pretty and the social distancing norms were not seen as a disruption to its business. L'Oréal, the cosmetic giant, was comfortable with its repertoire of digital armory.

The company unleashed its augmented reality technology along with its cloud prowess. Adding live streaming capability to the mix made it a combination that COVID-19 could not dent. Its online sales went up by 62 percent compared to pre-corona days.

The cosmetic industry relies on physical touch and proximity, so it was bound to be one of the most affected industries when the pandemic raged. Pushed against the wall, with social distancing rules in place, the company put together the next best thing with the combination of digital technologies.

The company acquired ModiFace in 2018, which is an augmented reality (AR) technology developed for the beauty industry. It seamlessly integrates artificial technology to give consumers a virtual dash of makeup on their skins, minus the physical touch.

The AR technology is embedded on popular platforms such as Facebook and Amazon, where consumers can try cosmetics using their mobile phone cameras in a video or a photo mode. All the shades and colors at their fingertips, without having to step outside!

This acquisition of ModiFace happened in 2018, a full two years before the pandemic hit, which shows the digital acumen of the people leading the digital transformation for the cosmetic major. Last year, after the pandemic, the company further added AR lenses to Snap Camera for their brands, including Garnier, Lancôme, and Maybelline. Furthermore, consumers can broadcast their live streaming of the virtual try-ons through Google Meet or Zoom.

L'Oréal reached out to its consumers through a new partnership in Livescale, which is targeted for the beauty industry. Influencers and beauticians often showcase a plethora of beauty products on this livestreaming app, and L'Oréal's partnership paid the company rich dividends. The company has also invested in Replika Software, a network for ecommerce through social networks.

The company started to modernize their applications and cloudify them well before the pandemic hit. The flexibility they possessed when they had to scale when all sales went digital was *feather touch.*

L'Oréal vs. Estée Lauder: A Digital Transformation Comparison

Comparing digital transformations from one organization to another is like comparing the talent of Messi against Hamilton. The baseline or the numerator will never be on the same scale. L'Oréal and Estée Lauder are on different stages of digital maturity. The size of the companies and their market reach and breadth are a gulf wide.

Yet, I find it coincidental that the top cosmetic companies in the world, when pitted against a common situation, leveraged the same technology but in their own capacities.

L'Oréal saw the writing on the wall (not the pandemic, but virtualization) well before the pandemic started and acquired the augmented reality technology. Estée Lauder was rather reactive in opting for the technology after the fact. Clearly, having the vision to foresee the future of virtual market through augmented reality has been the French company's biggest win.

Estée Lauder opted to build their own tool when the pandemic hit. When the stores were shut, the top priority would have been to reach the maximum market at the shortest possible time. A prudent decision would have been to go for a COTS product such as VTO (which they did eventually six months later). This case study will open the discussion for buy versus build and to me, the decision to go one way or the other is governed by the situation. Retrospectively, after seeing the pandemic for a year and a half and after having seen these examples in action, it is easy to say that the company should have opted for COTS in the first place rather than trying to build their own.

A positive aspect of Estée Lauder's case study is their decision to withdraw from the build decision six months down the line and opt to go for VTO. Many a time, especially when we spend six months building a product, we get too close and emotionally attached to the product, and we end up keeping our rational decisions out of the office. But the company pulled through with a tough decision and did end up saving a lot of money, plus they had a working solution that put their products back on the market.

Techniques and Architectures

Technology isn't just about codes and futuristic elements that can automate everything. It is not all knowing like *Skynet* (the artificial intelligence in the *Terminator* series). Applying logic to reasoning can make mountains look like molehills—I am referring to techniques that can be applied to make the technology look a whole lot more powerful than it is.

Consider this—a customer does not want to suffer any downtime during an overhaul of the web application. There are multiple ways to address this quagmire. It can be done on the infrastructure layer or on the application layer or both.

One of the common approaches is using the blue-green deployment methodology where two sets of production environments are maintained and work in conjunction with a load balancer. One of the environments is referred to as blue and the other is green. Let's say that at the time of deployment, all the traffic is routed to the blue environment and the application is deployed on the green environment. Since the green environment is inaccessible, users don't face any downtime. Once the deployment and testing is complete, the traffic from the blue environment is routed to the green environment. The blue environment gets the new software, and upon successful production testing, the load balancer can normalize by routing to both production environments. You can have as many parallel production environments as needed. It not only helps with zero downtime deployment but also serves as an effective rollback mechanism against bad releases.

A different variation of the blue-green deployment is when you have one set of production environments that hosts the current application. A new production environment is set up with the new application and all required integrations. At the time of the release, the traffic can cut over from old production to new production. Users will probably not notice it unless they are logged into active sessions, which will be terminated.

Golden Practices for Technology Implementation

The heights of technology is limited by our imaginations. Digital transformation is no different. A sound architecture and approach to planning and executing transformation determines the role of technology. Yet, technology is not omnipotent and its implementation comes with varied sets of challenges.

There are a number of ways to implement technology, and as long as the implementation is successful, all is well. The problems arise when things go south. Therefore, there are some golden practices that organizations should follow because they have worked time and again. The order of the practices is not important. What is key is that the practices point you in a general direction, and based on the context, organizations have to choose the specifics. In fact, within the same organizations, two different technology implementations may follow separate approaches.

Here are the seven golden practices that are universally accepted in organizations:

- Manage the change
- Timing is key
- Automation is normal
- Plan for scaling
- Evaluate technology
- Implementation partners
- Iterate implementation

Manage the Change

Change is always good when sitting outside of the box and driving it. People on the inside will have a different take on the change, when it rocks their worlds and takes them out of their comfort zones. If the people who use the products or services feel that the change was unwarranted, the outcome is not going to be pretty. A disgruntled user is not going to produce the best they can, and when faced with hostility, the feeling can be contagious.

Technology change is not just what changes in the backend. The beauty of technology changes is that they can bear a change to the process. In fact, they should. The process should improve in order to improve efficiencies and throughput. As this happens for the benefit of the greater good, it is critical that the people on the ground are taken on the ride as well. Bring in change management consultants to smooth out the effect of changes and to address any discontentment.

Timing Is Key

Changing technology has a bearing on the business process. If the business process has to change, the timing needs to be perfect. If you are doing it over a long weekend, who is going to test the production when it goes live? If you are planning to make a change during the end of the financial year, what is going to happen to the company's financial transactions and year-end closing if the technology change fails? Plan your release early and give enough time to evaluate the tools and to bring about the change with optimal planning. When you have to decide on a technology, you don't want to make a decision in haste, which could be perilous if the technology is not just right.

Timing is everything. Get sufficient time to plan and implement. Technology changes cannot be done in a jiffy, especially during the selection and design phases. Take as much as you need. When it's time to plan, consult with the business to understand their process timelines. Plan with them and around critical timelines that may be risky if changes go awry.

Automation Is Normal

Automation is normal. Manual processes are the exception. Generally, organizations start with manual activities, and when they are able to deliver manually, they look for automation options. With a good maturity of automation setting in, it is time to reverse the trend. Every activity that comes out of digital transformation must be planned to be automated. If any activity cannot be done, you must put in place a rigorous process to vet the use case. If it's satisfied, you label it is as an exception.

For IT related testing, there are a number of solutions like Tosca and Selenium that lend heavily in the testing space. Almost everything can be automatically tested, including the user test cases. On the business side, their activities can be picked up by the robotic process automation technology. Even the COTS and low code/no code products come with built-in automation options that need to be exploited.

Plan for Scaling

Organizations that don't grow wither away and die. This is the hard truth. Every organization must look toward growing. As organizations grow, their systems must be capable of handling more transactions, their infrastructure must be scalable, their data volumes should be managed, and, most importantly, their process must not break down due to big numbers.

The mantra should be *think big*. Options for scaling must be done right at the genesis and should not be an afterthought. After all, you may have to choose a different technology altogether if you are thinking of scaling possibilities, so factoring it during the design phase may not be sufficient. For example, cloud infrastructure is a shining example of scaling. You can extend horizontally or vertically without breaking a sweat. This was not the case a decade earlier. Moving to higher configuration servers required migration planning for weeks and months and the effort was not only extensive but the results were not guaranteed.

Evaluate Technology

The new norm for working in IT is in iterations and small batches. However, when it comes to decision making on the technology, it needs to be done at the beginning and preferably only once. The cost of deciding on a technology and changing midway is high and it needs to be avoided at all costs. In short, don't iterate technology evaluation. Spend as much time as needed to determine the technology that will work for you.

Many a time, we see organizations changing their processes and goal posts to suit the technology—this is not a good practice. Business processes and practices should always come first; they should be defined with specific defined goals. To meet the goals, and to solve the specific business problems, choose the best technology.

During the decision making process, identify all the stakeholders who are a part of the value stream. Make them an integral part of the decision process. With stakeholders from every quarter, new aspects will arise which help narrow down the technology that will solve the problems at hand.

During technology evaluation, we often do a proof of concept to put the technology to practical use. This helps you decide based on the actual implementation and usage rather than published features and capabilities of the product. In some cases, certain technologies like ERP solutions can be applied to multiple areas and value streams. In such cases, the scope of technology may spread to a wider part of the organization, which will bring in more stakeholders and delay the decision making process. Yet, at the end of the tunnel, you will have an integrated solution that solves multiple problems.

Implementation Partners

While choosing a technology is one major decision, the path to take for its implementation is another. A company may choose to implement the procured/acquired technology on their own. The question to ask is whether the company has the expertise to implement. Have they done it before? Successfully?

As the *digital* of everything widens, there are companies that specialize in niche areas—one of them being implementing particular technologies. Examples include implementing Salesforce, or SAP, or any other COTS product. It has become quite rare these days to build products from scratch and build bespoke products. With bespoke products, the chances of success is too low, and the effort and time taken is too high. There are products out in the market for every industry and for every application. Why not just get it implemented with a partner who has done this a number of times and get going? The priority today is to get up and running in the shortest possible time. The risk appetite for implementation success has gone down considerably. So, the best ploy is to find implementation partners who come in, implement, and hand over the operations to the company and leave. In some cases, the implementation partners will continue supporting the product after implementation. In either case, the company that is going to use the identified technology is not going to take it upon itself to implement it. There is too much risk.

Iterate Implementation

Implementation is an activity that yields the best results when done iteratively. Massive, Big Bang changes are harder to deal with, mainly due to the lack of data and anticipated bugs and challenges.

The advantage of iteration is that you can start small in a remote corner of an organization. Learn from the mistakes. Rectify it in another corner to be doubly sure that the second pilot is successfully. Once the implementation team is confident, they can roll it out in phases/waves. The data-driven implementation bolstered by the learning will increase the probability of success and decrease unnecessary disruption for the business.

When I plan implementation rollouts, it starts with a proof of concept, which deals with non-production data, and no practical uses for the product. When it meets the exit parameters, a pilot is planned in a not-so-busy part of the organization. For the pilot rollout, remember that you do not have any data on how the product behaves, and how the implementation will happen in this organization. Even though as implementation partners, you have experience from other organizations, a new organization is still a green pitch. A pilot is crucial to study the activities. Every step in the pilot is recorded and reviewed with various stakeholders. When the pilot goes live, you should give sufficient time for hypercare to identify all the possible issues. Don't look at the issues as issues but as learnings. A retrospective of the pilot program must include a detailed analysis of the steps undertaken, the outcomes achieved, the learnings, the optimization opportunities, and the mistakes. These would be improvised during the next wave of implementation, which will be a lot smoother thanks to the experience and the data that is gathered.

Data

Data is like nutrients in the digital age. There is plenty of food today, and food has its respective carbs, fats, proteins, and other nutrients. The food that is beneficial to us—namely protein, some carbs, and good fats—have to be chosen carefully from the assortment of foods. Data is like food. It is everywhere. Like food, there is abundance of data. We need to curate the data that is beneficial and discard the mundane. It is easy to state this, but the challenge is real. To put it simply, the abundance of data is a massive challenge because you need to start looking for specific datasets that help you in this data superset—much like finding a needle in a haystack.

Some organizations are methodical and disciplined about data. They create departments to manage, analyze, and make sense of the data. There are executive positions like a Chief Data Officer (CDO) who is made accountable for all the data functions. This is a good start, but is it good enough? I don't believe that data can be managed centrally because in every nook and cranny of an organization or a project, data is generated. A central team trying to discover and manage all such data is just not going to cut it. It is not practical and possible. Much like innovation, managing and analyzing data must be done at every service line, every team, every program, and every project. All those who are part of the digital exercises should be responsible for data—for identifying data points and analysis. Construing, interpreting, and decision making may happen either at leadership levels or the data is fed into predictive models. In essence, the decision making can happen based on identifying data sources and analyzing it effectively.

Digital transformation is often done on the back of almost no data to back the decisions data. Many programs are executed under the digital transformation banner and are either being done for the first time in the organization or being experimented with. So digital transformation often does not have the luxury of backing the roadmaps to undertake. Therefore, the importance of running the program in small batches and executing the pilot is critical. A lot can be learned from the pilot, and as you iterate, you learn a lot more. The learning does not stop, because digital transformation is not a destination but a journey.

DIKW Cycle

Before delving into data strategy and other related nuances, this section introduces a model that characterizes the different evolutionary stages of data. The data-to-information-to-knowledge-to-wisdom (DIKW) is often represented as a pyramid and is shown in Figure 12-5.

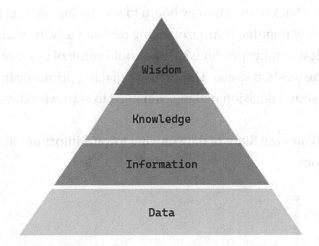

Figure 12-5. *DIKW pyramid model*

Data is the foundation and is (or can be) extracted at every stage. Imagine the data that Amazon can gather from your product buying habits, your spending trends, and the items that you browse and don't purchase. All this is data.

But data itself doesn't signify anything. I browsed Amazon for Isolate Whey Protein. So what? Unless you marry the data to a trend, it's not helpful. While I browsed for the product, I also filtered out certain brands and sorted based on reviews. Now this is good information. Because Amazon now knows that I don't buy something that is listed on the top of the screen (often paid engagements) but am specific, and I learn about the stuff that I am buying. This is information.

Knowledge is power is a popular aphorism derived from the Latin phrase *scientia potentia est*. It is powerful weapon because it is a culmination of people's experiences, ideas, thoughts, and insights. The result of all of these factors transforms information into knowledge. Amazon can gather information from multiple customers, analyze the information, and make corrections to their algorithms to showcase products that are popularly being sought. They can also join up with manufacturers to get sponsorship for promoting the products. No wonder they say knowledge is power!

In the process, knowledge tries to answer the how question.

How did the 54 incidents get raised? How are we offering 23 services to the customer? The answers to these questions, you need excessive analytical skills and sound analysis.

Wisdom is the highest echelon in the knowledge management area. While data, information, and knowledge capture the data, add context and meaning, and invoke actions, wisdom goes back to the strategy board to see the big picture. By promoting a product that is not very popular, is Amazon being partisan toward accumulating profits through (perhaps) low-quality products? These could some of the level of discussions that are hosted in the wisdom space. The decision making primarily happens in this realm and to get to sound decision making, you need to start with data and progress to wisdom.

Figure 12-6 indicates the flight of data moving toward information, knowledge, and finally toward wisdom.

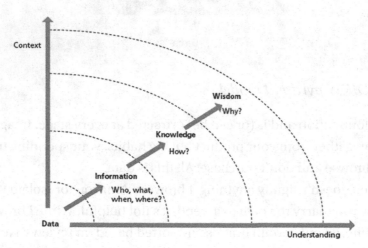

Figure 12-6. *Data to information to knowledge to wisdom*

Summary

This chapter introduced the battle tank framework for digital transformation. This framework addresses all the aspects of digital transformation—the areas that need to be considered before and during the journey.

The digital transformation exercise is a long-drawn game, where the end is not in sight. Therefore focus and effort need to be placed on the means and the journey. A sound strategy is needed before embarking on the program and the topic of digital transformation strategy addresses this need.

CHAPTER 13

People and Leadership

If you ask 100 people in IT what they are currently working on, 90 would say that it has something to do with digital transformation. A number of organizations are on their digital transformation journey. But the phrase digital transformation is an overly used, abused, and misused term. Many believe that digital transformation is about shifting to newer technologies and its offshoots. The truth is that digital transformation has very little to do with technology, and much more to do with people.

To state it even further, digital transformation is of the people, by the people, and for the people.

Digital Transformation Is People Centric

Before we get into this topic, let me reiterate about digital transformation.

The phrase digital transformation has a different meaning and connotation in every organization. Not only that, but people in the same organization interpret digital transformation differently as well.

Imagine that business and IT are woven into the same piece of cloth. The business processes and IT processes are not separate anymore, and IT is realizing the business' needs every step of the way. The business' outcomes have become IT's objective.

The common belief is that digital transformation is about the latest technological advancements, and organizations jumping onto the futuristic bandwagon of transforming digitally are all set for the future. Well, it may be partially true that organizations that keep up with technology can claim to be digitally forward, but there is more to the story that's often untold.

Technology is not at the center of digital transformation. Think about it. Organizations have capital and they can buy technology. But what are they doing with the technology? To make this technology remotely useful, you need people. You need people who can apply the problem on hand or innovate to improve business outcomes.

© Abhinav Krishna Kaiser 2023
A. Krishna Kaiser, *Reinventing ITIL® and DevOps with Digital Transformation*,
https://doi.org/10.1007/978-1-4842-9072-9_13

You need people who can creatively and constructively leverage the technology with the right mindset through Agile and DevOps. Added to this is the power of automation to accelerate processes and reduce human-induced delays.

Technology by itself is useless. Technology needs people. Or in fact, technology becomes functional when it is deployed by people.

Moving on in support of people driving digital transformation, an important element that drives digital transformation is the leadership. Digital transformation has to be driven using a top-down approach. Companies cannot make changes to a process here, and a technology there, and call it digital transformation. The vision of an organization to move into digital ways of working has to be set by its leaders. I cannot stress enough the importance of having the right leaders to lead the way for the organization to move forward digitally. Digital transformation is possible only with leaders who have an able vision, mindset, values, integrity, and competence.

For an organization to transform digitally, you need people who embrace change willfully. One of the new ways of working is moving from the project-centric model to the product-centric model. As this happens, the ways of working changes, roles change, responsibilities change, and in short, the entire mindset of working toward project completion is an old school of thought. So, for digital transformation to be successful, you need the employees to buy into the new ways of working, the new culture. If they don't, then no matter the best plans and technologies, digital transformation will stall before taking off. This shows why digital transformation is about people more than anything else.

With new ways of working, and having introduced new tools, technologies, and processes, the current employees will be upskilled and cross-skilled to meet the new challenges. In essence, you need the employees to undergo training, workshops, and do a lot of slogging to adjust to the digital ways of working. It's not easy. Learning new skills is hard unless you have the right mindset, but it must be done. To make it happen, you need leaders who can persuade their teams, and people who develop a mindset to yearn for new skills. If either one of these doesn't fall into place, you have a problem. Digital transformation will stall. It's not about just hiring people with the right skills and getting rid of the old people. Well, that may be easy to say, but in reality, you need people with organization and customer experience; people who are tenured to ensure continuity.

The COVID-19 pandemic gave rise to a new problem—the large-scale adoption of hybrid working environments. In fact, digital transformation has been used in conjunction with the flexibility of ultra-distributed teams working from homes.

The challenge with remote working is multi-fold. The work culture once revolved around proximity, meeting in conference rooms, water cooler discussions, and team lunches. That's largely in the history books. This changing work culture involving remote working does not foster natural collaboration, or team working and employee engagement. Organizations on their digital transformation journeys have to find ways to overcome these challenges to ensure that the transformation objectives are unaltered. I created a video about leading remote teams effectively (`https://youtu.be/s24H6dPCv8I`), which addresses solutions to some of the challenges.

I have only touched the tip of the digital transformation iceberg as far as the role of people. I am not discounting the role of technology, or downplaying its role in the journey. As long as you have the right people who are ready to take this arduous journey, there isn't anything that you cannot accomplish with technology. As you find new use business use cases, technology is there to bridge the gap. The challenge will always be training people to new ways of working. Realigning people to meet use cases is not straight forward and that's the argument around digital transformation being more about people than technology.

This chapter discusses how a digital transformation worker works, what works and what doesn't, and the leadership qualities that are essential for digital success.

The End of Work as We Know it

There was a time, not too long ago, when most of us worked out of offices. We had a time slot where work was expected from us—for some, it was flexible and for most, it was rigid, such as 9AM to 6PM. People came to offices, worked, and went back to their homes. This trend worked until COVID-19 hit us all. Overnight, we had to improvise and move from the familiar work environment to a space that meant everything other than work. A lot of people kept office work out of their homes until COVID-19 changed everything. Homes became offices, and with that, the thick redline separation between home and office vanished.

It was novel at first. Many employees were unsure how it would turn out, given the economic downturn and there was the anticipation of pink slips in the air. When there is a threat to existence, it is our human nature to adjust and do the best we can. And that is exactly what happened. People continued to work from their homes and delivered similar results to office work. The IT train chugged along. During the course of working from home, the clear distinction between office time and home time diminished. People worked round the clock, depending on their life circumstances and commitments. In the process, they involuntarily started to work more than they did earlier (perhaps because of the time saved on travel), and the productivity figures started to show this. Employers didn't have much to complain about, as they saw the writing on the wall. While the work from home model started to turn out favorably, they could see the saving potential from real estate, electricity, and other amenities that are a part of the office setup.

Work from home is a norm today, and while some businesses have opened back up, many others are hiring employees who work only from their homes. It's probably a win-win situation. As this is shaping up nicely, the often talked about business hours are no longer the topic of discussion. People have stopped declining meetings that are scheduled beyond office hours. Taking siesta naps after lunch is an accepted productivity booster. This is not just the beginning, but the declaration of work time as we knew it.

The Pitfalls of Legacy Working

It is no secret that the profitability of organizations has shrunk a great deal. There is a perceived economic downturn since the COVID-19 pandemic hit, and in a bid to survive, budget cuts is one of the tested methods. With cost cutting, one would expect digital initiatives to have been shelved, which is not exactly what happened. The business is still looking to continue IT with a lower budget, which translates to lower margins. What has added to the quagmire is the increasing costs of talent acquisition. Salaries of IT workers have gone up quite steeply, not for all, but for the top talent who showcase pie-shaped skills. All organizations are on the lookout for top talent. They are spending freely when it comes to acquiring smart and top talent, which is good, but it is essentially driving their margins lower.

With new targets and changing circumstances, organizations looking to go back to the legacy mode are faced with serious challenges. On the financial side, employees working from homes effectively is a boon. Employers have cut down on real estate, electricity, and Internet expenses. On the people side of things, there are essentially two areas that don't work anymore if we continue to work in legacy mode:

- Talent code
- Productivity equation

The Talent Code

Deloitte and Fortune conducted a joint survey in 2021 of approximately 120 CEOs from 55 sectors. Fifty-seven percent of them felt that the biggest challenge that organizations face today is finding good talent. They are on the money, as the talent pool today has not shrunk, but the demand has exceeded. Employees are not just looking for the compensation and benefits but are also considering aspects that will challenge them and teach them new tricks to take them to a different level. And, most importantly, employees are looking for flexible work options. The CEOs felt that the next biggest challenge at 51 percent was retaining top talent.

In the legacy work mode, companies set up offices in cities that attract employees with the required skills. Every city has a certain number of professionals who live in it and a percentage who are willing to relocate. Then there are employees who prefer not to travel, and they have their own areas of companies that they can work for.

From an organizational standpoint, getting good people is a critical factor, and the reason to have offices in expensive cities and in downtown areas is to attract the best talent. Instead of dealing with distance, if organizations can expand their catchment areas several times by hiring remote workers, they do themselves a favor by increasing the probability of getting good resources, and perhaps at a cheaper rate. When hiring talent is such a big challenge, organizations that require people to work in offices are at a disadvantage. To me, cracking the talent code begins by expanding the search to hedge the bets on getting the best of what the talent has to offer.

The Productivity Equation

Owl Labs conducts an annual survey called the *State of Remote Work* to get the pulse of remote working. In September 2021, they interviewed 2050 full-time remote workers in the United States, which is the fodder for their 2021 survey report. According to the study, 67 percent of the respondents reported that their productivity improved with remote working, while 24 percent said that it was more or less the same as in the office. That's more than 91 percent of the respondents claiming that their productivity has either gone upward or remained the same while working from home. This number makes a big statement and reveals the human psyche of working environments.

Another study conducted by Flexjobs that same year revealed similar results. Ninety-five percent of the respondents reported that their productivity has gone up or remained the same as in the office. Other studies conducted by universities and private institutions reveal similar numbers as well, which is a hard confirmation for the perceived productivity increase by employees. What would be interesting is a report from the perspective of the employer rather than employees. I would like to believe that the numbers would look more or less similar.

The revelation is this—a homogenous environment involving personal and work lives is best from the productivity angle. All employers would see better productivity!

However, what the studies doesn't show is the quality of personal lives as office work has shifted to personal spaces. In the Owl Labs report, it states that 55 percent of the respondents have worked more than they did at the office, while 12 percent worked less. The additional hours don't automatically equate to office work encroaching personal spaces, as there is the saved commute time to consider—maybe the additional hours are coming from the potential commute time.

The Flexible Model of Working

The current ways of working are not automatically mapped to work from home. Flexible working is about the freedom to work from any location and outside of a fixed time slot. With the flexi-work model of working, the output and outcomes are measured and not the time spent doing the tasks.

For example, if an employee is developing a functionality, in the legacy mode, the log in and log out times were captured, and the time spent was measured as the actual time spent working by the employee. Today, we look at the functionality delivery. We look at how quickly and efficiently a developer can turn around the requested functionality. They could work at midnight or any odd times, for all we care! The time spent developing the functionality is still measured due to academic importance for future estimations, but not for accounting the hours.

While there are several aspects to the flexi-work model of working, there are four areas that are of importance to digital transformation. They are as follows:

- No fixed hours or location constraints
- Asynchronous work
- Productivity as a KPI
- Employee engagement

No Fixed Hours or Location Constraints

Technology has freed us from the bounds of constraining employees to physical spaces and work shifts. Decades back, we did not have the means to allow employees to work outside office hours, mainly due to the lack of collaboration tools, high-speed Internet at homes, and organizations' urge to run the show by command and control. All this has changed now, mainly due to technology and aided by the cultural shift in thinking.

As the pandemic hit, many businesses saw the writing on the wall and got themselves ready for a spell of misalignment, confusion, and low productivity. But what they failed to realize was that the systems and tools that were in play enabled collaboration, and the work was as good as what the employees delivered in the office. As time passed and offices were shut down on precautionary grounds, they witnessed better than ever productivity. Better ideas and out of the box thinking emerged too. There was suddenly a splurge of creativity with new ideas and innovative designs taking shape. This was possible because employees were unshackled from location and time constraints, and this helped them unleash their creativity and produce better designs. I call this as a collateral benefit of the COVID-19 era.

Employees must be free to express themselves, and this freedom comes from a place of comfort and safety. While people work when they are their creative best, and this allows organizations to exploit their skills for better outcomes, leading to better business results and excited customers. Organizations should realize the multi-fold benefits stemming from letting go of control and letting employees take charge of the collective outcomes.

Asynchronous Work

There was a time when my colleagues and I arrived at the office at around the same time, and our work involved talking to each other, discussing specifics. We all sat in cubicles, so it involved plenty of in-cubicle discussions. When other parties were involved, we moved to a conference room and had meetings. Our work was hardly independent, although we were individual contributors. It is generally believed in project management that 70 percent of the projects were all about communication and with all the meetings and discussions, project managers believed that we were moving in the right direction.

369

As time changed, Agile came in. With Agile, there was a new concept of redesigning offices spaces. Cubicle walls were removed to increase interactions and foster collaboration. Co-location of teams became a trend again. Organizations started to build teams under the same roof. Then COVID-19 happened.

The Agile ways of working are synchronous ways. This is not bad, but it eats into efficiency. It invariably moves people into physical spaces that may not be their first option. There are benefits to co-locating teams, but it necessarily means that the team members have to travel to the office and, more importantly, have to work a common shift. Not for the digital age!

The digital age runs on asynchronicity. DevOps enables asynchronous work. Asynchronous work is where every contributor can contribute independently. They are not necessarily expected to be online during specific shifts, and every team member is assigned work, and they are able to accomplish the assigned work independently. Through this, you can build global teams where team members working in different time zones represent the principle of one team.

Meetings are not necessary as long as there is clear and crisp communication through various collaboration tools. DevOps is built to support this, where every developer, tester, and other roles carry out their tasks, and the feedback is seamlessly delivered to them or to the next person in the value chain. Every developer works on their own user story and on their own private branch. When the feature is ready, it gets merged. If there are conflicts, there is immediate feedback.

There is minimal dependence on each other to carry out work. Technology is backing collaboration ably. Even if a document needs to be created by multiple team members, they can work on the same document simultaneously. They don't need to create their sections separately and integrate them. Integration and development can happen together. Such is the power and backing of technology to support asynchronous work, which is the present and future of work and is an enabler for digital transformation to flourish.

Productivity as a KPI

The digital age promotes flexible work, with no constraints of *where* and *when*. Team members are not bound by constraints. This doesn't mean that team members have no accountability. The targets in the digital age are not about the time spent doing work but rather the outcomes. Taking an example of a developer, certain functionalities are assigned (generally self-assigned) with a target date for delivery. The team member can choose to work at any time and from anywhere as long as the feature is delivered within the target. The developer may take 25 hours or 3 hours; it does not matter, as long as the feature is delivered on time.

While the benchmark starts with delivery of outcomes, the KPIs intend to see the delivery of work as a product of improved productivity over time. In Agile, we call it the *velocity*, which needs to improve over time. It is not a preference to see productivity go up, but rather an expectation of leadership.

In other words, it is a kind of negotiation. The team member gets the freedom to work from anywhere and at any time. But the delivery needs to happen on time, and over a period of time, it must gradually increase. Sounds fair!

Employee Engagement

A common thread that existed in older ways of working was the challenge of engaging employees. Employee engagement has its roots in how they feel about work, whether they are satisfied with the work they are doing, and whether they are looking forward to working the next day (and the next).

Why do we care about employee engagement as long as the desired outcomes are being delivered?

Digital transformation is a journey. There are things that take shape on a daily basis. Team members have to be at their best every day to make a difference. That is possible only if they are motivated and have the zeal to do what is necessary. This is not an one-time effort, so employees need to be involved in the good work, day after day. This can only be done if there is motivation and sufficient engagement with the organization they work for, the customer organization, and with the people they work with.

The State of Global Workplace is an annual study published by Gallup about employee experiences. In their own words, employees state how they feel about their work and their lives, which reflect on an organization's resilience and performance.

In the 2022 report, Gallup notes that only 21 percent of the employees worldwide are actively engaged in their respective organizations. The majority of the engaged employees reside in United States and Canada. This is alarming, and organizations need to take notice and implement steps that will bring employees closer to work, to colleagues, and to the organizations.

While there are multiple benefits to the flexible working model, one of the downsides is that it is naturally hard to engage employees. Working at odd hours, and working out of their homes is not an ideal setting to create work connections. The interest in the work, although interesting and challenging, will wane over time in the absence of employee engagement. This is the last thing that organizations need, as they are already battling high attrition and talent scarcity.

Organizations need to go out of their way to build teams in which team members respect and back each other up. There must be various employee engagement initiatives that strengthens the bonds. A small organization that I have consulted with schedules team dinners every third Saturday of a month. The event is a big success as coworkers are eager to see other, talk about various topics, and connect to each other. Also, when employees feel appreciated, a sense of loyalty and connection are direct benefits, which go a long way in enhancing the employee experience.

On the other side, the digital age has enhanced employee engagement in unexpected ways. In legacy styles, when a question needed to be asked, team members had to raise their hands and ask their question, while the rest of the crowd turned their attention to the one speaking. Not everyone is comfortable being at the center of attention, and many people would probably not ask the question, thus reducing the engagement. In digital age, where meetings are remote, the process of asking questions becomes inclusive. Big meetings such as townhall meetings do not allow employees to ask questions directly but rather they are sent over chat and scrutinized before being posed to the chair. Maybe the digital age can unearth employee engagements that went under the radar in legacy settings, but mostly, employee engagement has suffered, and organizations and leaders have to think beyond their business to keep employees engaged.

The Framework for the Flexi-Work Model

Changes that alter the fabric of an organization need to be done methodically. Yes, even in the digital age, changes as big as flexi-work models cannot and should not be done without thinking them through. In other words, a framework (of sorts) is needed to ensure alignment of expectations.

The framework that is introduced here (Figure 13-1) is minimalistic and is a good starting point. The key elements, or the pillars for setting up a flexi-work model, are as follows:

- Digital envisioning

- Enablement for flexible model

- Digital culture fitment

- Performance management

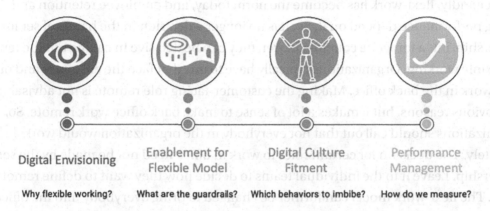

Digital Envisioning   Enablement for   Digital Culture   Performance
             Flexible Model   Fitment   Management
Why flexible working?   What are the guardrails?   Which behaviors to imbibe?   How do we measure?

Figure 13-1. *Framework for the flexi-work model*

Implementing each of the elements sequentially is best, considering that there are ample dependencies on the previous elements. Each element can be viewed as a guide to building an organization's flexi-work model, and you will find out soon enough that there is plenty of room to maneuver within the elements—flexibility starts from within!

Digital Envisioning

When an organization opts to adopt the flexi-work model, it must have strong reasons to back this decision up. This is a major shift in the way the organization works. It is a step toward digital transformation. But the rationale must be understood, and all the subsequent steps are dependent on knowing the *why*. As Simon Sinek puts it in *The Golden Circle* concept, it all starts with the question *why*. As a result of the pandemic, we all figured out what to do and how to do it even before thinking through the reasons behind it. It was justified during a crisis, but now when we start to look at the future, it is a pertinent question to ask.

One of the primary reasons organizations opt for the flexi-work model is to attract good talent. No matter how advanced the technologies they employ, organizations still need good talent to grow. Talent will always be the lifeblood and success and failures are directly dependent on the talent. There is absolutely nothing wrong for organizations to go on the record to state this. It is important for not only the employees to understand, but also to announce it to potential employees that you mean business when you say you follow flexi-work. In fact, employees and potential employees are always keen to understand the rationale behind senior leadership decisions, and they go the extra mile to support it. This is true with all decisions in the organization.

Secondly, flexi-work has become the norm today, and employee retention and hiring performance depend on it. So, it is no longer a decision in the hands of senior leadership, but a foregone conclusion. Yet, they can be decisive in calling out the tenets of flexible working. Organizations typically have teams that face the customer and others who work in the back office. Making the customer-facing role remote is not advisable for obvious reasons, but it makes a lot of sense to make back office work remote. So, organizations should call out that not everybody in the organization would work remotely. The decision for certain roles to work in office need not be made by the senior leadership. Leave it to the individual teams to decide how they want to define remote work. The flexi-work model can further be changed to bring everybody into the office once a week or once a month.

GitLab is one of the leading tools of DevOps orchestration. The company is global and houses around 1200 employees across 65 countries. The company's flexi-work policy is called all-remote because they do not have any physical offices. Even the executives work out of their homes. The company made a conscious decision to make remote working uniform across the board with the intent of a singular message—all employees are equal. Offsites are held once or twice a year, and employees are fully compensated for travel and accommodation. By not having offices, the company is serious about remote working and are intentional about it. They have removed the barrier between some people working from offices and others from home. Employees for their part know that they will work from homes, so their homes include home-offices, and some of them prefer to travel and not work from the same location more than a month at a stretch. GitLab does not have to spend a penny on office infrastructure, and these savings help their bottom line.

Enablement for the Flexible Work Model

GitLab employees work remotely every day. They may interact with their coworkers once or twice a year. But they don't feel isolated. Remote working is backed up by technology to ensure that team members can collaborate, interact, and share ideas as if they were sitting across from each other. The asynchronous nature of work aided by collaboration tools has made it possible for employees to work independently. When needed, regular communication channels through video calling can give the experience of social warmth.

Making a purposeful decision to flexi-work is the beginning. The company needs to make it happen by enabling employees to work from anywhere that provides the same experience as working from office. Target, the U.S. superstore, gave allowances to their employees to buy comfortable chairs and desks. They further ensured that the employees had laptops that would not constrain employees to work longer to complete the assigned work. Furthermore, they cut down on meetings to give employees the schedule flexibility.

It is the responsibility of employers to provide guardrails to employees that will help them succeed at work—this could be in the form of technology through collaboration tools, security systems, VPN for connecting to private networks, and self-healing tools to resolve laptop problems when they arise. The example that I quoted from Target are the physical amenities that provide a basic infrastructure, including reimbursing Internet and electricity expenses.

When organizations are intentional about flexi-work, they must live the talk by committing to cutting down on meetings. Essentially, meetings are harmful to flexi-work because they go against the concept of schedule flexibility. Leaders must push employees to communicate through chat, email, and other asynchronous forms. Furthermore, if an organization is serious about getting the best talent onboarded by claiming flexi-work policies, they must be intentional about it. The last thing organizations want is to chest-beat about flexi-work and then create disparities between employees who come into office and others who don't. Especially when customers and executives are involved in meetings, there is a notion that putting a face physically earns them visibility, respect, and attention.

Work Culture Fitment

A study conducted by Great Places to Work in the summer of 2021 revealed that a good majority of employees reported not feeling engaged at work. The study was conducted worldwide with 14,000+ respondents. Fifty-two percent of the European employees reported that they were sufficiently engaged at work. Numbers from other regions were better than Europe but not by much—United States and Canada at 53 percent, Asia at 56 percent, Africa at 58 percent, and Latin America at 60 percent. The broad message was that the employees did not make meaningful connections at work. Reasons quoted were that coworkers did not care about each other, employees had to pretend to be somebody else (not being their own), and emotionally and psychologically unhealthy conditions. A majority of them indicated that their work didn't feel like it was serving any purpose for the company—in other words, it was redundant or lower than their expectations. They had qualms about their leadership as well—not involving them in decision making, not caring for them, and not walking the walk.

The problems that the study points to has its root cause in the work culture. Remote working has its challenges, and the result indicates that companies have failed to adopt to new ways of working. When it's intentional, flexi-work does not end with the decision-making alone; leaders must change the culture and bring in an essence of togetherness and connectedness.

The MURAL Story

MURAL was successful in raising series B funding of $118 million in August 2020, all in the midst of first wave of COVID-19 pandemic. They wanted to announce it to all of their 250 employees spread across many countries in a celebratory style. A virtual meet was their only option. The job was entrusted to their head of culture and collaboration (interesting role!) Laïla von Alvensleben and she was given two weeks to plan it. Any other planner would have planned the date and time, and an agenda of items to go over. But she didn't do the normal.

The session was named 2020 MURAL World Tour, at a time when worldwide travel had come to an abrupt halt. The theme for the session was to take the team on a virtual tour for three hours from an airport lounge and in an airplane across snowy mountains, tropical islands, and finally into the outer space.

Images of various places to virtually visit were downloaded from the Internet and shared with all employees , and then they were used as backgrounds during the session. The intention was to create a sense of being in the same place by having the same backgrounds at every stage of the virtual tour. To make the experience physical, props such as disco lights, glow stickers, sunscreen, lip balm, and an a la carte of other items were shipped to the employees.

The day before the session, an invite was shared that looked like a boarding pass, with the itinerary along with the flight and ground crew. Team members were told of the part they had to play, and to dress accordingly.

The session was peppered with entertainment and puzzle-solving sections, which helped to break the tension of serious discussions.

The culture displayed at MURAL shows that the company and its leaders are willing to go beyond the ordinary to engage their employees; it shows that employees were important and the teams across locations were bounded through virtual space while they had fun with party props and zoom backgrounds.

An organization's culture is formed by its actions, the intent showed by its leaders, and the positive energy it generates. It becomes all the more critical that organizations put extra effort into creating a culture of growth and inclusion. It is not easy in a remote setting, but for the flexi-work model to bloom, it needs to be done.

Performance Management

When we design and implement DevOps, we measure everything, whenever possible. Measurements are at the heart of understanding the direction of performance. With accurate frequent measurements, we have an opportunity to course-correct if needed, rather than waiting until D-day to be surprised of the outcome.

The challenge with flexi-work is about assessing employee performance. As employees stay out of sight (literally), a common concern has been ability to accurately monitor employee's work and deliverables. From experience, I find this no different than when employees and their managers are co-located. Still, how do you monitor employees. Not by looking over their shoulders

A Gallup Workplace survey indicated that only 21 percent of the interviewed employees felt that they were fairly assessed and this motivated them to do outstanding work. On the other side of the coin, the majority of employees did not feel that they are being assessed accurately. There are various reasons this could happen:

- Employees may have feel the presence of exaggerated self-worth that leads to demeaning their supervisor's feedback.

- Supervisors may not be close to employee's work, so it may be possible that the employee may not be judged fairly.

- There is a mismatch between the expectation and the delivery. While supervisors expect certain outcomes, the employee delivers something else, but there could be a degree of misalignment between the expected and delivered, which could lead to discontentment.

These issues are not necessarily coming out of remote working. They existed earlier. The problem is with the structure of performance reviews. Typically in the past, organizations and managers insisted on certain work hours and they recorded the punch-in and punch-out hours. How many hours the employees spent in the office was an important measure of performance. Furthermore, the goals and expectations were quantified—the number of lines of code, the number of calls made to prospective customers, and the number of test scripts developed were the type of goals set during the legacy days. These goals did not work then and will definitely not work now.

Monitoring an employee's log-in and log-out hours is a cruel joke on the organization's resources and had roots in the industrial age. Even in the legacy era— before COVID-19—measuring an employee based on the hours spent in at work is not only unfair but also a waste of resources. The message is that the company does not trust their employees to do the job, and they feel that they must keep track of the work, either by monitoring the hours spent inside the office or monitoring login hours on the workstations. Although there is no data to suggest the fact, this could be one of the reasons for attrition in companies that practiced it.

The nature of performance goals in this age should be qualitative and not based on quantities. It does not matter if a developer writes thousands of lines of code if they do not work. The goals should be based on outcomes—rather than lines of code, provide the functionalities to develop something in a certain timeframe. The goals should be crisp, clear, and unambiguous. It should not say that development of functionalities in the project but rather specify what those functionalities are, and when they are required to be developed. Develop the API between *Applications A, B,* and *C* during *Sprints 11* and *12*. This objective is very clear. The developer is asked to develop APIs and the timeframe is specified clearly as well.

While clear goals are one part of the equation, the elephant in the room that is yet to be addressed is the frequency of performance reviews. In DevOps, we believe in providing rapid feedback, which is the basis for swift development of software. Likewise, frequent performance reviews with employees will help set short-term goals—say for about a month (equivalent to two, two-week sprints). The goals are immediate for the employee to start working toward, and the outcome is known within a matter of weeks so the manager can provide feedback accordingly. It's a win-win situation for the employee and the manager. For flexi-work to be successful, there should be no ambiguity in this department, with managers laying out clear and actionable goals. These should be followed up with frequent reviews, which will help set the course when employees are off target.

The second part of the equation in the digital age is the need to introduce or firm up employee satisfaction surveys. The organization needs to be aware of what has been going on with their employees—especially because good talent is gold and no organization wants to lose out in this race, especially when they have acquired them at a steep cost. Hear from employees on a frequent basis to understand if the employee's career goals are met, how their flexi-work is progressing, if they are stressing out, and most importantly, if they have sufficient time to do things outside of work.

Measuring performance is a two-way street, and it must happen methodically. In the digital age, organizations must make the extra effort to keep employees engaged, satisfied, and motivated to contribute to the organization. Fair assessment reviews, constructive feedback, and a healthy paycheck will do the trick.

Leadership in the Digital Age

We looked at how IT has changed from a decade ago, the ways of working that have changed, the way people prefer to work, and the technological aids that are driving transformations. One aspect that is much debated is leadership. The argument is that leadership is not new, unlike IT processes or technology. It has existed from time immemorial. There have been leaders with their own styles—leaders of people, leaders who led revolutions, and leaders who changed history. In the IT world too, there are leaders who led innovation and changed consumer behavior. The argument continues that leadership is not new since the same principles have continued over the years, and small refinements based on new generations should suffice. While this is true in principle, the digital age has turned leadership on its head and has redefined and reshaped it. The transformation in leadership is visible compared to the previous IT era. The most visible transformations are illustrated in Figure 13-2.

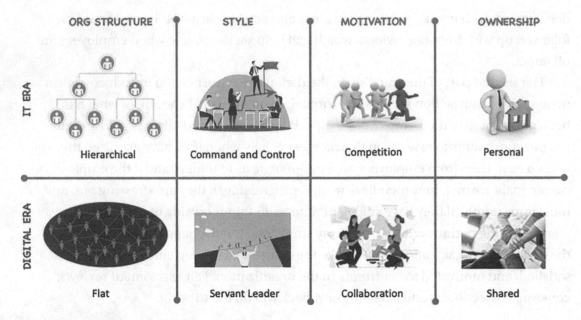

Figure 13-2. *Leadership in the digital age*

I address four dimensions of leadership that have changed drastically:

- Organization structure

- Style of people leadership

- Persuasion or motivation

- Ownership of assigned responsibilities

Organization Structure

The genesis of leadership in an organization stems from the way companies are organized. It is a critical success factor for them to succeed, and the majority of organizations find it tough to get it right even after multiple iterations. While organizing people into functions, projects, and different varieties of matrices plays a major part, the aspect that matters directly are the layers.

A hierarchical organizational formalizes the layers in an organization starting from executives to the developers and testers. At a non-executive level, you have a delivery lead, project manager, team leads, senior engineers (dev/test), and junior engineers.

The problem is not the structure itself. In fact, it has existed for a long time. With this hierarchy, every manager/supervisor has direct reports who need to be managed. Every employee should ideally get ample attention. In the digital ways of working, employees are expected to manage themselves. This is a key differentiator between the IT and digital eras where team members are empowered to manage their time and other aspects that determine outcomes. In a digital organization, leaders take center stage by guiding teams toward the true north, from the perspective of program outcomes, innovative ideas, and career aspirations.

In digital organizations, the structure is comparatively flat. It's devoid of multiple levels of hierarchy. A leader will a number of employees, including senior roles such as architects and junior positions, such as support and maintenance. Flattening the organization helps leaders reach the lowest of layers (in hierarchical organization) directly, and this motivates employees into delivering great outcomes.

The flat model aids communication, from both top-down and bottom-top. The communication from the organizations' leaders generally reaches down in a hierarchical model. However, in a flat organization, the communication takes fewer hops to reach the rest of the organization. Likewise, the grievances will reach the right set of the ears the fastest in this organization.

The decision-making ability is far greater in flat organizations. Generally, the decision makers sit at the top of the organization chain, and the intelligence from the ground that enables the decision makers lies with employees at the bottom. With a hierarchical structural, the possibilities of the ground level data reaching the leadership is hit and miss. Think about it like Chinese whispers (or the game telephone), where information passes through layers of hierarchy and is culled, modified, and transformed before it reaches leadership. With a flat structure, there is an efficient connection between the top and the bottom, thus enabling better decision making.

Leadership Style

Leadership comes in numerous styles. In fact, we don't believe that all the different styles of leadership could be catalogued, as there are new ways that are being created today.

A leader must necessarily have certain goals and objectives, which requires people to be able to deliver to achieve success. A leader can use any style to go past the end goal. Putin uses violence and aggression to attempt world domination, Gandhi used non-violence in support of Indian independence, Warren Buffet provides guidance and lets his team take success into their own hands with a laissez faire approach, and Richard Branson's charisma has taken Virgin to great heights.

Different situations require certain leadership styles to achieve results. For Apple to thrive, it needed a leader who had a vision, who could show the path and innovate together. The vision he set, that not only works great but looks beautiful, set the course of what Apple is today. There was a decade when Apple's fortunes looked south when Steve wasn't involved. His re-entry changed the fabric, and Apple became a different company altogether. Likewise, Walt Disney Studios' tells the story of a leader who was transformative in nature. Although Walty Disney himself did not say it, a widely associated quote, *if you can dream it, you can do it,* is true to the company. The company started with an idea, with Walt's skill as an artist to set in motion a transformation in the entertainment industry. In IT, although there are numerous leadership styles that exist—such as consensual, laissez faire, and participative—the chief among them that is of interest is the command-and-control style of leadership.

Command and control works well in a traditional organization where bureaucracy exists. The leadership makes all the decisions and passes down actions to be carried out by the rest of the subordinate employees. It was in vogue in military organizations, and when IT started, it followed the paradigm of the most commonly practiced style, and it worked. The approach is autocratic in nature with a view that the leadership knows everything and is capable of herding the sheep where they need to be. Developers, testers, server admins, and other individual contributors followed orders, and it was successful while it lasted.

As ideas dried up, the search for the next big thing was surprisingly hidden in the trenches of individual contributors. The flatter world required assimilation of joint venture between the top and bottom layers of the industry. Thus started the digital revolution.

The style of leadership has turned on its head. Barking orders from the top did more bad than good. The biggest problem however was this—lack of innovation. When new ideas did not breed, the leadership layer understood that they didn't stand a chance in infusing new thoughts, and they saw glimpses of hope in the bottom layers. So, they announced an innovation team, time for people to come together to innovate, and other workshops to bring out innovative ideas that they could leverage.

Guess what? It just didn't work. Innovation is like art. You can't cage artists and ask them to create a masterpiece. They were just able to scratch the surface. The real innovation needed a different kind of an environment—an environment that fostered freedom, away from the commands, blame, and restrictions. The siloed environment that was born out of the command-and-control culture did not allow freedom for innovation to happen. There were other problems that were generally brushed under the carpet—like lack of coordination between teams, lack of a one-team culture, and delivery not matching the expectations.

The root cause of the problem was the style of leadership—or rather, the main cause that had multiple ripple effects. It had to change, it had to invert. Leaders had to come off their high horses and work shoulder to shoulder with their teams. Leaders do not tell people what to do, but rather act as a bridge for what the team wants to achieve and aid the team by helping their goals be free of hurdles. Thus, was born a servant leader!

A servant leader wasn't conceived in the digital age. This style of leadership was used as early as 1970 in an essay by Robert K Greenleaf, a writer, a consultant, and a teacher.

He wrote, "The servant-leader is servant first... It begins with the natural feeling that one wants to serve, to serve first... The leader-first and the servant-first are two extreme types. Between them there are shadings and blends that are part of the infinite variety of human nature. The difference manifests itself in the care taken by the servant-first to make sure that other people's highest priority needs are being served. "

Simply put, a servant leader has the same set of objectives as a command-and-control leader. However, instead of passing orders from the top for others to follow, a servant leader makes the team successful by bringing the best out of every individual on the team. They do this by making decision making a team activity, building a sense of shared responsibility as opposed to individuals fending for themselves, and removing all the hurdles that lie between the team and their intended outcomes.

Servant leaders do not showcase their leadership credentials by hierarchy or authority but rather through the respect of team members, customers, and other stakeholders, by virtue of leading the team toward success democratically and with humility.

Mother Teresa served people. She did not ask her fellow nuns at the Missionaries of Charity to start serving people in need. She was hands-on; she cared for people and through the service, she led others into following her footsteps into serving others. A servant leader always leads by example and is ready to do anything that is asked of the team. The motivation for the team comes from the team watching the leaders and following their lead.

Motivation

What motivates a team member to contribute? What do the goals and objectives look like for team members? In the pre-digital era, the focus would be on the individual—the work produced by the team member—and the team members is measured on the delivery. This was the period of superstars. Certain team members would rise above the others, get coronated for their deeds. Motivation was through competition between team members. This internal competition would gel well for the organization in getting the best out of individuals. In the process, the overall program delivery would benefit by the fierce competition.

In theory, competing against one another is good, but the problem is that in the game on one-upmanship, the direction taken by team members may not be the same. For all we know, each of the team members could be working on something from scratch. This would result in duplication of work, and as a result, wasted efforts. Team members learn through experimentation and from their mistakes. In a competitive world, these lessons are internalized and serve the individual in becoming better at the trade. The learning is not necessarily shared with other team members, which indeed would make the organization poorer through the lack of empirical data and lessons learned.

I remember the days when I used to work for Dell. I was solving computer issues for remote customers who were sitting in the United States. The company had a recognition called the star of the week. The technician who resolved the most incidents and received the highest rating would get the coveted award, which included a cash award. Each technician started to build their own knowledgebase and with experience, the database grew, and so did the competition between us. The new joiners suffered with no help from others and the real loser was customers who had to work with the novice technician, while the solution was available all along with the technician sitting five feet away. I would presume that Dell also lost out on customer experience ratings owing to delayed resolutions. I didn't stay long enough at Dell to see the evolution of this reward but can surmise that as the world moved from competition to collaboration, the awards changed shape to reward collaborators than superstars.

Collaboration is the new competition. The greatest realization in organizations is the power of team members working as a single unit—rather than rats racing each other. The age of competition brought the best out of individuals, made them fiercely competitive and, as professionals, they gained profound knowledge. While the team members won this game, the organization lost. For the organization to remain on the winning side of competition, they needed team members to work shoulder to shoulder and think of the bigger picture rather than what they had to achieve as individuals. The focus became on the team or the organization delivering outcomes rather than on individuals. Organizations eventually changed the structure of the organization to promote collaboration by bringing in a host of changes, including the goals and objectives to reflect and measure collaboration between individuals. Although measuring collaboration is not straightforward, the vision from the leadership to collaborate, highlighting team efforts, and awarding teams has started to pay good dividends. Although the north star is for all the team members to collaborate seamlessly, it may never be fully possible, as every team has superstar wannabes. And yet, the overall team focus toward working as one team motivates the majority of individuals to shed their egos and support one another in delivering outcomes.

As the motivation to work moves from competition to collaboration, does it mean that individual team members are no longer accountable for their own work? While the intent of an organization is to promote team members to work as one unit, they need to carefully design the structure to measure individuals based on their individual performance. Team leaders must build hooks into every team members' work to be able to measure and provide constructive feedback. Let's take an example of a sprint delivery where several team members are working toward achieving the sprint goal. Every team member is assigned one or more user stories that they work on independently and collaborate as needed. The outcome of the user story delivery is a decent indicator of a team member from a technical standpoint. Even though the team practices blameless retrospectives, where individuals are not called out for the defects stemming from their work products, team leaders must notice and measure the performance—not in terms of drawing a bell curve, but rather to help improve and prevent such occurrences in the future. Case in point, SAP believes in setting goals that are measurable, and there are specific ways for managers to provide feedback.

However, the practice of rating team members based on their performance has been done away with. A rating, at the end of day, could either motivate or demotivate team members. This is not only toxic for the individual but for the organization as well. A team member who was docked in the rating system might find the fastest way out of the company rather than improve and fight on. The company would have lost a valuable team member, no matter what their rating is. What is more toxic to the system of measurement is the bell curve methodology. Placing team members in a bell curve necessitates competition—pitting one against the other, and comparatively placing certain team members at the bottom of the curve—even if the performance indicators are minute, and in some cases, the same. This practice of bell curving has long surpassed its use-by date, and it's a system designed to artificially create competition, to reward performers, and to penalize under-achievers.

Responsibility

Motivation and responsibility are like Siamese twins. Although they represent different aspects of leadership, they are generally connected.

While the industry worked on the system of competition, the responsibility of work products was handed over to individuals, and their standing, success, or failure was a direct result of the product delivery. There is little difference between the terms ownership and responsibility in this context. Both generally remained with the same individual. While this was a great motivation to get the job done, if the work product did not go as planned, it was a death knell for the individual involved. This was the practice that was generally followed across the IT industry before the digital age and Agile era set in.

With collaboration taking precedence, the ownership and responsibility with single individuals is counterproductive. Hence the concept of shared responsibility or shared ownership. In this, the team would succeed together or fail together. Say for example, a product feature consists of a few sub-features. Individuals in a team pick up one or more of these sub-features to develop. If six of the seven sub-features work as they should, and pass every indicator, and yet the failure of the seventh sub-feature renders the entire sprint release as incomplete, the entire team, including the team members who developed the successful sub-features, take responsibility for the failure. On the flipside, let's say that a developer is struggling to develop a sub-feature. The rest of the team helps the developer (either by sharing work, or by providing solution) to ensure that the sprint objectives are met. This ensures that the team that shared the responsibilities succeeds together. To reiterate, either the entire teams succeeds or it fails. At an individual level, each team member has their own set of responsibilities and work products assigned to them. Yet, the onus of delivering the individual work products is the commitment of the team, to ensure collective success or failure.

In the digital world, shared responsibility/accountability stands for doing the best that is possible by leveraging the assets that are available, sharing information with one another, acting in a responsible manner, and looking at the team's objectives as a true north star.

The other aspect of the digital era that is associated with shared responsibility is blameless postmortems. Delivery does not always follow a plan. Things can go bad. Failures may be fewer but it is not zero. When failures happen, the genetic human tendency is to blame an individual for it—the person blaming is usually not pointing fingers at themselves. My son is training to play competitive chess, and his first reaction to losing is always toward the opponent. He finds various reasons why he lost, and all of them point to the opponent. *My opponent had a higher rating, my opponent made an illegal move, or my opponent gave an unstoppable check are some of the reasons I have heard.* He hasn't thus far analyzed his games to determine the blunders he made. Likewise, when releases fail or when products fail customer's expectations, it is natural to shift the blame to individuals who are solely responsible—the users did not test sufficiently during the acceptance testing phase or the testers didn't think through of all the negative scenarios are some of the reasons that get handpicked when a release goes south. Blaming an individual or even the entire team is a bad practice. At the moment of failure, rather than questioning the *who*, the focus should shift toward the *what*. Analyzing the failures objectively will help find the root cause for the failure, and with it, a solution to move forward. Blaming people will take the delivery two steps back, demotivating individuals and team members, and with a low probability of finding a fix for releasing it in the near future.

You may have sat in on meetings where leaders talk endlessly about failures and how they have affected whatever they have affected. Instead, if they took a position of objectivity, rather than looking at the past, they can look toward what can be done to overcome the current situation. It is important to understand that analyzing objectively with a view on future is constructive and helps move forward. Blameless retrospectives are good options for analyzing work products, to understand how things went and to identify improvements or actions for the way forward.

Leadership Levers to Stay Relevant

Information travels much faster than any other time in history. Parallel inventions are a common occurrence. Leaders serve employees. These are strange times indeed, and it's common across digital industries worldwide. With new competition springing up rapidly, companies need to stay relevant to continue doing business. A strong and able leadership will help companies stay afloat, and leadership is put to test every day in the wake up of umpteen factors that could possibly go wrong.

While there are several ways that a company can shape their leadership, the following description makes it to the top five list in every organization. These levers drive the organization forward in the digital age and help it handle the challenges that digital technology throws at them. The top five leadership levers are as follows:

- The customer is still king
- Agile and nimble
- Experimentation and innovation
- Foster people in the new culture
- Be authentic

There are others that did not make the list, but are worth a mention, including leveraging emotional intelligence, limiting needless expenses, and an unparallel focus on quality.

The Customer Is Still King

Twenty years back, any time I walked into a retail store, it was hard to miss sayings on the walls stating that the *Customer Is King* and the *Customer Is Always Right*. At that time, the saying was so common that it meant nothing and customers weren't treated exactly like royalty. That saying is still appropriate. If I put up the sticker on my desk, it would still carry a lot of meaning and relevance.

The relationship with the customer has changed over the years. Customers no longer see internal and external IT providers (products or services) as what they are, but as partners. The status is an acknowledgement of the deep ties and dependency on one another. The service provider or manufacturer need continued business to stay afloat, and the customer's organization needs the IT companies for their survival. This mutual dependence has strengthened the bond, and in effect, the business outcomes of the customer organization is a result of their IT partner and has a bearing on the future of this relationship. It becomes all the more important that IT partners support businesses as though it is their organization, and businesses have to open up and be frank about their transactions and challenges, and more importantly, provide feedback rapidly to enable IT partners to course-correct.

The digital strategy in customer organizations has changed dramatically over the years. There was a time when organizations employed IT companies to build bespoke applications for their needs. This arrangement did run well until they realized that the cost of maintaining and upgrading was impacting their profit margins. The change has shifted to adopting commercial-off-the-shelf (COTS) products, leveraging the power of configurations, and consciously minimizing customization. This shift has put the onus on the IT product companies to develop products that are designed with customers' needs in mind. IT companies no longer have the freedom to introduce features based on their instincts, but rather they must be based on specific and perceived customer requirements. The practice is for customer organizations to request specific product enhancements and feature introductions, which once developed, are available for all the organizations. For the product manufacturer, while the freedom has been taken away in setting the roadmap, the gain is from the ideas that are generated through various customer organizations, which eventually set the direction for the future product roadmap. Again, this is a win-win scenario as long as the product manufacturer treats the customer as the centerpiece.

For IT service organizations, exciting the customers throughout the journey is paramount to their existence. Customer service is like medicine. You need to have it handy, and you hope you never have to use it. Businesses hope that they never have to use the customer service, because it generally means something isn't working as it should. The 2008 publication, *The Best Service is No Service* by Bill Price and David Jaffe, explains the emotion.

> We are in the times when customers expect instant responses and
> immediate delivery. A finite customer service personnel sitting
> in the global market can never satiate customer needs. Thus, the
> need to scale customer service through self-help solutions and
> employing bots. You might have observed that most companies
> have employed chatbots to assist customers with basic support.
> The problem is that the bot support is so minimal that its
> existence feels like a bane in some of the implementations that
> I have come across. What could be really useful is if the bot can
> take decisions and perform as a human customer service agent
> would. Embedding artificial intelligence with chatbots would be
> an ideal foil to keep the customers happy and mostly to not make
> them feel dumb by having them to interact with petty bots. Digital
> companies must put themselves in the shoes of their customers
> and think through if the bots make sense. You don't need a bot to
> fetch your tracking information. The generic page with tracking

information did just fine. What would be helpful is if the bots
could reach out to delivery agents if there are changes or delays in
the delivery.

In the book, *The Amazon Way*, John Rossman talks about Jeff Bezos' obsession with
customers. Bezos puts himself in the customers' shoes and thinks through what would
give them the best possible experience, and then the processes and systems are designed
based on these parameters.

The Amazon method is built on the holy trinity in the retail industry—price,
selection, and availability. To get customers on your side, price is a powerful parameter.
Amazon priced items competitively, ready to make smaller margins for a short period
of time. When customers got familiar with Amazon shopping, the prices went up in a
long run, but customers didn't go elsewhere. Customers love to have choices. So, it was
important for Amazon to enlist product lines from various manufacturers. The idea
was to establish Amazon as a store that had everything. Customers didn't have to go
anywhere. When a customer buys a product, they know exactly when the product will
arrive at their doorstep. The predictability element made customers trust Amazon. One
year, Amazon ordered 4,000 pink iPods and this version of the iPod had a hard drive
instead of a disk drive. Amazon customers had prebooked the iPods to arrive just before
Christmas. In November, Apple contacted Amazon and told them that they would be
unable to deliver the iPods before Christmas due to the excess demand. Instead of saying
sorry to their customers, Amazon went to retail stores like Best Buy and Circuit City
and bought the iPods at retail price. These were shipped to their customers who had
prebooked them. While the company suffered a loss on the pink iPods, they lived up to
their promise of delivering iPods for Christmas. Such customer-centric measures have
made Amazon the go-to store and happened because they treat their customers as kings.

Agile and Nimble

Leadership in the digital era is not about documenting, implementing, and auditing
processes. The days of hardcore processes are over. The implication is not that processes
and policies should not exist. They should. Otherwise, everyone would be running like
wild geese. Processes should be documented in a way that guides toward a general
direction, and not specifically nail down every single step. For example, if an employee
wants to work in a different role, depending on the role availability and the capability,

the organization should help to make it happen in the interest of all parties. In a process based bureaucratic organization, there generally lies clauses like minimum number of months/years in a particular role before switching to another role and the various approvals that are to be sought before making the switch.

Bureaucracy is good for certain types of organizations that come under the ambit of compliance audits. But for a digital organization, the concept of compliance is restricted to security and architecture related implementations. The organization needs to be in a position to pivot in the direction of favorable winds to derive the best possible outcome. Taking over the same example of an employee wanting to switch roles—if the employee is capable, and if there is an opening, then why not switch them? It is a win-win situation for the employee and the organization. Yes, the previous role that they were performing needs to be backfilled, and a transition plan can be worked out. But the principle is that there are no hardened policies and processes that will restrict an organization's workings.

Take the case of Agile project management. To develop new features, we frame a methodology that will help us get the best software possible in the quickest possible time. The internal workings of the Agile framework are so nimble that Agile implementations between two products may not look alike. The hierarchy of requirements will follow the path that suits the product to be developed. Some products may follow Initiative ➤ Feature ➤ Sub-Feature ➤ User Story and another may follow Initiative ➤ Sub-Initiative ➤ Feature ➤ Sub-Feature ➤ User Story. It does not matter what the hierarchy is; what matters is that a hierarchy exists to plan and organize the product roadmap, development, and deployment. If organizations start to harden the hierarchy, there is every possibility that the structure looks made up and tends to lose the flow.

The requirements' hierarchy is an example of how the Agile framework differs, giving complete freedom to the teams involved to set their own course. Of course, there are guardrails to move the project in the intended direction.

The essential element of designing processes is to look at the bigger picture. What is it that the process intends to achieve? Why do we have the process in place? Processes should exist to help concerned stakeholders achieve outcomes—the optimum way to do this is through simplicity. For the past few years, minimalism has become a lifestyle of choice, and for a reason. The reduced complexity helps in navigating the system with ease, and the entire experience of using a system or dealing with a process is uncluttered, thus infusing new ideas and better use of time for creativity.

Experimentation and Innovation

An organization will thrive in the digital age if and only if they improve continuously. Improvement to a product company can be regular product feature releases and enhancements, and to a service company, it could be new service offerings, better KPIs, and SLAs. Developing new product features and service offerings fairly regularly is not an easy ask. There are cash-rich product companies that invest in research and development, where their elite staff do nothing but innovate. The downside is that the process is waterfall-ish and more often than not, in today's competitive world, with parallel innovation, these companies lose out on first mover advantage.

Digital organizations have the ability to innovate quickly. They innovate, develop, and operate, all at the same time. The 360-degree experience involving operations provides the additional data point to make the transformation complete.

Gene Kim is a popular name in the digital world. He is a best-selling author and the founder of Tripwire Inc. His book, *The Phoenix Project: A Novel About IT, DevOps, and Helping Your Business Win,* has been read by the majority of folks in the digital industry. In the book and on his blog, *IT Revolution* (`https://itrevolution.com/the-three-ways-principles-underpinning-devops/`), he talks about three underlying principles for DevOps to operate in behavior and in function (see Figure 13-3).

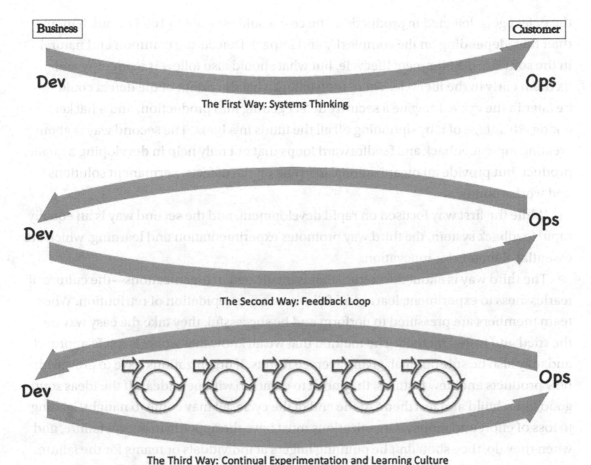

Figure 13-3. *DevOps principles: the three ways*

The first way is described as a fast left to right. The work product from the development side of things moves toward operations. The objective with DevOps coming into the picture is to deliver software as quickly as possible. This can be done in a combination of the following ways—working in small batches, automating the repetitive activities, identifying and fixing defects early in the cycle, simplifying the development process, and optimizing the flow.

The second way is in the reverse direction, and it represents an equally fast right to left feedback. As the saying goes, feedback is the breakfast of champions. Feedback is the backbone of the DevOps methodology. In order to create a quality product, feedback is prominent. It needs to arrive as soon as anomalies are detected, and it must be early in the cycle. It is generally believed that if a defect costs X to be fixed in requirement/design phase, it will cost 10X to be fixed in system/acceptance testing phase. What's worse is if the defect gets detected in production, the cost would escalate to 100X or much more than that, depending on the complexity and impact. Defects are common and natural in the software development lifecycle, but what should also follow is to identify and fix them early in the lifecycle. There is no telling what the extent of the defect could be later in the cycle. Imagine a security defect getting into production, and a hacker taking advantage of it by siphoning off all the funds in a bank. The second way is about creating rapid feedback and feedforward loops that not only help in developing a quality product, but provide an organizational learning on the defects, permanent solutions, and workarounds.

While the first way focused on rapid development, and the second way is an equally rapid feedback system, the third way promotes experimentation and learning, which are essential elements for innovation.

The third way is about the culture that is inculcated in organizations—the culture of fearlessness to experiment, learn, and fail without the trepidation of retribution. When team members are pressured to perform and be successful, they take the easy way out, the tried and tested method. The method that we all know that works is a safe approach, and may also be sub-optimal, giving average results. If organizations have to grow with new products and new features, they need to come up with new ideas. If the ideas sound good, then build and test them. At the end of the cycle, all may come to naught, leading to loss of effort and money. Organizations must have the appetite to accept failure, and when they do, they shouldn't be pointing fingers at individuals or teams for the failure. Team members have the best intent and the only way to know if something works is to build and test it. In failure, the team can objectively analyze and find the reasons behind it. They may turn up successful results during the subsequent iterations by learning from these experiments. These cycles of activity including ideation, experimentation, learning, and blameless retrospectives. This is the culture that the third way represents.

DevOps builds guardrails that help the team members experiment, fail, learn, and iterate in a rapid manner. It builds an environment that provides rapid feedback at any stage of the failure through the power of automation. This system helps teams experiment, and as soon as something does not go as planned, there is feedback immediately, and not at some cron-based feedback timeline. This immediate feedback helps team members to course-correct, without wasting further efforts.

The ability to come up with new ideas and experiment requires new learning. Organizational culture must be transformed inherently into a learning organizations for team members to have access to the best of training resources, mentors to help, and Key Responsibility Areas (KRA) that are aligned with learning objectives. Learning new tricks and skills must be inculcated, with leaders stepping up to lead the way. The trainings must be curated carefully to align to the direction of travel. The natural progression is to see skilled employees performing higher levels of work and leaving the lower bits to either the machines (automation) or somebody with fewer battle scars.

Build the Right Team and Foster People in the New Culture

People are everything. They determine success or failure. No matter how advanced our technologies are, businesses and digital technology will be led by the analog brain signals from the people who matter. Organizations therefore have to take care to onboarding the right people and fostering the existing employees in the new culture.

The new culture is nothing but new ways of working led by collaboration, experimentation, teamwork, and flexibility.

The top aspects that leadership should focus on to build a new team and to foster the existing people can roughly be laid out using the following methods:

- Hire the right talent

- Understand the team

- Agree on a team charter

- Communicate clearly

- Cultivate group thinking and decision making

- Address problems head-on

- Facilitate learning

- Measure teamwork performance

- Give rapid feedback

- Recognize good work

Hire the Right Team

I have often observed that organizations hire people for the technical and management skills of the roles they are positioned for, rather than for the alignment with the organization and its culture. Hiring people has become transactional in other words. You have certain work that needs to be done, so you find the right person and get it done. Whether that person is a right fit in terms of gelling with other team members, whether the person has the right attitude, and whether the person is motivated all take a backseat. The result could go many ways—the employee will quit soon after realizing they don't fit, or worse, other team members who were a good fit for the organization quit. Or worse, nobody quits and team members become individual contributors and the supposed one-team becomes multiple teams.

Hiring a team member is like adding a new family member. Leaders have to bear the brunt of time pressure for onboarding people and take utmost care while extending offers. In his book, *The Amazon Way,* John Rossman explains that the company created a role called *bar raiser* whose job is to review potential hire's candidature and make a decision based on a preset criteria. The *bar raiser* has the veto power over anybody in the organization. The role exists to ensure that the right people are getting hired, and to ensure that with the hiring decision, the collective IQ, capacity, and capability of the organization increases. By setting the bar high, it does two things—you get the right people onboarded into the organization family, and the value of being a part of the organization family is well known, so people will think long and hard before leaving. Talking of high standards, Rossman had to endure 23 interviews over a six-week period before getting an offer.

Understand the Team

Everybody is different. Some are good at certain aspects and some may find it difficult to accomplish the same set of activities. It is the job of a leader to understand all the team members and to use this information to assign the right set of activities to individuals.

I spoke about the team managing their own activities earlier in the chapter, which is true where team work is involved. Certain initiatives and activities should be handed to individuals. During such circumstances, knowing individual team members' strengths and weaknesses will increase success.

It is also important that a leader gets to know the team members, their professional history, aspirations, and bits of personal information. This will lead to a healthy professional relationship and a strong bond, which will serve the leader and the organization well.

Agree on a Team Charter

When it comes to working as one team, the team needs to come together and agree on certain hygiene factors to ensure no ambiguity.

A team charter is an agreement between the team member (facilitated by leaders) that draws boundaries. It could include the team members and their expertise, their roles, mode of work (remote/office), working hours for collaboration, communication means and frequency, among other aspects. In effect, the charter exists to align the team toward the common goal, and its charter is published to other stakeholders (such as leaders and other interested parties) to indicate the team's ways of working.

A charter can be done at a team level or at an unit level, as long as the group is properly sized to have a common goal and comes to an understanding.

Communicate Clearly

Most leaders fail to become great because they are poor communicators. Think of all the leaders around us—in politics, technology, health, and other segments. Leaders across the board know how to communicate. They know how to be heard, and they know how to send messages to the intended recipients. This is a skill to master—not only for leaders but for everyone.

Communication needs to be as direct as possible. Tell the message simply as is. Beating around the bush and speaking in metaphors is for the books and fiction, and not for the digital life. Leaders must make an effort to talk directly to their team members, and not play the game of Chinese whispers through the hierarchy.

Verbal and written communication have their respective places, and they must be used appropriately, depending on the message. Verbal communication is leveraged when the message requires a personal touch, and when the message is of significance. If verbal communication is employed, explore opportunities for face-to-face meetings. Although collaboration technologies are sophisticated, it cannot be the best possible alternate for physical face-to-face meetings. Written communication is generally employed when you are communicating generic information, like the company's quarterly performance.

While verbal and written communication is in complete control of the author, non-verbal communication is driven subconsciously. The words can be saying one thing while the body is saying completely something else. Mastering non-verbal communication is another muscle that leaders must work on. All it takes for teams to decipher whether a leader is trustworthy and honest happens a matter of seconds, and a leader who has worked hard all their life could lose the support of the team if the non-verbal cues do not match the words. Gaining it back, if it can be done, takes penance of sorts. Leaders must make an effort to work on their body language, smile when necessary, make eye contact, and not embody an attitude that will drive people away.

Cultivate Group Thinking and Decision Making

Teamwork was previously fostered through team-building activities, which were mostly physical activities that required the team members to work together to achieve goals. Today, with hybrid and remote working, bringing the teams to an offsite location can be challenging. Instead, leaders can bring the team members to work together through ideation and decision making.

The combination of remote, hybrid, and asynchronous work is the engine that drives IT delivery in the future. In this scenario, teams getting together to discuss, chit-chat, and communicate is not natural. Therefore, leaders have to make it intentional where the ideation or other brainstorming activities are done as a group activity. The power of multiple brains coming together will make the solution better, and equally importantly, the achievement that comes out of the exercise will build the team's collaboration muscle. Some of the areas where it can be done is during user story grooming sessions, along with the customer and sprint planning and retrospective sessions.

Extending the concept of team collaboration and understanding the need for digital teams to self-manage, the decision-making need not be done within the four walls of the leaders' group. But rather, involving the team through the process will enhance feelings of shared responsibility, and psychologically, team members will not be working for the leaders but for themselves, for the team, and for the objectives. Group decision-making is a powerful way to build empowered teams and to groom future leaders who can strengthen digital ways of working.

Address Problems Head-On

Conflicts happen, even in the best of teams. There is no way around them. They could be between team members, team members with other stakeholders, customers, or even leaders. A friend narrated his experience of having to deal with a conflict between a married couple who were part of the same team. The conflicts between them cropped up every second day, and the solution was never fully comprehended by both the parties. Without a positive way forward, the wife eventually moved to a different project.

Leaders, when forced with conflicts, have several tricks up their sleeve to deal with them. Some prefer to ignore and look the other way, in anticipation of conflicts being resolved on their own between the parties. This is not an ideal approach because what the leader is essentially doing is kicking the can down the road. Sooner or later, the problem will fester and the conflict will only be greater next time around.

Leaders should instead look to resolve conflicts head-on. Take the bull by its horns. I do not necessarily imply taking a dictatorial approach and passing judgment, but rather addressing the problem with the affected parties directly. Based on the situation, an appropriate conflict resolution approach may be applied. For example, if the parties are right to call out a conflict based on their perspectives, the leader may help find a middle ground for the parties to agree and move forward. Or if one of the parties is right, then the leader needs to be assertive in the resolution style. With time being limited, it is paramount that leaders take conflicts head-on and find solutions that are just and fair to all involved parties.

Facilitate Learning

Creating a culture of learning and development are the goals. The means to the goal are for the leaders to lay out the plans for setting up a digital academy. The roadmap essentially has a plan for training resources with skillsets that align with the organization's service and product capabilities. For example, an organization that predominantly operates on Microsoft Azure would expect all their employees to be capable of managing Azure services—some on the infrastructure, some on network, and a select few on native DevOps.

The training plan would still need to be mapped and overlaid with team members' career aspirations. You don't want to force a Big Data person to train in depth on networking, because you wouldn't see them doing it in a long run, and they wouldn't be motivated to learn. Therefore, it goes back to the hiring aspect of hiring the right people, and after getting the right people onboarded, understanding their career aspirations and formulating customized training plans based on them.

When I started working in IT back in the early 2000s, training was essentially classroom based. There was limited training and getting into a training was a matter of pride. We had to fight, beg and bother our managers to get nominated for trainings. These days, training is on-demand and self-paced. There are plenty of trainings available on any given topic. The problem of plenty has taken the sheen off the privilege of getting trained. Trainings are now seen as a burden, rather than a privilege. Leaders have to work meticulously with every team member to show how training leads to the work that is accomplished and to the goals. It is no easy process, but it must be done.

A practical problem that team members often face is that they are asked to give the training. And the work that is assigned for that particular day does not get shifted to others, or moved to another date. They are expected to manage the training and the work. This is definitely a burden and is the fastest way to ensure that team members detest training. Leaders must be cognizant of the day-to-day activities and lighten the load during training days. They should also ensure that the entire team, including customers, knows that certain team members are in training and are not to be disturbed.

Measure Teamwork Performance

Goals provide a high-level overview of the desired outcomes. The goal will not necessarily specify what must be done to meet the goal. It simply states what is required, such as bring in customer excitement and high-quality software. Actions are required to meet the goals. These actions are referred to as objectives. For example, increase the customer review ratings by more than ten percent and reduce the software bugs by 20 percent compared to the previous release.

The goals and objectives are generally spun around the outcomes that the team member is involved in delivering. The SMART principle is leveraged in drafting these objectives. SMART is an acronym for specific, measurable, achievable, relevant, and time-bound and is shown in Figure 13-4.

SMART Objectives

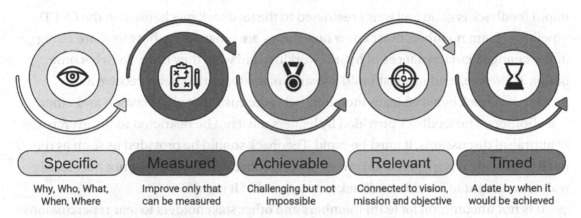

Specific	Measured	Achievable	Relevant	Timed
Why, Who, What, When, Where	Improve only that can be measured	Challenging but not impossible	Connected to vision, mission and objective	A date by when it would be achieved

Figure 13-4. *SMART objectives*

Every objective set forth needs to be spelled out as clearly as possible on the actions and outcomes to be achieved, and the leader must find a way to measure them. The objectives must also be relevant to the identified goals, and the targets must be achievable. If unrealistic targets are set, team members know that they are not going to succeed in meeting the objectives, and their motivation will sag. Finally, the objectives need to state the timeframe by which the objectives need to be achieved.

To promote collaboration, leaders must add goals and objectives pertaining to teamwork. The leaders can be creative in going about it. Under the goal of promoting collaboration, the objectives could read as follows:

- Establish good relationships with team members and demonstrate this by introducing at least five team members in a team meeting next quarter.

- Demonstrate teamwork by identifying initiatives for improvement along with three other team members before the end of the calendar year.

- Successfully plan and run the next townhall.

- Prepare and deliver the lessons learned from the project as a team in the next quarter's seminar.

Give Rapid Feedback

Rapid feedback is good and is not restricted to the feedback mechanism in the CI-CD pipelines. Team members must know how things are progressing, how they are faring in the changed circumstances of hybrid working, and what they must do to become better. Therefore, leaders must build a system of feedback that helps receive and provide feedback between team members, with the customer organization and other stakeholders. The feedback provided by leaders must not be restricted to the exercise of appraisal discussions. It must be rapid. Feedback should be provided as soon as the need to provide it is triggered. Likewise, other feedback channels must not necessarily wait for an event to provide feedback but ensure that it is swift.

It is not uncommon for team members and other stakeholders to fear repercussions stemming from the feedback. To ensure psychological safety, leaders must set up mechanisms to channel feedback anonymously to the intended recipients. Although digital organizations practice blameless cultures, it is hard for us to draw a line between objectifying a feedback and personalizing it. Therefore, depending on the team construct and the nature of the feedback, there should be sufficient provisions to qualify and pass on the feedback without identifying the provider.

Take care to ensure that the feedback is constructive and not meant to put down a colleague. The purpose of the feedback process is not to share opinions, however honest they may be. Feedback providers should think through this aspect and only if it checks all the positive boxes, should they pass on the feedback.

Recognize Good Work

No matter how high we climb the career ladder, appreciation and recognition of our work is essential. Look at it as an extension of the feedback mechanism. *Leaders gave me feedback that I have done an excellent job, but where is the reward? Forget about the reward, I would like to feel appreciated in front of the customer and my team.*

It does not matter if we are talking about a developer, team leader, or a customer representative. Appreciating good work in the presence of others gives employees the fuel for more good work. Studies show that being recognized in public for good work beats salary increases by a long shot. This is another way of making team members feel like they belong at the company and are an integral part of it.

The onus is on the leaders to establish a framework for recognition. Remember that without a formal process in place, recognition will not happen, as we get busy in our work cocoons. Leaders, in coordination with the human resources, should set up a framework and a process for identifying and rewarding performers. And it must be practiced diligently.

Be Authentic

There is a notion that leaders who do not hold back their thoughts, leaders who say it as is, and leaders who are genuine are authentic and can be trusted. There is another school of thought that authentic leadership is an innate quality, which means either leaders can be authentic or not. The choice is not for the leader to make, but the quality is embedded in some while it is absent in others. Both these notions are far away from what we consider authentic leadership.

Authenticity is when leaders remain who they are in the midst of any scenario thrown at them. An authentic leader is somebody who knows their strengths and leverages that part of their leadership acumen as the situation demands. Authenticity comes from who we are and how we act, and not how we want to be perceived. I talk further on the aspects of authentic leadership in the rest of this section.

Steve Jobs is a classic example of an authentic leader. He did not put on a mask for his followers and the public to see and perceive, as stated by his biographer, Walter Isaacson. He was generally difficult to be around, and he was highly impatient and a taskmaster. He has a passion to create products that stood out from the others in the market. He wanted to deliver perfection through his creation and wanted to do something great. Generally speaking, people don't like to be around other people with Steve's qualities. But it was different with Steve, even though he told people to their faces that their ideas were dumb. People stuck around and toiled day and night. They did not mind his brash behavior because they knew that it came from a good place, a mind that was set on a vision for the company and for the consumer. The result of this authentic leadership is that Apple makes top-notch consumer electronics. Through one man's authentic leadership, a company took shape and changed the way people used technology. The authenticity of Steve made people loyal to him, and this loyalty and the teamwork that ensued is one of the prime reasons for Apple's unparalleled success.

Steve never claimed to be an authentic leader. In fact, no leader should claim to be authentic. Because authenticity is a quality that's recognized from the outside rather than from within. Authenticity has meaning if others identify the leader that way, rather than a leader tooting their own horn of authenticity.

Leading with Authenticity

Leaders have certain traits that make them unique and that makes them what they are. A leader is expected to lead people. A leader who uses all their leadership traits in the leadership campaign will remain average at best. An authentic leader is somebody with a sound head on their shoulders, somebody who knows their strengths, and has the situational awareness to leverage those traits as they are deemed fit. Authentic leaders remain true to themselves when showcasing leadership capabilities, but leverage only those aspects that are necessary, while the rest are safely stacked away. In other words, leaders do not lose their identity in the midst of adverse situations.

Authentic leaders believe in walking the walk. They do what they say and say what they do. The rules are not different for others. A leader is authentic when team members can see the leader demonstrate the aspects that were asked of them. For example, if a leader expects every team member to communicate swiftly but fails to communicate with their own team members, that person will seem fake.

Be Self-Aware

Leaders need to know themselves if the intent is to be authentic. Understanding themselves will help them assimilate the strengths and weaknesses and take this knowledge in leading and supporting people. Leadership skills are an outcome of the experience gained over the years. The practicalities of the long road to leadership would have taught multiple skills and at varying complexities. Leveraging and displaying the varied skillsets creates self-awareness, a trait that can be gained through self-effort and practices such as meditation, yoga, and mindfulness.

In the whitepaper, *Authentic Leadership Development: Getting to the Root of Positive Forms of Leadership*, authors Bruce J. Avolio and William L. Gardner observe that self-awareness is not a destination but a journey toward discovering their own unique talents, strengths, sense of purpose, core values, beliefs, and desires. Further, to enhance self-awareness, leaders must practice to:

- Obtain feedback from the people they are connected to. This helps understand other people's perspectives who are closely involved.

- Use the down-time to reflect on their own actions and behavior. Take timeout every day by meditating or simply thinking through their behaviors and triggers.

- Learn to become self-aware of their feelings. When they are talking to a team member who is disgruntled and disrespectful, they should check if there is anger or other feelings lingering.

History Is Key

It is the experience that makes us who we are and what we turn into. When leaders take charge, they will have a repository of experiences and baggage that they may not want to reflect upon. Both of these are invaluable. Leaders can command respect and come off as authentic when they leverage their experience in dealing with people, issues, and delivery, among other duties. One way that I find effective to show my true self is by telling stories. I tell the stories of my past experience, good or bad, and how things turned out to be. The situation can be as simple as a scope creep discussion with a customer. By stating the experience, and the learnings that have come through it, I, as a leader, was able to prepare my team for the upcoming discussions and be as ready as I could be. The experiences and learnings of the past are stored in the long-term memory, and by vocalizing them, the learnings can help prepare people for future events.

The experience may not be from the professional world alone. With our team members, we may share the same language, culture, sporting interests, among others. We can enhance connections in our teams by drawing on these experiences, and firmly bonding the relationship between a leader and team members. That said, leaders should also be cautious about extending their reach to certain topics, and expressing opinions on topics such as politics, religion, body weight, and other sensitive and polar issues. It is hard to generalize the topics that could be deemed sensitive, as they depend on the region and culture. For example, while some cultures are open to talking about religion, others find it inappropriate to bring religion into the workplace.

Exert Self-Control

Leaders have to be careful about how much they reveal, which is dependent on the people, the environment, and the situation. While keeping a certain distance, the challenge is to also seem authentic. When leaders keep too much distance, they are perceived as aloof. This can break the barrier between leaders and team members. In fact, keeping distance is perceived as attractive, and it draws a lot of followers.

Some leaders restrain themselves based on internal standards they live by. Others are more fluid and set their level of constraints based on their gut feeling. There isn't a right or wrong method to determine this, as long as the distance is balanced and works As a result, leaders should not be rearing to showcase their skills or to confront others. They should be measured in their responses and wait for the opportune moment to act.

Summary

This chapter looked at two essential items: people and flexible working and leadership in the digital age. The flexi-model of working involves remote and asynchronous working. it's the new way work happens, and it is here to stay. Organizations and customers have to take note and make necessary adjustments to this new culture.

Leadership in the digital age has come a long way from where it was a couple of decades ago. The command and control culture is frowned upon, and servant leadership is the new style of leading teams.

CHAPTER 14

Techniques and Tools for Managing Digital Teams

The previous chapter looked at the new ways of working that turned homes into offices and made shifts antiquated. Leading such teams and drafting working charters is a different skill altogether. It requires a nimbleness that allows leaders to pivot decision making based on the situation, and yet be firmly grounded toward the true north.

This chapter delves further into the changes that teams, leaders, and organizations must ring in, to accommodate and adapt to digital ways of working. When team members came into offices, worked together in a physical bay, shared lunch, and other break times, knowing and understanding people was a lot simpler, and people generally got WYSIWYG (what you see is what you get). Asking teams to do certain work, such as chairing meetings, planning, and other tasks, was in some ways easier because the people were in the forefront. Their body language showed disagreements if any, and people picked up vibes that helped navigate the events and meetings. With remote working coming to the fore, it feels like a major weapon in the armory has been taken away, and the expectation is to deliver similar or better results. To excel, new techniques and tools are needed, which is the essence of this chapter.

How Do You Manage Remote Work?

There was a time when teams were co-located, and their work involved interacting and supporting each other to complete the task on hand. This was further enhanced with Agile workspaces, where the conventional cubicles made way for open desks.

© Abhinav Krishna Kaiser 2023
A. Krishna Kaiser, *Reinventing ITIL® and DevOps with Digital Transformation*,
https://doi.org/10.1007/978-1-4842-9072-9_14

The idea was to remove the barriers between people, which allowed them to communicate freely. Whether Agile workspaces resulted in benefits is a topic to debate, but what the co-working spaces eased was communication between team members, and it made Scrum masters able servant leaders, because they knew when there were impediments right then and there. They could act on them swiftly. Scrum masters could keep track of the progress, prepare beautiful reports with the latest information, and run all the ceremonies as planned.

With remote work, the Scrum master, who is the first rung of leadership, is affected the most. It is quite natural because Scrum masters work with the teams directly to deliver agreed outcomes, and although there is shared responsibility, Scrum masters are psychologically considered pseudo project managers. With the teams working remotely, including the Scrum master, what changes are needed to manage remote work?

Trust the Teams to Deliver

You must trust the teams to deliver on their promises. Not that the trust factor was absent earlier. But today, it becomes more critical with teams working remotely.

Trust is a two-way street. While the Scrum master trusts the team members to work diligently toward their commitments, the team members too should trust the Scrum master and other leaders to not look over their shoulders and verify the non-delivery aspects of work. Non-delivery aspects include log in and log out times, checking the logs to see if the team members are working for the required period of time, cross-checking social media accounts during sick days, among other things that do not contribute directly to the delivery of outcomes.

When team members know that leaders have their backs, they are more likely to ensure that deadlines are met, even if it means working through the night. This was true when teams worked in the same office, and it is true with people working remotely. The leaders and the Scrum master must trust the team members to deliver, and be vocal about trusting them to do the right thing.

Generally, trust is gained slowly and increases over time. Likewise, leaders should ideally start small—handing over low priority items to begin with. As a leader, do not micro-manage. Trust the team to deliver and asl them to come up with the goods. With the leaders leading the way, team members will reciprocate and trust will help the team achieve their objectives.

Putting trust in the people and people trusting their leaders is an outcome of the company's culture. If organizations maintain a culture of trusting their employees (like for example, not asking employees to submit bills for all claimed expenses), the employees feel accountable for actions, and will more likely be honest with their work, leading to a positive environment. Of course, organizations can have certain bad apples. Culture and norms should be developed for the majority and not for the exceptions.

Simon Sinek, the celebrity motivational speaker, has stated, "A team is not a group of people who work together. A team is a group of people who trust each other." To reiterate, the team has to work as a single group that trusts each other. Google's internal study of their teams reveals a similar sentiment.

Google's Team Effectiveness Study

Google's HR team wanted to answer a simple question, what makes their teams effective? They decided to conduct a thorough study (`https://rework.withgoogle.com/blog/five-keys-to-a-successful-google-team/`). This study is a well-known case study in the public domain. This was in 2015, but the revelations were relevant then and now.

Over a period of two years, the HR team, along with third-party psychologists and statisticians, interviewed over 200 employees and looked at more than 250 attributes of 180 teams in Google. It was generally believed that the team composition mattered if a team were to be effective, say a team of rockstars would outperform a team with "normal" team members.

The study elucidated a number of patterns. The result was that five key dynamics made the difference in how effective a team was:

– **Psychological Safety**

  The team members relied on an environment where they felt safe taking risks. They did not end up being mocked or embarrassed by other team members. This is the most important dynamic that affects team effectiveness. Having reservations in opening up for fear of retribution means brilliant ideas may not be shared. By not externalizing such ideas, the team is at a loss, and this can affect its effectiveness.

Team members lose their confidence and motivation if psychological safety is low. They are less transparent, and the natural tendency is to hide things and cover up mistakes for fear of embarrassment and possible penalty. This is particularly true in a majority of teams across industries where the rockstars in the team often do all the talking while others follow orders. A team cannot truly deliver when barriers restrict team members from opening up.

Team members who feel safe in a team, in other words, team members with higher psychological safety, are less likely to leave organizations. This not only lowers attrition rates but also preserves precious organizational knowledge.

– **Dependability**

Depending on other team members is a matter of trust. If team members feel they can depend on their team to complete the job, then there is a great opportunity for the team to collaborate and work as one.

Dependency further dives into the shared responsibility that the team has undertaken under Agile delivery. Taking shared responsibility by principle is one thing, while practicing it whole-heartedly is something else. When a team can stand up for one another and not compete in an internal rat race, this is a classic example of collaboration, and the effectiveness of the team is bound to improve.

– **Structure and Clarity**

Shared responsibility is good, and so is measuring success for teams altogether than individuals. However, every team member feels more comfortable when they know their respective roles— developer, tester, business analyst, Scrum master, and so on. Keeping the roles fungible appears to be made in the mold of Agile delivery, but it fails to provide clarity to team members on their goals and what is it that they have to do to succeed.

Team leaders have to treat every team member as a separate individual to set a role, define the structure, and lay out the charter to remove any hint of ambiguity.

– **Meaning**

Continuing from the previous dynamic, individual team members come from varied backgrounds, and each has their own strengths and weaknesses. They have their own career dreams and the path they want to tread on. The work they do with the team has to contribute toward meeting their career success. Or at least, they need to believe that the work they are performing is leading them to their dream destination.

Their effectiveness and hence the team's effectiveness will improve if the team members are set on their path of defining meaning to their work they perform, and if they are able to align it with their career aspirations.

– **Impact**

Moving from individual career aspirations to a worldly change their work brings in matters. The work they do, the software they are building, what does it change in the world? Will it affect how Internet banking will be used in the future? Will it change the user behavior while shopping online? These are some of the pertinent questions that team members like to get answers for. And with a clear view of the change that they are able to bring about, their work motivation goes up, and with it, the team's effectiveness.

Respect the Team

Like trust, respect is a two-way street. But unlike trust, which is a natural human behavior, respect is a learned behavior. It is a habit to cultivate, and to practice. Respect in the workplace means that the leaders believe that the team members can deliver, and the deliverables meet the requirements. For team members, respecting leaders means that they believe that the words are coming from a good place, and following the lead is the best way forward.

Respecting colleagues is not only about creating a friendly and cheerful environment to work in. There are numerous benefits, like employee engagement, work stress reduction, and delivery efficiency among others. A study conducted by Harvard Business Review (The Leadership Behavior That's Most Important to Employees (`https://hbr.org/2015/05/the-leadership-behavior-thats-most-important-to-employees`)) found that employees engaged better and were far more committed when the leaders respected them. The study was conducted with over 20,000 subjects across the globe. The study found that for employees, respect trumps everything else, such as being recognized and rewarded, the learning and growth opportunities, seeing a brighter vision, and receiving constructive feedback.

In a remote environment, we may not be sitting under the same roof, and the nature of the interactions may be different with video calls and text chats. However, the interactions still happen. People still need to talk to each other. Workplace respect is a major driver of success.

Respect is about how people conduct themselves during interactions. When a leader is under tremendous pressure and stress (for whatever reason), and that stress affects their interactions with their team members, it can be perceived as disrespectful, and can be detrimental to the organization's objectives. Therefore, leaders and team members need to pay attention to their interactions, to ensure that respect does not suffer because of external factors.

Respect can be shown in a number of ways. Being polite with one another is a good start. Have the patience to listen to what someone is saying. If a leader is in a meeting but not listening to what is being said, this can be perceived as disrespectful. If you are late to a meeting while others wait for you to join, you are being disrespectful of their time. Ensuring privacy is safe-guarded, not rushing to judge people or their actions, avoiding talking behind people's backs, and avoiding foul language are some ways people respect one another. This is true not just for the work environment but for all situations.

Everybody needs to be aware that with remote working, the only form of communication is remote. There are no more lunch chats and water cooler conversations. So, when a team member reaches out through chat, email, or any other method, the person on the other end must make it a point to respond. Not responding amounts to lack of respect . Not responding back to emails is one of the most common ways that employees face disrespect at work. So, care must be taken to respond to every email that is addressed to you, however trivial or uninteresting the information might seem.

When remote work started, people were waiting to turn on their cameras and see others on the monitor screens. The bottling up of people at homes due to COVID-19 made people desperate to see other people, even if it was remote. People have now used and overused their cameras and have stopped turning their cameras on. Video fatigue has set in.

Not turning on the camera is not a form of disrespect. But not turning it on when the other person has turned it on can be perceived as disrespectful. The expectation when one person turns on the camera is for the others to turn theirs on as well. Nobody intends to turn on the camera with the sole reason of showing off themselves. They probably want to have a face-to-face conversation. At times, we may not be wearing the right attire or we may have sleepy eyes. Let the other person who has turned on the camera know that you are unable to turn it on, so the other person gets a chance to either turn off the camera or be conscious that you have a genuine reason to not turn on the camera. When I am not camera ready (say if I am eating or not wearing a collared shirt), I generally say that I am having a bad hair day. People who generally talk to me know that I have no hair, and they get the humor that I am not camera ready.

How Do You Hire the Right People?

Hiring employees is a risky proposition. You just need a single rotten apple to spoil the whole bunch. Not many organizations hire the right set of people—the percentage of people hired vs. people who are the right fit for the company is small. Add to this another layer of complexity where hiring is done remotely, and the right fit for the digital age is still being defined and addressed. How do you hire the right candidate for this job?

This section looks at the best characteristics when hiring someone remotely for the digital age and how other companies are doing it.

The Fundamental Challenges with Hiring

Adding new team members to projects and organizations is the same as getting new family members through marriage or by other means. When new members are inducted, it is not just the bodies or skills that are brought into the equation, it is their work culture and their work habits as well. People working for an organization have certain ways of working, certain communication means, and expectations, among other norms. When you bring in a new person with opposite ways of working, there is bound to a disconnect and conflicts will arise.

413

Conflicts may not necessarily be with the new team member but with existing team members as well. Some existing team members could be influenced by the new team member and the changes could result in conflicts. Let's look at an example. An organization that is committed to responding quickly to each other brings in a new employee, who is laid back when it comes to communicating. This person does not respond as swiftly as others. Their project mates are taken aback at first with the person's attitude. After a while, some of them adopt this style of delayed communication. This, potentially, could change the fabric of the project team. Being lazy in communication is the easy way out and requires less effort.

People are often swayed toward taking the easy way out, and organizations that could have taken years to build a certain culture can possibly lose track, and lose out on the well-entrenched habits with a few bad hires.

Therefore, it is critical for companies and team leaders to put their weight behind the hiring process to ensure that the company makes the right hiring decision every time. Yes, there will be mistakes along the way. They need to introduce sufficient parameters to mitigate bad hiring risks and to ensure that similar mistakes and blunders do not happen repeatedly. This challenge not only applies to hiring remote teams but also to traditional teams.

Cheating on Interviews

With remote hiring, there are opportunities for fraudsters to cheat on the interview or appear in an interview using a different identity. With the traditional interviewing styles done remotely, such fraudsters find it easy to wreak havoc. When I was working in an organization as a service management head, we were conducting telephone interviews due to lack of time. It was in the evening, and I was interviewing a candidate for the position of a service manager. I needed somebody strong in ITIL and communication. Every question I asked was followed by a pause, fillers like *yeah, aaa, mmm,* and sometimes he would repeat the question back to me, which was perfectly fine by me. But what I could hear in the background was clacking on a keyboard, and the answers were pitch perfect. After a few questions, I had a hunch that the candidate was googling the questions and was reading the answers out to me. So I changed tact. I asked a scenario based question, the answer would flow from experience and not from Google. After some more fillers and clacking, he gave me a horrible answer. I tried another scenario. Same result. I confronted him and asked him how his answers were perfect for questions that were textbook based, and any question that was scenario-based were floundered. He hung up. He knew that I had caught him. During those days, we didn't have the luxury of video calls and it was possible for people to cheat on interviews.

After video calls and interviews became commonplace, I wasn't sure that I could catch interview cheats. During video interviews, the candidates look at the screen when they talk, and on the screen, you have the video of the interviewer. So, they are looking at the screen and not at the camera. So, it is possible that they may be able to pull up answers on their screen and read out of it. It has happened and during my interviews reviews, I have caught a few reading from their screens. Poor camera quality and the light source facing the camera (lens flare) distort the video, and are potential avenues for interview cheats to prosper. In such situations, interviewers have to ask scenario based questions, and must insist on candidates crossing their arms during the interview. During remote interviews, avoid asking direct questions. In fact, I avoid asking direct technical questions in any form of interview, because you are getting somebody onboarded for their experience and not their theoretical understanding. Instead, talk about their experience, and how they dealt with certain problem situations, and the way candidates answer to such questions, an interviewer should be able to ascertain the technical quotient of the candidate.

Identity Fraud

Impersonation is another major hurdle that hurts companies. People who were interviewed were not the people who turned up and joined the company. It would take a few months to figure out the fraud owing to poor productivity at job, and the lack of requisite skills.

Bengaluru is the silicon city of India and boasts of multitude of IT companies making the city as their offshore base. During the COVID-19 pandemic, while the rest of the world faced the great resignation, companies in Bengaluru were hiring people in bulk as cutbacks in the west resulted in new jobs at their offshore sites. An executive at EY who is close to the hiring market said, "The issue got significantly accentuated with high attrition and the present remote work culture because of covid. The number of such impersonation cases I've come across has doubled."

Companies who faced the brunt of hiring the wrong people resorted to capturing images during video interviews and comparing the visuals at every interview stage and during onboarding. The official documents and photo identity proofs are vetted along with the interview snapshots to ensure that impersonators don't get through.

The challenge of impersonation plagues bigger organizations that hire in bulk. The HR involved in sourcing is generally a team, the interviewers too may be disparate, and not exchange notes directly. The manager may not end up talking to the candidate until the day they join the company and the team. When the expected results don't come through, at that point, investigations begin to ascertain whether the person in the interview and the person who joined the organization is the same. In one such instance, a manager was surprised that a new joiner would not turn on the camera, while they were open to doing it during interviews. After repeated requests, the employee turned on the camera, and the manager was able to see that the person was different than the one they interviewed.

There are several identity verification applications that can be used to compare images. This helps, but frauds are generally a step ahead and they find ways to beat the system.

The Automattic Case Study

The company Automattic may not be famous, but their product Wordpress is most definitely well-known. It is an open-source content management software and it powers over 48 percent of websites, the world over. My first encounter with WordPress was in 2004, when I became a blogger and built my first blog. The software has come a long way since then and boasts a great community of contributors who are responsible for keeping it fresh.

I like the software very much, but this section isn't about WordPress. The founder of Wordpress is Matt Mullenweg; he went on to found Automattic in 2005. Apart from Wordpress, the company owns the likes of Tumble, WooCommerce, Gravatar, Akismet, and Day One. The company is valued USD 7.5 billion and boasts of over 2,000 employees across more than 200 cities all over the world at the time of this writing.

Harvard Business Review (https://hbr.org/2014/04/the-ceo-of-automattic-on-holding-auditions-to-build-a-strong-team) wrote an article on the company's transformation. Back in 2014, when working from the office was very much the norm, the company decided to let their employees work from anywhere (WFA). Although they had an office in San Francisco, it was mostly meant to be a showpiece for guests. While the company went remote, they also switched to asynchronous working and abolished the 9-5 shift working for their employees. They saw the writing on the wall, well before the rest of the world woke up. The company's culture did not believe in asking people to work during certain hours and mimic the way the company intended them to work. People were measured on outcomes and not process. One of their employees, Scott Berkun, penned a book called *The Year without Pants*, which explains the culture of the company.

Automattic's hiring was traditional to begin with. They would ask technical questions, and follow them up with brain teasers and riddles. They relied on past experience of the candidate to come up with the goods. They even took the candidates out to lunch. Despite their best efforts, they came up short with the people they hired. A number of them quit the company in search of greener pastures, while some of them made others' lives miserable.

The *aha* moment appeared when the key personnel of the company put their heads together to figure out where they were indeed going wrong. They realized an interview lasting for an hour is not a sample of time and interaction that could point them to their next employee. Good candidates could flounder and get rejected while average ones could talk their way into the company's rolls.

A candidate would go through the normal rigors of matching skills and technical rounds of interviews. When a candidate got through the initial hurdle, they would be hired on a contractual basis for about eight weeks. They are not expected to quit their existing jobs, but are asked to commit to a decent number of hours weekly. They are treated just like employees with logins and the work is democratically divided between employees and those on contract. The goal is for the candidates to get a feel for what they are getting into and for the existing team members and the company to vet the candidate on the job. The work done by the candidates is not free but are rather paid a standard rate.

Candidates who agree for the try-outs have cleared their first hurdle of having an open mind to stretch along with their regular jobs, and show the mettle to prove their worth. During the entire contract time, there is continuous feedback given to the candidate. A candidate who accepts the feedback and takes corrective action would have passed the next hurdle. The team then decides toward the end of the contract whether a candidate is fit to appear for the final hurdle.

If the team is happy to have a candidate as their long-term team member, then Matt himself interviews the candidate. He does not pick up a phone or video call a candidate. The interview is through a text messenger, as the majority of communication in Automattic is done through a text messenger. Matt is trying look for passion and culture in the candidate. The majority of those who appear for the final hurdle make it through, which is a testament to the fact that the try-outs and decision making by the team is a great success.

Contracting candidates to try out their work in a real environment is a practical approach to hiring people. The company can fire people if they don't seem a good fit—which is the outcome of traditional hiring. But, as I contended earlier, hiring and onboarding people is not like changing clothes. It takes plenty of effort to hire every person, and the bonds that are built, the time spent with each other cannot be wasted away by a hire-and-fire approach.

Dean Sas shared his experience of joining Automattic on this blog (`https://deansas.org/2022/01/02/being-hired-at-automattic/`). He explains the process in minute detail. A worthy read!

Self-Supervised and Self-Motivated

I stopped tracking the various roles that IT companies have on offer when I started seeing Happiness Manager and Chief Heart Officer (CHO) emerge from their thinktank hats. All organizations define their set of roles, at various levels and they are unlikely to be similar as the next company. No matter what the roles are, and what skillsets are needed to fulfill the role, there are certain common characteristics that are absolutely necessary if a digital organization dreams of thriving. The critical characteristics are:

- Self-supervised

- Self-motivated

- Collaborators

- Communicators

I grouped them in twos because of the synergy that exists between the aforesaid characteristics. Organizations must find a way to scrutinize candidates based on how well they display these characteristics. Testing them on an interview call may be difficult, but not impossible. Or they can employ the Automattic way of hiring, which gives them real-life exposure to the candidates.

Self-Supervised

Companies hire people because they can add value through the outcomes that are a result of the work they perform. They are people and not cattle. Cattle require cowboys to manage them. People don't need managers. The role of a people manager is outdated because companies have started to realize the positive effects of people managing themselves. Supervising one's own work makes the individual accountable for their work. This accountability will make them committed to what they have promised to deliver. Making and staying committed to work is the biggest form of motivation and can drive individuals and the teams toward success. Team members will not be order-takers and this lateral shift has several advantages—including the innovation that is an outcome of a free-thinking mind.

Self-supervision is not the end goal but rather the beginning of what is to come. The objective is to build a team that can manage, challenge, innovate, and deliver without getting prodded by project managers and delivery leads. Such a team is well situated to work in an Agile fashion, which roughly translates to keeping their ears to the ground and pivoting based on the customer's likes and dislikes. A team full of self-supervised individuals will tend to be self-autonomous by DNA and will be in a position to take full responsibility of their successes and failures.

A self-supervised team may not have managers and leaders who pass commands and demand updates. Rather, such a team will be ably supported by the leadership to provide them every opportunity to succeed including the deployment of Agile and DevOps coaches who can guide the team in their ways of working.

What are the tell-tale signs that a team has achieved the self-autonomous stage?

When you form a team, you wouldn't be in a position to understand the maturity from a self-supervision angle. However, you should have an intuition as a leader who put the team together. It is therefore important to slowly release the rope of control as the team starts to bond and work as a team. Holding onto control is addictive but it does no good to the team, the morale, the outcomes, and the overall working environment. The signs that you should look for to determine a team's self-supervision stage is through their collective decision-making ability, the trust between the team members, and the flow of information (communication) in the team. If these three aspects begin to flourish, it should be proof that the team is well formed. They are in their performing stage and can be depended on.

Self-Motivated

Motivation is a by-product of self-autonomous teams. Team members are high on energy and are on constant lookout for the next big thing. The support they need is vision from their leaders to put them on a path that takes them to new places. They don't need to be motivated by external factors. The motivation comes from within, and they have the energy, the interest, and the motivation to do it all on their own. For example, a project demands leveraging on a new technology, and the team members do not possess the necessary skills. A team that is self-motivated learns the technology and start to implement it in the project without a push from the management to tread the direction of learning and implementation. I have come across a few teams that learned and applied the learning on the job successfully. It doesn't necessarily take skill but the willpower and motivation to make things happen, even in the wake of uncertainty.

As a leader, here are some things that you can do to transform your team into a self-motivated team:

1. Give the team the autonomy to make collective decisions. The decision could be on their style of working, times when they meet, the artifacts they produce, among others.

2. The team must get the respect they deserve. As a leader, you must respect the team and their decisions. Instead of doubting the intentions, determine the rationale behind the decisions that you deem questionable. Unless leaders and other stakeholders respect the team for what they are and how they deliver, the team will not have the cudgels to build their motivational muscle.

3. Share the vision of the organization, the product roadmap, and the goals and objectives that the team is expected to march toward. Teams find meaning when they can see the flagpole and the crown perched upon it.

4. Include personal or team learning goals for the individuals to embark upon. A learning organization is an organization that grows, and the learning motivates the team to do greater things.

5. Provide constructive feedback at every possible juncture. We have discussed the power of providing rapid feedback in the earlier chapters. It is an essential component for self-motivated teams to continue performing.

6. Every team member has strengths—not referring to technical skills, which is the primary reason for their inclusion in the team. One team member could be good at analyzing requirements, another at problem solving, and so on. Employing ways of working will help form a team that is built around the strengths of individuals.

7. Reward the team when it is due. Recognitions are important for every individual to motivate them to do greater things at work and at life. One of my mentors was a fascinating character and he never missed praising his team members or other people he met before starting a conversation. The praise was not hollow. It came from a good place and was grounded on facts.

8. Penalizing people for the things that go awry is the fastest way to demotivate them. Don't do it unless it is absolutely unavoidable.

9. As a leader, it is important to keep track of the team, check in on regular intervals, and show that you care. You should do it in a way that you don't present a picture of micromanagement or being nosey, but rather somebody who is genuinely interested in the affairs of the team.

10. People are going to have bad days. They are going to reach out to you for comfort. Help the team approach the problem as an opportunity, to change the perspective of the situation to find a solution rather than dwell on the difficult situation. This is a life skill that can keep people motivated.

Collaborators and Communicators

The games of chess and golf are single-player games. This is unlike the game of football/soccer, where you need eleven players to perform at a certain level to win matches. The midfielders must ensure possession of the ball and deliver it to the strikers with great precision. The defenders must guard the post along with the goalie. In all, it's a game that requires teamwork. Digital ways of working are more like football and nothing like Chess. The entire project team must work as one unit to come close to succeeding. The project team is like a gear system, where one gear turns the other, and then the next one gets moving at a faster rate. In other words, digital teams have to collaborate, there is no way around it.

To begin with, collaboration is about sharing information. You aren't really building a house, which starts with a foundation, followed by walls, roof, stairs, interiors, and so on—you get the drift? Building a house is a sequential activity, and collaboration has a minimal role. Digital working is like constructing a bridge. The bridge that you construct is not done sequentially starting from one end. You start to construct the bridge from both ends, and the parts in between simultaneously. This exercise would take a great amount of accuracy to ensure that the bridge connects seamlessly between the parts that are getting built simultaneously, which is a byproduct of high-level of information exchange and collaboration. Throughout the construction journey, all the team members must communicate, at every step, multiple times in a time period, and communicate well by providing the exact data points, feedback, ideas, and solutions among others. No wonder digital projects take a great deal of collaboration and high precision communication to succeed.

Building a bridge is a physical activity. You can see the pillars, the piers, and the girders. It requires precise solution designs and equally precise construction. Seeing and building physical components is a level of comfort compared to digital projects where the designs, builds, and releases are all abstract. The team needs to be able to connect the dots of abstract components and do it seamlessly and accurately. This, in my view, is more complicated and complex compared to building bridges and other marvels that are built non-sequentially.

According to Francesca Gino (`https://hbr.org/2019/11/cracking-the-code-of-sustained-collaboration`), collaboration is natural for people with certain mental attitudes. They are:

- Respect for colleagues and their work

- Being open to experimenting on ideas generated by others

- Sensitivity of your actions toward colleagues' work and objectives

The reality is that most people are obsessed with their own ideas and are not open to accepting others' ideas. So, experimenting their ideas is a long shot! Collaboration may come naturally to a few people, so this doesn't mean that the rest of them should stay away from the digital industry. You can learn to collaborate, and leaders must pave the way for this. Especially when they hire people, while they scrutinize the collaboration aspects, they must also note a candidate's ability and willingness to learn.

Learning to Collaborate

Early in my career, during meetings, if I had something to share, I would wait for a prime opportunity to share it with the members in the meeting. I would rehearse the words in my mind, think about where I should pause for maximum effect, and how I would present it. And like a cheetah that would wait for an opportune moment to pounce on its prey, I would wait for a long pause, or an opening to start talking. Throughout this entire process, there were other people in the meeting, and they were sharing information, sharing important thoughts that did not hit my ears. I was deaf to their words and alert to jump in to talk. Even when I chaired meetings, I made sure that my ideas were heard early and gravitated the meetings toward my ideas and away from differing views.

What I did in my younger days should possibly be made a case study of what-not-to-do in meetings. Francesca Gino contends that leaders should train their team members to listen to each other, rather than focusing on their talk. By not listening, you are disrespecting other team members and possibly distancing them from you. They wouldn't like to work somebody who doesn't respect, and the team will effectively be working as multiple individuals, which brings down the delivery effectiveness.

If you lose your train of thought, write it down so you can refer to it when you need to speak. Listen to others' ideas and try to get more info on the ideas shared by asking more questions. If their ideas make sense, and if the general mood in the room is positive toward the idea, think through whether what you have is worthy to be shared at this point. The critical aspect to focus is not on highlighting yourself with the sharing of your ideas but to think on the lines of your contribution in the meeting toward the objective set forth.

The common reason why we do not listen to others is because we believe that we are smarter, and others do not have anything valuable to contribute. Try to understand what other people are trying to share, there is a good possibility that their views are going to drive more value to what you are building as a team, there is also a possibility that your understanding of the topic on hand was not aligned.

To collaborate successfully, everybody on the team must truly believe that everybody in the team is equally brilliant, have unique perspectives and ideas, they care about others and the objective on hand, and are fully committed. Most importantly, do not judge others. This needs to be default setting irrespective of people's roles and designations.

In a collaborative team, giving and receiving feedback should be seamless, unbiased and without the intention of putting down colleagues. Giving and receiving feedback is an art, and it needs to be learnt as well. Feedback given should be devoid of judgment, and possibly be accompanied with suggestions. When people receive feedback, they should know that the people giving feedback have their best interests at heart, and are not acts of one-upmanship.

Communicating as a CSF

Communication has long been considered a soft skill that embellishes and buttresses the hard technical skills. This was not true earlier during the waterfall years and it definitely isn't true now. Communication is a glue that holds digital work together. It is the bond that brings together various elements of a work product together. It is not an enabler but the core. When a hiring decision is made, communication needs to be on top of the list, and should be a decisive factor before rolling out the offer.

Good communicators don't just speak well. It is the message that they are trying to convey that should matter. I knew an individual who spoke well. His voice was music to others' ears, and he brought a definite level of professionalism to the table. When I worked with him, I realized that his message lacked substance. It didn't contain specifics but was rather generic—using wordsmithing to mask the actual message. Leaders need to hear the underlying message and make sense of it before making a hiring decision.

Not all good communicators are great orators. There are different types of communication and the exercise of making a communication an essential aspect is not to choose orators. Remember Matt Mullenweg's interview using text messaging—he was testing the communication most prevalent approach at Automattic. Likewise, when candidates are interviewed, hear what they are saying rather than how they are saying it. When I was running operations for a client, I worked with an incident manager who liked to document minutes, note actions, and update tickets. When I read his updates, I rarely had follow-up questions. His updates were complete, clear, concise, and importantly, he was able to predict the possible follow-up questions that some of the stakeholders may have, and would provide details around scenarios as well. I worked with others during the same tenure, who were excellent in writing process documents and standard operating procedures, but were average orators. People may be great communicators but not in all the forms, so it is important to hire appropriately.

Then there are communication preferences. Similar to how we have synchronous and asynchronous ways of working, there is synchronous and asynchronous communication. A video meeting is synchronous in nature because the information is exchanged in real-time. Communicating over email is asynchronous in nature because the exchange takes place when the team members are able to respond to emails.

Christoph Riedl and Anita Williams Woolley conducted a study (`https://behavioralscientist.org/bursty-communication-can-help-remote-teams-thrive/`) involving 260 software engineers spread across geographies. They were given a task—to develop an algorithm that could recommend the ideal contents of a medical kit on a space flight. Some participants were offered cash prizes in order to study the effect of perks on the quality of the delivery. Work efficiency picked up briefly, but the quality of the outcome was unchanged. Clearly, cash incentives (or perks to generalize) did not improve quality.

However, what did the trick was *bursty* communication. It is a term that the researchers coined which means bursts of back and forth communication between team members—similar to the rapid feedback concept that is leveraged in DevOps. The teams that employed *bursty* communication for exchanging information and ideas did well, and the quality of the product improved a great deal. The teams that did not lagged behind, and the quality remained the same. Reading this data points to quick and rapid communication having a direct effect on the quality of the work product. The data pointed out to a 24 percent increase in work efficiency when bursts were involved.

What the *bursty* communication is doing is aligning the thoughts and activities of team members and fostering collaboration. Team members get the necessary input and information to carry their work full stride. This also points to remote teams doing great when they are able to collaborate well.

Bursty communication or synchronous communication need not be over voice or video call. During the study, it was found that email exchanges were rapid and *bursty* in nature, and although it is categorized as asynchronous, it was used effectively as a synchronous form of communication.

Managing Virtual Meetings

I wouldn't go so far as to state that meetings are time wasters, but the time spent meeting is time that people are not working. It is a deterrent to productive use of time. So, should we stop meetings altogether? No, there is a place for meetings, and its place is right at the end. Meetings should be set up if the other forms of communications fall short. Meetings should be your last resort. My personal preference for communication is text messaging through collaboration tools, then email, then phone calls/calls on collaboration tools, then meetings.

My preference is also dependent on the type of message that I am trying to send. Information to be passed or received is usually not urgent, so asynchronous forms of communication using text messaging or emails generally work. If it's urgent, I generally call people using collaboration tools or via their cell phones. This is the fastest way to get a hold of people (if they are available). If nothing works, there needs to be a bit of planning, advance notice and carving out a slot for scheduling meetings. I talk about it more later in this section.

The need for meetings has been necessitated by remote working more than ever. Information exchange used to take place informally by the water cooler and over a cup of coffee. All these are now on track to be done to be through meetings.

Physical meetings are tiresome because of the effort required to plan, schedule, and to run them. A level of complexity for physical meetings is the location to meet in, its availability and participants' availability in the location. For people who shuttle between meetings, imagine the time and effort needed to move between buildings and floors. All this is wasted clock time, which is a potential saving in virtual meetings. There are debates in various circles on the effectiveness of virtual meetings over physical ones, the number of people who are siding with virtual outnumber those with physical meeting preference.

The argument for virtual meetings is its dynamism and the agility with which meetings can be scheduled and run. With teams spread across the globe, virtual meetings should be the norm and should not be seen as a rainy-day backup for physical meetings.

The proponents of physical meetings argue that they are impersonal, attendees lose focus and attention, and they are prone to technical glitches. The arguments on both sides are true, and as we move forward in the digital ways of working, we should acknowledge and accept that there is place for both kinds of meetings. Co-located teams may find it comfortable to attend physical meetings, and meetings involving executives and CXOs fair better physically because of the physical interaction and the potential impact.

How to Run Virtual Meetings Effectively

The pandemic has been a great teacher and has taught us how virtual meetings are to be run. When the pandemic started, participants mostly knew how to join meetings, but did not exploit the complete feature set of the meeting software. There were certain rumors in select circles on the security aspects of certain meeting platforms but over a period of time, they have been dispelled, and teams have started to use its features increasingly.

Either with physical or virtual meetings, the basic etiquette that is not followed enough is accepting or declining meetings. The meeting host needs to know who is attending and who isn't, because there is a potential to either reschedule or postpone a meeting based on the attendance. Managing virtual meetings is an art. The following are some of the areas that need to be covered reasonably to manage effective meetings.

Meeting Platform

There are a number of virtual meeting platforms—Microsoft Teams, Google Meet, Cisco Webex, and Zoom being the popular ones. The feature set among the platforms is more or less similar. The audio and video quality are alike. Certain organizations have opted for one over the other, so the choice of a platform is removed. Suppose this isn't the case. The meeting host needs to consider the features used during the meeting and choose accordingly. Microsoft Teams has an intuitive interface integrated with chat feature that remains as is even after the meeting has concluded. The participants can use the chat feature to continue discussing ideas long after the meeting is over. This is definitely a feature that would sway me toward MS Teams over the other biggies that do not include this feature. Also, some of the platforms may not be available in certain geographies, which could be a main consideration as well.

Technical Setup

There are constraints with our workspaces. Many people work in their bedrooms or in an empty room. The acoustics may not be studio class, but there are certain things that you can do to make the meeting experience better. The majority use laptops that have an integrated webcam and a microphone, which works well for the most part. Users of this setup need to ensure that they remain closely rooted to the laptop, as the microphones that are situated on the display screen are not very sensitive.

If you are using a docking station plugged with an external camera and microphone, opt for a non-wide angle camera mounted at eye-level. Webcams generally come with generic microphones, which do a decent job just like the laptop integrated ones. If you are going for a separate microphone setup, ensure it is a unidirectional microphone to avoid picking up feedback and other disturbances. If you don't want to invest in external microphones (as they can be expensive), any decent headphone with mic would do as well. I personally try to avoid it, as it tends to hurt my earlobes after long hours of usage. Yes, I spend a good number of hours in meetings.

Suppose you are sitting in an empty room. There is a possibility of echoing, which can be disturbing to other participants. Consider adding furniture or acoustic panels to the room.

Meeting Plan

A meeting needs to be planned after careful consideration. If the objective can be achieved by shooting some emails back and forth, go for emails rather than a meeting. After determining that a meeting is required, schedule the meeting at least 48 hours ahead of time. This time will help the participants prepare for the meeting (if needed), or move other meetings around if they are busy.

Every meeting invite should be thought through from the objective it is serving. What is it that you want to achieve in this meeting? Based on the answer to this question, the agenda needs to be set, and should go out along with the meeting invite. If there is preparatory work that needs to be done by the participants, call it out loud and clear. The goal is to make the most of the meeting and make the most of the time that is being invested.

Invite only those who have a role to play in a meeting. I have seen a practice that is rampant across organizations, inviting people just because they are part of a team or could influence others in joining the meeting. Every participant's time is precious, and the meeting host needs to respect that fact.

Meeting Props

In the digital ways of working, I find it hard to agree that we can have effective meetings without props. These could be presentations or certain templates that capture data or a whiteboarding tool so participants can contribute collaboratively. A presentation is a minimum requirement and the meeting host must ensure that it is in place before the meeting begins. What is even better is when the presentation is shared with all the participants. It will make the meeting efficient as the participants can directly get into discussing the differing views and the way forward rather than having to learn about the contents of the presentation during the meeting.

A mural board is a great addition to virtual meetings. It helps collaborate actively during the meeting. Of course, not every meeting requires the use of a mural board, but if collaboration is an expectation, a mural board is a good option.

Ground Rules

If there are a number of participants in a meeting, it is recommended that the meeting host draw up the ground rules and communicate them to the group during the meeting or along with the meeting invitation.

Ground rules can be as simple as participants keeping their microphones on mute when others are talking, keeping their camera on, and raising their hands before speaking.

If the meeting is being recorded, call this out before the meeting begins. It is a good etiquette to get agreement from all participants before recording. Some participants may not be comfortable with the meeting being recorded or some organization/country rules may not permit meetings to be recorded.

Meeting Etiquette

Virtual meetings are generally held from the comfort of our homes. So, it is possible that the participants may have just woken up to attend the meeting. It is therefore preferred to keep a professional outlook when you are in meetings with the camera turned on. When you are on a video call, look at the camera when you talk and not at your screen. I know that it is natural for us to address others by looking at their faces, but with virtual meetings, you need to see them eye to eye, and that effect can be brought about by looking into the camera. It takes some practice getting used to looking at the lens while you speak.

Whether there are ground rules in a meeting or not, keep your microphone on mute unless you are speaking. It can be annoying to have disturbances flow through participants while other members are talking. Also, raise your hand to talk, so that the current speaker or the meeting host can ask you to speak at the end of a logical conclusion.

Most importantly, we are meeting virtually using our laptops, where email and chat messages keep flowing in. We might have the urge to respond back to them as soon as the notification pops up, because we are in listening mode and not talking. Resist this urge, and if possible, turn off your notifications or the application itself to avoid getting distracted. I have heard participants asking for things to be repeated when it was said slowly and clearly the first time. This is annoying because it is not only a waste of everybody's time, but it also is a form of disrespecting other participants. If you need to respond to an email or take a phone call during a meeting, let others know that you are away from the meeting using the chat window.

The meeting host must also ensure that the topic discussed is on the agenda and not a digression. It is quite common for people to be taken over by emotion and discuss topics that lie outside of the agenda. Generally, you will find the dominant speakers move the meeting in a direction of their choosing. The meeting host needs to keep such things in check, and ensure that the goals of the meeting are moving toward completion.

Meeting Initiation

Meetings have to be initiated by the meeting host alone providing the context to the meeting, calling out what the objectives are, and the ground rules (if any). Depending on the people attending the meeting, a round of introductions needs to be on the cards. The introductions should not be a lengthy narrative of experience and span of control. It should be the name, geography, and the role/designation.

Depending on the participants in a meeting, an ice breaker could be a good call. This situation may arise if the participants are not known to each other, and if there is a certain level of tension in the virtual room.

Note Taking

My favorite aspect of a virtual meeting is the ability to take notes collaboratively. Platforms such as MS Teams have integrated a meeting notes feature inside the meeting. Anybody in the meeting can take notes, and everybody else can tracking them. Suppose additions need to be made; others can jump in and start making changes right away. There is no need of the minute taker to publish the minutes and receive feedback about changes. More importantly, the meeting notes remain in the same meeting construct, and can be referred to/modified by participants even after the meeting is closed.

Summary

This chapter was not about theory but about the practical aspects of managing a digital team. The majority of digital teams work remotely these days, and for this model to thrive and continue working, organizations and leaders have to create an environment, put things in place, and consistently work with the team to enhance the remote working experience. This extends to the routine task of hiring the right team members and running virtual meetings. The Automattic case study is an excellent example of how the conventional means of hiring may not be the right way to hire people who work remotely, and who work in a culture that is entirely different from what it was a few years earlier.

CHAPTER 15

Adopting a Product-Led Approach

For organizations to thrive, they need to focus on a pivotal aspect that will allow them to grow roots and put their strategies in place. Organizations often put customers first, they meet customers' needs and change strategies around what customers want. So does it mean that they are a customer-centric organization? Yes, they are. In fact, every organization survives because of its customers. But an organization that relies on customers alone, or rather an organization that is basing its approach on an outside entity alone, is not going to last long. Even with the best of efforts, customers may switch to a competitor, or the company may go bankrupt, which would threaten the IT provider's existence. Primarily looking outward toward customers is a recipe for disaster. Organizations need to balance this outlook with an inward-looking approach for their growth and everything else that makes them players in the market.

Organizations can broadly be classified under services or products. A company like ManpowerGroup is in the service industry of recruitment. They find the right people for organizations that are looking to hire. They act as a bridge between the candidates and the companies. Their offering in simplest terms is a service that understands customers implicit and explicit requirements and finds possible candidates who fit the bill. Such an organization grows through their service offerings, and their growth trajectory is centered around services. How they conceive their offerings, shape their service offerings, and execute on their offerings determines their fate. This is an example of a service-led approach.

On the other hand, we have a product-led organization which is gaining steam and is considered as the key pivot for organizations to grow and outperform in the digital age. A product-based organization centers its strategy around a product, and whatever decisions it undertakes, it does so through the lens of the product. LinkedIn is a website that is

433

© Abhinav Krishna Kaiser 2023
A. Krishna Kaiser, *Reinventing ITIL® and DevOps with Digital Transformation*,
https://doi.org/10.1007/978-1-4842-9072-9_15

social media for professionals, it is a place for recruiters to find prospective candidates, a platform for companies to showcase their capabilities, and a channel for sales partners to find leads. For LinkedIn, their existence remains on the basis of their website, which is the product they are centering around. All the various interactions between various stakeholders happen through this product. The experience of using the product by these stakeholders is defined by what the product can do and how effectively it gets done. The LinkedIn site has seen thousands (if not more) changes—to their features, UI, algorithms, and so on. These changes have been brought about from user feedback and a great deal of backroom ideation. LinkedIn is a classic example of a company that follows the product-led approach, which is discussed in the rest of this chapter.

A company could be in the business of selling products and sales could happen through cold calling, making visits to key personnel, or through targeted communications. A used-car showroom that houses multiple brands of cars is an example of such a company. Then there are companies that are into marketing. Their job is to market products and services, and they center their growth around their ability to bring positive interest to products and services by the potential market. WebFX is a digital marketing company that helps businesses promote their interests. Viewing sales-led and marketing-led approaches through a different perspective, we could categorize them broadly under service or product led companies. For instance, a company that sells, like the used car showroom, is a service that is being offered for car owners who are looking to sell, and car buyers who are looking for used cars. It is perhaps a service company. WebFX has become what they are today based on their Internet presence (website), which is mostly driven directly by customers who interact directly with the product (website). The customer experience is through the website and perhaps it can also be considered a product-led company.

The trend that we see in the market today is that organizations are looking to transform themselves into product-led companies. Gartner suggests (`https://www.gartner.com/smarterwithgartner/how-to-become-a-product-centric-organization`) that organizations should look to become product-centric to be in the best position to transform their digital businesses. They state that organizations should look beyond the current and transactional aspects of the business and focus heavily on developing their products, which will be the vehicles for future success.

What Exactly Is a Product-Led Approach?

The product-led approach does not give guidance on how to build products. It is an operating model that makes products the center of the company's universe, around which all other activities center, including the customer experience. Like how DevOps is more of a culture than a technology or any other aspect, this product-led approach requires a different thinking, which we refer to as a *product mindset.*

A product-based company strategizes the company's objectives and goals around the product. There are several digital examples of companies, like hotels.com and LinkedIn, whose identity is their product, and rightly so. Customers interact and experience with such companies through their product and product alone. If these companies want to diversify, they can add more features to execute their plans on their existing products or create additional products to meet their end goals. Yes, you read that right. A product-led company does not necessarily mean that they need to put all their bets on a single product. They can have as many products as needed at their disposal. Look at Google and Amazon, for example. They have several products in their armory. At the time of this writing, Google has 71 products in a stable state. They started with Google Search as their initial product and have added products over the years. They have retired several products as well, such as Picasa and Google+. By the time you are reading this, do not surprised to find that products have been added or removed from their repository.

Why Should Companies Swivel Around Products?

There has been a fundamental shift in the way consumers use products. A few decades ago, procuring software was seen as an investment by companies. It was generally a one-time expenditure and the companies realized perpetual revenue through the services and maintenance they provided. In this period, you typically had the sales folks who made the pitch and followed it up with promises until the transactions were confirmed. This was the time when every software purchase went through the CIO's office and there were elaborate approval processes to onboard into a company's environment.

Around 10-15 years ago, there was a shift in software use. Web applications hosted on cloud infrastructures were introduced. The increasing costs of data center maintenance and development of bespoke applications gave way to increased dependence on web applications that were hosted centrally (generally) by the product manufacturers. This further changed the licensing model from one-time to period based. This was attractive because companies could hold on to their purses as the payments were spread over years, and it prevented companies from having to invest heavily. The risks associated with this approach were also mitigated. The CIO owned and controlled software acquisition started to lighten up with individual teams and service lines opting for the tools of their choice. In fact, it was no longer considered a tool or utility for the team to deliver work, but rather a necessity to innovate and deliver.

The digital age can also be referred to as the age of tools because we depend on not just one but several of them. Take a look at the applications on your phone. How many applications do you use? I have a few dozen at least, and although these products appear to stand on their own, they don't. They are often integrated. A particular software program may leverage Google's sign-in service to authenticate users and may be integrated with PayPal or a UPI (unified payments interface) system to make payments. Google AdSense may fetch data (anonymously?) from other applications to display contextual ads. You can find several such examples just by looking at your phone, so imagine the depth of integration at an enterprise level. The digital age is the era of connectedness, an era where tools can be tightly knit and data flows are seamlessly integrated. In this period, there is all the more need to make the products as the center, and build an operating model around them.

Think about this—earlier software product investments or expenditures were quite hefty. Once a customer made a decision to move in a certain direction, there was no turning back. The digital age has moved into a subscription model where switching software products is like picking treats from a menu in a restaurant. You can have one this month, and change your mind the next. A software manufacturer is therefore forced to be on their toes and never let their guard down. The product should be attractive today, next month, and the next year too. This requires continuous innovation and faster feature delivery cycles. Product companies therefore need to remain competitive at all times to remain relevant in the market. They need to have their ears to the ground to hear what customers are saying. They need to know what the competition is doing. They need to be aware of the governances that could affect them. The decision-making process should be based on solid on-the-ground information and not based on gut feelings. In short, they need to be on top of their game to be a force to reckon with. Based on all the information received, they must act swiftly to be competitive and to retain and gain customers.

The marketing for software products does not take the traditional route either. Floating ads on television, print, and digital channels just won't do it anymore. The customer needs more proof that the software serves a purpose before making a *buy* decision. They offer the software on a trial basis, or even better is to offer the software for free with limited features. As the users get accustomed to it, the dependence on the software product increases, new habits form, and the quest for more will lead to a decision to buy the software. When customers start to see the value behind software products, they become the brand ambassadors of it by sharing the experience with their circle of influence. The digital play is a double-edged sword. While the customers have the option to pull the plug anytime, the manufacturers don't have to go hard after potential customers. If the software is worth it, a tactical play like offering freemiums will do the trick. YouTube is a good example. The product is free and is synonymous with video streaming. They offered a premium version of the software in 2014 for a small fee. The users could experience ad-free experience and access to certain titles that are restricted behind the paywall. You can try the Premium version of YouTube for free for a limited time—between 1 and 3 months depending on the time of the promotion. I watch plenty of stuff on YouTube and I can be quite impatient with the ads, especially those that interrupt midway through the videos. I signed up for Premium with a three-month trial period. The ad-free experience of YouTube was great. I loved the experience and to top it off, I could listen to YouTube with my phone screen turned off, another feature that I adored. I have now become a paying customer and more importantly, I turned some of my team members and friends into Premium subscribers as well.

The digital age is all about balance between external perspective and internal introspection. While sales and marketing is sorted out through testing by fire, the internal processes needs to stand up and be counted. Digital products run on data, and every click of a button, every feature accessed, and all events have to be recorded, analyzed, and feed into the decision making process. The recommendation videos on YouTube are one such feature. Based on the type of videos we watch, more videos are placed on our home screens. I used to follow a couple of YouTube channels that are about fitness and body building. Thanks to the recommendations by the YouTube algorithms, I have come across many such channels that I find worthwhile. As a user, I can see value from this feature. For YouTube developers, their data analysis systems ideally measure all the instances of recommendations being clicked on, and repeated videos watched on such channels. Based on the information gathered and analyzed, their algorithms can be tweaked to serve customers better. The other aspect of introduction of new features that has continued on from the DevOps period is the approach to releasing new major versions. A/B testing and feature flags are some techniques that have continued to dominate.

Why Should Products Exist?

A product should exist if it meets a business objective, if it can solve a problem for a customer or improve some aspect of life experience in customer's current view. Every initiative undertaken by software companies must therefore be clear about the business objectives they are trying to meet with the products. What is fancy these days is to get the funding for new projects, assemble teams, and move swiftly toward execution. The best of project management principles is applied to track the delivery. These practices were deemed good maybe a decade or two ago, but in the digital age, software companies should take a closer look at what they are building, why they are building it, and how they are going to proceed building.

You cannot build products with the project management approach, what is the need of the hour is product management, which will enable you to think about products, think holistically and measure differently. Author of *Project to Product: How to Survive and Thrive in the Age of Digital Disruption with the Flow Framework* (IT Revolution Press, 2018), Mik Kersten believes that project management tracks and measures triple constraints that are irrelevant. Tracking the number of activities completed and the budget consumed gives a sense of fulfillment that is superficial. These do not give the real story, the story of how the customer is receiving the output.

Product management, on the other hand, opts to measure the difference the product is making to the customers. The measurements are external, based on feedback from customers, rather than relying on metrics arising from triple constraints. A typical project plan executes a plan based on the features that need to be developed. A product roadmap is dynamic and is flexible enough to swivel based on the customer feedback.

In product management, you assess success based on the value delivered to the customer. This is in the form of feedback, which is expected to be subjective in nature. Therefore, it is important to give the customer access at the earliest opportunity—say in a beta stage with a limited set of features. A minimum viable product (MVP) is built and to test the waters, it is released to users—maybe a few or the whole public depending on the strategy the company wants to take. Invite users to experience the application before it goes mainstream. In my experience, users are often willing to don the role of beta testers and are eager to provide feedback. It's a win-win situation with the software manufacturer accomplishing live user testing, where an exhaustive testing cycle can often take plenty of time and resources.

Risks exist in both project and product management methodologies. In project management, it is more pronounced with the appetite to taking risks is limited to the conceived project activities—triple constraints. In product management, there is a long rope. You release an MVP to customers. They provide feedback. You can then release another MVP and then another. You can dig at it as long as it takes to get the right mix of features that help customers solve their problems and create a positive impression. The risks are further mitigated in product management by building product teams. A product team is a mix of cross-functional team members who come together to work as one team and for the product. Unlike project management, they do not sit in a matrix environment, and are not generally stretched between projects. And while the project teams require a certain strength depending on the size and budget, a product team often starts small and incrementally grows as the product starts to mature.

The DNA of a Product-Led Company

A company that is into software development can choose to take a path that is conventional and well tread or they can take a rollercoaster ride called product management that is apt for the digital age. It is a rollercoaster in a good sense that the road to fruition is an iterative exercise with no exact destination. The ride is filled with successes and failures, and most importantly, it celebrates successes and includes lessons.

A company that professes to undertake a product-led approach needs to tick off a few things. There are number of features that such a company must indulge in, and the critical ones are shown in Figure 15-1.

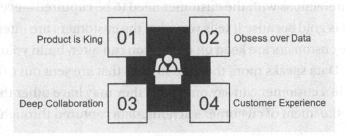

Figure 15-1. DNA of a product company

Product Is King

The product needs to have a seat at the table. Companies have to make business decisions through the lens of the product. By giving the product its rightful place, the product gets the right priority and focus to grow. There could be one product or multiple products for a company to manage, but the business decisions have to be made through their products and products alone.

LinkedIn is a product based company and their business actions should be driven to align with the product's roadmap and the value it delivers to its users. If the company intends to monetize further, their revenue plan will be drawn using the product—maybe like charging certain professionals a monthly subscription fee, similar to Elon Musk's plan to charge blue tick holders. If the company intends to expand further to students, they can make feature changes on the existing LinkedIn product or create a new product. When a company makes all its decision around a product, the product gets the right attention. If LinkedIn was to monetize by hiring talent specialists to work as a consulting company, they would lose their focus where the product is not receiving undivided attention and focus.

Obsess Over Data

There was a time when collecting data was not as rampant as it is today. We used to read and analyze the limited data that was available for trends and opportunities. Today, all the toolsets that we leverage are powerful to capture data that becomes hard to consume all of it. In other words, there is more data than needed, and sifting through what is required versus the junk is the critical success factor.

All product interactions with the customer need to be captured—every click or page viewed. This data is gold because it tells you what the customers are interested in. By knowing what the customers are keen on doing, you can alter/build your products to meet their needs. Data speaks more than the surveys that are sent out to customers from time to time. While a customer can say one thing, they may have other things on their mind. To capture the intent of customer's actions, data captured through the products is pure gold.

Deep Collaboration

Collaboration is an aspect that makes its presence in every digital area. I have discussed this aspect in various sections in this book, and yet it cannot escape the clutches when it comes to the makeup of a product-led company. A company that is truly product-led will find ways to foster collaboration between various stakeholders, and not just a one-team culture, but by bringing together various parts of the organization to consume data from the same source, align, and handshake on integration points and build a deep connection between the teams that build the software and the teams that interact with customers.

Collaboration between internal facing and external facing teams will give product companies an edge in building the products. The beauty of product-led companies is that the alignment of all business decisions around a product applies to congregation of teams around products, and working as a single unit in the unified success of products.

Customer Experience

Customers interact with products, and therefore it is key for companies to make the customer experience as friendly and fruitful as possible. Customers should form their opinions based entirely on their interactions with the product, and if these opinions are good, then the product would have created a deep impact for customers to continue using it.

Amazon's shopping application is a good example to invoke customer experience. The company has an intuitive interface. Other aspects of shopping—like modifying and canceling orders—are in the hands of the users. They treat their customers as king by providing the controls to their orders, and making the tracking information available at the touch of a finger. The customer feels empowered and in control of their purchases, and this experience encourages them to shop more. Contrast this with another marketplace whose name I wish to withhold. The products are cheaper than Amazon but the search feature is either missing or is hidden from the customer's view. Once you place an order, you have no control other than to track it. If you want to cancel an item, your options are limited. And there are no options to return a product unless you talk to a customer agent. Comparing the two experiences, a customer is much more likely to buy products on Amazon even if the price is higher than from the competitor, who has not made a good attempt at creating positive customer experiences.

The other aspect of customer experience is to anticipate what the customer would like to do next. By using data that is available to companies, data scientists can be employed to make educated predictions on the customer's future intent and a process of ideation can follow to identify the upcoming product roadmap.

Benefits of the Product-Led Approach

The product-led approach is relatively new. It has stood the test of time like other traditional practices have. However, given the experience of running products through a product-led approach, there are specific advantages that have been unearthed so far. Yes, there are several common ones with the DevOps benefits as well, as both are derived from the same family.

Enhanced Customer Experience

As the product is the center of the universe, and because the customer engagement is a derivative of the product experience, you can perhaps affirmatively conclude that you are putting customers first, considering their recommendations and delivering features that they need and embellishing the product based on gut instinct.

Product Growth

Molding a product to the customer's needs presents you with an opportunity to understand the customer better. As long as you are on the same wavelength as the customer, there are several collateral benefits like growth in business—either directly or through references. Customers praising your products is the fastest way to grow your business. The other problem that plagues the digital industry is customer retention, and this too can be handled successfully by delivering products that customers require.

The product-led approach also provides insights into the ways of customer needs, and this has the potential to generate new ideas for developing new features or new products. For any product to survive the test of time, it needs to add real features that solve new problems for customers, and it needs to be differentiated from the competition, which requires innovative thinking. The product-led approach ticks off all the boxes and helps achieve product's goal of surviving and thriving in the coming age.

Rapid Development

Developing quickly without hindrances, with the freedom to experiment with the aid of receiving swift feedback, which is a characteristic of DevOps, this adopted practice is a good product-led approach as well. Quick iterations of development followed by release to customers is the fastest way to get real on-the-ground feedback. Using feature-flags and A/B testing, you can create a subset customer base from whom you can expect feedback, without the need to release to all users.

With rapid development, customers realize value faster, which translates to better customer experiences, a new customer base, and better customer retention, among other benefits.

Understanding Value Streams and Value Stream Mapping

DevOps and Agile focuses on rapid development while keeping its ears close to the ground. The prime objective of these practices is to ensure that software development happens unhindered. To ease the hurdles, impediments are identified and sorted and automation is introduced. While the practices have shown great promise, there is a fundamental aspect of the operating model that needs to be considered to make Agile and DevOps work. Or, in other words, for a product-led approach to work, the operating model should be designed in a specific manner that allows information to flow seamlessly and to open all channels of collaboration.

Instead of considering projects, the concept of value streams has taken shape in a product-led approach. Consider Figure 15-2, which shows the structure of an organization that operates in a matrix type.

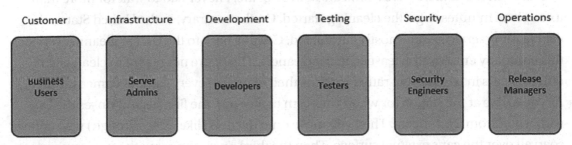

Figure 15-2. *Matrix type organization*

A matrix type organization is organized based on the capabilities of team members. You have functions created in such organizations catering to different skillsets. All the Java developers and architects could be listed under a Java function, ITIL professionals under the operations function, and manual and automation testers under the testing function. When a project needs to be stood up, select resources from each of these functions are handpicked to form a project team. Since projects are temporary, upon completion of a project, these team members will return to their respective functions. It works fairly well considering that the team members will have a permanent home with other team members with the same/similar skillsets. Functions generally exist with the objective of enhancing capabilities of individuals. On the downside, team members coming from various functions represent silos. The information that needs to pass from one team member to another, say for example from a developer to a tester, has to flow through from one silo to another. This information exchange is far from seamless for a simple reason that team members from different functions do not easily trust each other, and hence the collaboration effort toward the project is restricted to sharing minimal information. This will further result in delays due to multiple handshakes. More importantly, each of these silos engages in one-upmanship that works to highlight and showcase their work rather than working together for the outcomes that benefit the customer. The customer in such cases will not be the center of focus, which is a big problem.

The solution to this problem is to create value streams.

An Introduction to Value Streams

During my stay in the United Kingdom, I employed the services of a car cleaning company that was all manual labor and the efficiency at which they cleaned cars was a treat to watch. Even when there were a few cars in front of me, I never had to wait for more than a couple of minutes to get the cleaning started. On the contrary, in the United States, the car cleaning services were mostly automated. Coming back to the UK car cleaning service, this company employed at least eight car cleaners. They were not meant to clean eight different cars in parallel, but rather to focus their efforts on every car that comes through. As you arrive at the station (or when your turn comes up), the first person rinses the car with water from a jet stream. Then you move onto the next (like drive through) who applies soap all over the car's external surface. Then the third rinses the car with jet stream water. At the final juncture, you are asked to step out of the car, and four to six people vacuum the interiors, wipe the internal surface with semi-wet cloth, and dry the external surface—all in parallel. Before I could realize, I was looking at a clean car—inside and out. From start to finish, this would take less than ten minutes.

Putting on my analyst hat, I believe that the car cleaning system works so efficiently (and effectively), because the staff work as a single unit. They have minimal hand-offs, and the minimal are seamless, and it happens like clockwork. During the final phase of cleaning and drying, each knew what they were doing and there was no confusion about the division of labor. I barely saw them talk to each other to discuss what was done, what needed to be done, and so on. This car cleaning process is an excellent testimonial for collaborative work that we can use in IT offices. Value to me is a clean car, which is what I expected as I entered the car cleaning station. The activities they undertook to clean the car represent the value stream.

A value stream is a series of activities that are undertaken from the initial request until value is created (for the customer). Value is subjective, and in the eyes of the customer, something that is beneficial and expected. For example, if the car cleaning company gives me free car perfume while my car's cleaning rate is average, the free product does not make up for the sub-par cleaning service. As a customer, a clean car is at the core of value and needs to be delivered, anything on top may add value if and only if the core value is delivered. A value stream therefore is focused on creating value through the series of steps undertaken from start to finish. Sticking with the example of the car cleaning service, the value stream looks like Figure 15-3.

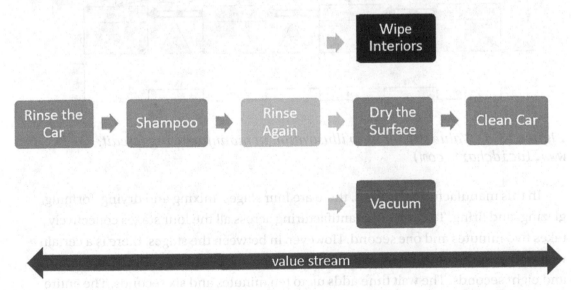

Figure 15-3. *Value stream illustration*

What Is Value Stream Mapping?

Value streams are visualized to understand how the activities progress, whether the activities are delayed at a particular stage, and what causes the delay. This visualization is referred to as value stream mapping.

This method of visualization has its roots in the manufacturing industry and is a popular concept in the lean manufacturing community. Early in the 20th century, Toyota was known to have employed this technique in their car manufacturing and assembly process. As the car goes through the assembly, Toyota engineers identified the reasons for slow production and where the bottlenecks were formed. It helped them immensely by identifying the root cause of the delays on the assembly line, and as a result, it made them productive. They reduced waste associated with delays. As they solved the problem, the company collaborated better, which was an unintended benefit of the exercise. An illustration of a value stream map is presented in Figure 15-4.

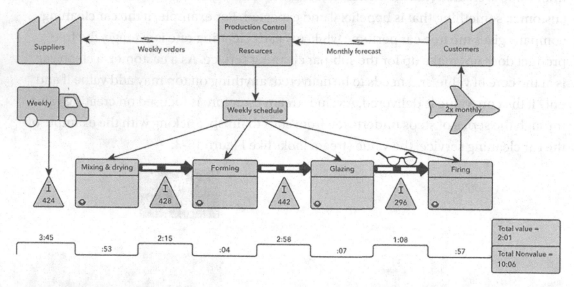

Figure 15-4. *Value stream map illustration in manufacturing (credit:* www.lucidchart.com*)*

In this manufacturing process, there are four stages: mixing and drying, forming, glazing, and firing. To carry out manufacturing across all the four stages collectively takes two minutes and one second. However, in between the stages, there is a certain wait time. For example, between glazing and firing, there is a wait time of one minute and eight seconds. The wait time adds up to ten minutes and six seconds. The entire manufacturing process therefore takes twelve minutes and seven seconds. The actual value adding work is only two minutes and one second, while the wait time (which is a waste) is ten minutes and six seconds, which is a non-value activity. The engineers behind this process can get a better understanding of the delays at every stage, and with non-value work running at five times the value work, improvements can be brought about to make the process productive and reduce waste.

In manufacturing, we have physical parts that move through various processing units and in a software, or digital industry, the setup is similar with sets of activities that succeed each other. The problems in manufacturing industries—like accumulation of waste and productivity loss—are common occurrences in digital industries as well. If value stream mapping could help manufacturing, it can help digital sector as well.

Value stream mapping has been adopted in the product-led approach to help visualize the development and operational processes. By measuring the process and wait times, engineering architects are getting a better feel for the loss of productivity, which is a major factor determining how quickly new software/features can hit the market.

The process of running a value stream mapping exercise and identifying current and future states, if done well, will lead to better productivity and reduce waste that exists in the system. However, the bigger collateral benefit is that through the process, while the architects get a better handle on the system, they develop and can engage in a systems thinking rather than looking at activities in isolation. A culture of strong collaboration starts to emerge because the team starts to come together to identify the problem, reflect on the possibilities, and arrive at solutions that can make them highly successful. The product team is better placed through this exercise to accurately estimate their velocity of delivering on features, get a better handle on measuring capacities, and gauge the complexity of features. It is my experience that teams become a lot more disciplined after being subjected to the value stream mapping exercise, because they can visualize the ill effects of not maintaining discipline, like not working in harmony and neglecting certain aspects of quality and guidelines. Team members will start to trust each other more than before and communicating about various aspects of work becomes second nature. The team becomes more efficient and effective, with information flowing both ways, giving and receiving feedback, and talking through the challenges . Nothing tastes better than success. With success at their backs, job satisfaction goes through the roof.

Carrying Out Value Stream Mapping

Before beginning this section, I want to make the disclaimer that this is not a masterclass for conducting VSM exercises. The intent of this section is to provide a glimpse at how it is conducted, what is measured, and how the improvements are brought about. Value stream mapping is a deep topic, and it warrants a book on its own. The mapping exercise uses several symbols, notations, and rules that are disregarded in this book.

Value stream mapping has evolved over time. There are several elaborate processes that can be undertaken for a full-fledged VSM implementation. However, the essential steps are listed here:

1. Document the current process

2. Identify value adds and non-value adds

3. Define a future state

4. Find the root cause of waste

5. Identify improvement initiatives

6. Plan and implement

7. Measure the value adds and non-value adds again

Step 1: Document the Current Process

The process starts by identifying the current sets of activities. It includes identifying the value stream, which essentially means where the trigger for value generation begins, and where the customers see value.

It is possible that there could be nested value streams. During the identification and documentation stage, it is critical that every step be documented.

Figure 15-5 illustrates a simple software development process beginning with ideation until the software is deployed into production. The example also considers that all the activities take place in a sequential manner, unlike the car washing value stream in Figure 15-4, where certain activities are executed in parallel.

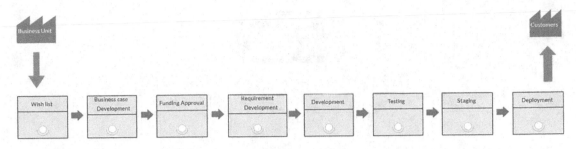

Figure 15-5. *Value stream identification and documentation*

Analysts who run VSM exercises first spend time with the team to understand the flow of activities in the value stream and then they sit and observe if the flow is indeed going as per the plan. The steps are documented based on the current practice rather than the documented processes in standard operating procedures.

Step 2: Identify Value Adds and Non-Value Adds

I talked earlier about the wait times that add to the delays and cause loss of productivity. It is true but a closer examination of the time spent on activities will typically reveal the nature of the activity—whether the activity itself is adding value or if it's a gold-plated step.

In Figure 15-6, the trigger for value creation starts by creating a wish list and then a business case is developed for each of the wish list items. During observation, the analyst identifies that the wish list, although is a trigger, is not considered seriously for building business cases. During the business case development activity, the product owner and key users get together and brainstorm to identify the next set of requirements. So in light of this information, it is possible that the wish list activity is a non-value add activity.

Next up in this step is to accurately measure the processing time—the time taken by the process step to complete the activity—and the lead time (or wait time), which is the time between two process steps. During the lead time, the value does not flow, so basically, the entire flow has stopped, which is potentially a delay and a waste. Also, the process step itself may not be adding value to the value stream. For example, if you are creating product documents before deployment that nobody reads, you are appending time for a non-value add activity.

The output at the end of this step is illustrated in Figure 15-6.

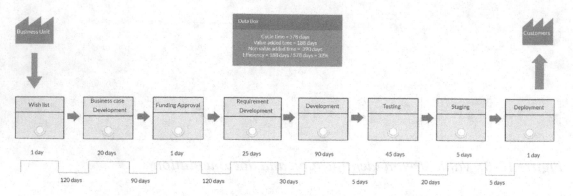

Figure 15-6. *Value stream map for a software development process*

As per the observed report, the value add activities is 188 days while the lead time/ waiting time between value add activities is 390 days. Combining value add and non-value add activities provides the cycle time, which in this case is 578 days. The cycle time points to the time that is required for a wish list item to go through all the hoops of getting documented, approved, developed, tested, and deployed, and this entire cycle takes 578 days. The efficiency is calculated as 32 percent (value add/cycle time).

Step 3: Define a Future State

The VSM objective is to reduce waste and improve productivity. If the current process is set as a base, and improvements are carried forward on top of the current process, it does not yield transformative results. Therefore, it is imperative that the analysts sit down with engineering architects and other stakeholders as necessary to define a future state that is forward thinking and leverages the digital thinking ways of working.

In the example, a few improvements have been identified, as illustrated in Figure 15-7.

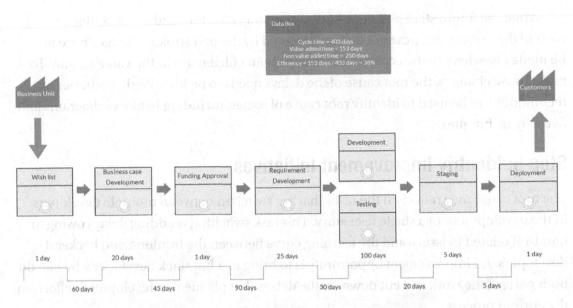

Figure 15-7. *Future state value stream map*

The future model considers fewer lead days between certain process activities. And most importantly, the development model will turn into a hybrid Agile model, where development and testing is carried out simultaneously, and not one after the other, as was the practice in the current method. As per the defined future state, the overall cycle time is estimated to cut down from 578 days to 403 days which is 30 percent more efficient. Customers can now expect to get their software product 30 percent faster.

The process time has seen an improvement as well, from 188 to 153 days. And the lead time has reduced significantly from 390 to 250 days. The efficiency of the planned future state process now stands at 38 percent, which is an increase of 6 percent from the earlier 32 percent.

Calculating efficiency in the process is an internal metric and does not necessarily reflect on the efficiency of the value delivered to the customer. From a customer's standpoint, the cycle time is absolute and reduction in it matters and the rest of internal processes like lead and process times are often ignored.

Step 4: Find the Root Cause of Waste

The current process, which includes process times and lead times, exists because of various reasons, which could include dependencies on other teams, resource mobilization, defects and batch uploads, among others. In fact, these external factors are typically the reasons for lead times, which elongates the overall cycle time.

While the future state plans and sets a vision for reduction and optimization in each of these areas, they cannot be implemented by the pen stroke. Changes have to be made elsewhere in the ecosystem to bring about efficiencies in the value stream. To make those changes, the root cause of the delays needs to be identified. A number of techniques can be used to identify root cause of issues, including Ishikawa diagrams and five why techniques.

Step 5: Identify Improvement Initiatives

The root cause may reflect on the tasks that are switched between multiple developers in the development of a single user story. This task switching is adding delays owing to hand-off related to issues and the learning curve between the frontend and backend developers. An improvement opportunity is to bring in a full stack developer who can do both parts of the work and cut down on the delays that plague the development efforts in the current process.

This example shows the importance behind conducting good root cause analysis exercises. Based on the identified causes, improvement initiatives are to be identified to move from current to future ways of working.

Drawing up improvement actions should be done as a team. The entire team should come together, understand the root cause, and find a solution or the way forward to mitigate it. As the team works together, it strengthens its resolve to make the value stream more efficient, and the team members end up owning the future state of working rather than being asked to follow new processes.

Step 6: Plan and Implement

The next logical step in the value stream mapping exercise is to prioritize all the improvement actions, plan for their implementation, and go through with them.

One of the blunders that architects/analysts make is to adopt all the changes at once in a Big Bang approach. This never works when you are trying to tweak multiple aspects of a process. Team members are people, and people do need time to get used to new ways of working, even if they support the initiation. The implementation must therefore happen in a phase-wise manner, typically in the order of priority. Carry out the first improvement initiatives, and once that settles down, do the next, and so on.

Step 7: Measure the Value Adds and Non-Value Adds Again

Let's consider that several changes were brought about, including the composition of the teams, the processes employed, technologies leveraged, the cutdown in the number of meetings, and other activities. How does the cycle time stack up now? Does it immediately follow the timelines designed in the future state?

To find out, another value stream observation exercise needs to be carried out by VSM analysts. Figure 15-8 illustrates the observed timelines after making all the identified improvements.

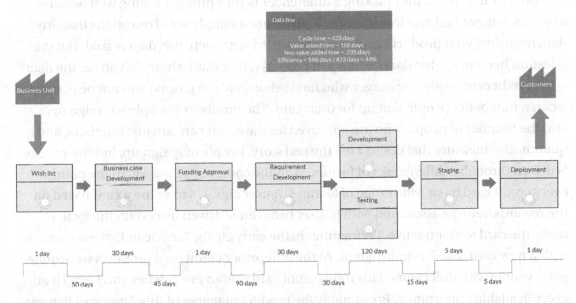

Figure 15-8. *Future state actual timelines*

When observed, it was found that the cycle time had improved, from 578 days to 423, which is an improvement of 155 days. Customers got the new product/feature 155 days earlier compared to earlier process, which adds value to the customer community. However, when the process activities were measured, the number of days spent did not improve, despite bringing in efficiencies in multiple activity areas and running development and testing in parallel. However, the lead times or non-value added time reduced from 390 to 235 days, which brought down the cycle time as well. This lead to further value to the customers. The efficiency of the value stream increased from 32 to 44 percent, while the future state plan predicted an efficiency of 38 percent.

The future state timelines are a north star and to reach the target, it may take multiple iterations. Or to state plainly, such VSM exercises need to be conducted on a regular basis to find opportunities for improvement and waste reduction, and to ensure that the value to customers is maximized.

Looking at Data and Metrics

As you develop new products or features, how do you know that these features are accepted by users? Are they making a difference? Is your product selling well because of your strategy to release features often? These are a sample set of questions that drive data regarding your products, and in a product-led approach, this data is gold. But the question becomes, what data should you process rather than where do you get the data?

A credit card product manager who has their ears to the ground will not be ecstatic when a number of people sign up for their card. The number of people who sign up, and the number of people who are approved for the credit card are just numbers, and a quantitative measure that doesn't tell the real story. People may sign up, but their usage is driven through a different set of factors. With the competitive market in the offing, every credit card has a wide range of features. A user chooses to swipe a card based on the rewards/returns associated with it. User behavior is driven by certain things that make the card look attractive. I remember in the early 2000s, American Express came up with a new card that was transparent. At the time, other credit card products were quite plain vanilla with dull colors. This transparent card was an eye catcher and I used it at every available opportunity. Presumably the product manager of this American Express card could measure the outcome—the number of swipes, daily active users (DAU), and monthly active users (MAU), among others. Product managers should measure the right things and go after what they really need in order to develop the product further and take it to new heights.

Data is a double-edged sword. If you know exactly what you are looking for, you can possibly influence the data collection process to suit favorable responses. For example, if a product manager is looking to tempt more people into trying software before the buy decision, they may start luring them with multiple months of freemium experience. Although this may increase the trial users, they may not all convert to paying users. I worked at Dell as a technical support specialist. My job was to fix laptop problems for my customers over the phone. One of the key metrics that we tracked was first time fix

(FTF). After successful resolution of problems, if the same customer returns (with the same or a different problem) within 48 hours, that would affect my FTF metric. So, I devised a method to help with the metric. After successfully resolving issues, I would tell customers to wait for at least 48 hours if they find the same issue or if they encountered a different one before calling back, as I, their *favorite* support specialist would be back to work after my weekly offs. It helped me a bit because I knew what I was measured on. But it didn't help the customers or Dell. While it's important to know what to measure, if product managers are too close to the data, the data may be interpreted not for what it represents but based on what it needs to be.

The Problem of Perspective in the Digital Age

With plenty of product data in our hands, it is often challenging to note which metrics do help and which ones don't. Yes, metrics such as revenue are commonly used, but it doesn't tell the entire story nor is it important to everybody in the product value stream.

When the pandemic hit, people switched to online shopping. Grocery companies were not thinking about their revenues or profits, but rather metrics around inventory management. As people ordered online, grocery stores had to ensure that their products were available and accessible when the orders rang in. With the brick and mortar stores, there was certain space restrictions and products were stocked. Shoppers came, looked, and bought off the shelves. When a product ran out, they opted for alternates or didn't buy them at all. With online shopping, the grocer had a problem of maintaining inventory to ensure that buyers don't end up paying online only to realize later that the product was not available. Different situations, different stakeholders, and a different set of challenges!

Products today have to be built with the ability to derive data from all aspects— to help further strategy, operational aspects, quality, marketing among others. So, it becomes imperative that products are embedded with full-fledged analytics engines that not only capture data but also make sense of it. The upcoming sections look at some of the common metrics employed today.

Operational Metrics

These are the metrics that are on the ground; the metrics that reflect the operational aspects of a product. To get a better handle on how the product is being perceived and how stable a product is, operational metrics (Figure 15-9) need to be studied and further actions are initiated based on them.

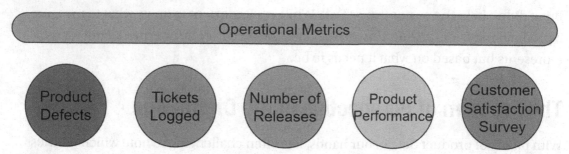

Figure 15-9. Operational metrics

- *Product defects:* A product's stability is defined by the number of defects, and how often these defects plague users. On Android phones, when an application stops working, you might have observed a notification that appears asking either to wait or report to the manufacturer about the crash. These notifications are the window for users to communicate to the shop floor engineers. Engineers behind the scene need to be vigilant, find patterns, and plug the gap as soon as possible. Bad experiences owing from defects will drive paying customers away, even if they have been loyal for a long time.

- *Tickets logged:* This metric may not represent the true nature of product stability, but it is a metric worth keeping. Tickets logged may not correspond to the number of defects, as there could be defects that users may not have logged in yet. In such cases, the products need to have built-in mechanisms to proactively auto detect problems and log tickets. There are several application monitoring tools on the market, and many product companies build their own monitoring solutions that are tagged onto the main product.

- *Number of releases:* A product that releases often can be construed as a product company that not only has ideas but is also doing well in terms of putting pen to paper. A product that releases often can do more good than bad. While new features are introduced and known bugs are fixed, some users may find it intriguing to try new features. Then there are others who can get fatigued by constant changes. Product managers have to play a balancing act to satiate both types of users.

- *Product performance:* This metric measures the speed at which the product loads. The product performs its action among other speed related aspects. During the engineering of products, the DevOps pipelines take them through the rigor of performance testing that tests product's performance in the test conditions. However in the real world, when different types of devices are used, the work for the engineering managers is cut out to ensure that the product stays above the benchmark to keep users from worrying about it.

- *Customer satisfaction surveys:* One of the most popular metrics around measures how well customers like the product. Generally a five-star rating system captures satisfaction levels, and the ripple effects of the rating can make the product more popular with other users making a buying decision based on other users' feedback. On the other hand, a product can simply be drown out if the feedback coming through is not favorable.

Usage Metrics

The usage metrics illustrated in Figure 15-10 provide insights into how well the feature development and marketing translates into users and customers using the product.

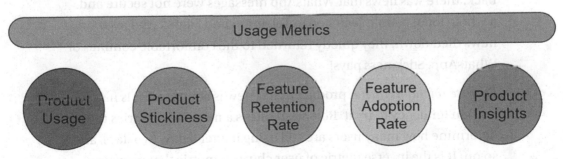

Figure 15-10. Usage metrics

- *Product usage:* Customer satisfaction ratings tell you how well a product is liked. But that doesn't translate into regular usage. For example, I have watched all the thriller movies on Prime Video. Although I like their interface, the product's stability and its UI, I don't use it often because of the lack of content. When we talk about usage, generally it is measured on a daily basis (Daily Active Users, Weekly Active Users and Monthly Active Users). A product like Prime Video would expect its users to regularly watch on a daily basis—hey may keenly measure DAU and WAU. A product that does taxes may indeed measure usage during the fiscal year end and during the tax payment window.

- *Product stickiness:* This is the next level of usage metric that measures how often a user lives out of a product. Some users may not use a product once or multiple times in a week, but rather use certain products throughout the day. Take the example of WhatsApp. With a high adoption rate, all my family, friends, and coworkers are fully entrenched in WhatsApp. All the messages we share, the forwards we enjoy, and the birthday wishes are predominantly on WhatsApp. We have also started calling each other using WhatsApp to avoid long distance calling charges. Meta, the company that owns WhatsApp, would look at the stickiness metric as the calling card to introduce more features that could involve subscription charges. The advantage of this metric is that people who are sticky to certain products are loyal to a fault. They don't move unless there is significant reason to. So, product companies look for opportunities to make their products sticky. Talking about moving out of sticky products, a few years back, there was news that WhatsApp messages were not secure and a whole lot of people switched to Telegram and Signal. And, as the news died down, they quietly returned to the comfortable confines of WhatsApp. Stickiness pays!

- *Feature retention rate:* A product that is new is shiny, and it is natural human tendency to try it. Retention rate is a measure that tries to determine how many users are still using it after a day, two days, and so on. It is the inverse metric of user churn, a metric that measures how many users have left. Retention rate is not as straightforward as some of the metrics that we have discussed thus far. Retention of product usage depends on the category of users, which is referred to as the *cohort*, and the analysis involving them is *cohort analysis*. A cohort of college students might have a higher retention rate of products such as Instagram than a cohort of senior citizens.

- *Feature adoption rate:* New features or products are released fairly regularly. The feature adoption rate metric takes into consideration the number of users who continue to use the feature, or in other words, have adopted the feature for their regular use. It is a metric that tells product managers that they have hit gold if the feature adoption increases over time. In fact, in any product, it is preferred by product managers that users adopt multiple features, which makes it harder for them to migrate out of it. For example, I have been using OneDrive since they introduced it with free 7 GB storage. Since then, I have paid for their subscription which includes 1 TB of storage data and five licenses of Office 365. After losing tons of precious data on portable hard drives, I find OneDrive a memory keeper, and with multiple computers lying around, there is always a need for MS Office product. Even though I know that there are other cloud providers that are much cheaper than OneDrive, my dependence on it has kept me glued and I have basically adopted it as something that I cannot live without. Great news for Microsoft!

- *Product insights:* This is a holistic analysis of a user's experience with a product. It includes not only how often users use the product, but also how comfortable they are with the UI, the features, and the interactive touchpoints of the product. Before a product is launched, product companies build variations of the same product, and will ask select groups of users to try it and provide feedback. The feedback is received through a detailed survey using the Likert scale (Figure 15-11). The feedback is analyzed and feature changes are made before releasing the product on a larger scale.

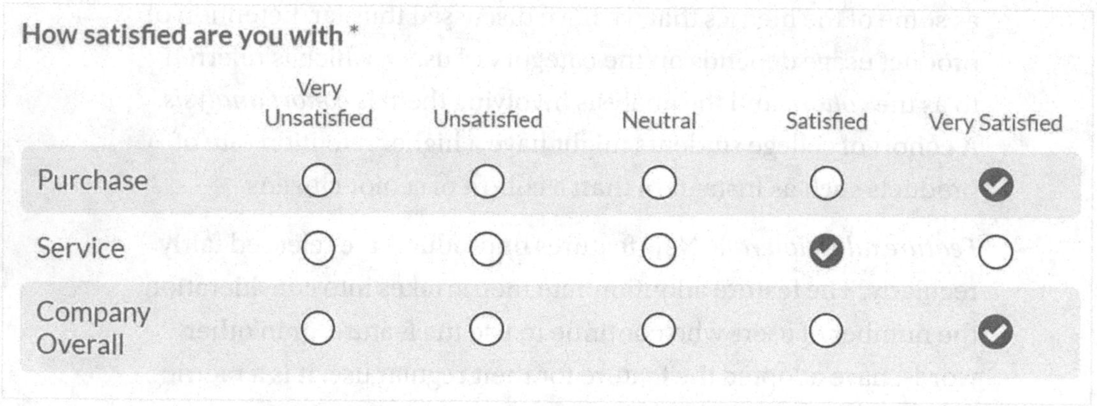

How satisfied are you with *

	Very Unsatisfied	Unsatisfied	Neutral	Satisfied	Very Satisfied
Purchase	◯	◯	◯	◯	✅
Service	◯	◯	◯	✅	◯
Company Overall	◯	◯	◯	◯	✅

Figure 15-11. *The Likert scale*

Business Metrics

While operational and usage metrics measure the output and outcomes associated with the product usage phase, business metrics are holistic. They look forward and backward in time for trends, for a way forward, and of course, at revenue-related metrics. This is illustrated in Figure 15-12.

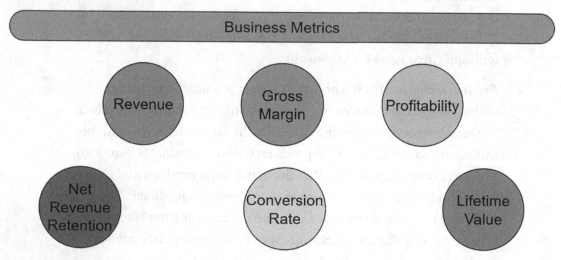

Figure 15-12. *Business metrics*

- *Revenue*: Measuring revenue is the lifeblood of a product company, especially in the digital age due to the nature of subscriptions and dynamic pricing. Revenue is typically measured on a monthly, quarterly, and annual basis. There are a number of factors that influence revenue during a certain time. For example, marketing campaigns are expected to bring in new customers, and with that, additional revenue. Holidays like Christmas and Diwali are expected to ring in new customers. This metric by itself is half useful. To estimate accurately, the marketing campaigns, the time of the year, and any new rollout of features must be considered.

- *Gross margin:* This is the money that the company gets after covering the cost of goods sold. It goes toward product development, maintenance, research, and infrastructure costs, among others. My grandfather (and Ben Franklin) used to say that every penny that you save is like the penny you earned. The saying is apt for product companies (or any other company for that matter), which should drive the company to make judicious economic decisions.

- *Profitability*: While gross margin considers direct expenses alone, the real deal in a company's performance is based on its profits or losses. Profitability considers direct and indirect costs that are attributed to the development and maintenance of the product. Indirect costs include seating costs for employees, sales, marketing, and so on.

- *Net revenue retention:* This measures the revenue that is expected from repeat business—as in subscription costs on a monthly basis. If all the existing customers continue to subscribe, a certain monthly recurring revenue is guaranteed. This is the best case scenario. It is possible that customers may cancel the subscription or opt for a cheaper package. It is also possible that new customers sign up or existing customers choose a more expensive package. In both cases, the monthly recurring revenue is impacted. Therefore, the product company must find a factor/formula to consider all the possible cases to calculate net revenue retention.

- *Conversion rate:* We have had the concept of shareware and freeware for a number of years. They either were available for trial for a limited period of time or had limited features available. The software manufacturer did not have a good handle on the number of people who were trying them out. With the dawn of the digital age, where SaaS products and thick clients strongly linked usage metrics, any trial period user or free version user who switches over to a paid version is tracked. This movement from free version to paid version is called the conversion rate.

- *Lifetime value:* This metric looks into the future based on the current crop of customers. It estimates the revenue that the company can expect from its existing customers over their lifetime. The company can further enhance the data by adjusting for inflation and new feature rollouts. This is a key metric that gives the company an accurate picture of its financial position in the upcoming years and is used to drive economic decisions.

Summary

This chapter looked at the product-led approach and covered how the methodology of product management in conjunction with Agile, DevOps, and the digital transformation looks at creating and managing products. Product-led companies are organized around value streams rather than in silos or based on projects. Developing and running value stream exercises is a continuous process that needs to be undertaken to improve the cycle team, reduce leads, and deliver value to paying customers. Finally, the chapter ended with measurements that provide companies information about performance and how customers feel about their products.

Index

© Abhinav Krishna Kaiser 2023
A. Krishna Kaiser, *Reinventing ITIL® and DevOps with Digital Transformation*,
https://doi.org/10.1007/978-1-4842-9072-9

Printed in the United States
by Baker & Taylor Publisher Services

Printed in the United States
by Baker & Taylor Publisher Services